The Anatomy of Justice

The Anatomy of Justice

On the Shape, Substance, and Power of Liberal Egalitarianism

GINA SCHOUTEN

OXFORD
UNIVERSITY PRESS

Great Clarendon Street, Oxford, OX2 6DP,
United Kingdom

Oxford University Press is a department of the University of Oxford.
It furthers the University's objective of excellence in research, scholarship,
and education by publishing worldwide. Oxford is a registered trade mark of
Oxford University Press in the UK and in certain other countries

© Gina Schouten 2024

The moral rights of the author have been asserted

All rights reserved. No part of this publication may be reproduced, stored in
a retrieval system, or transmitted, in any form or by any means, without the
prior permission in writing of Oxford University Press, or as expressly permitted
by law, by licence or under terms agreed with the appropriate reprographics
rights organization. Enquiries concerning reproduction outside the scope of the
above should be sent to the Rights Department, Oxford University Press, at the
address above

You must not circulate this work in any other form
and you must impose this same condition on any acquirer

Published in the United States of America by Oxford University Press
198 Madison Avenue, New York, NY 10016, United States of America

British Library Cataloguing in Publication Data
Data available

Library of Congress Control Number: 2024941793

ISBN 9780198898634

DOI: 10.1093/9780191999772.001.0001

Printed and bound by
CPI Group (UK) Ltd, Croydon, CR0 4YY

Links to third party websites are provided by Oxford in good faith and
for information only. Oxford disclaims any responsibility for the materials
contained in any third party website referenced in this work.

For my parents

Contents

Acknowledgments	ix
Introduction	1
0.1 Outline of the Case	4
0.2 How Mainstream? How Rawlsian?	10
0.3 How Feminist? How Egalitarian?	14
1. Two Pluralisms about Justice	17
1.1 Two Ongoing Debates	18
1.2 Conceptual Pluralism: Aspirational and Verdictive Justice	21
1.3 Substantive Pluralism: Distributive Egalitarian Aspirational Justice, Relational Egalitarian Legitimacy	31
1.4 Values Pluralism and Incommensurability	37
2. Distributive Equality as Aspirational Justice	43
2.1 Distributive Equality in Context	46
2.2 Luck Egalitarianism and Equal Respect	50
2.3 Luck Egalitarianism and Opportunity Pluralism	60
2.4 Equality and Social Reform	65
3. The Distributive Demands of Mutual Respect	67
3.1 Relational Egalitarianism and Distributive Equality	71
3.2 Pluralism and Priority	80
3.3 Plausible Priority *at the Cost* of Action Guidance?	90
4. Relational Equality as Legitimacy	93
4.1 Mutual Respect and Legitimacy in Political Liberalism	95
4.2 Distributive Justice Silenced?	105
4.3 The Substantive Role of the Aspirational: Distributive Justice Speaks Up	108
4.4 Justice, Legitimacy, Authority	118
5. Values Tradeoffs under Injustice: The Feminist Debate over Basic Income	121
5.1 Basic Income and Values Tradeoffs	125
5.2 The Values at Stake: A Distributive Justice Assessment	128
5.3 Mutual Respect and Gender Egalitarianism	131
5.4 The Values Tradeoff and the Anatomy of Justice	140
5.5 Reframing Gender Egalitarianism, Reframing Justice Theorizing	144

viii CONTENTS

6. Liberalism, Culture, and the Subject Matter of Justice 146
   6.1 Culture and Ideology Critique 148
   6.2 Varieties of Liberalism and the Basic Structural Focus 153
   6.3 What Can Stingy Liberal Justice Impugn? 157
   6.4 What Can Stingy Liberal Justice Prescribe? 168
   6.5 Liberal Feminism and the Anatomy of Justice 177

7. Reflective Equilibrium and Social Critique 179
   7.1 "Applied Ideal Theory" 180
   7.2 The Epistemic Problem of Ideology 183
   7.3 Reflective Equilibrium's Abstemiousness and Outlier Judgments 185
   7.4 Is Normative Theory Necessary? 194
   7.5 Is Normative Theory Adequate? 198
   7.6 Is Liberalism Ideology? 207

Bibliography 211
Index 221

Acknowledgments

I have many people to thank for their generous engagement with the arguments in this book. I have still more to thank for their support of me while I wrote it. However much better I'd have liked for it to be, it would be much *worse* without the village that helped me get it this far.

The arguments were developed and refined over many valuable conversations at many conferences, workshops, and colloquium visits. I presented chapters for the Society for Philosophy and Psychology, the Feminist Philosophy Grad Conference at University of Arizona, the September Group, the Symposium on Discrimination and Subordination at University of Toronto, the New Directions in Social Justice Theorizing workshop at UC San Diego, the Analytic Legal Philosophy Conference, the SUNY Albany Grad Conference, the Conference on Inequality, Religion, and Society: John Rawls and After, and the Kamm Lecture at Harvard University. I presented related work at the Workshop for Oxford Studies in Political Philosophy. I shared parts of the project for colloquia at University of Kentucky, Brandeis University, University of Pennsylvania, University of Bristol, University of Arizona, University of Vermont, Boston University, UNC Chapel Hill, Northwestern University, Stanford, UCLA, University of Chicago, and Johns Hopkins University. I discussed these ideas with the NYU Law Colloquium, the Harvard Law School Faculty Colloquium, the York Political Theory Workshop, the Centre for Ethics and Critical Thought at University of Edinburgh, the Center for Law and Philosophy Workshop at University of Southern California, the University of Warwick's Centre for Ethics, Law and Public Affairs, the Workshop in Law, Philosophy, and Political Theory at the Kadish Center at Berkeley, and the Political Philosophy Workshop at NYU. I discussed it as a visiting guest in classes at the University of Oslo and Humboldt University, and in an interview for the Just Theory podcast. I gained a great deal from all these discussions, and I thank participants for questions and challenges that improved my thinking.

I especially want to thank the many colleagues, at home and away, whose correspondence, written comments on chapters, and other contributions have tested and strengthened these ideas over the years: Brian Berkey, Tommie Shelby, Lucas Stanczyk, Selim Berker, Tim Scanlon, Eric Beerbohm, Zoë Johnson King, Jenna Donohue, Jeff Behrends, Harry Brighouse, David O'Brien, Lori Watson, Christie Hartley, Tom Parr, Kathryn Joyce, Christopher Lewis, Paul Weithman, Josh Cohen, Niko Kolodny, Annette Zimmermann, Patrick Tomlin, Philip Cook, Clark Wolf, Sabine Tsuruda, Mihaela Mihai, Ding, Aleksandra Wawrzyszczuk, Emilia Mickiewicz, Jeremy Waldron, Liam Murphy, Samuel Scheffler, Daniel Viehoff,

Sharon Street, Sophia Moreau, Robert Gooding-Williams, Juliana Bidadanure, Steve Wall, Shanna Slank, Minji Jang, Daniel Muñoz, Ram Neta, Noah Feldman, Samuel Freeman, Kim Brownlee, Nico Cornell, Jonathan Gould, Andrew Sepielli, Dick Arneson, Serena Olsaretti, David Estlund, Paula Casal, Peter Vallentyne, Anca Gheaus, George Sher, Kasper Lippert-Rasmussen, Amanda Greene, Seana Shiffrin, Andrew Williams, Thomas Christiano, David Brink, Melissa Ann Schwartzberg, Marcel Twele, Daniel Roberts, Livia von Samson, Markus Furendal, Amy Baehr, Asha Bhandary, Amia Srinivasan, Ruth Chang, Henry Richardson, Herb Leventer, Taylor Koles, Collis Tahzib, Jon Quong, Martha Nussbaum, and Dan Brudney.

Although I'd been toying with these ideas for years before, I really started work on this book during a year I spent as a Fellow in Residence at the Edmond & Lily Safra Center for Ethics. I'm grateful to the Center for the financial support and wonderful working conditions, and to the staff for their contributions to my work and for graciously accommodating my needs as a new mother.

I owe thanks to several current and former Harvard graduate students for valuable exchanges about these ideas, and for valuable exchanges about their own ideas that kept me energized: Yunhyae Kim, Britta Clark, Eva Yguico, Cat Wade, Lidal Dror, Bethany Cates, Isaijah Shadrach, John Abughattas, Ayo Ajimoko, Reuben Owusu, Krupa Appleton, and Matt Macdonald.

Thanks to Abby Zachary for her wonderful close reading, to Cat Wade for her expert help with the pictures, to Joyce Lu for her help to prepare the manuscript, and to Isaijah Shadrach for his superb work preparing the index.

Two chapters of this book engage critically with arguments from Sally Haslanger. Because my general feelings toward Sally's work are less critical than appreciative, I agonized over those chapters, and I agonized about sharing them with Sally. Of course, I needn't have. I am grateful to Sally for writing philosophy that so richly repays engagement. I'm even more grateful to her for ably showing how to welcome critical engagement with grace and openness.

Two chapters draw on work from my previously published papers. I'm grateful to the publishers for their permission to use that work here, and to the editors and anonymous reviewers whose input helped to improve both the earlier papers and this book. Those papers are:

- "Distributive Egalitarianism as Aspirational Justice." In *Conversations in Philosophy, Law and Politics*, edited by Ruth Change and Amia Srinivasan, 343–71. Oxford University Press, forthcoming 2024
- "Justice and Legitimacy in Caregiver Support: A Proposal for Managing Tradeoffs between Gender Egalitarian and Economic Egalitarian Social Aims." In *Caring for Liberalism: Dependency and Liberal Political Theory*, edited by Amy Baehr and Asha Bhandary, 266–91. Routledge, 2021

ACKNOWLEDGMENTS xi

Thanks to Peter Momtchiloff for his guidance and patience, to Imogene Haslam for editorial assistance, and to three anonymous reviewers of this manuscript for their very helpful advice.

I'm fortunate to have truly good friends in this profession. The combined support of the Harvard Philosophy Department, the Edmond & Lily Safra Center for Ethics, and an Arts and Humanities Manuscript Workshop Grant enabled me to invite several of them to a manuscript workshop to help with this project. I thank Harry Brighouse, David O'Brien, Lori Watson, Christie Hartley, Tom Parr, Christopher Lewis, Kathryn Joyce, Britta Clark, Yunhyae Kim, and Lucas Stanczyk for their generous engagement and discussion during that event. None of these participants was reading the work for the first time, but each brought enthusiasm for the book and patience with my slow pace of improvement. Beyond strengthening the finished project with their challenges and suggestions, their company and encouragement were a shot in the arm at a moment when my enthusiasm was flagging. I haven't addressed all their objections, to my own satisfaction let alone to theirs, but I'll keep trying as I look forward to our next opportunity to think together.

I thank Shanna Slank and Hayley Clatterbuck for being the most brilliant and loving long-distance philosopher friends a girl could hope for. I thank Samantha Matherne and Candice Delmas for being brilliant and loving close up. Thanks to Candice for her patience, advice, and good humor as I complained about this book over dozens of rounds of drinks. Thanks to Samantha for being the third grownup in our household, for helping me survive this book, and for sharing the joys and confusions of this strange, wonderful "job" we both have.

Harry Brighouse and David O'Brien have done more than anyone to improve this book over the years I spent writing it. Harry did more than anyone to equip me to write it in the first place. As if that weren't enough, Harry and David remind me, with each of our workshopping sessions, that this work is great fun under the right circumstances. And, with each workshopping session, they help realize those circumstances for me. Thanks to David for being such a kind and generous critic and such a wonderful friend. Thanks to Harry for believing I could write this, for the mountains of time and energy he gave to it, and for making it all possible to begin with.

My parents love me so much that they will probably actually read this book. It's a dang lotta love, shown every day in countless ways, and it's a genuine pleasure to try to be worthy of it. This book is for them. I hope they won't *actually* feel any compulsion to read it. But like all the good things in my life, it wouldn't have been possible without my first and best teachers.

This book begins and ends with my kids. I was pregnant with Frank when I started putting pen to paper. Rudy was born just as I sent the manuscript off for review. And as I write this paragraph, which I've saved for the very end, I think of

xii ACKNOWLEDGMENTS

the joy I've felt in the year and a half since, watching our wild, loving, deep-feeling Frank become a caring big brother to our sweet, laughing, rampaging Rudy. My kids' curiosity reminds me that our lives are full of beautiful, intricate puzzles. Their boundless affection and explosive giggles remind me that it's all actually pretty simple. Thanks to Frank and Rudy for making this book take longer and for making the years it filled immeasurably fuller. I'm grateful to the teachers who've cared for them, keeping them happily playing and exploring while Jeff and I were doing easier work. I'm grateful to Faith and Samantha, their dear friends who see in them people worth knowing well. I'm grateful to my parents and Jeff's parents for all the love and fun they bring as Oma, Opa, Mimi, and Papa.

Finally, thanks to Jeff: for all his help with the book and for all he did to keep the fires under control when it outgrew the compartment I meant to keep it in. But mostly, thanks to Jeff for standing by me through my very worst, and still believing in my very best.

Introduction

This book argues for a reorientation in liberal egalitarian theorizing about justice. I argue that the orientation I propose supports compelling resolutions to long-standing disputes and difficulties internal to egalitarianism and compelling defenses of liberalism against feminist and egalitarian critics.

On the orthodox approach, a theory of liberal egalitarian justice comprises a set of *normative principles* to guide the design and workings of social institutions. Normative principles purport to tell us what we should do, even if only defeasibly or in particular circumstances. For example, John Rawls's normative principles of justice tell us that in relatively favorable circumstances, when citizens are generally motivated to act rightly, we should design basic social and political institutions so that, working together, those institutions protect basic liberties, ensure equal opportunities in competitions for advantageous social positions, and ensure that any advantages attached to particular social positions work to the benefit of those who are least well off within the institutional scheme. Following Rawls, many think of these normative principles as realizing liberal egalitarian *ideals*. Whereas normative principles tell us what we should do, ideals capture what we aim to attain by so doing. By arranging institutions to comply with Rawlsian principles of justice, for example, we might aim to achieve *fairness* and *political equality*.

At the least ambitious level of description, my proposal is to redirect the flow of theoretical attention to the ideals that liberal egalitarian principles of justice aim to realize. My approach is decidedly *not* idealistic, so to avoid being misread in that direction, I'll generally refer to liberal egalitarian ideals as "values." By "values" (or "ideals"), I mean to refer to the *things that matter*. Among the things that matter to egalitarians, for example, are civic relationships of a certain character and fair distributions of social goods. Though we'll see that it has substantive implications for our thinking about justice, this redirection on its own is purely methodological. I'm not arguing that justice is consequentialist. I simply propose that those thinking about justice should take a longer look at the things that matter, aiming to discern the relative moral importance of those things that matter and the kinds of reasons they generate, before we turn to the work of systematizing answers to these questions in the form of normative principles. In a slogan: Rather than *normative principles*, our theorizing should principally aim to produce *evaluative discernment*. This book sets out a framework for doing just that. Call that framework "the schema."

2   THE ANATOMY OF JUSTICE

But the redirecting of attention is only part of the reorientation I want to propose. My proposal is for the schema in harness with a substantive way of filling it out: a partial set of liberal egalitarian values, or things that matter, and a ranking of the moral importance of those things. I argue that the proposed combination of schema and values—call it "the anatomy" of justice—constitutes an appealing approach to theorizing liberal egalitarian justice. It resolves difficulties internal to liberal egalitarianism; in part by resolving those difficulties, it shows liberal egalitarian theorizing to be helpfully action-guiding in circumstances of injustice; and it supports answers to feminist and egalitarian criticisms of liberalism.

My case for the anatomy's value with respect to disputes internal to liberal egalitarianism draws on two sets of considerations. First, I engage the longstanding dispute among egalitarians about whether equality is fundamentally a relational or a distributive value. The anatomy partially deflates that dispute by accommodating the increasingly common conviction that relational and distributive equality *both* matter, each in its own right. I argue that it is a mark in favor of the anatomy that it incorporates both distributive and relational egalitarian concerns and sets a principled and plausible priority relation among them. The second set of considerations that supports the anatomy from within liberal egalitarianism involves another longstanding dispute among egalitarians: the dispute about the *concept* of justice, between those who think justice just means fair shares (but that we sometimes have most reason *not* to pursue it because other things matter politically) and those who think justice is a complex concept that incorporates multiple distinct things that matter politically (and that we always or nearly always ought to pursue it). With respect to that dispute, too, the anatomy underpins a pluralist picture: Liberal egalitarian justice theorizing should employ both a pure concept of justice as fair shares *and* a broader concept of justice that encompasses additional evaluative considerations to more directly inform normative political judgments.

A second and related part of the case in support of the anatomy concerns its guidance for addressing injustice. By attending to and precisifying the things that matter, the anatomy supports a unified liberal egalitarianism that *could* be developed to describe the ideally just society, but that also, and more importantly, provides guidance for improving a highly *unjust* society. That's because the very same values that are optimally realized in a just society also provide guidance in circumstances of profound injustice. The normative principles these values issue may vary with circumstances, but these various, circumstance-dependent principles are underpinned by the single set of values, and we can theorize those values so as to render them at once concretely action-guiding and applicable across circumstances. Because the anatomy offers a modular framework for theorizing justice across a wide range of (just and) unjust circumstances, it is more broadly and concretely helpful than normative political theorizing is often thought to be.

INTRODUCTION   3

Finally, the anatomy I propose is valuable for underpinning compelling defenses against criticisms of liberalism from the left. These criticisms allege that foundational commitments of liberal justice theorizing render it inadequately responsive to injustice and inadequately permissive in licensing structural reform. I consider two criticisms, both longstanding charges against liberalism and both given new life in recent work by Sally Haslanger. First is the charge that liberalism's theoretical focus on the state renders it unable to address unjust culture; second is the charge that liberalism's method of moral justification renders it inadequately responsive to the empirics of existing social injustice and the wisdom of social movements. In both cases, I grant the foundational commitments attributed to liberalism—its state focus and its method of moral justification—but argue that those commitments don't have the alleged liabilities. Even if it focuses on the state, liberalism *can* adequately address unjust culture; and despite its method of moral justification, liberalism *can* respond adequately to the empirical nuance of existing injustice. In each case, my defense of liberalism draws on the liberal anatomy of justice I'm advancing.

Together, these three sets of arguments make a case for the anatomy of justice. More importantly, they make the case that liberal theorizing can help us think well and fruitfully about the injustices we confront. To many ears, terms like "left liberalism," "radical liberalism," "liberal egalitarianism," and "feminist liberalism" sound oxymoronic. To other ears, such terms simply ring hollow, as theoretical exercises that offer little guidance in the face of injustice, or, worse, as theoretical exercises that offer the *wrong* guidance, because normative political insights shouldn't come from a seminar room.[1] This book undertakes to show that liberal egalitarianism is viable and moreover that it is *valuable* for progressive politics. I do not shy away from the Rawlsian tradition that has become so unfashionable. Instead, I draw on the raw materials of that tradition, on what I take to be the fundamental, definitive commitments of liberal egalitarianism, and I assemble them in a way that lets them speak to the injustices we confront. Nor do I shy

---

[1] Here, I'm understanding "normative" broadly to include the kind of evaluative theorizing I do in this book. The terminology on offer is not ideal for my purposes. Because I judge it the least bad and most intuitive option, I use "normative" in two distinct ways depending on whether I'm using it to modify principles narrowly or theorizing broadly. For the narrow use of "normative," to modify principles as exemplified by Rawls's normative principles of justice, I might instead have used "prescriptive" or "deontic." But "prescriptive" sounds *too* narrow, as if implementing Rawls's principles were a matter of following simple instructions, and "deontic" sounds too substantive, as if I were defending a consequentialist picture of justice in opposition to Rawlsian deontological principles. And they both sound too technical for what I take myself to be doing. The broader use of "normative" is used to encompass narrowly normative principles as well as evaluative discernment I want to redirect our energies toward, and to contrast both with, for example, critical social theory or social ontology. For this, I might instead have used "political philosophy," but that risks suggesting I think critical theory and social ontology either aren't philosophy or aren't political. Or I might have used "philosophy in the Rawlsian tradition," but that is too narrow. Generally, context will make clear whether I mean normative *principles* in contrast with evaluative discernment, or normative *theory* to include evaluative discernment. When context doesn't clarify, I will do so explicitly.

4 THE ANATOMY OF JUSTICE

away from the methodology of analytical, broadly normative theorizing about justice. Instead, I show that normative theorizing is indispensable, including when it draws insights from, and when it counsels deference to, the boots on the ground. In short, I defend the anatomy of justice—and with it, the radical potential of liberal theorizing generally—by letting it flex its muscles.

0.1 Outline of the Case

In Chapter 1, "Two Pluralisms about Justice," I present the anatomy as a pluralist accommodation of two longstanding debates in political philosophy: a debate about the *concept* of justice and a debate about its *substance*. On the conceptual front, John Rawls and G. A. Cohen are flag-bearers for the opposing camps. Cohen sees justice as an input into the question of what we ought to do, politically speaking, and thinks that the justice input may have to be balanced against other considerations, like stability or efficiency.[2] On this way of thinking, we might sometimes have most reason *not* to pursue justice, for example because our circumstances are such that the measures necessary to pursue justice would be illegitimate, or too inefficient, or would make some worse off to nobody's gain. For Rawls, in contrast, justice is (closer to) an all-things-considered assessment of how social and political institutions ought to be arranged, which already incorporates those other considerations.[3] I think normative political theorizing needs *both* a pure, "aspirational" concept of justice as fair shares *and* a more-things-considered, "verdictive" concept that orders fair shares and other value inputs.

On the substantive front is the debate between relational and distributive egalitarians. On Elizabeth Anderson's formulation, this is a disagreement about "how to conceive of equality: as an equal distribution of non-relational goods among individuals, or as a kind of social relation between persons—an equality of authority, status, or standing."[4] I join a growing camp who think that distributive and relational equality *both* matter, and each in its own right. The anatomy of justice casts distributive egalitarianism as an account of fair shares, or aspirational justice, and it casts the relationally egalitarian value of mutual respect as an account of legitimacy. Legitimacy concerns the constraints we must abide by as we arrange the political institutions that set the terms on which we all will live cooperatively, or, within those institutions, as we seek collective political solutions to our shared social problems. Suppose you and I agree about what kind of social arrangement would be most just, or about how to remedy a particular injustice we confront. Suppose we're right, and we *know* we're right. And suppose we have the capacity to bring about the just arrangement or remediation. May we

---

[2] Cohen 2008.   [3] Rawls 1993, 1999a.   [4] Anderson 2010b, see also 1999.

do it? Suppose others disagree with us, and, although they're wrong, they have good reasons for believing as they do. Liberal legitimacy describes the permissible uses of political arrangements and political interventions to make things just or less unjust given that we will inevitably reasonably disagree about what justice is, about which current features of our society are *un*just, about which injustices take priority, and about the costs we should be willing to incur to make things better.

On the anatomy of justice, legitimacy adjudicates aspirational justice and all other value inputs into verdictive justice. Because on my substantive account of the things that matter, the relationally egalitarian value of mutual respect is the ideal that underpins the constraints of legitimacy, the anatomy is a version of "public reasons liberalism": a liberalism on which the legitimacy of some political action or political arrangement depends upon that action or arrangement being justifiable to reasonable citizens on the basis of reasons they can accept. (Figure 0.1.)

One challenge for values pluralists is to explain how a plurality of mutually irreducible values can underpin rational choice or provide practical normative guidance. This challenge evidently led Cohen and Rawls to agree on at least this much: We can't *both* theorize justice at the level of plural fundamental political values *and* have a theory that provides genuine and principled action guidance. We apparently can have at most one of these, because irreducible value plurality

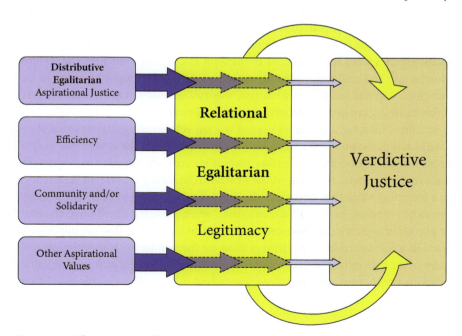

Figure 0.1 The anatomy of justice

6 THE ANATOMY OF JUSTICE

apparently entails that no metric exists by way of which we can weight distinct values within that plurality. Without such a metric, we apparently are forced into intuitionism or an *ad hoc* ranking, or we cannot rank the values at all. My book tackles a first-order normative project: describing and defending the anatomy of justice. I'll for the most part set aside the work of filling in the moral metaphysics that underlies it. But because so much of my argument relies on the relative moral weightiness of mutual respect relative to aspirational social values, I'll need to make the case that priority rankings *are possible* among irreducibly plural values—that we can avoid the route taken by some prominent defenders of values pluralism, which is to accept that the evaluative facts radically underdetermine what we ought to do.[5] In its final section, Chapter 1 makes that case.

The overarching aim of Chapters 2, 3, and 4 is to show that the anatomy locates the value of relational equality and the value of distributive equality in a way that can appeal to proponents of both, that is plausible in its own right, and that furnishes practically useful action guidance. Chapter 2, "Distributive Equality as Aspirational Justice," makes the case for distributive equality as an account of aspirational justice. It aims to convince relational egalitarians—who defend relational equality as the *sole* requirement of justice—not to reject the anatomy just because distributive equality is an irreducible part of it.[6] I make this case by defending responsibility-sensitive, or so-called "luck" egalitarian, distributive equality.[7] The chapter is structured as a response to some longstanding[8] and some more recent[9] objections to luck egalitarianism as a theory of justice. I argue that distinguishing luck egalitarianism as an account of aspirational justice within the conceptual picture I endorse enables luck egalitarians to answer objections, including by giving more content to answers already on offer based in values pluralism.[10] The anatomy equips us to defend a theory thought by many to be defective, without sacrificing what that theory's defenders rightly insist it gets right: its strong condemnation of distributive inequality.

In effect, Chapter 2 will have argued toward relational egalitarians that they should accept the presence of distributive egalitarianism in the anatomy of justice because the role distributive equality plays is securely contained. That argument casts mutual respect, the value at the heart of relationally egalitarian legitimacy, as a trumping value that constrains the force of other values to bear on the judgments of verdictive justice. This means that, when pursuing distributive equality or any other aspirational value comes at a cost to legitimacy, that pursuit always leads to a less valuable social arrangement on the whole, no matter the magnitudes of the gain or loss in question. Many theorists find lexical or trumping value relations deeply implausible. Indeed, many find it "more than a little mad" that

---

[5] See, for example, Raz 1999, 100; Berlin 2013, 11.   [6] Anderson 1999, 1; Scheffler 2003.
[7] See Anderson 1999.   [8] Anderson 1999, 2010b.   [9] Fishkin 2014.
[10] Temkin 2003; Voigt 2007; Stemplowska 2009; Huzum 2011.

any one consideration could have such priority that its presence always makes a state of affairs better in whole, no matter the loss in terms of other considerations.[11] The task of Chapter 3, "The Distributive Demands of Mutual Respect," is to make the case for the lexical priority of relational equality over distributive equality. I argue that the lexical priority ranking in the anatomy, unlike the one we find in Rawls, is intuitively plausible and extensionally adequate. This is because the lexically prior value of mutual respect is complex and multi-faceted, extensionally *seconding* a lot of the reasons independently furnished by aspirational values. I make this case about distributive equality in particular: Relationally egalitarian legitimacy is robustly distributively egalitarian, even more so than has so far been recognized. Because mutual respect cares about distributive equality as such, casting mutual respect as lexically prior does not implausibly subordinate distributive equality.

Chapter 2 will have defended a distributive egalitarian account of fair shares by emphasizing its position as a lexically subordinate value consideration, outweighed by any concern of the lexically primary value mutual respect. Chapter 3 will have defended the lexical priority of relational egalitarian legitimacy over distributive egalitarian aspirational justice largely by arguing that mutual respect is *itself* substantively very distributively egalitarian. This can all make the distributive egalitarian suspect that her favored version of equality does no real work within the anatomy of justice. In Chapter 4, "Relational Equality as Legitimacy," I argue that the anatomy of justice enables us to redeem the surpassing political importance of relational equality *without* unduly eclipsing the distributive egalitarian commitment to mitigating unearned disadvantage as a source of reasons of justice in its own right. I do this by describing two ways in which distributive equality can "speak up" even from within its lexically subordinated role. First, mutual respect *allows* the political pursuit of distributive equality to a greater degree than it *demands*, so distributive egalitarianism can direct us to go further toward equality than legitimacy requires us to do. Second, the anatomy shows how considerations of fairness can remain practically salient even when legitimacy forbids acting on them. Distributive egalitarians who are open to hybrid or pluralist accounts of justice should find that mine affords a plausible role to distributive equality.[12] More broadly, the argument of Chapter 4 describes how the *true* demands of justice can weigh in political deliberation and action even when legitimacy precludes acting on those demands as such—for example, when citizens reject the true account of justice as overly demanding, and when that account therefore cannot supply shared reasons that legitimize political action in pursuit of its realization.

---

[11] Goodin 1995.   [12] Wolff 1998; Lippert-Rasmussen 2015; Moles and Parr 2019.

8 THE ANATOMY OF JUSTICE

Chapter 5, "Values Tradeoffs under Injustice: The Feminist Debate over Basic Income," shows that the anatomy can provide plausible and illuminating guidance for policy in circumstances of injustice. I make this case by considering a values tradeoff case of particular concern for feminists: Universal basic income would materially benefit disadvantaged citizens, who are disproportionally women. On these grounds, feminists should welcome it. But basic income is also likely to lessen women's attachment to paid labor, because it will enable more of them to afford to prioritize caregiving. And more women prioritizing caregiving at a cost to their paid labor attachment will reinforce norms associating women with caregiving. On *these* grounds, feminists seem to have reason to *resist* basic income.[13] I consider the feminist debate over basic income as a case study illustrating how the anatomy of justice adjudicates tradeoffs among social aims that liberal egalitarian feminists ought to endorse, in light of the fact that unjust circumstances can place those aims at odds with one another. In previous work, I have argued that the gendered division of labor is best diagnosed as a problem of legitimacy, rather than a problem of distributive justice.[14] If considerations of legitimacy constrain what we may do in pursuit of distributive justice, as they do on the anatomy I advance, then a diagnosis of the gendered division of labor as a problem of legitimacy may seem to strongly subordinate the goal of distributive justice to the goal of gender equality. This would be a problematic consequence, and this lurking worry resonates with the charge that liberal egalitarianism is inadequately responsive to intersecting injustices. In response, I deny that the anatomy implausibly subordinates distributive equality to gender equality and show that it underpins nuanced, plausible, and context-responsive judgments regarding the values tradeoff in question.

Chapters 6 and 7 consider two lines of criticism against liberal theorizing of the sort this book exemplifies. In recent work, Sally Haslanger criticizes "mainstream political philosophy" for its focus on the state as the primary subject matter of justice and for its methodology of reflective equilibrium for theorizing about justice.[15] Using the anatomy of justice to illustrate the capacities of "mainstream" political philosophy, I defend against these criticisms. My defenses embrace the features of theorizing that Haslanger disparages and defend them against Haslanger's charges: Neither a focus on the state as the primary subject of justice nor a methodology of reflective equilibrium undermine the adequacy of the anatomy of justice, and any inadequacies with the "mainstream" generally must be found elsewhere.

In Chapter 6, "Liberalism, Culture, and the Subject Matter of Justice," I take up the first of these charges. Haslanger argues that a focus on the state renders

---

[13] For contributions to this debate, see Robeyns 2001; Bergmann 2004; Baker 2008; Elgarte 2008; Gheaus 2008; Orloff 2013.
[14] Schouten 2019.   [15] Haslanger 2017, 2020, 2021b.

theorizing inadequate for critiquing ideological culture. I distinguish two challenges. The first is to liberalism's *diagnostic* adequacy: Does liberalism's focus on the state as a subject of justice prevent it from impugning ideological culture in plausible ways? The second is to liberalism's *rectificatory* adequacy: Does liberalism's focus on the state render it impotent to prescribe plausible rectification for ideological culture? I acknowledge that certain versions of liberalism *do* lack the capacity to call culture unjust and to issue certain demands of justice that apply directly to individuals. But I argue that this limitation is well motivated and substantively not very restrictive. Moreover, I argue, the anatomy of justice enables us to see how liberals can impugn culture in justice-rich terms by observing that culture erodes the values that just institutions are arranged to realize.

In Chapter 7, "Reflective Equilibrium and Social Critique," I address Haslanger's second criticism: that the methodology of mainstream political philosophy renders it inadequate for addressing (sexist) ideology. Haslanger argues that the methodology cannot underpin adequately contextualized social critique and cannot incorporate the wisdom of social movements. Drawing on the anatomy of justice, I argue that the methodology in question *can* supply context-responsive normative guidance and *can* incorporate insights from social movements. I show that Haslanger's case to the contrary owes to a mischaracterization of the methodology and an underappreciation of its capacity for incorporating diverse kinds of evidence about injustice. The anatomy of justice constitutes a feminist egalitarian liberalism that withstands prominent objections from the left. If sound, my case for that anatomy undermines categorical rejections of liberalism as overly status quo biased and shows that liberalism's feminist and egalitarian potential is not undermined by some of liberalism's most derided, most emblematic commitments.

In whole, my case for the anatomy rests on its theoretical and practical usefulness. The anatomy is *theoretically* useful because it supports intuitively compelling resolutions to longstanding difficulties in political philosophy, in large part by deflating longstanding disputes: Distributive equality and relational equality *both* matter as fundamental values. We need *both* a pure concept of justice as fair shares and a more-things-considered concept of justice that can inform judgments about what we should do politically in our circumstances. The anatomy is *practically* useful because it furnishes action guidance across circumstances of injustice that's appropriately responsive to interacting and mutually supporting injustices along lines of economic inequality, race, and gender. It unifies judgments about what a just society looks like with judgments about what steps we should take now to make things better. It clarifies ideals of justice, illuminates shortcomings, and calls for radical corrective reform. And by doing all *that*, the theory underpins satisfying answers to criticisms from the left. Although some liberalisms may be undermined by those criticisms, *liberalism as such* is not ill-fitted to support radical social critique. The anatomy of justice shows this by

10 THE ANATOMY OF JUSTICE

doing what critics claim mainstream (liberal) theorizing cannot do: recognizing and impugning injustice and calling for structural change to confront it.

In short, this book makes the case for the anatomy of justice simply by describing it and exploring the things it enables us to say and do. Because these are things that we should want to be able to say and do using normative political theorizing, I think this constitutes a strong case that the anatomy merits consideration, both from liberal egalitarians and from egalitarian and feminist critics of liberalism. Rather than to settle any of the particular debates I consider in light of the anatomy, I hope to nudge an ongoing conversation in a new direction. I think the new direction can be a fruitful one. It enables us to see that many ongoing debates within liberal egalitarianism are overblown, and that different camps' cherished convictions about justice can be explored and developed non-oppositionally. And it enables us to glimpse possibilities for fruitful engagement between liberal egalitarians and liberalism's egalitarian critics—both oppositional engagement that may previously have seemed futile, and collaborative engagement in cases wherein distinct but non-oppositional inquiries might prove mutually illuminating.

If you feel adequately well introduced to the project, you can now proceed to Chapter 1. If you have lingering questions about my (mis)use of Rawls or about the mainstream-critical and Rawls-critical audience I'm hoping to engage, the final two sections of this Introduction might hold the answers.

0.2 How Mainstream? How Rawlsian?

The ideals that feature in the anatomy are clearly liberal and recognizably Rawlsian. They include the values embodied by the two principles of justice and the values emphasized in Rawls's later development of justice as fairness as a public reasons liberalism.[16] Some readers of this book have found in the anatomy a mere repackaging of Rawls's theory; they think this mere repackaging does little more than show that Rawls all along had the resources to move beyond ideal theory. Other readers reject my claimed affinities with Rawls, arguing that I'm distorting the raw materials I claim to find in Rawlsian public reasons liberalism and understating my departure from it. I am open to the possibility that one (both?) of these charges is apt. My interest is in securing the practical upshots and the theoretical gains that can be had by looking at things as I propose we do. My use of Rawls is friendly but mostly utilitarian. My aim is not to defend Rawls's theory, though I'm not opposed to a defense being drawn from my arguments and I think certainly a defense of the *usefulness* of Rawls's work is there ready to be drawn.

[16] Rawls 1993.

I invoke Rawls throughout this book mostly because he serves as a touchstone for the various debates I use the anatomy of justice to (re)consider and because many readers will better understand how I propose to see things by comparing my vision with Rawls's. This section offers a preview which such readers may find clarifying. It outlines some of the ways in which my way of seeing things differs from—though is not necessarily much at odds with—the ways in which Rawls oriented our attention. (For readers who *don't* find this clarifying, I aim for the book's main argument to presuppose no deep knowledge of Rawls.)

Most significantly, I want to propose that we can get more bang for the theoretical buck by focusing our attention on a different and earlier span in the range of normative inferences. Rawls thinks about *what we should do* politically—about how we should arrange our social and political institutions. In contrast, I focus on *what value considerations should inform* what we do institutionally—on what goods we should arrange institutions to realize. For example, whereas Rawls defends a theory of justice that tells us that a just society must protect basic liberties above all else, I propose to think about the value that underpins the moral urgency of prescriptions like the one the basic liberties principle encompasses: Protections for the basic liberties matter quite a lot because *mutual civic respect* and *political equality* matter quite a lot.

Looking back at the picture of the anatomy above, imagine an additional arrow in the top right-hand corner. Imagine that this arrow begins at the top part of the verdictive justice box and reaches rightward into a new box. Imagine that new box is labeled, "normative principles of justice under persistent full compliance." Imagine that this box contains the principles derivable from the anatomy of justice that apply to the very most favorable range of circumstances—namely, circumstances of present full compliance and with no history of injustice that limits the extent to which we can now realize the values of justice. We'll see that verdictive justice as I understand it is an *evaluative assessment*. It orders the political values that a social arrangement might realize so that we can discern of some arrangement how good it is by the lights of those values. From my account of verdictive justice, it is open to someone to argue that Rawlsian justice as fairness comprises the *normative principles* most fit to regulate a society under favorable circumstances and full compliance—that justice as fairness belongs in the new box we just imagined. But my focus is on verdictive justice itself, and on what it can do for us even without us needing to work out what normative principles it supports under what kinds of circumstances.

The substantive implications of focusing on evaluative assessment are significant. For one thing, when we theorize justice as a framework of things that matter rather than as a set of normative principles for realizing those things, we can render theory robust across a wider range of circumstances. To anticipate a running illustration throughout the book, consider Rawlsian fair equality of opportunity, which calls for our prospects for attaining desirable social positions to be

12 THE ANATOMY OF JUSTICE

unaffected by race or social class.[17] In circumstances of deep injustice, *the value* of fair equal opportunity plausibly calls for radically progressive educational practices, reform to economic institutions, and strict regulation of inheritance and bequest. And, when it comes to selection for positions, that value might call for affirmative hiring practices. After all, we won't reach a point at which prospects for attaining desirable positions are unaffected by race or social class if we don't correct for the mechanisms by way of which race and class currently do influence prospects.[18] But in more just circumstances, when it comes to selection, that same value might call only for anti-discrimination. If fair equal opportunity is theorized as a value, then a social arrangement is always less good, other things equal, insofar as that arrangement tolerates unequal opportunities. But what the value tells us *to do* depends on the nature of the inequalities in question. Understood as a value or a thing that matters, we'll see, fair equality of opportunity issues unified but distinct guidance across relevantly different circumstances.[19]

Now notice a second substantive implication of the shift in focus from normative principles to the value considerations that underpin them: This shift enables us to make progress and gain clarity about the relationships among the various things that matter; indeed, it enables us to see that theorizing justice as a set of normative principles actively obscures important possibilities about how various things that matter might relate. For example, Rawlsian lexical priority is notoriously implausible: Roughly speaking, it is notoriously implausible that protecting basic liberties is *always* more important than achieving distributive fairness. But we *might* be able to countenance a lexical priority relation *among the values* that underpin the principles. I'll argue that lexical priority among values is consistent with a nuanced, principled, and context-responsive relationship among the normative principles those values underpin.

A second point of departure from Rawlsian orthodoxy makes the substantive divergence seem more significant. Among the alternative (types of) theories of justice to which Rawls opposes his own principles, utilitarianism features most prominently. Second comes intuitionism. Rawls defines intuitionism as a form of values pluralism which includes "no explicit method, no priority rules, for weighing these principles against one another: we are simply to strike a balance by intuition, by what seems to us most nearly right."[20] The anatomy of justice is a political values pluralism that *does* include priority rankings. Rawls rejects intuitionism on the grounds that intuitionism helps us not at all in the ubiquitous cases of values tradeoffs. But he never explicitly raises the possibility of a *non*-intuitionist values

---

[17] Rawls 2001, 42–4.
[18] On corrective justice and fair equality of opportunity, see Shelby 2004, 2013; Shiffrin 2004; Mills 2013.
[19] This approach to theorizing about justice in circumstances of injustice has affinities with that suggested by Adam Swift in his Swift 2008.
[20] Rawls 1999a, 30.

pluralism, despite the facts that his own principles aim to *realize values* and that his ranking of principles plausibly is underpinned by the unequal moral importance of the values those principles realize. Seen from this angle, the anatomy of justice appears to be a substantive alternative to Rawls's theory, though we agree a lot with respect to the things that matter. Arguably, mine is an approach to theorizing justice that Rawls didn't address as a contender: a non-intuitionist political values pluralism.[21]

To illuminate the contrast, note that Rawls's original position argument, by his lights, yields a different type of principles for institutions than for individuals. On the institutional front, we've seen, the original position argument yields all-things-considered normative principles meant to guide the design of social and political institutions. On the individual front, Rawls claims that the output of the original position argument is a set of *prima facie* duties, which we thereafter have to weigh and balance in cases of conflict.[22] He never gives a reason, that I can find, for why we can derive all-things-considered principles for institutions but only *prima facie* principles for individuals. But it is significant that his discussion of civil disobedience in the context of individuals' duty of justice comprises his only extended work on non-ideal theory in *Theory of Justice*. Because he theorizes individuals' duties of justice as *prima facie* duties, or sets of defeasible reasons that derive from certain value commitments, Rawls is better equipped in the case of individual duties to apply his theorizing across a wider range of circumstances. For example, the same considerations that tell us why we should generally support just institutions also tell us how *un*just institutions may become before they lose their moral authority to compel us. I propose to construe a theory of justice for institutions on the model Rawls employs when he turns to principles for individuals. I won't employ the constructivist device of the original position, but the values I endorse overlap with those that justify its design features and that show up in the Rawlsian strand of public reasons liberalism—hereafter "political liberalism"—to regulate legitimate political action. The values of mutual respect and fairness feature especially prominently in the anatomy I endorse.

I see the anatomy of justice as a politically liberal egalitarianism that is Rawlsian in spirit and that owes a very great deal to Rawls's work, but that departs in practically and theoretically significant ways from justice as fairness. Maybe at the end of the day I'm merely repackaging justice as fairness, or maybe I'm departing from it more significantly than I advertise. I'm interested in having that conversation and will continue having it with those who are likewise interested.

---

[21] What Rawls called "intuitionism," Cohen called "radical pluralism." The "radical" part comes from the lack of method for weighting principles in cases of conflict. Accordingly, understood in Cohen's terms, what I aim to stake out is a *non*-radical pluralism (which imposes substantively radical demands for reform). See Cohen 2008, 4–5.

[22] See for example Rawls 1999a, 308.

14 THE ANATOMY OF JUSTICE

But in this book, I'll focus instead on what we can do with the anatomy of justice, setting aside the question of just how Rawlsian the anatomy is.

0.3 How Feminist? How Egalitarian?

This book is congenial to the critical reader who wishes political philosophers would stop litigating textual questions about what Rawls said or what he meant. I litigate such questions rarely, only when I think the litigation helps us better understand the content of justice. But a different kind of critical reader, tired not only of talk about Rawls but of theorizing justice in left liberal, Rawlsian terms, may find her patience tested. I ask this reader to bear with me. This book is written largely *for her*. I think that she and I share some important political convictions, and I think the tradition I'm working in does more for us than she thinks it does. I want to try to persuade her of this. In my view, Rawls *did* correctly discern fundamental political values: Reciprocity matters. Democratic governance based on our status as free and equal matters. The interests of the most vulnerable among us matter. These observations alone seem to defuse a lot of what masquerades as criticism of Rawlsian liberalism. For instance, Nancy Fraser wrote in 2001 that "the central political question of the day" is "how can we develop a coherent orientation that integrates redistribution and recognition."[23] On this count, she found Rawlsian liberalism lacking. But Rawls's theory is a coherent integration of just those evaluative considerations; as others have pointed out, it is a mistake to construe Rawls as offering only a theory of *distributive* justice.[24] My reorientation of liberalism does stick close to the parts of Rawls's view that provide foundation for not only a coherent but a *compelling* answer to the still-central question Fraser posed. But when we try to build out the values of justice *before* encoding them in normative principles, including especially building out a view about the relative weightiness of those values, we get a theory that looks importantly different than Rawls's. And the differences prove crucial to answering some of the more persistent challenges to liberalism.

The objections I consider are motivated largely by the thought that liberalism isn't helpful—indeed, in some cases, by the thought that it is downright *inimical*—to progressive social movements. I come at this challenge primarily from the direction of liberalism's feminist critics, drawing the substance of the criticisms largely from recent work by Sally Haslanger. I'll consider Haslanger's criticisms of "mainstream political philosophy" and argue that my proposed anatomy of justice is not undermined by them. To the contrary, my proposed approach to theorizing liberal egalitarian justice can underpin a feminism that

---

[23] Fraser 2001, 38.   [24] See for example Robeyns 2003.

is emancipatory and appropriately responsive to the intersections of gender injustice with racial and economic injustice. I make the case both by refuting arguments to the contrary conclusion and by demonstration: Because this book draws on the tools and answers the questions that typify mainstream political philosophy, and because it uses those tools to defend answers that critics allege are inaccessible by way of the tools in question, the book constitutes a defense of the tools and questions themselves.[25]

On Haslanger's characterization, we'll see, "mainstream political philosophy" undertakes to develop and apply theory that can provide guidance about justice across contexts: It attempts to refine theory as a set of tools that we can use to discern and rectify injustice under various circumstances. To that end, it employs certain kinds of abstractions. It proceeds in part by testing tools against problems that we already know how to solve: In these "test" cases, we know what a theory of justice should say is unjust or what it should tell us to do about it; we know what a good tool will do. *Everyone* who wants to think carefully about right and wrong employs test cases in some way. So far, we have parity between mainstream theorizing and its detractors. But in allowing that the tools we need may be complex and need fine-tuning, mainstream theorizing goes further. If a tool seems good but imperfect, we might try to adjust it before we discard it. And if we're still trying to figure out whether it's ready to go, we might test it in complex ways: Sure, this tool did pretty well on this job, but what if the contraption needing repair had a little more rust *right there*? Would it still have worked? What if our circumstances changed in this foreseeable way or that? Will the tool still do the job? The tool metaphor illustrates one way in which this book is an instance of mainstream political philosophy, and one way in which that positions it to address methodological criticism of mainstream political philosophy: Because its methodology often relies on projections about how theory will fare under a wide range of circumstances, the argument of this book inherits mainstream political philosophy's appearance, to some, as being overly abstract and disengaged.

But its methodology isn't the only thing that makes the book "mainstream." Its aspiration and the particular tools it seeks to refine and employ also play a role. The book aspires to shed light on the moral domain. It doesn't assume that all the

---

[25] In some cases, I draw on my previous work and other liberal feminist scholarship to serve as further evidence that "mainstream" tools and questions can accomplish just what their detractors deny they can do. I see *The Anatomy of Justice* as a natural extension of my first book, *Liberalism, Neutrality, and the Gendered Division of Labor* (Schouten 2019). That book argued that progressive social policies aimed at eroding the gendered division of labor constitute legitimate exercises of political power, even though those policies undertake to change social norms by burdening some reasonable choices individuals make about how to configure their domestic lives. I made the case by grounding a certain vision of gender equality on the complex value of mutual respect, which I argued is the core value at the heart of liberal democratic legitimacy. *The Anatomy of Justice* undertakes a further exploration of that value and situates it within a broader framework for theorizing justice. The anatomy thus undergirds my earlier work, and the earlier work in turn joins some of the arguments of this book to illustrate the anatomy's implications.

16 THE ANATOMY OF JUSTICE

answers, or indeed *any* of the answers, will be settled by the verdicts rendered by democratic processes or by the claims advanced by social movements. This is what can make mainstream political philosophy seem elitist, anti-democratic, technocratic. The particular tools the book works to refine are the tools of feminist liberal egalitarianism. In making its refinements, it draws on the contributions of the *quintessential* mainstream thinker of contemporary political philosophy, John Rawls. This is what can make mainstream political theorizing seem hegemonic, exclusive, campy.

I thus draw liberally on Haslanger's attempted takedown of mainstream political philosophy because it captures and gives credibility to something heavy in the air: the sense that analytic, normative political philosophy in the post-Rawlsian tradition is disengaged, elitist, hegemonic. There is a current mood of antipathy toward anything that smacks of Rawls, of liberalism, of orthodoxy. Insofar as that mood manifests the desire to see things done in more and different ways, I'm all for it. We should continue the move, already well underway, to disrupt the hegemony of post-Rawlsian liberalism. Indeed, I'll argue that the "mainstream" methodology Haslanger criticizes directs normative theorists to be in deep conversation with those who use different methodologies to address different kinds of questions. But insofar as the mood manifests the desire to move away not only from the *hegemony* of mainstream or Rawlsian liberalism but from *mainstream or Rawlsian liberalism itself*, I think it's misguided. That is the case that I hope to make through deep engagement with an influential spokesperson for these criticisms.

The Anatomy of Justice: On the Shape, Substance, and Power of Liberal Egalitarianism. Gina Schouten, Oxford University Press. © Gina Schouten 2024. DOI: 10.1093/9780191999772.003.0001

1
Two Pluralisms about Justice

The project of the book is to develop a particular approach to theorizing liberal egalitarian justice and to argue for that approach on the grounds that it supports compelling resolutions to longstanding disputes and difficulties internal to egalitarianism, and compelling defenses against external challenges coming from egalitarian and feminist critics of liberal theorizing. The task of this first chapter is to set out the approach in question. As a way in, consider some views I endorse about the substance of justice:

1. We have reasons of fairness to equalize citizens' shares of social goods. These reasons of fairness are often not decisive. They must be weighed against other evaluative considerations.
2. Among those other evaluative considerations are considerations of mutual respect. Mutual respect favors our acting politically only in ways that respect the civic equality of all citizens, including those who disagree with us about what social ends are worth pursuing. When some way of pursuing fairness runs afoul of mutual respect, we should avoid pursuing fairness in that way.

These statements reflect the convictions that some degree of distributive equality is among the things that matter (1), but that our pursuit of distributive equality is constrained by the requirement that we treat others as equals (2). This can be summed up using terms of contemporary political philosophy like this: Distributive equality and relational equality both matter; distributive equality is the consideration at the heart of *fairness*; relational equality is the consideration at the heart of *legitimacy*. I now add: Both fairness and legitimacy matter for *justice*, and neither is reducible to the other.

This chapter draws out these convictions and assembles their component parts into what I call the "anatomy of justice." The anatomy begins with the *things that matter* for justice, like relational and distributive equality. I think that if we theorize them in a certain way, these things that matter can tell us a great deal both about what a just society would look like and about how we ought to act now to reform our *un*just society in light of the tradeoffs and feasibility constraints that our circumstances present. For simplicity, I often refer to the things that matter as "values" or "ideals." This doesn't mean I think justice is consequentialist. We'll see that on my view, the things that matter include civic relationships of a certain

18 THE ANATOMY OF JUSTICE

character and fair distributions of social goods. On this framing, justice can remain deontological, just as Rawlsian liberals commonly take it to be.[1] The proposal as I've described it so far in this paragraph is purely methodological: When we theorize about justice, we should take a longer look at what things matter—and at how their mattering stacks up against the mattering of other things that matter—before we try to systematize those answers in the form of normative principles for the design of social institutions.

But the proposal this book develops goes beyond the methodological. I also want to populate the schema just described with a certain set of values—namely, relational and distributive equality—and to defend a certain relationship among those values—namely, one wherein relational equality enjoys strong priority. And I want to show that the anatomy cogently makes use of two distinct concepts of justice—one referring to the single consideration of fairness, the other referring to a more encompassing evaluative judgment. I argue for the resulting anatomy of justice on the grounds that it enables us to say and do things with normative political theory that we should want to be able to say and do. That case is multifaceted. I want it to speak to those who think distributive equality is all there is to justice; to those who think relational equality is all there is to justice; to those who think that distinct things matter but that we can have no systematic weighting mechanism to guide us in cases of values conflicts; and to those who suspect that all this is merely academic, that none of it helps us to make things better. Concretely, this chapter does two things: It explicates the anatomy of justice as advancing two pluralisms about justice, and it shows how from the anatomy we can derive normative guidance under circumstances of injustice.

1.1 Two Ongoing Debates

To understand how the anatomy of justice advances two distinct but related pluralisms about justice, it helps to see it as intervening within two ongoing debates in political philosophy. The first is a debate about the *concept* of justice; the second is a debate about the *substance* of justice. To present the anatomy and show how it intervenes within these two debates, I'll first sketch the landscape of each.

We can elucidate the conceptual dispute over what "justice" means by considering the figures cast as flag-bearers: G. A. Cohen construes justice as *one input* into the question of how we should arrange the terms of social cooperation, while John Rawls formulates principles of justice that broadly encompass evaluative considerations bearing on how we should arrange the terms of social cooperation.

---

[1] On the anatomy of justice, we can construe the things that matter such that the right remains prior to the good. This is due to the content of the things that matter within the anatomy. See Kymlicka 1988; Rawls 1999a, 26–7.

For Cohen, judgments of justice must be balanced against other value consider-ations, like stability or feasibility, in order to provide practical guidance; for Rawls, these value considerations bearing on what we should do are *part of* justice.[2]

The second debate that my project engages concerns the substance of justice's demands. This is the debate between distributive and relational egalitarians. On Elizabeth Anderson's formulation, it's a debate about "how to conceive of equality: as an equal distribution of non-relational goods among individuals, or as a kind of social relation between persons—an equality of authority, status, or standing."[3] Distributive egalitarians take justice to impose fundamentally *distributive* demands. The best-known variant, so-called "luck egalitarianism," holds that "it is bad—unjust and unfair—for some to be worse off than others through no fault [or choice] of their own."[4] A common positive formulation has it that luck egalitarians are unified in the conviction that justice demands seriously reducing or eliminat-ing involuntary disadvantage—that is, disadvantage for which those on the losing end are not responsible or not to blame.[5] Relational egalitarians, in contrast, don't find fault with distributive inequalities *as such*. For Anderson, rather than eroding unearned disadvantage, "the proper negative aim of egalitarian justice is...to end oppression."[6] The proper positive aim is "to create a community in which people stand in relations of equality to others."[7] This is a *democratic* equality, where "democratic" means "collective self-determination by means of open discussion among equals, in accordance with rules acceptable to all."[8]

The conceptual and substantive debates are not unrelated. The most influen-tial luck and relational egalitarians are divided on what justice *is* even as they argue about what it *demands*. Coming down on the Rawlsian side, Elizabeth Anderson claims that justice generates all-things-considered "oughts." As such, the right account of justice will abide by certain constraints: Justice "adheres to the maxim that 'ought' implies 'can'"; principles of justice must be "*publicly artic-ulable*"; they must be "*stable* such that people can be motivated...to follow [them] over time"; and they must "satisfy a *Pareto improvement* condition: that they not forbid actions or block events that advance some people's interests to no one else's disadvantage."[9] Anderson defends her relationally egalitarian view—and criticizes

---

[2] See, for example, Rawls 1999a, 3; Cohen 2008, 7.   [3] Anderson 2010b, 1.
[4] Temkin 1993, 13. The term "luck egalitarian" was first leveled as disparagement in Anderson's early critique of the views she referred to by that name. See Anderson 1999.
[5] Luck egalitarians disagree about what kind of fault, choice, responsibility, or blame is relevant here. For a survey of this and other disputes internal to luck egalitarianism, see Lippert-Rasmussen 2016. Two canonical defenses of luck egalitarianism are Arneson 1989; Cohen 1989. (But see Arneson 2008.) Dworkin 1981 is often taken as a canonical defense of luck egalitarianism, but Dworkin rejects that construal of his view in Dworkin 2003.
[6] Anderson 1999, 289.   [7] Anderson 1999, 288–9.
[8] Anderson 1999, 313. Other canonical defenses of relational egalitarianism include Miller 1997; Scheffler 2003.
[9] Anderson 2010b, 17; italics from the original.

20   THE ANATOMY OF JUSTICE

luck egalitarianism—on just these counts. But Cohen, a luck egalitarian, regards Anderson's constraints as "alien to justice."[10] For Cohen, a principle of political action that incorporates considerations of feasibility, publicity, stability, or efficiency is not a principle of justice at all, but rather a "rule of regulation": The former tells us what someone is due, while the latter tells us, roughly, what should be done to provide them with it.[11] Only the latter are subject to constraints of feasibility, publicity, stability, and Pareto optimality.[12] So, feasibility, publicity, and stability don't affect *what someone is due*—on Cohen's definition of the term, they don't affect the substance of *justice*—but they can of course affect what should be done to *secure* it.

In this way, the debate between luck and relational egalitarians is bound up with the debate over the concept "justice." For Anderson, justice gives final judgments on what we ought to do politically, and relational equality captures those judgments. For Cohen, justice is one input into what we ought to do politically, and that input calls for distributive equality. Both debates, like most debates about justice, proceed largely by way of consulting intuitions about what justice could or could not plausibly demand. And both sides seem to have a powerful case to make: If justice tells us fairly directly what to do politically, then a substantive account of justice that includes such considerations as efficiency, Pareto superiority, and democratic legitimacy will seem much more credible than a substantive account focused only on distributive equality. But if justice is *only one part* of what we should do politically, we can mount a powerful case for distributive equality as exhausting its demands. How are we to situate the philosophical import of either argument—or even to know whether or not we share the intuitions being invoked—if the parties are in fundamental disagreement even about what kind of a thing justice *is*?

We might begin by ensuring that all parties are talking about the same concept, one concept at a time, even if they don't yet agree that that's the one to call "justice." This is the strategy I employ. I want to explicate the following suggestion, and by the end of this chapter make it seem like a plausible hypothesis worthy of further consideration: Political philosophy needs both an *aspirational* and a *verdictive* concept of justice. *Aspirational justice* lines up with Cohen's concept of justice: It simply means fairness understood as each getting her due. The right substantive account of aspirational justice, I'll argue, is straightforwardly distributive. *Verdictive justice* is an evaluative ranking of social arrangements. It can tell us which social arrangement we have most moral reason to bring about

---

[10] Cohen 2008, 337.   [11] Cohen 2008, especially 275.

[12] For arguments (which I find persuasive) that Cohen cannot regard any ethos that includes productive requirements as an ethos of *justice* if he insists that Paretian considerations are extrinsic to justice, see Quong 2010; Tomlin 2010.

once all sources of political value are accounted for.[13] Neither luck nor relational egalitarianism, I'll contend, is a plausible account of verdictive justice. What relational egalitarianism plausibly *does* capture, though, are the demands of another moral concept that *informs* verdictive justice: *Legitimacy* imposes constraints on what we may do politically, in a liberal democratic society, to realize political values including aspirational justice.

What, then, should we call justice? Perhaps the two concepts equally merit the name, and we'll need to attach "verdictive" or "aspirational" in perpetuity. Perhaps we would do better to reserve "justice" for only one part of the anatomy. I leave that question open in favor of addressing the parts of the two debates that don't reduce to disagreement about the names of things. The thing that Cohen calls "justice" matters; so does the thing that Rawls and Anderson call "justice." Distributive equality matters in ways that are irreducible to relational equality; so too does relational equality matter in irreducible ways.

There is ample enthusiasm for hybrid, pluralistic, ecumenical, and deflationary accounts, both of the concept of justice and of the (seeming) disagreement between luck and relational egalitarians.[14] The anatomy of justice brings these conversations together, provides a theoretical foundation for a pluralism about the concept of justice and about relational and distributive equality, and offers guidance for confronting injustice. It does this through the lens of a kind of Rawlsian political liberalism, thereby making strides too toward showing how that framework can be action-guiding in circumstances of injustice. In the next section, I sketch the *conceptual* anatomy. Then, in section 1.3, I propose *substantive accounts* of two key concepts. Finally, in section 1.4, I locate my political values pluralism within the broader values pluralism literature.

1.2 Conceptual Pluralism: Aspirational and Verdictive Justice

At its most modest, I've said, the aspiration of this book is to propose a new schema for thinking about justice: to theorize justice as a weighted specification of the *things that matter*. The anatomy's conceptual accommodation comes from recognizing that, once we take that schematic approach, we really need a concept of justice that captures what Cohen had in mind *and* a concept of justice that encompasses more of the considerations that Rawls and Anderson (but not Cohen) regarded as intrinsic to justice.

---

[13] Verdictive justice is not the same thing as Cohen's "rules of regulation," we'll see, because it doesn't aim to give prescriptive guidance on what to do. On Rawls's and Cohen's respective concepts of justice, see Williams 2008.

[14] On the substantive front, see Wolff 1998; Schemmel 2011; Tan 2012; Lippert-Rasmussen 2015, 2016; Vallentyne 2015; Gheaus 2018; Moles and Parr 2019. On the conceptual front, see Tomlin 2012; James 2018.

22 THE ANATOMY OF JUSTICE

In the anatomy, the things that matter come in two importantly different varieties. First are aspirational social values. These things that matter comprise the attributes by virtue of which a social arrangement may be *in one way better* or *in one way worse*. For us, the most important aspirational social value is distributive fairness, which I call "aspirational justice." This value gives us reasons to arrange the terms of social cooperation to give each citizen her fair share of social value.[15] Set aside the question of what comprises a fair share; for now, we just want to get a sense of the concepts in play. To the degree that our social arrangement secures for each citizen her fair share, that social arrangement is in one way better; to the degree that it doesn't, it's in one way worse. "Efficiency" plausibly names another aspirational value: This is the value of having more social product to go around rather than less. After all, apart from a fair distribution of whatever social value happens to exist, we want enough so that a fair share equips each citizen to live a good life. We want social value to be distributed fairly *and* to be abundant. We can defer the work of defending a particular conception of efficiency, but minimally, a social arrangement is less efficient insofar as it is worse for some and better for none.[16] Plausibly, still other aspirational values name yet more attributes by virtue of which a social arrangement can be in one way better: "Community" or "solidarity" might name ways in which social arrangements can be better by virtue of citizens' interpersonal relations. A "prioritarian" or "humanist" aspirational value might strengthen our moral reason to benefit people in proportion to how badly off those people are.[17] Plausibly, these aspirational values are unequally important, and their importance plausibly varies with circumstances. For example, humanity is plausibly of relatively great importance when the worst off suffer greatly.

The second type of thing that matters *adjudicates* these aspirational social values. This type I call "legitimacy." Legitimacy tells us whether some aspirational value may be pursued by use of state power, and whether any particular use of state power is a permissible means of pursuing it. The distinctness of legitimacy captures the intuitive thought that it is one thing to ask whether some policy would make society fairer or more solidaristic or even better by the lights of *the*

---

[15] Here and throughout the chapter, I describe the anatomy as one on which values give rise to types of reasons. That might suggest that I'm committing myself to the view that values or "things that matter" are explanatorily more fundamental than reasons. In fact, I want to remain as neutral as possible on matters of normative metaphysics. I am open to the idea, for example, that reasons are normatively fundamental, and that what I'm describing as values are valuable because they are sources of reasons. Thanks to Jeff Behrends for helpful discussion about this.

[16] Some might argue that Pareto or constrained maximizing considerations are *part of* aspirational justice. I tend to think that the abundance of social value and the fairness of its distribution are conceptually distinct evaluative considerations, and only the latter a matter of aspirational justice, but I'm not sure. I will suggest in due course that certain aspects of both are implied by relational egalitarian *legitimacy*, and that meeting those distributive and Paretian/maximizing requirements is therefore a limiting condition for any liberal democratic political arrangement.

[17] See Parfit 2000; O'Neill 2008.

balance of aspirational values, and another thing entirely to ask whether that social policy is one that it would be permissible to enact. Conceptually, then, legitimacy judges the moral permissibility of social aims to be pursued by way of political power and the moral permissibility of political action to pursue those aims: May exercises of political power be justified by invoking this or that account of fairness? May an account of fairness be pursued using this or that policy? As I understand it, the concept legitimacy is such that an account of legitimacy need not settle the distinct question of what individual citizens should do in response to political actions or arrangements. Democratic legitimacy concerns how citizens of a democracy may exercise their shared power—or authorize the state to exercise power on their behalf—in the form of political action. An answer to that question needn't settle distinct questions concerning individual citizens' obligations to obey—for example, whether citizens always are morally bound to comply with legitimate political action, or whether they *never* are bound to comply with *il*legitimate political action. (Figure 1.1.)

For the concept legitimacy, it's illuminating to preview my favored substantive account at the outset: Substantively, on my view, the demands of legitimacy are set by the relational ideal of mutual civic respect among free and equal citizens. In a liberal democratic society, political action to pursue or preserve some aspirational social value is legitimate to the degree that it is congruent with mutual respect, and the social arrangement generally is legitimate to the degree that it

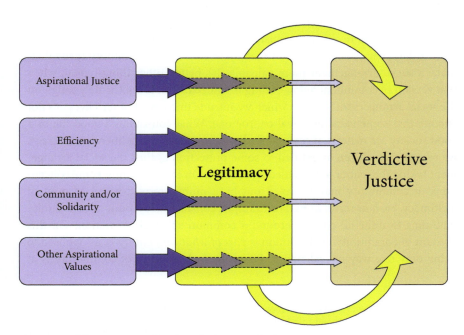

Figure 1.1 The anatomy of justice, depicting only the concepts

24   THE ANATOMY OF JUSTICE

and the political exercises that take place within it are congruent with that ideal. This account makes legitimacy scalar: As we'll see, political arrangements and exercises can be more or less (in)congruent with mutual respect, and a social arrangement can have more or fewer political exercises that are (in)congruent with mutual respect.

My account of legitimacy occupies a distinct role within the conceptual schema I'm forwarding simply because it *adjudicates* aspirational social values. We can illustrate by foreshadowing the substantive view I'll endorse concerning the relationship between aspirational values and mutual respect: On my view, mutual respect acts a trump card. The goodness that realizing some aspirational value lends to a social arrangement is always outweighed by badness when realizing that aspirational value comes at any cost at all to mutual respect: when the *means* of pursuing the value are impugned by mutual respect, or when the aspirational value itself can't be recognized as a value consistent with mutual respect.[18] Because legitimacy acts of a strong, trumping value, it is rhetorically most perspicuous to formulate its judgments in deontic terms: to say that legitimacy adjudicates what we *may* do and what we *must* do to pursue the values of aspirational justice or any other aspirational social aim. But because legitimacy's commands are themselves derived from a complex value, and because they're applied to a complex social system the various parts of which legitimacy may judge differently, we can nonetheless speak of a social arrangement *gaining* legitimacy as *more* parts of it *better* comply with the balance of demands and prohibitions issued by the value of mutual respect among free and equal citizens.

To make this more concrete, consider the candidate aspirational value of community. Suppose you're convinced that some version of community really does make a social arrangement more valuable: It's better, other things equal, when that version of communal fellow-feeling is realized. Still, to legitimately weigh on the social arrangement through which we intrude into one another's lives, it's not enough that some value be a real or true one. What constitutes a good life or a good society are matters of reasonable disagreement, and in a liberal democracy, we regard each citizen as entitled to some protection against the social arrangement taking the matter to be settled against her. On these grounds, some conceptions of community may be ruled out by a mutual-respect-based account of legitimacy, *even as social aims*. For example, consider an account of community that aims to unite all citizens around a common spiritual conviction: On this account of community, such a union is *part of what community is*, as opposed to being only one way of realizing it. Plausibly, such an ideal of community is at

---

[18] Though like Cohen I am a pluralist about political value, I here depart from his "*radical* pluralist" denial that we can have systematic mechanisms for weighing values. See Cohen 2008, 3–4. For a case against *radical* pluralism that doesn't undermine the *systematic* pluralism I defend in this book, see Schemmel 2021, 30–1.

odds with the conviction that all citizens should be able to "pursue their diverse conceptions of the good within a framework that embodies an ideal of reciprocity and mutual respect."[19] If so, then legitimacy impugns *the aspirational value itself*: This version of community can't politically be recognized as a value without running afoul of mutual respect. Different accounts of community plausibly are consistent with mutual respect in the sense that they *can* be recognized as valuable without running afoul of mutual respect. Even in these cases, though, mutual respect may impose limits on the *means*: on how community legitimately may be pursued. For example, mutual respect plausibly rules out political efforts to achieve spiritual unification of all citizens, even as a mere means of achieving a value of community that does not favor spiritual unification as an end in itself.

By calling mutual respect a trumping value, I mean to say that a social arrangement that better realizes the balance of institutional demands of mutual respect is always more valuable than one that realizes those demands less well, no matter the tradeoffs in terms of aspirational values. Insofar as aspirational values are rightly thought of in realist terms, they *continue to be values* when they're trumped by mutual respect; in that case, they just can't legitimately be recognized *politically* as values. (I consider the practical upshots of this distinction in Chapter 4.) And even when some aspirational social value *can* act as a political value, we've seen, some means of achieving it may be ruled out as illegitimate by mutual respect. In either case, the truth of the value in question ensures that a social arrangement really is better to the extent that the value is realized. But when its realization comes at a cost to mutual respect, it's always a loss on the whole. In other words: Among equally illegitimate social arrangements, some can be better and some worse depending on their realization of aspirational value. But the worst legitimate arrangement (the one that optimally realizes mutual respect but little aspirational value) is still better than the best illegitimate arrangement (the one that optimizes aspirational value but runs afoul ever so slightly of mutual respect).

There's plenty here to unpack and defend, but first we have one final concept to introduce. Aspirational justice, remember, refers to a single thing that matters: fairness in the distribution of social benefits and burdens. It's *internally* encumbered by none of the considerations that Cohen thought alien to justice, like feasibility, stability, or publicity, though those might comprise *distinct* things that matter that can weigh against aspirational justice. (Indeed, we'll see, some of them are grounded in the trumping value of mutual respect among free and equal citizens.) What I'll call "verdictive justice," by contrast, can tell us which social arrangement we have most evaluative reason to bring about—which has the most value, or realizes the best balance of the things that matter—once aspirational

---

[19] Scheffler 2003, 28.

justice is balanced against other aspirational social values and adjudicated by legitimacy. Verdictive justice comprises an evaluative ranking of social arrangements from which—in harness with facts about our circumstances, history, and feasibility set—we can derive judgments about what we should do.

In principle, this ranking is massively if not infinitely long. The judgments of verdictive justice are fully determined by the weighted values that inform it, but of course, the value of a social arrangement depends on more than just an evaluative specification of what matters: Additionally, the value of a social arrangement depends on the facts on the ground that determine which values are realizable—and to what degree, and at what costs to other values—in our circumstances. For instance: It may be that the value of community is realizable to a higher degree in a society without a long history of racist oppression than in a society *with* such a history, even if all other facts are held constant. And of course, it may be that this difference in the achievability of community is moderated by historical facts about what's happened in the intervening years. If so, then the ranking of social arrangements won't be indexed *only* by their institutions and social policies, because institutions and social policies underdetermine the extent to which a social arrangement realizes even a simple value, let alone a complex cocktail of things that matter. It will be indexed and cross-indexed as well by conditionalized historical facts, cultural facts, and other descriptive facts on the ground. This is the sense in which verdictive justice is fully determined by the things that matter and yet still accommodates the reality that facts matter to the goodness of any particular social arrangement. Verdictive justice ranks social arrangements by the extent to which they realize the things that matter, and the extent to which any arrangement realizes the things that matter depends not only on what matters but also on the circumstances and the cultural and historical facts on the ground.

Because of *our* history and culture, entire regions of the verdictive justice ranking plausibly are unreachable for us. Plausibly, for example, our history of racist subordination makes optimal realization of some social values either out of reach or only very distantly within reach.[20] We'll see too that verdictive justice's ranking of social arrangements is cross-indexed with yet another set of facts on the ground: the outputs of legitimate democratic procedures for setting our social ends together. These observations show that verdictive justice will be complicated and opaque on any plausible way of filling in substantive accounts of the things that matter. Luckily, the fruitfulness of the anatomy doesn't depend on the possibility of clearly discerning any particular range of verdictive justice's ranking of social arrangements. It's enough that we can draw inferences about it on the basis of premises invoking the things that matter.

---

[20] See Mills 2017, for example, 213.

To illustrate, notice that before I even introduced the concept of verdictive justice, I obliquely foreshadowed one conclusion that I'll reach about it: I said I'll argue that the legitimate arrangement that's least valuable by the lights of all aspirational values taken together is still more valuable than the *illegitimate* arrangement that's *most* valuable by the lights of all the aspirational values. This amounts to saying that verdictive justice ranks every legitimate arrangement above every illegitimate arrangement, whatever else may be true of them. More modest claims will be easier to come by, though still informative. For example, in the next chapter, I'll defend a particular account of aspirational justice, from which we can conclude that a social arrangement is always better, other things equal, to the extent that it is more distributively egalitarian. Verdictive justice is a concept for which we need no substantive account, since the ranking issued by verdictive justice is determined by the weighted values that inform it indexed to configurations of facts on the ground. But it's there, as an evaluative ranking of social arrangements; and in principle, we can derive all-things-considered judgments about what social arrangement is most valuable for us given our history, culture, feasibility set, and conditional projections about the outputs of democratic processes. More importantly than discerning the most valuable arrangement, though, is the possibility of discerning the arrangements and reforms by way of which we could make things better relative to our particular unjust status quo. As I'll argue, we can even discern when we'd be able to make things better by changing the very facts on which verdictive justice's ranking is indexed. Alas, we can't change our history. But in many cases, we *can* change culture. This possibility will be crucial for my defense of the anatomy against feminist criticism in Chapter 6.

To review: On the conceptual picture I favor, "*aspirational justice*" refers to a (set of) principle(s) that specifies fairness in the sharing of benefits and burdens of social cooperation; "*legitimacy*" refers to a (set of) principle(s) that specifies how our social cooperation may permissibly be regulated or political power exercised, in a liberal democracy, to bring about any aspirational social value; and "*verdictive justice*" is the all-things-considered ranking of social arrangements furnished by the things that matter.

Though I've foreshadowed some substantive commitments within it, this *conceptual schema* on its own leaves open much of what is substantively in dispute among different types of liberal egalitarian. It leaves open, for example, how constraining or permissive legitimacy is in adjudicating aspirational values. It leaves open how distributively egalitarian liberal justice is. It also leaves open the question of whether the subject matter of justice is restricted to political institutions. Both verdictive and aspirational justice are assessments about the value of arrangements of social cooperation, and it so far remains an open question how culture or individual behavior can affect such assessments and how to appraise

28 THE ANATOMY OF JUSTICE

them when they do. I hope the anatomy can be helpful already, for diagnosing, clarifying, and shifting disagreements among liberal egalitarians in fruitful ways. Figuring out whether we disagree about the things that matter, about their relative importance, or about the way in which the value of a social arrangement informs what we should do can help us to make progress on the substance. It would be illuminating, for example, if strands of Cohen's disagreement with Rawls could be catalogued in these terms—even if cataloguing them doesn't solve them. And, of course, the anatomy equips us to notice when apparent disagreement may be *merely* apparent. Perhaps luck egalitarians and relational egalitarians are in substantive disagreement about the demands of justice. Or perhaps they're offering accounts of different concepts, neither of which we should do without. Perhaps we can, with Cohen, work toward discerning fundamental political values, but insist, with Rawls, that political philosophy needn't resort to intuitionism in (at least many) cases of value conflict.[21]

In saying that the conceptual schema on its own leaves many substantive questions open, I don't mean to deny that it will face reasonable opposition. Neither aspirational nor verdictive justice comprises a set of normative principles of justice that tell us directly what we should do. Once the values are filled in, the anatomy will *inform* prescriptive judgments in light of feasibility considerations, but the relationship will not be direct, as we can have reason not to aim for the most valuable social arrangement in our feasibility set.[22] So, getting it right about the things that matter won't suffice to settle all questions of political normativity, even in harness with social science and knowledge of the feasibility set. This means that we give up the kind of straightforward prescriptive guidance that we might hope to get from normative principles of justice. We can use verdictive justice to *derive* such principles to guide us within a relatively narrow range of circumstances. For example, a politically liberal Rawlsian might construe legitimacy as a contractualist procedure for working out the implications of premises like the moral arbitrariness of our social class background as a determinant of our income and wealth. She might endorse justice as fairness as the normative principles derived from verdictive justice for the arrangement of our basic institutional structure under full compliance and reasonably favorable conditions.[23] But even fully populated with the things that matter, the schema is less directive than a set of normative principles.

The anatomy of justice thus holds no promise that some set of concretely action-guiding normative principles can direct us robustly across circumstances of justice and injustice. Instead, it offers a modular evaluative framework for theorizing justice. Getting it right about the things that matter and ordering them

---

[21] See Rawls 1999a, 30; Cohen 2008, 3–4.   [22] See Simmons 2010, 22–5.
[23] On the compatibility of justice as fairness with luck egalitarianism as an aspirational social value, see Rawls 1999a, 86; Cohen 2008, 85; Tomlin 2012, especially 387–9.

within the schema won't settle what we should do, but it will provide a consistent grounding in value for contextually varying normative judgments. The same values that are optimally realized in the just society guide us in thinking about how to reform or recreate our institutional arrangement to pursue justice from within a wide range of circumstances of injustice. Theorizing and refining political values and the relationships among them will equip us to discern the institutional arrangement and practices of a just society given our history and culture, the relative value of the various arrangements immediately or distantly accessible from where we are now, and what we could do now to move toward a more just social arrangement from our particular unjust status quo.

Suppose verdictive justice deems social arrangements more valuable to the extent that any distributive inequalities that arise within them attach to positions in competitions for which nobody is disadvantaged in virtue of her social class background.[24] In shorthand: Verdictive justice favors robustly equal opportunity, including robustly equal *developmental* opportunity. To achieve this end, *ideally*, economic institutions would be regulated or arranged "so as to prevent excessive concentrations of property and wealth,"[25] high-quality education would be ensured so that all could develop the qualifications on the basis of which subsequent positions are awarded, and protections would be in place to ensure non-discrimination in selection for those positions. Because robust equal opportunity is a value of justice, a just society (if it contains positions to which unequal rewards attach) will be one wherein institutional mechanisms and practices are in place to ensure robust equal opportunity. But now suppose that economic institutions are *not* arranged effectively to prevent accumulations of wealth. The wealthy purchase competitive developmental opportunities for their children, and although educational institutions can offset developmental advantage to some degree, they cannot ensure fully fair distributions of developmental opportunities in the presence of the wealth disparities. In these circumstances, non-discrimination in selection will be inadequate to realize robust equal opportunity. Now suppose this injustice has persisted for generations, compounded by racist oppression on every front. In such circumstances of deep injustice, robust equal opportunity *as a thing that matters* straightforwardly calls for something different than non-discriminatory hiring and admissions practices. Arguably, it calls for affirmative selection practices—explicitly and publicly justified as a measure of correction for injustice—as well as reform of economic institutions and strict regulation of inheritance and bequest, just for a start. The value calls for corrective action for the simple reason that we can't realize the value if we don't reform the social conditions that currently obstruct it: We won't reach a point at which our prospects for attaining desirable positions are unaffected by our race or social

---

[24] On Rawlsian fair equality of opportunity, see Rawls 2001, 44.   [25] Rawls 2001, 44.

30 THE ANATOMY OF JUSTICE

class if we don't correct the mechanisms by way of which race and class currently do influence our prospects.

We'll explore the implications of robust equal opportunity for corrective justice further in coming chapters. For now, the crucial point of this example can be appreciated whatever our substantive disagreements about equal opportunity as a thing that matters: On the anatomy of justice, when we ask how to make things better, what guides our answer is neither the institutional arrangement we'd have in a perfectly just society nor the principles that purport to help us answer that ideal theoretic question. What guides us are the *things that matter* and the way verdictive justice orders them into a ranking of social arrangements indexed to our circumstances. This point matters for three reasons. First, as we just saw, *the value* can straightforwardly license corrective action in unjust circumstances. Robust equal opportunity may call for affirmative selection procedures that favor members of certain groups precisely in order to move toward greater realization of equal opportunity. In contrast, normative principles that helpfully guide our social arrangement in some circumstances may provide no guidance—or they may provide bad guidance—when applied beyond those circumstances. The values the anatomy of justice systematizes will be invariant: If mutual civic respect matters, as I'll argue it does, then it *always* matters. But circumstances matter greatly for how best to realize it, and verdictive justice will favor different social arrangements and policies depending on the circumstances and constraints to which we index. These divergences may be extensive. Social reform may call for sectors or institutions that wouldn't even exist in a fully just society, or in a society with a different history, to perform functions that will no longer be necessary once justice is better achieved. For this reason, we should bring creativity to the question of what social arrangements might conceivably be among those ranked by verdictive justice and indexed for our particular set of facts on the ground.

Second, a focus on values at the foundational level of theorizing makes a difference because it can help us to see why prescriptive priority rankings that make sense in a just society are implausible in circumstances of injustice. For instance, *maintaining* institutions that realize equal opportunity may be morally more urgent than maintaining institutions that optimize the prospects of the least well off, but things look different when we turn to circumstances of injustice. Realizing institutional arrangements that are conducive to pursuing some value might matter little if we lack other institutional preconditions for that value being realized. Maybe fairness in hiring has diminished value as a guarantor of background justice so long as some positions carry unjustly large or unjustly small shares of social rewards.[26] In that case, (part of) the value of equal opportunity is simply unrealizable absent reform to the reward structure within which competitions take

---

[26] See Gheaus 2020; see also Mills 2015.

place. Even if fairness in hiring is particularly important in a just society, then, it may be that in an *un*just society, circumstances are not in place to make fair hiring meaningfully serve robust equal opportunity. If so, then pursuing it may bring less value than pursuing some other reform, whatever their relative importance in other circumstances. As we'll see in Chapter 3, part of the case for the anatomy of justice rests on the ways in which priority rankings among values differ from analogous rankings among normative principles. A priority ranking among values can unify and explain the judgments explored here, even if the analogous priority ranking among normative principles goes wrong.

Third and finally, conceptualizing justice in terms of values enables us to see that different kinds of values may retain importantly different kinds of reasons-giving force when they are decisively outweighed, in our circumstances, by other values. My case for the anatomy will rely on the ways in which aspirational social values can retain some kinds of reasons-giving force even when they are constrained by legitimacy—as, for example, when aspirational justice cannot be pursued because its pursuit is disfavored by a legitimate democratic majority. When legitimacy condemns our pursuit of aspirational justice because a legitimate democratic process condemns that pursuit, legitimacy trumps aspirational justice. But, I'll argue, it does not render aspirational justice practically impotent. Outweighed values can give us reason to change the contingent facts that bring about the very values conflict in which the aspirational value gives way. For now, it's enough to note that by conceptualizing justice in terms of the things that matter, we can attend to particular such things even when the circumstance-specific prescriptions we derive from verdictive justice fully subordinate those values to other considerations.

1.3 Substantive Pluralism: Distributive Egalitarian Aspirational Justice, Relational Egalitarian Legitimacy

Beyond a conceptual schema for theorizing justice, the anatomy of justice includes a set of values to populate the schema: distributive egalitarian aspirational justice and relational egalitarian legitimacy. (Figure 1.2.)

Broadly, distributive egalitarian aspirational justice holds inequalities (as measured by the relevant currency of justice) to stand in need of justification and defeasibly to stand in need of rectification. Because distributive egalitarianism on my picture is an account of *aspirational* justice—of *one input into* verdictive justice—the "defeasibly" qualification works on two levels. I leave open what can defeat the case *internal to* aspirational justice for rectifying inequality—that is, what can make it the case that aspirational justice itself does not favor rectification. Luck egalitarians, for example, variously take responsibility, choice, or desert to do this work. My suspicion is that few inequalities will turn out to be

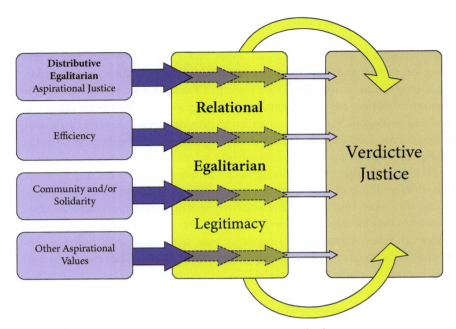

Figure 1.2 The anatomy of justice, depicting concepts and substance

internally justified on the right account of fair shares, but this book won't make that case. *Externally*, we'll see, other aspirational values can weigh against, and legitimacy can trump, the reasons aspirational justice furnishes: That we cannot *legitimately* rectify a distributive inequality, for example, will mean that rectification doesn't lead to a more valuable social arrangement on the whole, even though rectification is favored by aspirational justice. Here, aspirational justice is decisively outweighed by legitimacy. Note that the view just described stands inequality in need of justification but leaves open whether equality is subject to analogous treatment.[27]

The account of relationally egalitarian legitimacy I favor is centered on the liberal principle of legitimacy. The liberal principle of legitimacy specifies that "our exercise of political power is fully proper only when it is exercised in accordance with a constitution the essentials of which all citizens as free and equal may reasonably be expected to endorse in light of principles and ideals acceptable to their common human reason."[28] This substantive account of legitimacy makes the anatomy of justice a version of political liberalism, which aims to respect a constraint of broad, public justifiability for political action. Beyond favoring procedural democratic processes for social ends-setting, we'll see, this principle of legitimacy also imposes some substantive prohibitions and demands. Negatively,

---

[27] See Segall 2014; Neufeld 2015.   [28] See Rawls 1993, for example xliv.

the liberal principle of legitimacy prohibits as illegitimate any account of an aspirational value, and any means of pursuing an aspirational value, when the account or means cannot be given suitably public justification. Effectively, it filters out certain aspects of the aspirational things that matter, such that those aspects can make a difference only in comparisons with other equally illegitimate arrangements. Positively, on my view, legitimacy *demands* that our social arrangement ensure the protection of essential interests that follow from the ideal that animates the constraints of liberal legitimacy to begin with: the relational ideal of mutual respect among free and equal citizens.[29] In this way, the ideal of mutual respect among free and equal citizens generates what I regard as *mandatory* shared reasons: reasons on which a social arrangement cannot legitimately *omit* to act. The aspiration of the liberal principle of legitimacy is to secure conditions that are justifiable in light of reasons we all can recognize as such in our capacity as free and equal citizens. Our reason to preserve such a community of justificatory reciprocity is based in mutual respect: By preserving justificatory community, we secure mutual respect among free and equal citizens. The ideal of mutual respect among free and equal citizens thus sources reasons that *demand* to be recognized as such, because that is the ideal that underwrites the importance of the justificatory reciprocity that constrains our public reasoning in the first place. In issuing mandatory shared reasons that we cannot legitimately omit to act on, mutual respect can constrain, supplement, or *second* the reasons supplied by aspirational values.

So, on my view of political liberalism, the ideal of mutual respect is the animating evaluative commitment, and the commitment that justifies imposing a requirement of justificatory reciprocity to begin with.[30] In a liberal democratic society, citizens will inevitably differ deeply in the fundamental values that guide their lives, and they will thus inevitably be unequally burdened by the political pursuit of any social end. As I understand it, the aim of politically liberal, relationally egalitarian legitimacy is to maintain mutual civic respect among free and equal citizens despite this profound ideological disagreement, and to do that by insisting that shared democratic power be exercised only in ways that can be justified to all parties, using values that all parties can accept as such, whatever else sets them at odds. Because mutual respect is the whole point of public justification and the reciprocity requirement, mutual respect supplies reasons that reciprocity demands we heed as such. Figure 1.2 depicts the constraints and positive

---

[29] See Schouten 2013. For an account of legitimacy that is in some respects resonant, see Dworkin 2000. For a well-elaborated account of relational egalitarian justice explicitly centered on this ideal, see Schemmel 2021.

[30] See Larmore 1999; Nussbaum 2011; Schouten 2019. Justificatory reciprocity is also instrumental for realizing stability for the right reasons: In a society that abides by a principle of reciprocity—in which citizens hold themselves to burden one another only in ways that are mutually justifiable— ideologically divided citizens can assent to their political arrangement even when they are personally burdened by it. See Rawls 1993, xli–xlii.

34   THE ANATOMY OF JUSTICE

demands issued by mutual respect: Shrinking purple arrows show mutual respect adjudicating considerations of aspirational value, while prominent yellow arrows flowing from legitimacy to verdictive justice represent mutual respect's positive substantive demands.

As we'll see, the account of politically liberal legitimacy that I defend is resonant with Elizabeth Anderson's democratic equality view: "Democratic equality regards two people as equal when each accepts the obligation to justify their actions by principles acceptable to the other, and in which they take mutual consultation, reciprocation, and recognition for granted."[31] On the anatomy of justice, relational egalitarian *legitimacy* regards a social arrangement as overridingly more valuable insofar as political intervention into citizens' lives abides by the criterion of mutual justifiability, one requirement of which is to ensure for each citizen the positive conditions necessary for participation in the democratic system of self-governance on mutually justifiable terms. In her rejection of distributive egalitarianism, Anderson says that relational egalitarianism is a superior way to understand the "demand to act only on principles that express respect for everyone."[32] I agree that relational egalitarianism is a superior way to understand that demand. But in the anatomy of justice, I construe that demand as a demand of *legitimacy*, which is only one among the things that matter—one among the determinants of verdictive justice—and which operates by adjudicating all the others. For instance, relational egalitarian, politically liberal legitimacy holds that the value of fair shares is outweighed by the *disvalue* generated whenever fair shares is achieved in ways that fail to express equal civic respect. And it holds that, as a requirement of legitimacy, fair shares *must* be pursued politically insofar as the reasons of fair shares are seconded by reasons of mutual respect.

In sum: The liberal principle of legitimacy constrains us in acting on the reasons generated by aspirational social values, so that our pursuit of those values remains consistent with mutual respect among citizens, many of whom dispute the very values in question. This constraining, we've seen, sometimes appears as a positive insistence: Legitimacy demands (yellow arrows) that our social arrangement realize the value of mutual civic respect, even when the necessary political steps impose costs as measured by aspirational social values. Let's consider an example. Suppose the right balance of luck egalitarian aspirational justice and other aspirational values like efficiency favors socializing goods that markets undervalue, like private caregiving and law enforcement. Still, private caregiving is treated as *partly* a personal consumption decision—for example, parents can make tradeoffs at the margins between more time with their children and less income on the one hand, or more income and less time with their children on the other. (Plenty will disagree that this is what aspirational social values favor, but

[31] Anderson 1999, 313.   [32] Anderson 1999, 337.

just assume it for the sake of illustration.) By stipulation, then, private caregiving, for instance caring for one's own children or one's aging parents, imposes some marginal earnings tradeoffs, even when it is fairly socially supported. Now suppose that, due to gender norms, more women than men choose to trade off remuneration for extra time with their children.[33] If so, then the social arrangement favored by aspirational social values may be one wherein women have marginally less income, on average, than men.

Arguably, though, such a social arrangement would be condemned by legitimacy. That's because the inequalities in question are arguably objectionable at the bar of mutual respect among free and equal citizens.[34] Consider one schematic argument for why this should be so: Given the way in which gender historically has functioned both to channel women into caregiving and to ensure that caregiving be devalued and marginalized, aggregate gender differences resulting from gendered take-up of caregiving will threaten the equal standing of women caregivers. If this is right, then legitimacy ensures that verdictive justice rank any social arrangement that includes mechanisms to offset this problem of mutual respect (and that otherwise complies with demands of mutual respect) as more valuable than any arrangement that lacks such mechanisms. For example, verdictive justice might favor caregiver support provisions that incentivize take-up of caregiving among men and labor market attachment among women—so-called "daddy quotas"—and it might favor these incentives even if they lead to distributions that would be *sub*optimal looking only from the perspective of aspirational social values.

Note the parenthetical in the formulation a few lines up: "and that otherwise complies with mutual respect." Verdictive justice always favors bringing society into closer compliance with reasons sourced by mutual respect unless doing so comes at a net cost to that very value. Mutual respect won't favor criminalizing the choices women make that lead to the marginal pay gap, for example, because even if mutual respect does impugn the pay gap, it will impugn more strongly still political measures that criminalize reasonable lifestyle choices. Mutual respect is multi-faceted, and it's this multi-faceted-ness that enables it to set ambitious social ends without approving any and all political means necessary to achieve them. (It's also this multi-faceted-ness that will enable the anatomy to prioritize mutual respect so strongly without being subject to damning counterexamples. For example, I'll argue in Chapter 3 that mutual respect calls for a high degree of distributive equality. No society that realizes mutual respect will be *very* aspirationally unjust, then, because mutual respect itself seconds much of what

---

[33] Even if these choices reflect preferences that are socially constructed, they must be respected as authoritative for our purposes. Social policy cannot disregard as non-authoritative all choices that result from gendered social conditions. But social policy *can* aim to change the forces of social construction over time. See Schouten 2019.

[34] Watson and Hartley 2018; Schouten 2019.

36   THE ANATOMY OF JUSTICE

aspirational justice favors. Insofar as reasons of mutual respect co-extend with reasons of aspirational social values, the counterintuitive tradeoffs we associate with strong priority rankings are avoided.)

The gender equality case is an example of a *positive demand* of legitimacy that, because legitimacy is an evaluative trump, necessarily gets reflected in verdictive justice even when it means deviating from the arrangement most favored by aspirational social values. Consider now an example to illustrate how legitimacy *negatively* constrains aspirational social values (shrinking purple arrows).[35] On my view, whatever inequalities it condones among adults, the right account of aspirational justice disfavors all inequalities among children, because the choices of children lack the moral attributability to render resulting disadvantage innocent from the perspective of justice. Even when children's choices merit deference, those choices aren't agential in the right way to justify disadvantage. I haven't argued for this here, but for purposes of illustration, suppose I'm right.[36] In that case, plausibly, aspirational justice favors educational institutions (and other political institutions that influence children's life prospects) ensuring that all children enjoy equally good life prospects as they begin to enter adulthood.[37]

Other aspirational values will moderate this. For example, a society that realizes *community* or *efficiency* may leverage the talent of some for the good of all. So, when the institutional mechanisms are in place to do this, the balance of aspirational values plausibly favors some educational inequalities that aspirational justice on its own condemns, on the grounds that those inequalities redound to the benefit of all. But just to see how *legitimacy* enters the fray, let's simplify matters and stipulate that equal prospects through education is not only what aspirational justice favors but also what the balance of all aspirational social values favors. Still, legitimacy will prohibit some measures that this balance of values favors. Consider one possible strategy for realizing educational equality: Ramp up public education spending and starkly means-test public primary education, leaving all those with private means to find their way in a private education market while intensely concentrating increased public educational resources on those who lack private means. Suppose the public system could then outbid private schools for the best teachers, set small classes, and provide lavish support. Imagine that this strategy really would promote equal life prospects through education. Even so, plausibly, means-testing primary education is inimical to the legitimacy value of mutual respect. That's because educating students to relate on terms of mutual civic respect plausibly requires educating kids from different

---

[35] This distinction isn't deep. Whether the legitimacy value of mutual respect demands some political action that isn't favored by aspirational values or rules out some political action that *is* favored by aspirational values, in each case it justifies a deviation from the state of affairs that's favored by aspirational values taken in isolation.

[36] I've argued for it elsewhere. See Schouten 2012a, 2012b.   [37] Schouten 2023a.

walks of life together, not segregating them by economic class into a private system for those with means and a public system (even one flush with resources) for those without.[38] If that's right, then legitimacy condemns means-testing primary education, at least in circumstances like ours; thus, other things equal, verdictive justice favors social arrangements that do not means-test primary education. It renders that ranking even though, by supposition, means-testing is favored by the weight of aspirational values. In this case, mutual respect prohibits as illegitimate a measure that aspirational justice favors.

In this book, I won't work out priority rankings among aspirational values. Plausibly, some of that prioritization gets settled by democratic processes. If so, then in those cases, democratic processes not only legitimize political action but also *settle evaluative facts*. For example, how to manage tradeoffs between fairness and community when both are already fairly well realized may just depend on what citizens have to say about it. In other cases, plausibly, there are evaluative facts that *should guide* democratic processes. Because I won't try to work out those facts, there will be eliminable evaluative incompleteness in the anatomy as I present it. I hope to show that we can do a lot, even with an (as yet) incomplete anatomy of justice.[39]

And, at the end of the day, what principally speaks in favor of the anatomy of justice is its fruitfulness. It accommodates the multi-faceted-ness of political normativity while ordering the values that bear on the goodness of a social arrangement in a way that is plausible and informative. It enables us to theorize both about a just society and about what steps we should take to make our unjust society better. The conceptual schema on its own can accommodate a range of plausible substantive sets of principles of justice—like justice as fairness—while ordering the evaluative inputs of those theories so as to generate guidance beyond their explicit range of applicability. Over the next few chapters, I'll show that the anatomy in whole makes visible a plausible way of retaining the truth in relational egalitarianism without succumbing to objections raised by distributive egalitarians, that it makes visible a plausible way of retaining the truth in distributive egalitarianism without succumbing to objections from relational egalitarians, and that it equips both, together, to be more helpfully action-guiding than either appears to be on its own.

1.4 Values Pluralism and Incommensurability

A general challenge for values pluralism deserves an airing at the outset. On the anatomy of justice, pluralism about the concept "justice" enables substantive

---

[38] See Anderson 2007.   [39] See Sen 2006, 225.

38   THE ANATOMY OF JUSTICE

pluralism about justice. Conceptual pluralism presents no great problem *qua pluralism*: I'll need to make the case for the specific claim that we need two distinct concepts *of justice*, but the general thought that we need multiple concepts to theorize political normativity is unremarkable. Substantive pluralism is a different matter. As I construe it, substantive values pluralism holds that there are multiple distinct values, and that these values are not reducible to each other.[40] The problem is that positing an irreducible plurality of values seems to entail that there's no common metric by way of which we can compare distinct values within that plurality. Without such a metric, we apparently can't rank values in a principled way. So, a looming question for pluralism generally is how principled choice is possible when values are irreducibly plural. Our version of the question concerns the possibility of principled political guidance: If the anatomy's values are irreducibly plural, how can the anatomy give principled guidance when values conflict?

This book tackles a first-order normative project: describing and defending the anatomy of justice. For the most part, I set aside the work of filling in a moral metaphysics. But because so much of my argument relies on the relative moral priority of mutual respect and aspirational social values, I do need to make the case that priority rankings are possible among mutually irreducible values. And because so much of my case relies on the fruitfulness of the anatomy, I need to show that we can avoid the route taken by some prominent defenders of values pluralism, which is to allow that evaluative facts *radically* underdetermine what we ought to do.[41] Finally, because I think that political justification needs to be *public* justification, I need to show that we can avoid this route even if it can be

___

[40]   On some definitions of values pluralism, the anatomy doesn't qualify as pluralistic. Consider the claim that "value-pluralism holds that there can be true, incompatible but rationally inarbitrable normative judgments" (Skorupski 1996, 109; see also Stark 2018). Or consider the claim that a theory is *monistic* "if it either (a) reduces goods to a common measure or (b) creates a comprehensive hierarchy or ordering among goods" (Galston 2002, 6). I don't take the anatomy of justice to support incompatible normative judgments (though the values that underpin those judgments will not always be in harmony). And I *do* take the anatomy to create an ordering among goods. By each of these definitions, then, the anatomy is categorized as a non-pluralism. I think the view I defend nevertheless is intuitively recognizable as a (political) values pluralism. Either way, it clearly faces the challenge described here.

[41]   Isaiah Berlin argues for a version of pluralism on which "there are many different [ultimate] ends that men may seek and still be fully rational, fully men, capable of understanding each other and sympathizing and deriving light from each other..." See Berlin 2013, 11. Joseph Raz defends a view of practical reasoning which allows for rational choice among options when no reasons favor one over others. He argues that "most of the time people have a variety of options such that it would accord with reason for them to choose any one of them and it would not be against reason to avoid any of them." See Raz 1999, 100. For a defense of the view that genuine values *cannot* conflict and in fact are mutually supportive, see Dworkin 2011. See Winter for an argument that Dworkin is actually endorsing a form of pluralism, but "an idiosyncratic pluralism which differs from orthodox pluralism in denying that those separate values can ever conflict with one another" (Winter 2016, 465).

made more palatable by the invocation of a personal facility for practical wisdom which guides us where reasons run out.[42]

In response to this challenge, I deny that we must choose between pluralism on the one hand and practical, public-reason-based action guidance on the other. So, how can we have both?

In the much-cited introduction to her edited volume on the subject, Ruth Chang argues that *incommensurability* does not entail *incomparability*.[43] "Incommensurability" is the lack of a common unit of value by reference to which precise comparisons between two things can be made. "Incomparability" is the lack of possible comparison relations between two things, such as "better than" or "as good as." Applied to values, Chang's argument concludes that one value might matter more, but not in virtue of having more of any common unit of value. In that case, the values are comparable but not commensurable. To work this out, Chang introduces the notion of a "covering value": a relatively comprehensive value of which incommensurable but comparable values are parts. In a similar fashion, Michael Stocker posits a "higher level synthesizing category"—goodness—with respect to which plural values are constituent means,[44] enabling evaluative but not quantitative value comparisons. We might understand the anatomy of justice as a political values pluralism for which verdictive justice is a covering value: It's the relatively comprehensive value of which aspirational social values and legitimacy are parts.

We *needn't* understand things that way, though, because the pluralism I'm setting out needn't be a *foundational* values pluralism. Foundational pluralism posits plural values at the ground level, denying that plural values reduce to *any* value or property, like goodness. In contrast, my political values pluralism might maintain that the values of justice are *mutually* irreducible but that those mutually irreducible values reduce to a distinct common unit of value. Perhaps the mutually irreducible values of justice that I discern are valuable precisely in virtue of realizing political value, verdictive justice, goodness, or some other more foundational value. Still, the anatomy is recognizably pluralist *about justice*, because distinct values of justice are irreducible *to each other*. For instance: On my view, neither distributive nor relational equality is valuable only in virtue of its contribution to the other. And, though both might be valuable in virtue of realizing verdictive justice, we still want to theorize the realizer values in order to better

---

[42] Nagel, for example, argues that, "provided one has taken the process of practical justification as far as it will go in the course of arriving at the conflict, one may be able to proceed without further justification, but without irrationality either. What makes this possible is judgment—essentially the faculty Aristotle described as practical wisdom, which reveals itself over time in individual decisions rather than in the enunciation of general principles." Nagel 1979, 135. See also Larmore 1987; Anderson 1993.

[43] Chang 1997. See also Williams 1981, 79–80, 1985, 17. But see Raz 1986, chap. 13.

[44] Stocker 1990, 172.

40 THE ANATOMY OF JUSTICE

understand verdictive justice and its rankings. In short, my pluralism treads lightly. Perhaps, with Stocker and Chang, we have value comparability without value commensurability. Or perhaps we have a non-foundational pluralism with both comparability *and* commensurability.

I've previewed that I'll explicate certain features of the anatomy of justice by comparison with Rawlsian justice as fairness. In thinking about value comparability, it's helpful to notice that, while Rawls resists political values pluralism, his own theory of justice apparently relies on the very possibility on which my pluralism's viability also depends: the possibility of comparison among mutually irreducible things that matter. Throughout his work, he regularly writes of the "values" or "ideals" that inform the principles of justice or that the principles of justice embody in circumstances of full compliance.[45] Moreover, consider his observation that

> part of the value of the notion of choosing principles is that the reasons which underlie their adoption in the first place may also support giving them certain weights. Since in justice as fairness the principles of justice are not thought of as self-evident, but have their justification in the fact that they would be chosen, we may find in the grounds for their acceptance some guidance or limitation as to how they are to be balanced.[46]

The choosers in the original position aren't motivated by moral considerations, but moral premises do justify the original position with its veil of ignorance as a mechanism for modeling impartial concern, and moral premises justify including justice as fairness among the choosers' options. For Rawls, the principles that these moral premises support are ranked by a priority relationship, which is defended not by invoking some unitary value which all the ideals are valuable in virtue of realizing, but by considering "the [plural] grounds for their acceptance."

The anatomy's conceptual schema aims to make theorizing more broadly helpful, including for circumstances of injustice, by focusing on the plural ideals that might subsequently ground (the choice or acceptance of) particular normative principles. Compared with justice as fairness, it moves up a level in abstraction: It aims to theorize the things that matter that a set of normative principles like justice as fairness would realize for some range of circumstances, like circumstances of full compliance. I propose that we linger longer with the work of refining those things that matter so that they themselves can constitute a broadly applicable, evaluative political theory. The things I find mattering won't correspond exactly with the ideals underpinning justice as fairness, but I'm not alone in positing

---

[45] See, for example, Rawls 1999a, 138, 231, 284, 2001, 66.   [46] Rawls 1999a, 37.

mutually irreducible things that matter for political normativity. Rawls evidently had just such a picture in mind.

Although I part ways with values pluralists who embrace radical incomparability, there's plenty to learn from their embrace. Bernard Williams argued that ethics is complicated and that we should *expect* the evaluative domain to resist arithmetic adjudication.[47] His is a good reminder that we can easily err by expecting too much of normative theorizing. But when it comes to political value, I'm not yet willing to give up on the possibility that normative justice theorizing can provide fairly extensive action guidance. And, when the political values themselves underdetermine what we should do, those values favor a certain procedure—deliberative democratic decision-making—which itself confers value on its outputs. Even when values alone underdetermine the right course, then, they guide us in filling in the gaps. Conversely, when conflicts between mutually irreducibly plural values *can* be adjudicated, a decisive judgment supported by the anatomy of justice still leaves room for rational moral regret: We'll see that we can reasonably regret doing what we have most reason to do, and we can have reason to work over time to ease the values conflict that forces the tradeoff.[48] So, although I am a pluralist "systematizer" and an optimist about rational adjudication of values conflicts,[49] I can agree with more radical pluralists in some of their observations about our moral lives. Political values may underdetermine the best course of action, and even when they settle the best course, we can have "moral remainders" from outweighed values. The anatomy of justice makes sense of these observations.

One final clarification is in order. Some have tried to *justify liberalism* by invoking the premise that there are irreducibly plural human values.[50] Put roughly, the thought is that a broadly liberal deference to individuals' own values is called for on the grounds that distinct, contradictory worldviews or ways of life can be equally genuinely valuable and equally worthy of pursuit. My pluralism isn't about plural human values yielding plural kinds of valuable lives; it's about plural values of justice. And while the book defends liberal theorizing, it doesn't aim to *justify liberalism*, for example to those who reject basic liberal commitments like freedom and equality in favor of an alleged natural hierarchy. The critics of liberalism I engage with in the later chapters of the book are critics of *liberal theorizing*, not proponents of illiberal political ideologies. But even if

---

[47] Williams 1981, 1985. See also Stocker 1990.

[48] See Williams 1981 and Stocker 1990 for arguments in favor of pluralism that draw on the possibility of rational regret. (But see Hurka 1996 for an argument that rational regret is compatible with monism because a morally right choice can be regretted on *non*-moral grounds.) See Wiggins 1980 and Nussbaum 1986 for related arguments in favor of values pluralism, this time drawing on weakness of the will.

[49] See Williams 1981, 71.

[50] See for example Berlin 2002, 43–8, 212–17; Crowder 2001; Galston 2002, 2005. See also Kekes 1993.

42 THE ANATOMY OF JUSTICE

I *were* to mount a case for liberalism to proponents of illiberal political ideologies, it wouldn't rely on values pluralism. I don't think that liberal respect for individuals' values is called for on the grounds that distinct contradictory values can be equally genuinely valuable or equally worthy of pursuit. Rather, I think liberal deference is called for because we all are presumptively entitled to live to some degree according to our reasonable worldviews *whether or not* those worldviews are evaluatively correct. This is, of course, a *liberal* conviction, and I leave open whether it can be justified to those who don't already share it. My point is only that the pluralism I set forth in this book is not the sort of pluralism in which some are inclined to find a broad external justification for liberalism.[51]

To those who agree that reasonable worldviews merit some measure of political deference, interpersonal political justification should matter greatly. When our reasonable pursuit of our own reasonable values is burdened or curtailed by the actions or arrangement of political institutions, we might hope for a justification that we can understand and reason through ourselves. Indeed, we might be *owed* such a justification. Insofar as interpersonal justification matters, intuitionist or incomparability pluralism is theoretically and politically unsatisfying. Ultimately, it may be the best we can do. But I think it's worth seeking a systematic, theoretically plausible liberal pluralism that supports public, interpersonal justification across a range of circumstances. A working hypothesis of this book is that the search is not futile.

The Anatomy of Justice: On the Shape, Substance, and Power of Liberal Egalitarianism. Gina Schouten,
Oxford University Press. © Gina Schouten 2024. DOI: 10.1093/9780191999772.003.0002

---

[51] On internal and external justifications of liberalism, see Quong 2011, 5–7. See also Brighouse 1996, 1994.

2
Distributive Equality as Aspirational Justice

In his work defending relational egalitarianism, Samuel Scheffler says that "shares are fair when they are part of a distributive scheme that makes it possible for free and equal citizens to pursue their diverse conceptions of the good within a framework that embodies an ideal of reciprocity and mutual respect."[1] I agree with Scheffler that our social arrangement should make it possible for citizens to pursue their diverse conceptions of the good within a framework that embodies an ideal of reciprocity and mutual respect. But I want to argue that this is a standard of *liberal legitimacy*, and not, as Scheffler claims, a standard of *fairness*. A social arrangement meets the distributional demands of *liberal legitimacy* when it enables free and equal citizens to pursue their values within a framework of reciprocity and mutual respect; but a distribution is *fair* only if it meets a different, more stringent standard of equality.

Recall the basic picture: Political philosophy needs both an aspirational and a verdictive concept of justice. Verdictive justice gives an ordering of social arrangements by value once all sources of political value are considered. The substantive work of theorizing justice involves discerning and weighting the value considerations that inform verdictive justice. Aspirational justice is one such value consideration. The concept "aspirational justice" simply means fairness understood as each getting her due. The substantive account of aspirational justice I'll endorse is distributive egalitarianism. Some other aspirational social values are relational values: Community and solidarity were the examples I invoked in Chapter 1. Like distributive equality, community and solidarity plausibly name attributes in virtue of which a social arrangement may be more or less valuable. But the most important aspect of relational egalitarianism—mutual respect among free and equal citizens—comprises my account of *legitimacy*. Like aspirational social values, legitimacy informs the judgments of verdictive justice. But legitimacy informs verdictive justice in a different way: Whereas aspirational social values pick out the things that give value to a social arrangement, legitimacy *adjudicates* those things and our pursuit of them. (Figure 2.1.)

Let's return to Scheffler's standard: "Shares are fair when they are part of a distributive scheme that makes it possible for free and equal citizens to pursue their

---

[1] Scheffler 2003, 28.

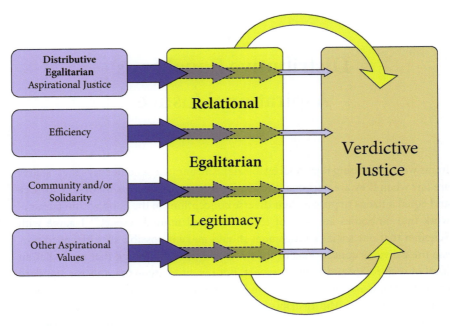

Figure 2.1 The anatomy of justice

diverse conceptions of the good within a framework that embodies an ideal of reciprocity and mutual respect." I embrace that standard as an account of legitimacy, the weightiest input into verdictive justice. But I *reject* that standard as a standard of *fairness*, or *aspirational justice*. The difference is significant. To put the point roughly: It might be perfectly legitimate for our social arrangement to feature some inequalities of income and wealth, including inequalities over which those on the losing end have no real control. Scheffler's standard may be perfectly well realized, consistent with some such inequalities. But meeting Scheffler's standard, I want to insist, doesn't make the inequalities *fair*. For now, I leave open the precise substantive demands that Scheffler's standard imposes: the question of what distributive inequalities really are consistent with reciprocity and mutual respect among free and equal citizens. I take up that question in the next chapter. In this chapter, I want to argue that, whatever distribution is compatible with mutual respect, *fairness* impugns distributive inequality directly. Aspirational justice cares about equal distributions as such, and not only to the degree that they are part of a distributive scheme that embodies reciprocity and mutual respect. So, contra Scheffler, our reasons to care about equality aren't exhausted once those broadly relational egalitarian achievements are secure.

I make this case through critical engagement with a series of arguments *against* distributive egalitarianism. First are the objections leveled by Elizabeth Anderson in her canonical case against distributive egalitarianism. Second are the objections developed by Joseph Fishkin in his work on equal opportunity. Canonical relational egalitarians don't just argue positively that relational equality matters; they argue critically, against distributive egalitarianism, that distributive equality matters only when it serves relational equality. My aim, then, is to persuade critics that distributive equality is fit to play a role in political evaluation and that we *need* it: First, distributive equality does not succumb to the criticisms relational egalitarians have leveled; second, it makes a difference—and a plausible difference that we should welcome—to our ultimate judgments of verdictive justice. Following that, in Chapters 3 and 4, I'll take up the work of convincing distributive egalitarians that distributive equality's role in the account is one worth having.[2] Across these chapters, the role of relational and distributive equality *within the anatomy of justice* is crucial to the defenses that I mount. This means I will at once be defending substantive accounts of aspirational justice and of legitimacy *and* building my case for the anatomy of justice by showing how it situates those accounts. I hope to show that the anatomy is practically and theoretically preferable to a pluralist intuitionism on which we lack any systematic mechanism for weighing values. It equips political philosophy to be action-guiding even when values conflict, thus showing that though these are academic debates, their import isn't *merely academic.*[3]

I defend distributive egalitarian aspirational justice by defending responsibility-sensitive egalitarianism, or so-called "luck egalitarianism."[4] Distributive egalitarianism generally holds inequalities (along some dimension) to stand in need of justification and defeasibly to stand in need of rectification. Because distributive egalitarianism on my picture is an account of *aspirational* justice—of *one input into* verdictive justice—the "defeasibly" qualification works on two levels. On the matter of what can defeat aspirational justice *from without*, we've already seen the answer: Other aspirational values like community or efficiency might do this, as might considerations of relational egalitarian legitimacy. If other aspirational values outweigh aspirational justice, or if legitimacy condemns some means of realizing it, then these suppressions will be reflected in the ranking of verdictive justice. I leave imprecise what can defeat the case *internal* to aspirational justice for rectifying inequality—that is, what can make it the case that *aspirational justice itself* does not favor rectification. Responsibility-sensitive egalitarians variously take (responsible) choice or desert to do this work. I think that vanishingly

---

[2] Distributive egalitarians don't advance the corresponding critical claim that relational equality matters only in service of distributive equality, so the structure of the chapters addressed to skeptical distributive egalitarian readers doesn't parallel that of the chapter addressed to skeptical relational egalitarians. See Lippert-Rasmussen 2016.

[3] See Rawls 1999a, 30–6; Cohen 2008, 3–4. For other pluralist, hybrid, or deflationary accounts of relational and distributive equality, see Moles and Parr 2019; Lippert-Rasmussen 2016; 2015; Tan 2012; Wolff 1998; Gheaus 2018; Schemmel 2011; Vallentyne 2015.

[4] The term "luck egalitarian" was first leveled as disparagement in Anderson's early critique of the views she referred to by that name. See Anderson 1999.

46   THE ANATOMY OF JUSTICE

few inequalities are justified by the lights of the right account of aspirational just-ice, but this chapter won't assume as much or argue for it. The egalitarianism I defend stands inequality in need of justification but leaves open whether *equality* also stands in need of justification. On my view, distributive egalitarianism is fundamentally egalitarian, not fundamentally anti-luck.[5]

The great bulk of criticism of luck egalitarianism invokes that view's alleged implausible implications. The most compelling defenses against this criticism invoke values pluralism to deny that luck egalitarianism has the implications that critics find so implausible.[6] Defenders point out that luck equality—or distribu-tive equality generally—is not claimed to be the only thing that matters. Since luck equality is not a unitary moral consideration, implausible guidance that it would issue *were* it a unitary moral consideration is no counterexample to the view. This chapter builds upon this basic model of defense, using the anatomy of justice to mount a theoretically unified defense of luck egalitarianism that rela-tional egalitarians can accept without abandoning their commitment to relational equality as an overriding requirement of justice. I argue that situating luck egali-tarianism as an account of aspirational justice within the anatomy of justice enables luck egalitarians to answer objections, including by unifying and expand-ing answers already on offer based in values pluralism. Section 2.1 does the situat-ing, briefly reviewing the anatomy and then motivating the constraining role of legitimacy that's so crucial for the arguments of this chapter. Sections 2.2 and 2.3 answer objections to luck egalitarianism in light of its place within the anatomy. They show how the anatomy equips us to preserve luck egalitarian insights while avoiding the apparent defects that its detractors regard as damning.

2.1 Distributive Equality in Context

Like Cohen's "justice," aspirational justice is a matter of a single consideration: each getting what she is due, shorn of considerations like feasibility, stability, and publicity. Verdictive justice gives a ranking of social arrangements by political value once aspirational justice is balanced against other aspirational values and approved or impugned by the constraining considerations of liberal democratic legitimacy. On the *substantive* pluralism this conceptual picture enables, luck egalitarianism as aspirational justice coheres with the role many luck egalitarians claim for their view. It rates a social arrangement as more valuable to the extent that that arrangement features less undeserved disadvantage, and it provides

---

[5] See Segall 2014; Neufeld 2015.

[6] As Temkin puts it, "any reasonable egalitarian will be a pluralist. Equality is not the only thing that matters to an egalitarian" (Temkin 2003, 63). See also Parfit 2000; Segall 2007; Eyal 2006; Cohen 2008; Brighouse and Swift 2008, 2009b.

defeasible reasons—to be balanced against other aspirational values and constrained by legitimacy—to pursue or maintain an arrangement with less undeserved disadvantage rather than more.

My defense of distributive egalitarianism as aspirational justice depends on the ways in which reasons of aspirational justice get defeated by considerations of relationally egalitarian legitimacy. Before that defense can fully come into focus, then, we need a bit more to motivate the pieces of the picture that *surround* aspirational justice: first, to motivate an account of legitimacy underpinned by mutual respect; second, to motivate the view that legitimacy underpinned by mutual respect acts as a decisive constraint.

The full case for associating relational egalitarian mutual respect with liberal legitimacy draws on arguments from across this book. But the *prima facie* case is simple: It is *intuitively plausible* that, in a liberal democracy, a political arrangement exercises power legitimately only insofar as that arrangement—and its exercises and omissions—comply with the relational ideal of mutual civic respect.[7] The ideal of mutual respect imposes a reciprocity requirement: A social arrangement is consistent with mutual respect only insofar as that arrangement and the exercises of democratic power that occur within it are mutually justifiable among citizens construed as free and equal—only insofar as they can be justified on terms that all free and equal citizens can accept. Imposing a reciprocity requirement on social arrangements and exercises of political power, relational egalitarianism's mutual respect commitment animates a theory of *politically liberal legitimacy*.[8] Though some relational egalitarians may resist this association, they shouldn't. Political liberalism is the consummate development of the relational strand in Rawlsian liberalism from which subsequent relational egalitarians draw support. And political liberalism's signature commitments—like to justificatory reciprocity and the substantive requirements for political conceptions of justice—derive from the value of mutual respect among free and equal citizens.[9] Politically liberal legitimacy undertakes to maintain mutual civic respect by insisting that democratic power be exercised only in ways justifiable to all citizens, within a constitutional structure that protects fundamental interests that all citizens share. An exercise of political power might comply with mutual civic respect because it is *substantively* consistent with, and is approved by a democratic process that is *procedurally* consistent with, constitutional principles that comprise a reasonable framework for ensuring the status of all as free and equal citizens, and because it is justifiable on the basis of interests that we share as free and equal citizens. Recall that Anderson's canonical relational egalitarianism regards two people as equal "when each accepts the obligation to justify their actions by principles acceptable to the other, and in which they take mutual consultation, reciprocation,

---

[7] For an account that is in important respects resonant, see Dworkin 2000.
[8] See Rawls 1993, for example xliv.   [9] See Larmore 1999; Nussbaum 2011; Schouten 2019.

and recognition for granted."[10] Relationally egalitarian, politically liberal legitimacy regards a social arrangement as more legitimate—and therefore overridingly more valuable—insofar as political intervention into each citizens' life abides by the criterion of mutual justifiability and ensures for each person the positive conditions necessary to undergird their standing as a free and equal citizen. In short, legitimacy concerns the moral status of uses and omissions of political power, and in a liberal democracy, mutual respect plausibly is the ideal according to which such adjudication should proceed.[11]

Remember, the anatomy doesn't cast liberal legitimacy as *exhaustive of* relational egalitarianism. Plausibly, some version of community or solidarity operates as an *aspirational* relational value. I now add that legitimacy doesn't even exhaust the reasons of *mutual respect*. On my account, legitimacy comprises the *institutional* face of mutual respect, but mutual respect plausibly supplies directly *interpersonal* reasons as well.[12] While a society is legitimate insofar as its *institutions* are mutually justifiable among free and equal citizens, and while this presumably includes fostering conditions for *interpersonal* mutual respect, legitimacy doesn't directly condemn all interpersonal failures of mutual respect among citizens. For example, we'll see, a social arrangement will be less legitimate by virtue of failing to promote social conditions that discourage racist behavior and preserve racial status equality; but it is not less legitimate when, though the discouraging conditions obtain, some instances of racist behavior persist.[13] Though not exhaustive of relational egalitarianism, then, liberal legitimacy comprises the signature political demands of relational equality: the institutional demands of mutual respect among persons construed as free and equal. Because relational egalitarianism and political liberalism both impose positive demands and negative constraints on political action and political aspiration, and because both rest those demands and constraints atop the value of mutual respect, we should not reject a construal of relational egalitarianism that casts mutual respect in the role of liberal legitimacy—at least not on its face.

---

[10] Anderson 1999, 313. This resonates with Scheffler's standard articulated at the start of the paper: free and equal citizens pursuing their diverse values within a system of reciprocity and mutual respect.

[11] To recall a point from Chapter 1, legitimacy is scalar because social arrangements and exercises of political power can be more or less (in)congruent with mutual respect, and because a social arrangement can have more or fewer political exercises that are (more or less) (in)congruent with mutual respect.

[12] Because I do not *equate* politically liberal legitimacy with relational egalitarianism, the anatomy does not rule out perfectionist relational egalitarianism as incoherent. Indeed, one might even endorse the anatomy *and* a perfection-based relational egalitarianism, so long as one endorsed subordinating perfection-based considerations to mutual respect for purposes of political evaluation. Thanks to Tom Parr for encouraging me to clarify this point.

[13] Some such behaviors raise problems of verdictive justice by way of aspirational values. Whether all do—or whether some raise problems for values *outside of* justice—is a question the anatomy leaves open. See Miller 1997; Wolff 1998; O'Neill 2008; Cohen 2009; Mason 2012, 2015; Schemmel 2021, 132–43.

But why think legitimacy underpinned by mutual respect has such strong priority over aspirational justice?[14] To recall, the role of mutual respect as a trumping value relative to aspirational values entails that a social arrangement is *always* politically worse insofar as it fails the test of mutual justifiability imposed by mutual respect. Aspirational values *remain values* when their pursuit is impugned by mutual respect. But in judgments of verdictive justice, the cost at the bar of mutual respect is decisive, no matter the magnitude of the gain to aspirational values that the cost would purchase: Illegitimate progress toward fair shares does improve our social arrangement *in one way*, but the way in which it makes it worse is morally more important. Mutual respect plausibly takes such strong priority because mutual respect is the very value that adjudicates our pursuit of all other values in a liberal democracy given inevitable, reasonable disagreement over those values and how to pursue them. To be sure, the value of mutual respect may itself be disputed. But disagreement over the value of mutual respect is different than disagreement over the value of, for example, distributive equality. Mutual respect is what gives disputes over other values political significance: It is because we want to preserve mutual respect that we must find a way to deal fairly with disagreement. If some political strategy could bring about greater compliance with fair shares but at a cost to mutual respect, then, it is plausible on principle that pursuing that strategy would result in a less good social arrangement—by the lights of *political* evaluation—no matter the magnitudes of the gain and cost in question. Mutual respect is the precondition for gains in terms of other values to be *publicly recognizable as such*. In sum: Mutual respect is a plausible value to underpin legitimacy because mutual respect plausibly regulates the moral permissibility of exercises or omissions of democratic political power; and legitimacy is plausibly overridingly weighty because mutual respect is precisely what determines whether and how other values may politically be treated *as* values.

Now, we might expect such a strong ordering of values to issue verdicts we cannot accept upon reflection. Intuitively, there are cases in which great gains by the lights of distributive equality generate more value than tiny improvements by the lights of, for example, the basic liberties. But we can accept mutual respect as a trumping value without denying that possibility. That's because mutual respect *on its own terms* condemns the kind of distributive inequality that other lexical weighting claims implausibly subordinate. Minimally, mutual respect demands that every citizen have enough to stand as an equal citizen, including adequate food, shelter, medical care, knowledge and deliberative capacities, the conditions for autonomy, access to education to develop talents, occupational choice, and conditions for participating in civil society without shame.[15] Moreover, relational

---

[14] For general skepticism about trumping values, see Goodin 1995. For skepticism about legitimacy's supremacy over justice, see Stemplowska and Swift 2018.
[15] Anderson 1999, 318.

50 THE ANATOMY OF JUSTICE

equality plausibly demands even more, distributively, than adequacy so understood.[16] On my picture, a society cannot legitimately fail to make good on these distributive demands of mutual respect, *whatever* account of aspirational distributive justice orders its institutions. The distributive inegalitarian implications that lurk as counterexamples to mutual respect as a trumping value simply may not arise, because mutual respect is robust and multi-faceted, calling on its own terms for much of what distributive egalitarians care about non-instrumentally. I'll say more in the next chapter to defend this ranking of legitimacy over aspirational social values. For now, for a chapter meant to convince relational egalitarians that they can and should accept a pluralistic anatomy of justice that includes distributive egalitarianism as a value in its own right, this will suffice.

The coming sections defend luck egalitarian aspirational justice as one component of the anatomy of justice. They also show that the anatomy of justice is crucial to the defenses I mount: The anatomy enables us to vindicate the conviction that (undeserved) distributive disadvantage is unfair while avoiding the problems that seem to challenge that conviction. We'll see that the reconciliation the anatomy supports is systematic, and that it avoids a radical pluralism of intuitionism. It therefore shows how theorizing can help us know better what to do—what kind of social policy to reach for to combat injustice—and that theorizing can help us to engage in public, interpersonal deliberation about what to do. This possibility should matter even to those with no stake in the debate over luck and relational egalitarianism. When theorizing justice, we can easily feel as though we face a choice: We embark either on a purely utopian project to envision the perfectly just society or on a merely critical project to describe existing injustice. The anatomy of justice helps us chart a third course. It can unify our thinking about what a just society looks like, about what is wrong with the society we inhabit, and about how to evaluate the relative merits of the reforms and institutional reconfigurations accessible from where we are now. That this methodological unification is one worth having can be established by the plausibility of the verdicts the anatomy issues and by the substantive unifications it enables. These are virtues whether we're invested in any particular egalitarian debate or not. Liberal egalitarians, after all, are hardly alone in thinking that justice requires both distributive and relational achievements, and hardly alone in seeing the appeal of integrating the two.[17]

2.2 Luck Egalitarianism and Equal Respect

Luck egalitarians disagree about how disadvantage is to be measured, about what it means to be disadvantaged undeservedly, and about whether the demand to

---

[16] Schemmel 2011, 2021.   [17] See, for example, Fraser 1997, 11–40, 2001.

mitigate undeserved disadvantage is strictly egalitarian.[18] For the most part, the defenses I mount are available across these disagreements, including to luck egalitarians who accept the two unifying commitments that Anderson attributes to that view in leveling her attack against it: "that people should be compensated for undeserved misfortunes and that the compensation should come only from that part of others' good fortune that is undeserved."[19] But for my purposes, we might think of luck egalitarianism as a stringent equal opportunity principle that approves inequality only if the disadvantaged enjoyed a robust opportunity to avoid it.[20]

Anderson's objections to luck egalitarianism share a common structure: She finds luck egalitarianism implausible because of what she takes it to tell us to do and what she takes it to express in so directing us. My defense shall be to deny that luck egalitarianism, *as aspirational justice*, tells us to do what Anderson says it tells us to do, and thus to deny that it expresses what she takes it to express in so directing us. Luck egalitarian aspirational justice simply tells us when shares are fair. Assuming fair shares is a value, the right account of that value supplies reasons. But how and whether we should act on those reasons depends on further considerations. Heeding the reasons sourced by fair shares would make a social arrangement in one way better. But to see how reasons to eliminate undeserved disadvantage filter into all-things-considered evaluative or normative verdicts of justice, we need to put luck egalitarianism in evaluative context.[21] Accordingly, an objection to luck egalitarianism misfires insofar as it misconstrues luck egalitarianism as a theory of how our social arrangement should be ordered, rather than as *one input into* our thinking about that question. In my terms, the ranking of social arrangements that *aspirational* justice generates will be different than the ranking that *verdictive* justice generates, because aspirational justice is only one among the values that inform verdictive justice. Whether a gain by the lights of aspirational justice makes a social arrangement better on the whole depends on how aspirational justice weighs relative to other values and on how its reasons diverge from or align with the reasons supplied by those other values.

To some degree, any generic political values pluralism can de-fang objections to luck egalitarianism that ride on claims about what it directs us to do: It is no mark against some value that, were we to pursue it at a cost to more important values, we would be making a mistake. Anderson argues that luck egalitarianism

---

[18] For an overview of debates within luck egalitarianism, see Lippert-Rasmussen 2016. Works canonically classified as defenses of luck egalitarianism include Dworkin 1981; Arneson 1989; Cohen 1989; Temkin 1993; Roemer 1994. Dworkin denies that his view is luck egalitarian (Dworkin 2003). Arneson now defends a view he calls "responsibility catering prioritarianism" (Arneson 2000, 2008, 2010; see also Parfit 2000). I leave open the scope and metric of luck egalitarian justice and the question of what it is in virtue of which unearned disadvantage is unfair.

[19] Anderson 1999, 290. I don't claim that my defense is consistent with every particular way of working out or contextualizing the implications of those commitments.

[20] Cohen 2008. But see Stemplowska 2011.   [21] See Brighouse and Swift 2008.

52 THE ANATOMY OF JUSTICE

fails to express equal respect for all citizens.[22] But luck egalitarianism as a theory of aspirational justice is not *meant* to capture reasons of equal respect, and it is also no mark against some value that it fails to express a different value.[23] Consider an example: As plenty of egalitarians have pointed out, the institution of the family obstructs equal opportunity. Even if effective egalitarian social institutions were in place, we could not fully offset the advantage one can accrue from being loved and favored by a parent who has even marginally super-equal social and material capital to confer. Luck egalitarianism, taken alone, therefore favors severely restricting individuals' interactions within their families or abolishing the family altogether. In this, it seems clearly to counsel the wrong course of action. But this implication is not a good basis for an *objection* to luck egalitarianism, because luck egalitarianism is not meant to be *taken alone*. Similarly, efficiency is plausibly a political value. It doesn't express equal respect, and taken alone, it may counsel action that *violates* equal respect. But this doesn't mean we don't care about efficiency; it just means we don't care *only* about efficiency. Like efficiency, luck egalitarianism captures a different value. Now, the strongest version of Anderson's charge takes issue not with what luck egalitarianism tells us to do but with what luck egalitarianism tells us that *justice* tells us to do. To this, *conceptual* pluralism has a ready response: Luck egalitarianism is not a theory of the concept of justice that helps us think about what to do; it is a theory of a concept meant only to tell us what each is due.

Still, I think we should hope for more than this from a pluralist defense of luck egalitarianism. To see why, notice that it *would* be implausible if *verdictive* justice favored abolition of the family. So far, the pluralist response establishes that all-things-considered (verdictive) judgments of justice *needn't* favor abolition of the family just because luck egalitarianism is one input into those judgments. But nothing in the generic pluralist response so far assures us that all-things-considered judgments that incorporate luck egalitarianism *won't* favor abolition of the family. The anatomy of justice provides this assurance. It supports theoretically unified and non-*ad-hoc* verdicts that preserve the intuition that Anderson's objections rely upon: the intuition that it would be a surpassingly bad thing for our political institutions to fail to express and preserve mutual respect. Within my proposed anatomy, distributive equality—like all aspirational values—yields to mutual respect. Mutual respect demands protection for associational liberty, which in turn favors protection for (some version of) the institution of the family. Relational egalitarian liberal legitimacy thus dictates that some version of the family must be afforded those protections. Meanwhile, put into context, luck egalitarian aspirational justice favors doing what we can—consistent with those

---

[22] Anderson 1999, 289.
[23] I do not say that no luck egalitarian theories have been cast as accounts of equal respect. For one intriguing attempt, see Stemplowska 2011.

DISTRIBUTIVE EQUALITY AS ASPIRATIONAL JUSTICE   53

protections—to offset or limit the family's dis-equalizing effects. With this example in mind, let's consider the specific mutual-respect-based objections Anderson levels against luck egalitarianism.

Victims of Bad Option Luck

First is the allegation that luck egalitarianism fails to treat with equal respect victims of "bad option luck," or those whose disadvantage results from choices they deliberately and responsibly made.[24] These may be condemnable choices—like avoidably driving uninsured—or laudable choices to take on a dangerous or ill-paid but socially valuable occupation—like de-prioritizing paid work to care for dependents. Because those who suffer bad option luck are not entitled to support by the lights of luck egalitarianism, Anderson argues, luck egalitarians must rely on paternalism to justify social support to ensure that such citizens enjoy the material preconditions for equal standing as citizens.

In assessing this objection, we should first note that, while luck egalitarians disagree about what constitutes a *fair* disadvantage, mere choice will not suffice. For one thing, our choices are often a product of our natural and social endowments, for which we are not responsible. Anderson could stipulate that the badly off in her case *really are* responsible in the relevant sense, but even so, luck egalitarians may impugn the disadvantage in question if the *choice set* was unfair by the lights of luck egalitarian justice. In many cases of deliberate choosing, we may have reason to doubt the fairness of that choice set. Recall that Anderson's concern is about ensuring for each citizen the basic material preconditions for equal standing as a citizen. In the case of at least some such material conditions, we might credibly doubt that anyone would with full responsibility sacrifice their holdings. We might argue that nobody *responsibly* and *against a background of fair options* chooses to go without housing, or care in old age, or education for their children. In the case of goods like these, luck egalitarians needn't reach for paternalism to justify social provision. They can claim, credibly, that such deprivation is never a deserved disadvantage.

Independent of any skepticism about responsibility attributions in these cases, luck egalitarians can argue that luck egalitarianism sometimes condemns disadvantage that results from option luck. For instance, those who construe their principle on the model of equal opportunity might endorse certain forms of public insurance as included with the equal opportunity set to which luck egalitarianism holds all of us equally entitled.[25] Alternatively, luck egalitarians may add to

---

[24] There is a large literature on this "harshness objection" to luck egalitarianism. See, for example, Voigt 2007; Stemplowska 2009; Huzum 2011.
[25] See Stemplowska 2011.

luck egalitarianism a set of commitments about the moral permissions individuals have to expose themselves to risk at public cost, and from this derive a (non-paternalistic) insurance scheme consistent with responsibility-sensitive egalitarian commitments, like a tax on gambling to insure gamblers against the risk of destitution.[26] If public insurance against certain avoidable disadvantages is part of an opportunity set to which luck egalitarianism deems us all equally entitled, or if we otherwise have reason to limit the disadvantage to which responsible choice can give rise, then luck egalitarians can disavow a blanket policy of non-compensation for the avoidably disadvantaged, and they can do so on non-paternalistic grounds. Here again, luck egalitarians can deny that luck egalitarian reasons favor withholding social support.

Suppose, though, that luck egalitarianism does indeed sometimes favor leaving victims of bad option luck without even the basic material necessities for equal citizenship. It still does not follow that luck egalitarians can endorse measures to secure equal citizenship only by embracing paternalism. Luck egalitarians may hold that someone who responsibly forfeits her own share of the social product is not entitled *as a matter of fair shares* to subsidy financed at a cost to someone else, but fair shares is only one value. Here, luck egalitarian pluralists can turn to defeaters external to luck egalitarianism. Defenders of luck egalitarianism have endorsed protections for victims of bad option luck on grounds of solidarity or compassion, both of which can supply reasons that do not rely on paternalism.[27] Critics like Anderson may rejoin that this pluralist defense of luck egalitarianism fails to justify support for victims of bad option luck *as a requirement of justice*.[28] The anatomy of justice answers this rejoinder by locating aspirational values like solidarity and community internal to verdictive justice (even if *external* to *aspirational* justice); thus, we can say that support for the disadvantaged is favored by an account of a concept of justice meant to provide such guidance (even if not by an account of a concept of justice meant only to pick out fair shares).

More importantly, the anatomy systematizes the pluralist defense against Anderson's objection: It *ensures* that the material prerequisites of equal standing will be called for by that broader concept of justice. This it does by casting mutual respect as the value at the heart of legitimacy, the input into verdictive justice that constrains aspirational justice. Relationally egalitarian legitimacy demands for each citizen unforfeitable protection for her standing as equal citizen, including the material preconditions for that standing, and it demands this on the very grounds that Anderson is keen to emphasize: Where material prerequisites of equal citizenship are at stake, measures to ensure that everyone unconditionally

---

[26] See A. Williams 2008; Moles and Parr 2019.
[27] See, for example, Segall 2007; Markovits 2008.   [28] See Huzum 2011.

have enough are demanded by mutual respect.[29] Even above that threshold, subsidy for victims of bad option luck might be favored by verdictive justice on the basis of aspirational values like community or efficiency. But *below* that threshold, verdictive justice will *always* condemn *any* social arrangement that fails to secure the preconditions for equal standing. And this condemnation is a strong one: A social arrangement that fails to secure the precondition for each citizen's equal standing is not only an *unjust* arrangement; it is to that degree a *less legitimate* arrangement. In this way, the anatomy of justice provides assurance of a strong condemnation of any social arrangement that subordinates victims of bad option luck, whether their choices are laudable or condemnable, and whether their subordination occurs by way of material inequality or otherwise.

Victims of Bad Brute Luck

Second, Anderson claims that luck egalitarianism fails to express equal respect for the *blamelessly* disadvantaged, or those whose misfortune comes about through bad *brute* luck. This failure of mutual respect concerns the reasons that luck egalitarianism allegedly gives us to aid those who are disadvantaged through no fault of their own: On luck egalitarianism, Anderson charges, "people lay claim to the resources of egalitarian redistribution in virtue of their inferiority to others, not in virtue of their equality to others"; and an attitude of pity underlies our obligation to aid the disadvantaged.[30]

Here again, luck egalitarians have plenty to say in reply even before contextualizing their view within the anatomy I'm forwarding. Nothing in luck egalitarianism entails that pity is the appropriate attitude toward victims of bad brute luck. Anderson seems to think that pity is bound up in luck egalitarian assessments because those assessments are comparative, but we need not pity someone in order to regard her as lacking her fair share of a social good. If you and I are equally entitled to the fruits of some venture but wind up with unequal holdings at the end of the day, the observation that one of us is owed the sum by which we fall short of equality certainly needn't involve pity. Nor does the luck egalitarian assessment of why the blamelessly disadvantaged are owed recompense imply that the blamelessly disadvantaged are inferior. Rather, it plausibly implies that they are equally entitled to the fruits of our shared social venture but have been left at the end of the day with less in their apron pockets.

---

[29] See Anderson 1999, 301. The anatomy offers a "developed view of what the 'stakes' of responsible choice might be, and how one could go about fixing them within a luck egalitarian framework." Schemmel 2021, 156.

[30] Anderson 1999, 306.

56 THE ANATOMY OF JUSTICE

Now, it is true that, if the value of a social contribution were determined solely by the price it can command in a market, then luck egalitarianism may imply that the blamelessly disadvantaged are owed an equal share not because they have made an equal contribution but because it's not their fault that they haven't. But luck egalitarians needn't and shouldn't reduce the value of every social contribution to its market price. When a social arrangement equates social value with market price, it demeans contributions that markets undervalue. Luck egalitarians should oppose such an arrangement, not only because it institutionalizes an evaluative mistake about social contributions, but on distinctively luck egalitarian grounds: A social arrangement is unjust by luck egalitarian lights if it systematically makes some citizens feel inferior, through no fault of their own, because of what social contributions they are (un)able to make. On any plausible metric of luck egalitarian justice, after all, the social bases of self-respect will matter for interpersonal comparison. The price one's skills can command is a function of institutional arrangement, and one way to lessen undeserved self-respect deficits is to ensure that the institutional arrangement makes room for social contributions by way of a diverse array of skills. Plausibly, then, citizens owed compensation because their skills are not well rewarded in the institutional arrangement are not owed that compensation "because their innate inferiority makes their labor so relatively worthless to others, as judged by the market."[31] They're owed compensation for the unearned bad fortune to live under a social arrangement that does not make good use of the skills they are able to contribute.

So, nothing in luck egalitarianism need entail that those whom some arrangement of labor markets leaves out are innately inferior as people or workers, and luck egalitarianism can impugn an arrangement that avoidably leaves some out. Nor need the reforms it favors take the form of after-the-fact compensation. In developing this objection, Anderson invites us to imagine a dystopian luck egalitarian fund to compensate the undeservingly ugly for their misfortune. But supposing the misfortune of being ugly registers as a problem of justice on the metric luck egalitarianism employs, luck egalitarians needn't think that monetary compensation is the remedy justice favors. Along some dimension of disadvantage, I think distributive justice *should* condemn social arrangements in which beauty norms systematically disadvantage those who don't meet them.[32] Perhaps antiracist or gender-egalitarian educational interventions can help to erode harmful beauty norms. If so, then luck egalitarianism plausibly favors such interventions on just those grounds: They are necessary to erode unearned disadvantage. Indeed, I suspect such interventions are justifiable not only as means to erode unearned *distributive* disadvantage, but as means to rectify certain forms of *relational* subordination as well. If so, then the extensional divergence between

---

[31] Anderson 1999, 352.
[32] For illuminating discussion, see Rhode 2011; Widdows 2018; Mason 2021.

relational and distributive egalitarianism when it comes to policy responses to culturally sustained injustice is smaller than Anderson's dystopian examples suggest.

For these reasons, I doubt that luck egalitarianism *on its own* expresses disrespect to the unfairly badly off in the ways Anderson alleges. But the pluralist anatomy I'm proposing disarms this charge in any case, for if the grounds for luck egalitarian concern sometimes *do* involve a pity that mutual respect condemns, the legitimacy constraint will subordinate that consideration as an input into verdictive justice. To see how, let's begin a few steps back and use one of Anderson's own examples. Anderson argues that equal democratic citizenship demands that some capabilities be ensured unconditionally. On behalf of the mobility impaired, for example, democratic equality demands "good enough access to public accommodations that they can function as equals in civil society"; but for Anderson, this "does not require that one's access be equally fast, comfortable, or convenient."[33] If she's right about what equal standing requires, then "good enough access" exhausts the demands of relational egalitarian legitimacy.

But luck egalitarianism favors more, and on the anatomy of justice, when we can do more without running afoul of mutual respect,[34] verdictive justice favors more as well. What functions as a disabling condition or as a marketable talent is largely a matter of institutional design, and luck egalitarian fairness favors arrangements that minimize the influence of natural and social endowments on life prospects. Surely, we can institutionalize these considerations to *some* degree without running afoul of mutual respect: If we can take the necessary steps to ensure *good enough* access to public accommodations, we can plausibly sometimes go *somewhat* further toward making that access comparably comfortable and convenient. But whenever considerations of luck egalitarian fairness *do* exceed what's permitted by mutual respect, verdictive justice rightly treats the latter as decisive. Suppose a city faces feasibility constraints such that the only way to provide fully equally comfortable and convenient public transit to those with mobility impairments would be to provide them with a fully *separate* transit system. Should the city tolerate the unequal convenience of a mobility-integrated system or pursue equal convenience through mobility segregation? Is segregated transit more like wheelchair ramps on buildings and mobility carts at airports, which (I assume) enable the *inclusion* of the mobility impaired? Or is it more like mobility-segregated schooling, which (I assume) facilitates their *exclusion*? The answer presumably depends in part on the baseline of comparison: on how far short of equality the integrated system falls on measures of comfort, convenience, and ease of access. I think the case is genuinely morally complicated. In such a case, arguably, mutual respect favors consulting the views of those most directly

---

[33] Anderson 1999, 334.

[34] And without running afoul of other aspirational values that weigh relatively heavily in the circumstances at hand.

58 THE ANATOMY OF JUSTICE

affected: the mobility impaired. Suppose that, after robust consultation, we conclude that, all things considered, a separate transit system would be marginalizing
rather than inclusive, and not worth the gains in convenience. We conclude, in
short, that mutual respect *overrides* the distributive egalitarian case for equal
comfort and convenience. If that's right, then verdictive justice favors the integrated system even though (by supposition) aspirational justice *dis*favors it on
grounds of distributive equality.[35]

Now consider the case through the lens of a different account of aspirational
justice: one which favors making public transit faster for the mobility impaired
in order to compensate those with mobility impairments *for their alleged
intrinsically lower wellbeing*. Mutual respect plausibly condemns *this* account
of aspirational justice wholesale, on the grounds that the very reasons it
supplies—as distinct from the available means of acting on those reasons in
our circumstances—are inconsistent with mutual respect. A theory of fairness
animated by a conviction that the mobility impaired live intrinsically worse lives
is demeaning in a way that renders that theory ineligible to inform political evaluation. Now, luck egalitarianism can't credibly be saddled with the constituent
conviction that people with mobility impairments have inherently worse lives.
The point is only that any such account would be screened off, by mutual respect,
as an illegitimate source of justification for political action.

The likelier conflict scenario was the first one. Luck egalitarianism will favor
some political action that mutual respect condemns. In such cases, legitimacy simply adjudicates the recommendations accordingly. Similarly, the value of efficiency
might in some circumstances favor action that mutual respect impugns. This
doesn't entail that efficiency doesn't matter; it only means we must situate efficiency within a scheme of political evaluation that subordinates it to other considerations. We may think it a stranger thing to say that *justice* can favor policy that
mutual respect impugns. But I think that within the context of the anatomy of justice, we should feel perfectly comfortable saying that *aspirational* justice cannot be
realized perfectly without running afoul of mutual respect. After all, on that anatomy, mutual respect is surpassingly weighty relative to aspirational justice when it
comes to the judgments of verdictive justice. And, as we'll see, it's an advantage of
the anatomy that it enables us to register the parts of aspirational justice that we
(rightly) leave unrealized for the sake of preserving mutual respect.

Intrusive and Moralizing

Finally, Anderson charges that luck egalitarianism fails to express equal respect
because it "requires the state to make grossly intrusive, moralizing judgments of

---

[35] In this case, aspirational justice might still give reasons to ease the feasibility constraints that
present the tradeoff. I consider this possibility in Chapter 4 (4.3).

DISTRIBUTIVE EQUALITY AS ASPIRATIONAL JUSTICE   59

individual's choices" in order to distinguish the cases of disadvantage that call for redress from the cases of disadvantage that do not.[36]

But this simply isn't true. Even where the principled case for remediating some disadvantage depends on that disadvantage owing to brute luck, other considerations might favor using rules of thumb so that institutions can avoid making individual responsibility attributions. For example, the balance of considerations might favor treating all disadvantage below some level of deprivation as disadvantage that calls for compensation. Reaching for heuristics or rules of thumb when it comes to politically pursuing luck egalitarian fair shares may be justified on the grounds that individual responsibility attributions are difficult to make and impossible to implement in a fine-grained way by the kinds of institutions that are responsible for realizing and sustaining distributive justice. And the specific rule of thumb just mentioned might be called for by a justified risk aversion about wrongly leaving severe deprivation unrectified, or by the premise that very severe deprivation is relatively unlikely to have been responsibly chosen.[37]

More importantly, in the anatomy of justice, insofar as any particular attempt to discern responsibility would erode or jeopardize mutual respect, that attempt is impugned by relationally egalitarian legitimacy. As we've seen, luck egalitarian reasons are always subordinated in the ranking of verdictive justice when those luck egalitarian reasons favor political action condemned by mutual respect. This includes luck egalitarian reasons to build institutional capacity for making individualized responsibility attributions.

In Chapter 1, when setting out the anatomy of justice, I imagined an aspirational value that violates mutual respect on its face: a conception of community on which the unification of all citizens on a common spiritual conviction is not only a way to *realize* community, but *part of what community is*. Community so understood is ruled out by mutual respect as an illegitimate *social aim*, even before we ask how it is to be realized. Distributive egalitarian aspirational justice isn't like that, even by Anderson's lights. We just saw that distributive egalitarian aspirational justice cannot plausibly be regarded as constitutively illegitimate on the grounds that it includes a constitutive conviction that the mobility impaired have intrinsically inferior lives. It includes no such constitutive conviction. Nor is its *actual* constitutive conviction—that undeserved inequality is unfair—*itself* intrusive and moralizing. The worries for distributive egalitarianism arise instead when we look at what that conviction appears to direct or license us to do. But these worries are not ultimately good grounds for objection. As we've seen, distributive egalitarianism is not undermined as a worthy social aim by the observation that, unconstrained, it would favor some on-the-whole-dis-valuable social arrangements or policies.

---

[36] Anderson 1999, 310.   [37] Compare Roemer 1993.

60   THE ANATOMY OF JUSTICE

Meanwhile, distributive egalitarianism can "speak up" even when it *is* constrained by mutual respect. The purpose of this chapter is not to justify the anatomy to luck egalitarians worried that it subordinates distributive equality *too much*; it's directed, instead, to relational egalitarians disposed against countenancing distributive equality as a value at all. The next section continues to address objections to luck egalitarianism. But it hints, too, at one way that distributive egalitarianism finds a voice even when constrained by mutual respect. I'll then take up that topic directly in the following two chapters.

2.3 Luck Egalitarianism and Opportunity Pluralism

I've argued that the anatomy of justice can strengthen pluralism-based defenses of luck egalitarianism against Anderson's challenges. It does so by theoretically unifying pluralism's disavowals of implausible supposed implications of luck egalitarianism, thereby making those disavowals less contingent and *ad hoc*. But plenty of luck egalitarianism's critics don't reject luck egalitarianism (only) because of what it entails or expresses; they simply find distributive egalitarianism unappealing and unmotivated from the start. Such critics will be unimpressed even if my defenses are compelling. In this section, I consider more objections to luck egalitarianism, but my aim is to work in the direction of a new way to *motivate* distributive equality as a value. In his book *Bottlenecks*, Joseph Fishkin refreshes and redeploys some perennial objections to luck egalitarianism.[38] I argue that luck egalitarianism as aspirational justice can answer those objections. But I also suggest that distributive egalitarian aspirational justice plausibly plays an essential role in justifying Fishkin's appealing positive vision for social reform. That is, we have a complete case for that vision only if distributive equality matters in its own right.

Fishkin argues for "opportunity pluralism" as a principle to guide the design of the "opportunity structure": Opportunity pluralism calls for an opportunity structure that fosters a wide diversity of views about what rewards are worth striving for and preserves myriad pathways to achieving those rewards.[39] Beyond *diverse* pathways to a flourishing life, opportunity pluralism calls for as many as possible of the valued goods and roles to be *non-competitive* and for as many as possible of the valued goods and roles to be *independent* of one another and *multiply achievable*.[40] Fishkin contrasts this vision with a "unitary" opportunity structure model, on which everyone competes for a small number of universally

---

[38] Fishkin 2014.   [39] Fishkin 2014, 80.

[40] I set aside Fishkin's methodological requirement concerning who has the authority to determine what the roles and goods are because I regard that as a consideration of legitimacy rather than of fairness.

coveted rewards within a "single pyramid of merit."[41] He illustrates a unitary opportunity structure by invoking a (somewhat) hypothetical "big test society." In the big test society, "there are a number of different careers and professions, but all prospects of pursuing any of them depend on one's performance on a single test administered at age sixteen."[42] The big test society occupies the extreme end of the spectrum ranging from unitary to pluralist opportunity structures. But, on Fishkin's telling, it exemplifies the kind of opportunity structure luck egalitarianism takes for granted: Along with other prevailing accounts of equal opportunity, luck egalitarianism allegedly takes a unitary structure for granted and asks only what the "big test" would need to look like in order for the outcomes to be just. It sees a landscape of constrained, scarce, and competitive pathways to a bundle of universally coveted rewards, and it seeks to minimize unearned disadvantage within that landscape. This accords as well with the popular notion of equal opportunity, which imagines life as a sport or race for which the playing field should be level or the starting gate fair. This image invites us to take a unitary opportunity structure for granted and ask only how access to opportunities within that structure should be arranged. The game is set; we ask only how to make conditions for competition fair. In contrast, Fishkin's opportunity pluralism "asks us to renovate the structure itself... to open up a broader range of paths and allow people to pursue the activities and goals that add up to a flourishing life."[43]

On Fishkin's view, luck egalitarianism is fatally flawed because it is unrealizable—and because it favors an unappealing social vision—within a unitary opportunity structure. Its flaws include:

1. The problem of the family: Luck egalitarianism is impossible to realize so long as advantaged families privilege their members over others.[44]
2. The problem of merit: Luck egalitarianism requires us to disentangle the features of a person's lot that are *due to her*, but this cannot be done because our circumstances shape both the effort we put in and the ends to which we put it.[45]
3. The problem of individuality: Luck egalitarianism discourages individuals from forming and pursuing their own conceptions of the good because by regulating competition within a unitary reward structure, it fortifies "one hegemonic set of institutions, values, and ends."[46]

---

[41] Fishkin 2014, 80.

[42] Fishkin 2014, 13. Fishkin bases this case on Williams's classic "warrior society" case. See Williams 1973.

[43] Fishkin 2014, 23.   [44] Fishkin 2014, 55–6.   [45] Fishkin 2014, 56, 108.

[46] Fishkin 2014, 80. Because luck egalitarianism is not a "starting gate" theory, I set aside the "problem of the starting gate" (Fishkin 2014, 65). I also set aside Fishkin's "problem of harshness," the substance of which I addressed in the previous section (Fishkin 2014, 67).

62   THE ANATOMY OF JUSTICE

But crucially, these three "problems" comprise *problems for luck egalitarianism* only if luck egalitarianism really does approve a unitary opportunity structure. If luck egalitarianism instead favors a pluralistic opportunity structure, then by Fishkin's own lights, the objections are defused. My defense against the objections consists in arguing that luck egalitarianism is consistent with and indeed favors opportunity pluralism because opportunity pluralism is the way to overcome the very obstacles to realizing egalitarian fair shares that these "problems" spotlight. With Fishkin, I think opportunity pluralism is a favorable institutional arrangement for pursuing fair shares; but I argue that opportunity pluralism's appeal is a mark *in favor of* luck egalitarianism, because luck egalitarianism favors opportunity pluralism and indeed helps to explain why it's such an attractive institutional reform agenda.

Consider the problem of the family. We've already seen that the anatomy of justice subordinates distributive fairness to mutual respect and thus ensures some protection for the institution of the family, even at a cost to distributive equality. What distributive equality favors, then, is a social arrangement that *minimizes the tradeoffs* between distributive equality and protection for the institution of the family. We can better realize luck egalitarian aspirational justice, consistent with respecting the family, under an opportunity structure that preserves diverse pathways to myriad good ways of life, and in which more of the goods that comprise such lives are non-competitive and independent of one another. In our current unitary-reward-structure society, the material conditions for living well come in a bundle, in the form of well-paid, high-status jobs that require at least an undergraduate college degree. Developmental opportunities like college admission spots are highly competitive goods whose value for their possessor is significantly a function of that person's place in the overall distribution of the good.[47] Competitive goods exacerbate the problem of the family because they direct everyone's pursuit of success in the same direction: Parents compete for the scarce goods that will enable their children to emerge successfully from the unitary gateway to social rewards. But by reforming the opportunity structure to make more social goods non-competitive and unbundled, and by establishing more distinct pathways to attaining them, we spread opportunity broadly and render the family less obstructive to distributive equality. In short, opportunity pluralism makes the family less disruptive to equality because it lessens the extent to which privileged parents can advantage their children in ways that work to the *dis*advantage of others.

For similar reasons, luck egalitarianism constrained by mutual respect plausibly favors opportunity pluralism as a means of easing the problem of individuality. Here again, as the value that gives way to mutual respect, distributive equality

---

[47] See Hirsch 1978.

effectively favors institutional arrangements that lessen the need to make tradeoffs. I don't argue that mutual respect or any other input into verdictive justice favors individuality *as such*, but mutual respect as I'll understand it *dis*favors institutional arrangements that systematically undermine citizens' ability to form and pursue their own conceptions of the good. If opportunity pluralism enables greater realization of distributive equality while supporting citizens' capacity to form and pursue their own conceptions of the good, then, subject to other aspirational values, verdictive justice favors opportunity pluralism. Fishkin's argument *just is* an argument for the antecedent of that conditional: A diverse opportunity structure lessens social incentives for individuals to conform to a particular narrative of success and enables citizens to share more equally in what matters to them. The anatomy of justice, featuring luck egalitarianism, favors opportunity pluralism.

Opportunity pluralization also enables luck egalitarianism to overcome the problem of merit. Fishkin points out that our traits and capacities "result from an ongoing, continuous, iterative interaction over time between a person and the various facets of her environment"; he goes on to claim that "most advantage does not derive 60 percent from choice and 40 percent from chance, but rather 100 percent from choice and 100 percent from chance."[48] But if Fishkin is right, then "most" advantage is equally and wholly saturated with brute luck. And, if graded responsibility attributions are incoherent or impossible, luck egalitarians can conclude that their view favors complete equality. That conditions could be such that luck egalitarianism favors complete equality is not a problem for luck egalitarianism; if disadvantage is never deserved in the relevant way, luck egalitarianism simply impugns all inequality.[49] And, even if it doesn't impugn all inequality on principle, luck egalitarianism will, when balanced against the value of efficiency, trade off some accurate discernment of responsibility for the sake of lessening undeserved disadvantage. After all, luck egalitarianism as I understand it does not *favor deserved disadvantage*; at most, it *approves disadvantage when it is deserved*. So, an opportunity structure that minimizes *all* disadvantage, or that minimizes certain types of disadvantage irrespective of responsibility attribution, is not in virtue of that condemned by luck egalitarianism. If minimizing disadvantage without a responsibility audit is the best way to reduce undeserved disadvantage without violating mutual respect, that strategy is positively favored by luck egalitarianism put into context of the anatomy of justice. In part to avoid the very problems of discerning merit, then, luck egalitarianism favors opportunity pluralism: Unitary opportunity structures make valued opportunities scarce, and

---

[48] Fishkin 2014, 108. I think Fishkin sometimes overstates his case on this matter, but I won't argue for that. The argument in the main text suffices to show that luck egalitarianism is not undermined by his argument in any case.

[49] See Cohen 2008, 60. But see also Stemplowska 2008.

64   THE ANATOMY OF JUSTICE

many go without through no fault of their own. In a pluralistic structure, there is simply less disadvantage to go around, including less disadvantage in opportunities to develop valued competencies and capabilities. When more of the things we have reason to want are non-competitive and unbundled, and when diverse pathways lead to attaining them, we lessen the need for comparative desert attributions simply by avoiding much of the disadvantage that *can't* be avoided in unitary opportunity structures.

Opportunity pluralism is not a normative theory but a way of arranging social institutions. Ways of arranging social institutions can be favored or disfavored by verdictive justice. Luck egalitarianism is an account of aspirational justice. As such, it's an *input* into verdictive justice: It's one consideration that informs verdictive justice's evaluation of opportunity pluralism. Once we see that luck egalitarianism and opportunity pluralism answer two distinct questions, we see that Fishkin goes wrong in treating luck egalitarianism as a rival to opportunity pluralism. The two are not incompatible. And we see too that they are in fact closely allied: Considered in the context of constraining values, luck egalitarianism favors opportunity pluralism, because opportunity pluralism enables us to realize distributive equality without violating those value constraints. In short: Opportunity pluralistic social arrangements will be favored by verdictive justice because they preserve legitimacy *and still* realize a great deal of aspirational value.

The goodness of opportunity pluralism is no challenge to luck egalitarianism, then, because verdictive justice informed by luck egalitarian aspirational justice plausibly favors opportunity pluralism. Pluralism enables fuller realization of distributive equality without running afoul of mutual respect as compared with a unitary opportunity structure wherein practical and values-based hurdles to eroding unearned disadvantage are more obstructive. Since, by Fishkin's own lights, opportunity pluralism is the way to ameliorate the problems he construes as objections to luck egalitarianism, it follows from luck egalitarianism's compatibility with opportunity pluralism that luck egalitarianism can answer Fishkin's objections to the satisfaction of his own standards.[50] If opportunity pluralism is the solution to these problems and if nothing in luck egalitarianism's basic commitments is at odds with opportunity pluralism, then opportunity pluralism *just is* luck egalitarianism's defense against Fishkin's objections.

But there's yet more to say. Distributive egalitarianism broadly is a crucial piece of what *justifies* opportunity pluralism. Opportunity pluralism is a vision for a social arrangement, and we can cogently ask what values make it a *worthy* vision. Fishkin should answer that pluralism is favored by egalitarian justice. But by what standard of egalitarian justice? I've argued that opportunity pluralism is favored by an account of verdictive justice that includes distributive egalitarianism as an

---

[50]   Differences in the shape of the opportunity structure "determine the severity of the...problem of the family, the problem of merit...and the problem of individuality" (Fishkin 2014, 131, 139).

aspirational political value constrained by relationally egalitarian mutual respect. That's because opportunity pluralism enables a social arrangement to achieve more distributive equality without running afoul of mutual respect. Fishkin himself argues that opportunity pluralism lessens the distributive disadvantage a social arrangement must tolerate before incurring the kinds of costs to other values that alternative social arrangements would impose. Plausibly, then, distributive egalitarian commitments are a crucial part of what makes opportunity pluralism appealing in the first place. Maybe relational egalitarianism could provide an adequate values grounding for opportunity pluralism without distributive equality furnishing reasons of its own. But on Fishkin's own rendering, *distributive* equality does the motivating. Opportunity pluralism is a compelling vision, and I submit that it's compelling in part because distributive equality matters in its own right.

2.4 Equality and Social Reform

The canonical defenses of relational egalitarianism tell us that the demands of relational equality exhaust the demands of fairness. I think the standard these defenses get closest to articulating is a standard of *legitimacy*, and that a distribution fully compliant with that standard may yet fall short of fairness. We have reasons to pursue a social arrangement that realizes mutual respect *and* reasons to eliminate (undeserved) disadvantage. Relational egalitarian legitimacy accounts for the former, and distributive egalitarian aspirational justice accounts for the latter. We can accommodate this pluralism by embracing another, which is appealing in its own right: Political philosophy needs a pure, aspirational concept of justice as fair shares *and* a concept of justice that tells us how well a social arrangement realizes *all* aspirational political values balanced against each other and subjected to the constraints of legitimacy. This framework enables us to say that, although less important than mutual respect, distributive fairness matters; and it enables us to answer powerful challenges to that claim. As a theory of aspirational justice within a full anatomy of political value, luck egalitarianism withstands prominent challenges. Indeed, some of those challenges may help to show that distributive equality does matter in its own right.

This anatomy of justice is not meant to accommodate Rawls's theory of justice, but noting likenesses and differences will be illuminating to some readers. Luck egalitarian aspirational justice is Rawls's "principle of redress," which holds that "undeserved inequalities call for redress."[51] Rawls thinks the principle of redress is plausible, "as most such principles are, only as a prima facie principle"; but he

---

[51] Rawls 1999a, 86.

66 THE ANATOMY OF JUSTICE

holds that "whatever other principles we hold, the claims of redress are to be taken into account."[52] Rawls's difference principle is, I contend, a plausible balance between luck egalitarian aspirational justice and the aspirational value of efficiency.[53] On the anatomy, better realizing that balance adds value in whole only insofar as better realization is compliant with mutual respect, the demands of which include *but are not exhausted by* protections for the basic liberties. Most notably, mutual respect also demands robust distributive adequacy. Crucially, verdictive justice does not consist in normative principles that apply only in circumstances of full compliance. Instead, it comprises a pluralist specification of values from which we can derive evaluative comparisons of social arrangements and guidance for reform. The *most* valuable social arrangement in some set of circumstances may be the well-ordered society of Rawlsian justice as fairness. But the anatomy is a framework to systematize the values that should guide political action in circumstances of justice *or* injustice.

The picture I'm forwarding departs significantly from customary usage of some core concepts, especially legitimacy. On my picture, legitimacy comes in degrees, and full legitimacy—full compliance with the weighted institutional reasons sourced by mutual respect—is a demanding standard that would require massive social reform to achieve. This conceptual disruption has implications beyond those addressed here. For example, if we accept that full legitimacy is this demanding, we'll probably conclude that something *less* than full legitimacy suffices for democratic *authority*—for political institutions to morally compel.[54] More work is needed to show that the anatomy of justice repays this disruption. I take that up in the coming chapters. For now, we can have a theoretically unified pluralism about justice that includes both distributive and relational equality as fundamental values. That pluralism can support systematic defenses of distributive egalitarianism against criticism, on terms critics should find congenial. And it can underwrite an appealing vision of social reform that aims to pluralize and diversify the opportunity structure: If distributive and relational equality play the roles I propose for them, then verdictive justice will rank arrangements more favorably insofar as they realize opportunity pluralism.

The Anatomy of Justice: On the Shape, Substance, and Power of Liberal Egalitarianism. Gina Schouten, Oxford University Press. © Gina Schouten 2024. DOI: 10.1093/9780191999772.003.0003

---

[52] Rawls 1999a, 86. But see Scheffler 2003.
[53] The difference principle favors the social arrangement with the highest floor: the arrangement wherein the worst off are better off than they could be under any other arrangement. See Rawls 1999a, 65–6.
[54] But see Sleat 2015.

3

The Distributive Demands of
Mutual Respect

Chapter 2 argued that relational egalitarians should accept the presence of distributive egalitarianism in the anatomy of justice because the role of distributive equality is relatively minor. That argument situates mutual respect—the value at the heart of relationally egalitarian legitimacy—as a trumping value that constrains the force of other values—like distributive egalitarian aspirational justice—to bear on the judgments of verdictive justice. This chapter defends the claim that mutual respect acts as a sort of evaluative trump card with respect to distributive egalitarian fairness. My defense draws on the substantive convergence of mutual respect and distributive egalitarian aspirational justice. Most who endorse mutual respect among free and equal citizens as a political ideal agree that that ideal imposes some distributive demands. This chapter argues that those distributive demands are quite demandingly egalitarian.

It then elaborates the upshots of that argument for the plausibility of mutual respect as a trumping value within the pluralist anatomy of justice this book defends: Because mutual respect *itself* favors distributive equality, I argue, situating it as a trumping value *vis-à-vis* distributive egalitarian aspirational justice does not implausibly subordinate distributive equality. It may seem surprising that the plausibility of a strong priority ranking would depend on the substance of the two values in question. But objections to strong priority rankings rely on cases that strong priority rankings allegedly adjudicate wrongly. And yet, whether those rankings in fact adjudicate the cases as they're alleged to do depends on precisely what the values being ranked give us reason to do. And so, this chapter explores my ranking of mutual respect over aspirational justice in light of the exacting egalitarian distributive demands of mutual respect.

The relationship among values matters greatly if we want the pluralist anatomy of justice to guide us as we think about *what we should do*. The social configuration that produces the greatest amount of valuable social product will not always be the configuration in which that product is most fairly distributed. As we'll see later in this chapter, the social configuration in which social product is most fairly distributed won't always be the one that best realizes the value of mutual respect among free and equal citizens. Because we face tradeoffs among the various things that matter, a pluralist anatomy of justice must, if it's to be helpful,

68   THE ANATOMY OF JUSTICE

incorporate some principled way to judge the relative importance of the various things that matter.[1]

To be sure, if justice were minimal in its demands, we might plausibly think that all failures to realize those demands are equally dis-valuable. Suppose you think that justice demands only that we protect basic liberties and secure for everyone a very modest social minimum. In that case, you might plausibly think that each type of injustice is categorially as morally bad as each other type. But if justice demands *a lot*, then some types of failure to realize it plausibly will be morally egregious and others merely bad.[2] Suppose that justice also demands the elimination of all (undeserved) disadvantage. In that case, we're going to want a principled explanation for why eradicating childhood poverty matters more, morally, than combatting the underrepresentation of women in leadership positions at Fortune 500 companies. And we're going to want that explanation to help guide us in far less obvious cases. The principal aim of this book is to defend a picture of liberal egalitarianism that is broadly helpful, including in circumstances of injustice. On that picture, justice demands a *lot*; in circumstances of profound injustice, we'll see, its demands are quite radical. Because I think that justice demands a lot, and because I also want it to guide our thinking about what to do, it is crucial for me to have something to say about which of the things that matter *matters most*, and by how much, and why.

One particular approach to answering priority questions generally—the *lexical priority* approach—enjoys outsized attention. In its evaluative formulation, lexical priority tells us that a gain by the lights of the lexically prior value is always a gain on the whole, even if it comes at a cost of any size to any lexically secondary value(s). Evaluative lexical priority seems to offer an appealing sort of political action guidance in the form of tidy, decisive evaluative judgments whenever the lexically weightiest value is at stake.[3] But some of those judgments can seem highly implausible, especially in circumstances of injustice. To illustrate, consider a view that ranks equal opportunity as a lexically weightier value than the prioritarian value of benefitting the least well off among us. This ranking seems implausible, at least in circumstances of injustice: It seems implausible, for example, that breaking top-floor glass ceilings—rectifying unequal opportunities for very advantageous positions between a few high-earning women and men—is a more valuable social improvement than massively benefitting a large number of very disadvantaged citizens. This case illustrates only one conceivable type of

---

[1] On the matter of what practical guidance we should hope for a theory of justice to provide, see Rawls 1999a, 34–6; Cohen 2008, 3–6.

[2] By "morally," I mean only to clarify that the issue at stake concerns the relative importance of *values*. This is how I shall generally use the term "moral" and its cognates, but I'll sometimes use "political" as distinct from "moral" in the sense standardly associated with political liberalism. My meaning in those cases will be clear from context.

[3] Even decisive evaluative judgments on their own won't suffice to settle normative questions about what to do. More is coming on that later in the chapter.

THE DISTRIBUTIVE DEMANDS OF MUTUAL RESPECT   69

lexical priority ranking, a simplified distortion of Rawls's lexical priority of fair equality of opportunity over the difference principle.[4] But it hints at the reason why plenty of people find it "more than a little mad" that any one consideration could have such priority over all others that its presence always makes a state of affairs better on the whole, no matter the loss in terms of other considerations.[5] The priority ranking is so extreme that any formulation of it seems likely to face damning counterexamples. Yet the distributive demands of mutual respect give us reason to rethink this prognosis. This chapter argues that the distributive demands of mutual respect are more robustly egalitarian than has so far been appreciated, and then argues that we need to evaluate the plausibility of a lexical priority weighting of mutual respect over distributive fairness in light of those distributive demands. Even if that lexical priority weighting is not ultimately fully defensible, it doesn't have the implausible implications that seem to embarrass it.

In section 3.1, I argue that the relational egalitarian value of mutual respect among free and equal citizens imposes a defeasible baseline of distributive equality and rules out differential talent as a justification for deviating from that baseline. The case rests on two premises. First, mutual respect among free and equal citizens requires that we treat each citizen's interest in pursuing their own values—their "conception of the good," as I'll say—as equally morally important with each other citizen's like interest.[6] Second, the requirement to treat all citizens' pursuit of their conception of the good as equally morally important in turn imposes distributive egalitarian requirements: It requires that we observe a baseline of equal shares of social product—that is, that we stand inequalities in need of justification. And it requires that we regard unequal talent as ineligible for justifying deviation from that baseline of equal shares.

In section 3.2, I explore the upshots of section 3.1's distributive argument for views according to which justice comprises multiple values including fairness and mutual respect. First, we might think that the robust distributive demands of mutual respect undermine the motivation for pluralism. If mutual respect does indeed impose a defeasible baseline of distributive equality, then it conditionally favors distributive equality as such. And if mutual respect conditionally favors distributive equality as such, it may seem that relational egalitarianism gives us everything we should want—even everything distributive egalitarians should

---

[4] See Rawls 1999a, 77. The illustration distorts Rawls's ranking because it assumes benefiting the very disadvantaged citizens won't also improve equal opportunity (whereas in the relevant circumstances it almost certainly would), because it ignores the Rawlsian basic needs principle, because it applies lexical priority in circumstances of injustice and, arguably, because it formulates lexical priority in evaluative terms. On basic needs, see Rawls 1993, 7, 164. It will matter to my defense that the lexical priority I consider is a ranking among *values*. More on that to come.

[5] Goodin 1995, 47.

[6] More expansively, "conceptions of the good," are conceptions (sometimes partial) "of what is of value in human life, and ideals of personal character, as well as ideals of friendship and of familial and associational relationships, and much else that is thought to inform our conduct, and in the limit to our life as a whole." See Rawls 1993, 13.

70　THE ANATOMY OF JUSTICE

want—from a theory of justice. I'll urge that we resist this take-away. Distributive fairness matters independently of relational equality, and this makes a practical difference because fairness favors distributive equality even when the stringently distributively egalitarian demands of mutual respect run out.

Second, and despite the extensional divergence just noted, I argue that the robust distributive demands of mutual respect weaken the intuitive case against the lexical priority of mutual respect over distributive egalitarian fairness. That case against lexical weighting relies on instances in which great gains by the lights of distributive equality seem more valuable than tiny gains by the lights of mutual respect. Lexical weighting allegedly contradicts this intuitive judgment. But I'll argue that the distributive inequalities that lexical weighting appears implausibly to subordinate are in fact condemned by mutual respect, the priority value. Thus, the implausible subordinations are only *apparent* implications of lexical weighting. Evaluative lexical priority does entail that a tiny gain in terms of mutual respect always has more value than any gain at all in terms of fairness, and fairness does impugn distributive inequalities that mutual respect finds unobjectionable. But the unfairnesses that mutual respect finds unobjectionable are not the ones that fuel the conviction that a lexical priority weighting is implausibly strong.

Remember the context: I want to defend mutual respect as the value at the heart of *politically liberal legitimacy*. Accordingly, when I argue in this chapter that mutual respect's distributive demands are more robust than they are commonly taken to be, that amounts to arguing that *legitimacy* is more distributively egalitarian than it is commonly taken to be. And when I argue that one upshot of this is that a lexical weighting of mutual respect over fairness is more plausible than it's commonly thought to be, that amounts to arguing that *legitimacy* can just as plausibly act as an evaluative trump relative to aspirational justice. In this chapter, this context remains largely in the background. I frame the discussion mostly in terms of what *mutual respect* demands with respect to distribution, rather than in terms of what relationally egalitarian *legitimacy* demands. In Chapter 4, we'll recontextualize and extend the argument, using it to explore the ways in which aspirational values like fairness can "speak up" even when trumped by mutual respect and, thus, by legitimacy. We'll turn, in other words, to the question of what role the truth about justice and about values broadly can play within a politically liberal scheme.

For now, my argument for the distributively egalitarian demands of mutual respect is robust: Neither its soundness nor its importance rely on my way of framing it. It can be translated into other frameworks. For example, we might render it as an argument about the distributional demands of relational egalitarianism construed—as its proponents cast it—as a theory of justice. Relational egalitarians take the demands of relational equality to exhaust the demands of justice. On this framing, then, my argument would conclude that the distributive demands in question are demands of justice at all—that relational egalitarians should by their own lights be distributive egalitarians rather than sufficientarians. For purposes of defending the anatomy and assessing its action guidance, what matters is that the distributive demands of mutual respect are egalitarian enough that distributive egalitarians can countenance the evaluative lexical priority of that value.

Of course, distributive equality is not the only consideration we might worry about in this context. On my picture, mutual respect politically subordinates *all* values; it can exclude some values from eligibility even to supply reasons for political deliberation. The lexical subordination of aspirational justice is the most important challenge for me to address given my argumentative aims in this book. But in this chapter and, mostly, the next, I suggest that the defensive strategy I deploy can extend to other subordinations that some see as problems for political liberalism broadly: subordinations of all ethically contentious values distinct to particular moral outlooks.

3.1 Relational Egalitarianism and Distributive Equality

In the next chapter, I'll offer a principled case for lexical priority of mutual respect over all other political values. *This* chapter defuses the intuition that such a ranking could not plausibly be true because its implications for distributive equality will be so implausible. Can we accept a lexical priority ranking in light of the judgments it renders with respect to relational and distributive equality? At least for purposes of assessing candidate reforms against the backdrop of an unjust society, we might expect to encounter clear cases in which great gains by the lights of fair shares generate more moral value than tiny improvements in compliance with institutional demands of mutual respect. I challenge this expectation, arguing that the value of mutual respect favors a very great deal of what is also called for by fair shares. If I'm right about the distributive demands of mutual respect, then lexical priority simply won't render the sorts of judgments that seem to tell against it. The dire tradeoffs we imagine—just a tiny bit more mutual respect, at the cost of *so much distributive inequality*—simply won't arise, because mutual respect itself condemns *so much distributive inequality* in the cases that prompt incredulity. If that argument is sound, and if the principled case for lexical priority is persuasive, then we have good reason to rethink opposition toward the evaluative lexical priority of mutual respect over fair shares.

Notice that the relational value of mutual respect among free and equal citizens can be construed as an *interpersonal* ideal, of actual citizens relating on terms of respect within their actual social environment; or it can be construed as a *structural* ideal, realized to the degree that institutions are set up in accordance

72 THE ANATOMY OF JUSTICE

with reasons supplied by that ideal. These two fronts of mutual respect are connected, and relational egalitarianism applies the ideal at both levels: The value of mutual respect regulates not only what the state may do—what democratic citizens may do together through the state—but also how citizens comport themselves toward each other directly. My argument focuses on the *institutional demands* imposed by the value of mutual respect among free and equal citizens: the demands that the arrangement of social institutions comply with the reasons supplied by a commitment to realizing that value. In this section, I first review some egalitarian distributive demands of mutual respect that are widely recognized as such. I then argue that mutual respect's egalitarian distributive demands go further still.

The Received Wisdom: An (Egalitarian) Adequacy Threshold

Though relational egalitarianism is not in the first place a view about fair distribution, the ideal of mutual respect among free and equal citizens straightforwardly requires that material resources be distributed in a manner consistent with citizens standing in relations of equality. Here again we can draw on Anderson's work on equal citizenship, and in particular her view about the institutional requirements for enabling citizens to relate as equals. Negatively, Anderson argues, "people are entitled to whatever capabilities are necessary to enable them to avoid or escape entanglement in oppressive social relationships. Positively, they are entitled to the capabilities necessary for functioning as an equal citizen in a democratic state."[7] This includes the ability to exercise political liberties and to participate in civil society and the economy. Effectively, democratic equality demands for each citizen adequate food, shelter, and medical care; the conditions for autonomy; access to education to develop skills and deliberative capacities; occupational choice; and conditions for participating in civil society without shame.[8] For Anderson, then, mutual respect doesn't require capability *equality*, but it does impose a high threshold of distributive *adequacy* and requires that institutions be arranged so that all can meet it.

Though Rawls does not measure shares of distributable goods in terms of capabilities, the relational egalitarian commitments of his theory impose similar requirements. Distributionally, a political conception of justice must ensure that each citizen have "adequate all-purpose means to make effective use" of her rights, liberties, and opportunities, and to stand as an equal citizen.[9] Equal standing in turn requires access to the food, shelter, education, medical care, economic

---

[7] Anderson 1999, 316. Anderson attributes this idea of measuring justice in terms of capabilities to Amartya Sen. See Sen 1995. See also Nussbaum 2000.

[8] Anderson 1999, 318.   [9] Rawls 1993, xlvi, 6.

THE DISTRIBUTIVE DEMANDS OF MUTUAL RESPECT 73

opportunities, and other material goods necessary for full participation in civil society.[10]

In both cases, the adequacy threshold is partially dependent on strictly egalitarian considerations. To see how, consider G. A. Cohen's case of the market maximizers, to which we'll later have occasion to return.[11] Market maximizers are people with talents—stipulated to mean abilities prized on the market[12]—who command high earnings for exercising their talents. Cohen uses the market maximizers to support his rejection of the Rawlsian basic structure restriction, which is the view according to which justice (directly) judges only the institutional structure of society.[13] Because the market maximizers leverage their talents for higher salaries, their labor market participation makes society less egalitarian. For distributive egalitarians like Cohen, a less egalitarian distribution should mean a less *just* distribution. Assume, though, that this market maximizing happens within the context of fully just social *institutions*, including just labor markets and a just tax-and-transfer system. In that case, if we accept the Rawlsian basic structure restriction, then the market maximizers' labor market behavior cannot be said to make society less just, even though it makes society less egalitarian. Cohen thinks that distributive egalitarians should regard this as grounds for rejecting the basic structure restriction. More generally, whatever principles of justice we endorse, the basic structure restriction entails that individual behavior within just institutions cannot make society less just, even if that behavior frustrates the very distributive values just institutions are arranged to serve.

Whether Cohen's market maximizers give us reason to reject the basic structure restriction depends, I think, on how much space a just basic structure leaves open for market maximizers to disrupt equality. If market-maximizing behavior interferes with legitimate ends of the liberal state, then the basic structure can include institutions and institutional practices aimed at interrupting it: educational institutions that propagate an egalitarian ethos of justice, for example. If a just institutional structure leaves little room for inequalities due to market maximizing, it won't be so implausible that two societies with fully just institutions are

---

[10] Samuel Freeman writes that for a liberal political conception to satisfy the all-purpose means requirement, that conception must provide for: "(i) public financing of political campaigns and ways of asuring the availability of information on matters of public policy...(ii) fair equality of opportunity especially in education and training; (iii) a decent distribution of income and wealth; (iv) society as an employer of last resort, needed in order to provide security and meaningful work, so that citizens can maintain their self-respect; and (v) basic health care assured to all citizens." See Freeman 2007, 402. In making this case, Freeman cites Rawls 1993, lviii–lix.

[11] See Cohen 2008, 138.

[12] For Cohen and for me, "talented" just means that these individuals "are so positioned that [they]...command a high salary and...can vary their productivity according to exactly how high [that salary] is." Cohen 1997, 6–7. What counts as a talent on this definition of course varies with contextual features of the society in question.

[13] See Rawls 1999a, 6.

74 THE ANATOMY OF JUSTICE

both fully just, even if marginal incentive inequalities make one marginally less equal.[14]

For now, what bears emphasis is a point about the value considerations that rightly determine the shape of the basic structure: The extent to which the basic structure should include institutional arrangements to disrupt market maximizing may partly depend on distributive egalitarian fairness. But *some degree of equality is also favored by the relational value of mutual respect among free and equal citizens.* That's because the behavior of those far above the adequacy threshold can affect the standing of those right on its cusp. Indeed, the behavior of those far above can determine whether those on the cusp reach that threshold or fall short of it. To illustrate, consider one part of the adequacy threshold: Equal citizenship requires ensuring that each citizen has adequate all-purpose resources to enjoy the full value of her basic liberties. With respect to the political liberties, full value means *fair* value, meaning that what counts as an adequate share of resources depends in part on how well resourced *others* are. This is because the "limited space of the public political process" makes the material preconditions for exercising the political liberties *positionally* valuable:[15] My share becomes less valuable as a means of leveraging political influence insofar as others' shares grow relatively greater than mine, even if the absolute amount of my share hasn't changed. The adequacy threshold is defined by the capacity of citizens to stand as equals, and although we (apparently) can stand as equal citizens even if we are unequally materially well off, we can't stand as equals if we are *very* unequally materially well off.[16] So, citizens can fall below the threshold for equal standing, though the absolute quantity of their share stays the same, if those above it move *far* above it. The adequacy threshold for legitimacy is thus somewhat distributively egalitarian in effect, and it equips us to impugn institutional tolerance of market maximizing on egalitarian grounds.

Whether this should assuage worries about the basic structure restriction is a question I set aside. The point is to remind us that mutual respect is fairly robustly distributively egalitarian, even on the conventional reading: On the basis of that value, relational egalitarianism imposes an adequacy threshold, and that threshold is responsive to strictly egalitarian considerations.

More Egalitarian Still: A Baseline of Equality

Mutual respect imposes robust distributive demands, and even on the conventional view, some of those demands are effectively egalitarian. But on the

---

[14] See Cohen 2001; Ronzoni 2008; Schouten 2013. I take up the basic structure restriction directly in Chapter 6.

[15] Rawls 1993, 328.   [16] See Scanlon 2003b.

THE DISTRIBUTIVE DEMANDS OF MUTUAL RESPECT   75

conventional view, the egalitarian demands are derivative, and many inequalities are wholly unobjectionable. I now want to argue that the ideal of mutual respect at the heart of relational egalitarianism *also* provides a basis on which to object to distributive inequalities *as such*, and not only when they erode interpersonal realization of mutual respect. But first, an apparent conceptual oddity must be addressed: How can the interpersonal value of mutual respect issue institutional reasons that go beyond reasons to secure the institutional prerequesites for citizens to realize that interpersonal value?

It is no surprise that the interpersonal value of mutual respect furnishes reasons that apply to the institutional arrangement of society. The apparent oddity is in thinking that those institutional reasons *include but are not exhausted by* reasons to arrange institutions to make interpersonal mutual respect possible. This substantive claim requires argument, but the apparent *conceptual* oddity is *merely* apparent. Consider another interpersonal value that plausibly supplies institutional reasons: solidarity. If solidarity is a political value, it may coherently ask more of our institutional arrangement than to secure the minimal conditions for making solidaristic fellow-feeling possible. We might coherently say, "solidarity favors this institutional arrangement over that, even though both are consistent with solidaristic fellow-feeling." The preferable arrangement may make fellow-feeling *likelier*, or it may be more befitting of a solidaristic society in some other way. In the case at hand, I want to argue that the value of mutual respect favors an institutional arrangement that: 1) imposes a baseline of distributive equality against which deviations must be justified, and 2) precludes talent as a justification for inequality.[17] I can coherently say, "mutual respect favors such an arrangement even if such an arrangement is not strictly speaking necessary for securing relations of mutual respect among citizens." The question is whether a case can be made that this is *true* in addition to *coherent*.

The argument that it's true goes like this: First, the value of mutual respect among free and equal citizens favors treating each citizen's interest in pursuing her conception of the good as equally morally important to each *other* citizen's interest in pursuing *their* conception of the good. Second, treating each citizen's interest in pursuing her conception of the good as equally morally important to each other citizen's like interest means that inequalities in the shares of (relevant) social product with which citizens can pursue their conceptions of the good stand in need of justification, and it means that unequal talent cannot furnish the needed justification.

---

[17] For a related, respect-based argument to the conclusion that relational egalitarians should endorse a defeasible presumption of equal distributions of social goods, see Schemmel 2011, 2021, chap. 8. On the distributive demands of relational egalitarianism, see also Gheaus 2018; Moles and Parr 2019.

76   THE ANATOMY OF JUSTICE

Let's start with the first premise: the inference from mutual respect to the equal moral importance of each citizen's interest in pursuing her conception of the good. Notice first that the *interest itself*—the interest in pursuing our own conceptions of the good—is paradigmatic among the interests of free and equal citizenship. Indeed, that interest is the feature of citizens (partly) in virtue of which we are to regard ourselves as equals. And the *equal moral importance* of each citizen's interest in pursuing her conception of the good is bound up in the foundational commitment to securing mutual civic respect among citizens construed as such: The *equal* in "free and equal citizens" either denotes or entails the very commitment I'm here trying to infer.

We can see this, for example, in the relational egalitarian commitment to preserving justificatory community: Citizens will come to divergent but reasonable convictions about the good life, and we must find some way to arrange social institutions to deal fairly with this disagreement. Insofar as our social arrangement makes it costlier for citizens to pursue substantively illiberal values than substantively liberal values, for example, we owe those who favor the former a justification for that unequal burdening that they can accept despite their allegiance to the burdened values. All reasonable citizens—roughly, all those who respect the basic political equality of other citizens—are owed inclusion in the justificatory community, and that is due to the equal importance of their interest in pursuing their own conception of the good: Because our interest in pursuing our own values matters equally—because we are free *and equal* citizens—we owe each other justification for features of our social arrangement that impose asymmetrical burdens in terms of our abilities to live out our values. In some version or other, this requirement of justificatory community is widely accepted as an implication of mutual respect. I'm suggesting that that implication is mediated by a more foundational implication or component of mutual respect among free and equal citizens: a commitment to the equal moral importance of each citizen's interest in pursuing her conception of the good. *Because* citizens' interests in pursuing their conceptions of the good matter equally, mutual respect among citizens means that we cannot justify some social arrangement by invoking reasons peculiar to your conception of the good or peculiar to mine. It must be justifiable on the basis of reasons that we can *all* recognize as such, even if they asymmetrically burden some of us in terms of our ability to live our values. Mutual respect demands that we treat each citizen's interest in pursuing her values as equally important, and through that demand, it calls, too, for justificatory community.

The relational egalitarian case for preserving justificatory community illustrates something important about the commitment to treating citizens' interest in pursuing their values as equally morally important: That commitment is either part of what we mean when we say that citizens are free and equal, or it is closely entailed by what we mean when we say that. Turn now to the second premise of my argument: the inference from the equal moral importance of citizens' interests in pursuing their values to the distributive egalitarian implications. Here I draw on an argument due to Seana Shiffrin, in which she considers what justice has to say about the market maximizers introduced earlier.[18] Though our interest concerns only one small move that Shiffrin makes, it's worth briefly rehearsing the larger argument for context. Shiffrin argues that, once *institutional* justice is realized and society is otherwise well ordered, we can level a justice-related complaint against the market maximizers *whether or not* we agree with Cohen that principles of justice apply to individual behavior. That's because even if the primary subject of justice is institutions, as Rawls holds, the *justifications* for the principles that apply to institutions have implications for what is required of individuals in a well-ordered society. By the Rawlsian definition of "well ordered," in a just and well-ordered society, citizens accept the principles of justice *and their major justifications.*[19] That includes accepting the "major justification" for the difference principle: that although my talents are relevant to the matter of what job I should do, *they are arbitrary*, from a moral point of view, with respect to my share of the distribution of income and wealth; and that distributions of income and wealth should not reflect what is arbitrary from a moral point of view with respect to those distributions.[20]

Shiffrin's interest in these claims concerns citizens' acceptance of them in a well-ordered society: Citizens' acceptance of these two claims as justification for the difference principle restricts the motivations on which those citizens may act. If I accept that talent is morally arbitrary with respect to the distribution of income and wealth, then I shouldn't try to leverage my talent for higher income. To do so would be a kind of failure of integrity: It would be "to affirm one conception of equality but through our actions to subvert that conception."[21] In a society in which citizens accept this justification for the difference principle—in a Rawlsian well-ordered society—we can criticize market maximizers on just these grounds. So, while Cohen and other parties to the debate about what justice judges write as though judgments about incentive inequalities and market maximizing depend on answers to the big question of whether justice applies only to the basic structure of society, Shiffrin's main point is that we can criticize market-maximizing behavior directly, even without rejecting the basic structure restriction.

This book is not especially concerned with what is true about the well-ordered society, nor is this chapter especially concerned with the integrity of market

---

[18] Shiffrin 2010.

[19] This is by virtue of the publicity condition for well-orderedness. See Rawls 1993, 63–4.

[20] Shiffrin 2010, 121–4. As Shiffrin notes, Rawls offers other distinct justifications for the difference principle. See Daniels 2003.

[21] Shiffrin 2010, 131. The argument assumes that special labor burdens are adequately accounted for in the metric of justice so that salary differentials are not justified on grounds that certain kinds of work are especially onerous.

78   THE ANATOMY OF JUSTICE

maximizers. Instead, I want us to zoom in on an early move in Shiffrin's argument: I want us to look at what grounds the arbitrariness claim, which in turn, on Rawls's view, justifies the difference principle. The arbitrariness claim was the claim that talents are arbitrary, from a moral point of view, with respect to income and wealth. Talents are arbitrary in this sense, Shiffrin argues, because income and wealth afford access to resources and opportunities that enable each of us to pursue our conception of the good, and *because each of us, regardless of talent, has an equally morally important interest in developing and pursuing our conception of the good.* Our talents (unlike our race or sex) are relevant to what occupation we should perform, and thus to how we should *contribute to* the social product. But talent is *not* relevant to our *claim on* the social product. That claim is based on a feature of us that we are all taken to share in common—indeed, the feature (partly) in virtue of which we are to regard ourselves as equals: our interest in developing and pursuing a conception of the good. The moral importance of this interest does not vary according to our level of marketable talent, so the presumptive claim to social product that this interest generates does not vary with our level of marketable talent, either. Here we see Shiffrin defending precisely the second inference on which my argument for the distributive demands of mutual respect relies. She sums up her case like this:

> Our equal interest in pursuing a conception of the good motivates the initial presumption of an equal distribution of income and wealth and explains why talent is arbitrary with respect to income and wealth. Because possession of a talent is arbitrary, it cannot serve as a reason for an unequal distribution.[22]

This small move within Shiffrin's argument is sound. In a liberal democratic society, our interest in pursuing our own values is morally important. In a liberal *egalitarian* society, we commit to treating that interest as *equally* morally important. The equal moral importance of our interest in pursuing our values doesn't mean we always must devote equal resources to each citizen, and it doesn't mean citizens' values are equally good. But the equal moral importance of our interest in pursuing our values *does* mean we hold unequal investment *in need of justification.* And it means that talent—the good fortune to live in a social arrangement that is well matched to our particular social endowments—cannot serve as the needed justification. The moral importance of citizens' interest in pursuing a conception of the good does not vary according to their level of marketable talent. Since that interest is what underpins our base claim to social product, that base claim also does not vary with our level of marketable talent, either.

In sum: Mutual respect among free and equal citizens favors treating citizens' interests in pursuing their values as equally morally important. In turn, the equal

---

[22] Shiffrin 2010, 125. See also J. Cohen 1989.

moral importance of each citizen's interest in pursuing her conception of the good favors social arrangements that observe a presumption of equality and treat talent as unfit to overturn that presumption. In conclusion, we have reasons *of mutual respect* to establish and preserve such social arrangements.

Can we resist this conclusion by maintaining that the argument equivocates across two different notions of mutual respect? No. It may be that *some* notion of mutual respect is relevant to matters of fair shares and is distinct from the value of mutual respect I have located at the heart of legitimacy. But the value of mutual respect that I claim underpins a crucial premise in the argument for the arbitrariness claim is recognizably the very value of mutual respect that I claim lies at the heart of legitimacy. On my argument, the complex value of mutual respect among free and equal citizens that grounds justificatory reciprocity *also* grounds the equal moral importance of each citizen's interest in developing and pursuing her conception of the good.[23] If that equal moral importance in turn justifies a presumption of equality and designates talents as unfit to overturn that presumption, then those verdicts have the import that follows from being verdicts of *that* value commitment, whatever distinct commitments may go by the same name.

Shiffrin denies that her grounding for the presumption of equality is relational.[24] In extending her argument to the context of relationally egalitarian legitimacy, I might appear to ignore this denial. But Shiffrin is clarifying that her grounding for the presumption of equality is not based on the *instrumentality* of equal distributions to securing interpersonal relations of equality among actual citizens. My use of her argument is in perfect agreement on this point. I just want to insist that the commitment which *does* do the grounding—our equal interest in pursuing our conception of the good—is in one sense relational: The equal importance of each citizen's pursuit of her own values is supportable by or comprised of the relational ideal of mutual respect among free and equal citizens. After all, the "equal" in "free and equal citizen" doesn't refer to distributive equality but to relational equality: to equal standing *vis-à-vis* other citizens. With Shiffrin, we do not impose a baseline of equality because doing so is instrumental to securing a certain character for citizens' interpersonal relations; we do it because a baseline of equality is favored by an interest that fundamental relational values demand we treat as equally morally important. Remember, mine is an argument from the *structural* face of relational equality: an argument about the demand to arrange

---

[23] Mutual civic respect is a demanding ideal, and some liberal theorists favor less demanding civic relational ideals. See, for example, Galston 1995. The argument just rendered does not address those who deny that mutual civic respect is an important value. It only identifies implications of that value for the many liberals who affirm it.

[24] She says that Rawls's relational arguments for distributive equality "turn upon the ways that *significant* inequalities and class differentials may create social divisions that interfere with well-functioning communities and politics and that provide grounds for inescapable envy. The relational arguments do not provide the basis to object to less significant resource inequalities." Shiffrin 2010, 125; italics hers. Here she cites Rawls 1999a, secs. 80, 81.

80   THE ANATOMY OF JUSTICE

social institutions in accordance with the reasons supplied by the value of mutual respect among free and equal citizens.

Our equally morally important interest in pursuing a conception of the good justifies a baseline of equality and rules out unequal talent as a justification for departing from it. The equal moral importance of this interest is underpinned by the value of mutual respect. That means that the distributive implications of the equal interest are called for not only as demands of some construal of distributive fairness, but also on the basis of relational egalitarian mutual respect. The value at the heart of relational egalitarianism is conventionally understood to favor arrangements of political institutions that ensure everyone has enough to stand as an equal. That adequacy threshold has egalitarian implications of its own. But the value at the heart of relational egalitarianism supplies reasons to go beyond enabling interpersonal mutual respect. These are reasons to arrange institutions in ways that cohere with the conviction that we *are* free and equal citizens who *should* cooperate as such on terms of mutual respect. The argument of this section concludes that this conviction favors a baseline of distributive equality from which unequal talent does not license departure. Meeting an adequacy threshold is a material prerequisite for mutual respect, and securing its material prerequisites is plausibly mutual respect's first order of business. But that value makes still more robustly distributively egalitarian demands than that.

3.2 Pluralism and Priority

Mutual respect stands inequalities in holdings of social product in need of justification and disqualifies differential talents from providing justification. These robust distributive egalitarian demands of mutual respect might seem to undermine the motivation for values pluralism. Specifically, they might seem to show that a single value—mutual respect—can account on its own for what we thought we needed fairness to explain: the fact that distributive equality matters even when *in*equality doesn't jeopardize interpersonal equal standing among citizens. In this section, I first argue that distributive egalitarian fairness issues its own distinct reasons that diverge extensionally from the distributive demands of mutual respect. I then argue that the extensional overlap between mutual respect and fairness nevertheless does lessen the force of the intuitive case against the lexical weighting of mutual respect over fairness.

Why Distributive Egalitarians Should (Still) Be Pluralists

Mutual respect underpins a case for distributive equality as such: It imposes a baseline of distributive equality and precludes talent from justifying deviations from that baseline. In light of this conclusion, we might think that mutual respect alone supplies everything that seemed to motivate the inclusion in the anatomy of a distinct value of fairness. On the contrary, distributive egalitarians should think the case for distributive equality goes beyond the arbitrariness argument from mutual respect. It's *unfair* for some to have more than others, along some dimension and under some circumstances, independently of our status as free and equal citizens or relations among us construed as such.[25] Despite a significant extensional overlap between the two values, fairness impugns more (and different) inequalities than those impugned by mutual respect.

If the distributively egalitarian demands of mutual respect are so robust, what remains for fairness to do? Notice first that the presumption of distributive equality that mutual respect imposes can permit inequalities that *correlate* with talent; it's just that unequal talent as such can't override that presumption.[26] Mutual respect impugns inequalities that would be justified only if (counterfactually) talent were morally relevant, but it doesn't forbid all inequalities that happen to track talent.[27] Inequalities might track talent without differential talent justifying the institutional arrangement that permits this. Salary incentives might be used to draw those with certain skills into socially valuable work, for example. Whether something goes wrong when the workers in question *demand* salary incentives,[28] mutual respect needn't impugn an institutional arrangement that allows the incentives, if those incentives can be justified on the basis of the value they realize. Or consider the institution of the family. Because raising children involves privileging those children's interests to at least some degree, and because parents are unequally well equipped to confer advantage by privileging their children's interests, the parent-child relationship disrupts efforts to achieve or maintain distributive equality. Because the advantage in question includes both material benefit and investment in talent acquisition, the resulting material inequalities may well track differences in (developed) talent. Here again, mutual respect needn't impugn this, if it can be justified on grounds other than differential talent itself.

---

[25] Plausibly, distributive egalitarians should remain pluralist for another reason as well: to account for values beyond mutual respect *and* fairness. Community or solidarity and efficiency are plausible contenders.

[26] Richard Arneson and Jonathan Quong both argue that Rawlsians can defend the difference principle against certain objections by construing equality as the *prima facie* (rather than *pro tanto*) just distribution. If equality is only *prima facie* the just distribution, then inequalities need carry no residual injustice. Analogously, in my argument, because equality is only *prima facie* favored by mutual respect, inequalities *needn't* offend against that value. See Arneson 2008; Quong 2010.

[27] More precisely, it impugns any *institutional arrangement* that avoidably allows inequalities that would be justified only on that counterfactual condition. The institutional qualifications are left out of the main text for readability.

[28] Shiffrin's argument concluded that, *in a well-ordered society*, something *does* go wrong in this case.

82 THE ANATOMY OF JUSTICE

What values might justify talent-tracking inequalities that result from parental investment or salary incentives? Efficiency is the most obvious candidate answer. Where occupations are well matched with genuine social needs,[29] social value is more abundant insofar as the skills necessary for those occupations are well matched with the skillsets of the people who fill them. In some cases, the efficiency value to be gained from matching skillsets to occupations might favor salary differentials across roles. In a still smaller subset of such cases, the efficiency case may be seconded *by mutual respect*: In very unfortunate circumstances, salary incentives may be necessary to generate adequate social value to secure all citizens above the adequacy threshold. If so, then mutual respect will favor deviating from its own baseline of equal shares as a necessary measure for realizing distributive adequacy. Mutual respect also favors freedom of association, including citizens' ability to form intimate cooperative domestic partnerships and to raise children. If some talent-tracking inequalities are unavoidable byproducts of freedom of association—for example, because they unavoidably result from a constitutive part of the parent-child relationship—then those inequalities too are favored on grounds of mutual respect.[30]

When mutual respect approves but does not positively call for some inequality, fairness may oppose it and thus make it dis-valuable on the whole. This might occur, for example, where the aspirational value of efficiency favors some inequality that correlates with unequal talent but where that inequality is not necessary to secure anyone above the adequacy threshold. In such cases, mutual respect *tolerates* the inequality so long as aspirational values on balance favor it; efficiency *favors* the inequality; and fairness *impugns* it. In at least some such confrontations with efficiency, fairness will win out. But even when fairness does *not* win out, even when it is trumped by mutual respect or outweighed by efficiency, it matters that it dissents from the judgments of verdictive justice. For a proponent of distributive equality, it is in one way bad—because *unfair*—for some citizens to have more than others only in virtue of their good fortune to have talents that their social arrangement makes good use of. And it is in one way bad—because *unfair*—that parental partiality generates unearned privilege. In both cases, fairness may issue these verdicts even as mutual respect or some other value weighs in to determine that removing the unfairness would be all-things-considered dis-valuable.[31] In the next chapter, we'll see that unfairness can be practically salient even if weightier values preclude rectifying it, as when it

---

[29] This condition significantly constrains the current real-world cases in which this argument applies.

[30] If those inequalities are *not* unavoidable byproducts—if they can be removed without undermining freedom of association, for example through progressive taxation or provision of high-quality in-kind goods—then freedom of association no longer constitutes a positive justification for them. Compare Brighouse and Swift 2009a.

[31] Compare Cohen 2008, 7.

supplies reasons to work over the long run to ease the very tradeoff in question: for example, to establish institutional conditions that discourage market maximizing and parental partiality. For now, we need only note these ways in which distributive egalitarian fairness diverges from mutual respect, even though the latter is itself robustly distributively egalitarian.

Consider another kind of case in which egalitarian fairness can bear on the value of a social arrangement in ways that diverge from egalitarian mutual respect: Fairness can give us reason to deviate from mutual respect's defeasible baseline of equal shares because fairness might operate with a different metric of equality. To grasp this possibility, focus first on the interplay *within* mutual respect between its adequacy threshold and its defeasible baseline of equal shares. Each citizen must meet the threshold for standing as a social equal, and equal standing is understood in terms of what citizens *can do*: whether they can effectively exercise basic political liberties, for example. The defeasible baseline of distributive equality that mutual respect imposes operates over a different metric: shares of distributable social product. Because citizens vary in the amount of distributable social product they need in order to be secure in the capacities that comprise the adequacy threshold, mutual respect favors certain departures from *social product equality* so that everyone achieves *capability adequacy*. For example, citizens with mobility impairments may need certain provisions—wheelchairs, curb cutouts, accessible public spaces—to exercise basic political liberties. Because these provisions require an outlay of social resources for the benefit of the citizens in question, *equal standing* requires *unequal shares* of social product. When this occurs, unequal shares are favored by mutual respect as a justified departure from the defeasible baseline of equal shares imposed by that very value.

This matter of metric conversion points us toward a case in which fairness legitimately supplies reason to depart from mutual respect's defeasible baseline of equal shares: Fairness may employ a different metric of equality. If so, fairness favors departing from mutual respect's baseline of equal shares of social product in order to attain equality along some other dimension. Suppose fairness cares about capabilities all the way up: It favors removal of capability inequality irrespective of the adequacy threshold. In that case, fairness acts directly within the space above mutual respect's adequacy threshold, asking us to deviate from mutual respect's defeasible baseline of equal shares of social product in order to realize capability equality.

Despite its robust distributively egalitarian demands, then, the value of mutual respect does not second *all* considerations of distributive egalitarian fairness. Distributive egalitarian fairness will oppose efficiency- or associational-freedom-based departures from distributive equality, even when mutual respect would approve those departures. Fairness can justify departures from mutual respect's defeasible baseline of equal shares of social product to achieve equality along

84 THE ANATOMY OF JUSTICE

some other dimension. And it can condemn mutual respect's tradeoffs of distributive equality in favor of some other good of free and equal citizenship. Notwithstanding the robust distributive egalitarian demands of mutual respect, distributive egalitarians should (still) be pluralists, insisting that distributive egalitarian fairness is a non-reducible social value.

A (Partial) Defense of Lexical Priority

Among liberals who endorse it, the value of mutual respect is thought to enjoy *some* priority over distributive fairness. It's fairly non-controversial, in broader terms, that *political* equality matters more than *distributive* equality. This is why, for example, most distributive egalitarians would not have us bypass legitimate democratic processes to bring about just any gain at all in terms of fairness. It's also (part of) why section 3.1's conclusion is significant: Distributive inequalities and political inequalities remain two distinct problems of justice, but that argument establishes that many actual cases of distributive inequality are *failures to realize the value that underpins political equality.* Within a widely embraced hierarchy of justice, then, section 3.1's argument gives a vast category of distributive concerns a significant promotion.

Less settled is the question of *how much* priority political equality enjoys over distributive equality. *Lexical* weighting has received a great deal of attention, much of it critical.[32] In evaluative terms, the case against lexical priority draws on the apparent implausible implications of adjudicating any (huge) gain toward distributive egalitarian fairness as always less valuable than any (tiny) gain in terms of mutual respect. This case against lexical priority needs reconsidering, though, in light of the distributive demands of mutual respect.

To begin, recall that the lexical priority in question is *evaluative* lexical priority: a lexical weighting of *values.* An evaluative priority ranking enables pluralism about justice to supply decisive *evaluative* judgments. But such judgments won't suffice to settle normative questions about what we should do in our circumstances to make our societies more just. Although Reform A would realize more political value, perhaps we should nonetheless opt for Reform B, which has a better chance of successful implementation for contingent circumstantial reasons, or which is likely in the long run to bring about still more political value than Reform A would bring about now.[33] When we evaluate the apparent implausibility of lexical priority, then, we have to keep in mind just what values pluralism purports to offer: a set of evaluative judgments that are relatively robust across

---

[32] For general skepticism about evaluative lexical priority, see Goodin 1995. For skepticism about the supremacy of legitimacy over justice in particular, see Stemplowska and Swift 2018.

[33] See the discussion of transitional and comparative justice in Simmons 2010, 22–5.

circumstances, and that can *inform* normative prescriptions in light of contingent circumstances. Evaluative lexical priority does not prescribe the course of action that yields a tiny gain as measured by mutual respect even at a massive cost as measured by fairness, because it does not prescribe any course of action at all. It tells us only that a gain in terms of mutual respect is always a gain on the whole, even if it comes at a huge cost to fairness.

This difference matters, because—as Reforms A and B foreshadow—we may have good reason not to maximize with respect to verdictive justice. We may have good reason, in other words, not to pursue the most valuable social arrangement in our feasibility set: Maybe the most valuable arrangement is less of a sure thing than the next most valuable, and the next most valuable is nearly as valuable as the *very* most valuable. Maybe the most valuable feasible arrangement is likely to generate backlash among those who resist it, and thus risks subsequently restricting the feasibility set in regrettable ways. For the purposes of assessing evaluative lexical priority, then, we need to focus on apparent implausible evaluative implications. Objections based on derived normative prescriptions might rearise at a later stage, when we ask how political values concretely should guide reform in circumstances of injustice. (Should we maximize *expected* verdictive justice? Over what time horizon, with what discount rate?) Once we have an account of *that* on hand, we can ask whether circumstances could ever arise such that we all things considered should subordinate the lexically weightiest value. But it's worth first asking whether evaluative lexical priority is plausible *as* evaluative priority: Is it plausible that greater compliance with reasons of mutual respect always makes for a more valuable social arrangement now, no matter the cost—including the opportunity cost—in terms of fairness? Even for comparisons made against the benchmark of a deeply unjust *status quo ante*?[34]

My defense of evaluative lexical priority is underpinned by a simple point: Because mutual respect is itself so distributively egalitarian, the reasons it supplies overlap quite significantly with the reasons supplied by distributive egalitarian fairness. And because of *that*, lexical priority simply does not render the sorts of judgments that seem to embarrass it. The dire tradeoffs we imagine don't arise, because mutual respect itself condemns distributive inequality in the cases where subordinating distributive equality would be too great a bullet to bite.

Begin with the (true but incomplete) conventional wisdom about the distributive demands of mutual respect: that mutual respect imposes an adequacy threshold for equal standing. No extensional adequacy case against the lexical priority of mutual respect can exploit the urgency of extreme distributive disadvantage because mutual respect's adequacy threshold rightly condemns extreme disadvantage as unjust. So, if a lexically prior mutual respect implausibly licenses

---

[34] For the moment, I take for granted that, if mutual respect is plausibly lexically weightier than fairness, it is also plausibly lexically weightier than other political values like efficiency.

86   THE ANATOMY OF JUSTICE

disadvantage, the disadvantage in question cannot be disadvantage below the adequacy threshold, because below the adequacy threshold mutual respect *condemns* disadvantage. And, if a lexically prior mutual respect implausibly licenses great *inequality*, the inequality in question cannot be inequality arising *across* the adequacy threshold, because across the adequacy threshold mutual respect condemns inequality. Recall, too, that that threshold is quite demanding and has egalitarian content due to the positionality of the goods that underwrite equal standing. To the extent that adequacy is demanding, the conventional wisdom already vastly constrains the range of cases that opponents of lexical priority can invoke to support their opposition.

Now add the conclusion that mutual respect condemns all material disadvantage that would be justified only if (counterfactually) talents were morally relevant to the distribution of income and wealth. What grist remains for the lexical priority opponent's mill? To evaluate the plausibility of lexical priority, we need cases of inequality that are condemned by the candidate lexically subordinate value (distributive egalitarian fairness), but that are *not* condemned by the candidate lexically prior value (mutual respect). Among such cases, some involve mutual respect dispositively favoring that we leave an inequality intact. This occurred above when equality could be achieved only by curtailing associational freedom: Fairness favored curtailing associational freedom to secure distributive equality, but mutual respect's priority ensured that doing so would result in a less valuable social arrangement on the whole. Other divergence cases feature mutual respect *permitting* the rectification of some inequality because fairness favors rectification, though still de-prioritizing that rectification when alternative reform would yield gains by the lights of mutual respect itself. This occurred above in the example of metric conversion: when fairness favored capability equality above the adequacy threshold.[35]

From these types of divergence, opponents of lexical priority can certainly build challenge cases. But for either type of case, the distributive demands of mutual respect will significantly constrain possibilities. Mutual respect itself condemns any inequality that causes relational subordination or leaves someone below the adequacy threshold. It condemns any inequality that cannot be justified, from a baseline of equality, on some permissible grounds other than unequal talent. (For instance, if inequality yields an efficiency gain but only against a background of pre-existing inequality, mutual respect does not approve it.) And, although I am not yet entitled to this premise, I'll argue in due course that mutual respect also condemns any inequality that results from or gives rise to unequal

---

[35] Other divergences between fairness and mutual respect might result from differences in the respective sites or scopes of those values. I set aside these candidate divergences for the moment except to note that their extent will matter for an ultimate assessment of the extensional plausibility of lexical priority.

developmental opportunity—that is, unequal opportunity to develop the capacities that count as talents in our social context. Only with respect to *mere* unfairness—with respect to inequality that meets none of these conditions—does some measure that *is* favored by mutual respect enjoy evaluative lexical priority. If a bullet remains here for defenders of lexical priority to bite, it's vanishingly smaller than critics of lexical priority have thought. This is thanks to the egalitarian distributive demands of the lexical priority value and to its role as a priority *value*. On the priority ranking under consideration, we don't lexically prioritize a set of political prescriptions—for example, to secure the basic liberties—to the exclusion of the other social aims that are favored by the very value that underpins those prescriptions. Rather, we prioritize *all* the social aims—basic liberties *and* distributive aims—that are called for by the value of mutual respect among free and equal citizens. The lexical priority under consideration cuts between values to prize mutual respect holistically.

Let's look closer at the type of divergence between fairness and mutual respect that was illustrated by the issue of metric conversion: Fairness plausibly favors certain departures from mutual respect's baseline of equal shares of social product, because *un*equal shares of social product will be necessary to achieve equality along the metric that fairness employs. Is it plausible that great progress toward equality as measured by the metric of fairness is less valuable than any gain, however miniscule, as measured by mutual respect? Let's assume for illustration that the metric of fairness is capabilities: Fairness favors an equal distribution of capabilities and so favors resource inequality where necessary to realize capability equality.

Now consider Della, a woman with a mobility impairment, who meets the adequacy threshold—she has enough mobility capability to stand as an equal citizen—but whose mobility impairment otherwise leaves her less than equally capable of getting around. There are things we could do about this by way of political institutions: better wheelchair lifts on public transit, for example, or better upkeep of sidewalks. Fairness favors doing just that; thus, if it would come at no cost to mutual respect,[36] doing just that would make our social arrangement better on the whole. But compare Reva, a woman with a mobility impairment who lives in a community whose infrastructure leaves her unable even to meet the adequacy threshold imposed by mutual respect. Lexical priority would tell us that bringing Reva up to the threshold for equal standing *always* generates more value than enriching Della's capability set—no matter how many Dellas we stack against a single Reva, and no matter the relative total magnitudes of capability gain.

---

[36] And setting aside any other political values that bear on this matter.

88   THE ANATOMY OF JUSTICE

In assessing the plausibility of this implication, we must bear several things in mind. First is the lesson of the market maximizers: Della may stand above the adequacy threshold *now*, but that threshold is itself modestly egalitarian. If those who are better off than Della grow *much* better off, the positional value of their gains may press her below the threshold. The adequacy threshold thus continues to limit the extent of inequality that mutual respect tolerates, even once everyone reaches that threshold and the absolute shares of those with least remain constant.

Second is the lesson of the stringently egalitarian distributive demands of mutual respect: Even above that adequacy threshold, mutual respect sets a baseline of equal shares of social product, and it precludes talents from justifying a deviation from that baseline. So, mutual respect impugns any economic system that is predicated on the notion that the price talents can command in a market is morally relevant with respect to the distribution of income and wealth. The lexical priority of mutual respect may indeed hold Della(s) hostage to Reva and in so doing may subordinate a (much) greater net capability gain to a lesser. But it does so only when the unfairness that afflicts Della arises above the robust egalitarian capability threshold, only when the inequality can be justified on grounds of some admissible social value against a baseline of equal shares of social product, and only (yet to be defended) when the inequality does not result from or give rise to unequal developmental opportunities. It's not clear, to me at least, that a lexical subordination under these circumstances will be an *implausible* subordination.

And one lesson remains to bear in mind: Remember that an evaluative lexical priority ranking won't directly supply political prescriptions. The ranking in question *does* entail that bringing one Reva up to the adequacy threshold *has more value* than equalizing capabilities for any number of Dellas above that threshold, relative to the Dellas' status quo baseline (assumed for illustration) of equal shares of social product. But this doesn't entail that we all things considered *should* prioritize Reva lexically. New considerations may enter at the stage of drawing prescriptive inferences, and these considerations can attenuate the distinctly evaluative considerations. Prioritizing Reva will bring about a more verdictively just arrangement *now*, no matter how much more capability equality we could secure above the adequacy threshold by prioritizing Della, but we might rightly accept less verdictive justice now if doing so expands the feasible policy options in ways that will promote the weightiest values over time—for example, by empowering constituencies motivated to serve the interests of citizens with mobility impairments. On its own, evaluative lexical priority neither forbids nor recommends this. It punts on the question of when to defer value now in order to make more value realizable later. This may seem a liability, but other theories on offer similarly punt on the question of when we should accept less justice now for the sake of more justice later. Like those other theories, the anatomy of justice will eventually need to answer this question. In the meantime, the punt hardly leaves it toothless. By equipping us to rank social arrangements according to their realization of weighted political values, we've seen, the anatomy offers valuable political guidance.

Once we appreciate the distributive demands of mutual respect, the lexical priority of mutual respect over distributive egalitarian fairness seems far less extensionally implausible. Even if this defense doesn't fully vindicate lexical priority, it bears on the question of how far from lexical priority we must retreat—if we must retreat at all—to arrive at a viable priority ranking between relationally egalitarian mutual respect and distributively egalitarian fairness.

The discussion so far is limited in two rather important ways. First, I've defended the stringent priority of mutual respect over distributive fairness by showing the high degree of extensional convergence between those two values, but I've focused on the cases wherein mutual respect and distributive fairness agree about the *scope* of distributional considerations. I've not considered cases of inequalities arising among non-contemporaries or among distant strangers among whom only weak political ties exist. Luck egalitarian aspirational justice plausibly condemns many such inequalities; mutual respect may appear indifferent to many of them. In fact, I think mutual respect's indifference to inequalities among distant strangers and some non-contemporaries has been overstated. I suspect we can get a robust adequacy threshold of global distributive justice and robust obligations to future generations from a value of mutual respect that *principally* regulates relationships among political subjects of a common state or set of shared political institutions. But I haven't made that case, and I won't, explicitly, in this book.

Second, while I claim to have rendered less implausible the thought that mutual respect is a trump with respect to aspirational values broadly, I've only made the case with respect to distributive egalitarian aspirational justice. I don't think this omission is hugely significant in the case of the other aspirational values I've identified as bearing on the rankings of verdictive justice. As I made the case for its distributive egalitarian demands, I showed too how mutual respect seconds certain considerations of efficiency, for example when we need to generate enough social product to secure everyone above the adequacy threshold. Mutual respect surely also seconds a range of the reasons sourced by community or solidarity. If so, an extensional convergence argument could be made for the plausibility of a strong priority relation between mutual respect and those values, too. We would need to distinguish the parts of these aspirational values that mutual respect seconds from the parts that it doesn't second and render it palatable that the former are lexically more important than the latter. Though I won't work out the details, I think this can be done. But what of putative values I *haven't* identified as plausibly bearing on the rankings of verdictive justice? What about the values that politically liberal mutual respect apparently rules out as *wholly* unfit for political deliberation? What about, for example, the putative value of

90 THE ANATOMY OF JUSTICE

reverence for life, which some think favors restrictions on abortion or stem cell research? Is it plausible that mutual respect lexically subordinates *those* values?

The next chapter continues its focus on distributive aspirational justice among co-citizens. But it also charts a course for answering these remaining questions about the scope of egalitarian concern and the values that legitimacy renders unfit for political justification.

3.3 Plausible Priority *at the Cost* of Action Guidance?

The evaluative lexical priority of mutual respect over fairness resembles Rawlsian lexical priority, but the divergence should by now seem significant: The lexical priority I'm defending is evaluative,[37] and the priority value is more robustly distributively egalitarian.[38] Still, while the substance of our priority rankings diverges significantly, Rawls's *case for* lexical priority resonates with my own. Rawls argued that protection for the basic liberties "is a condition of the adequate development and full exercise of the two moral powers of citizens as free and equal persons."[39] Because protecting basic liberties is a fundamental interest *of citizenship*, protection for those liberties has priority over other social aims. My argument in this chapter amounts to this: A baseline of distributive equality and the unfitness of talent to justify deviations from it are *also* implications of a fundamental citizenship interest—in this case, the fundamental interest in treating each citizen's own particular interest in pursuing her conception of the good as equally morally important with each other citizen's. Failure to live up to the distributive demands of mutual respect is *of a kind* with failure to institutionalize protections for the basic liberties.

And the ideal of mutual respect among free and equal citizens is distributively egalitarian indeed. This conclusion is significant for anyone who thinks that mutual respect is a consideration of justice. For those who think that mutual respect is an *especially weighty* consideration of justice, the conclusion matters for the evaluative importance of equality. Suppose Shiffrin is right that the arbitrariness argument supports the difference principle.[40] If so, my argument would establish that the difference principle is a demand of relational egalitarianism that

---

[37] Though Rawls doesn't explicitly frame his priority ranking in evaluative terms, he does intend it to tell us "which elements of the ideal are relatively more urgent" and thus which injustices "are most grievous as identified by the extent of the deviation from perfect justice." (The exact measure of departure is left to intuition.) Rawls 1999a, 216.

[38] Though the divergence on this front should not be overstated. As we've seen, Rawlsian basic liberties themselves impose distributively egalitarian demands.

[39] Rawls 1993, 297.

[40] I've argued that mutual respect underpins the case for the presumption of equality and the inability of talent to overcome that presumption, but I have not committed to the Rawlsian take on what normative distributive principle those conclusions support.

relational egalitarians ought to endorse as an implication of their theory. Meanwhile, Rawlsians must rethink the categorical lexical priority of protections for basic liberties over distributive fairness, because the very value that explains the moral importance of the basic liberties also underpins the case for the difference principle. And, in Rawls's estimation, "part of the value of the notion of choosing principles is that the reasons which underlie their adoption in the first place may also support giving them certain weights," that "we may find in the grounds for their acceptance some guidance or limitation as to how they are to be balanced."[41] In the next chapter, I will contextualize these conclusions as conclusions about the distributive demands of *legitimacy*. But those who reject the anatomy of justice are not thereby relieved of grappling with the distributive demands of mutual respect. That conclusion is robust.

How does that conclusion square with the thought—which partially motivated the weighting question in the first place—that a theory of justice should provide guidance for political reform in cases of values tradeoffs? The robust distributive demands of mutual respect show lexical priority to be more plausible than we might have given it credit for, but at the cost of sacrificing some of the tidiness that we might have hoped for it to provide. Lexical priority enables decisive judgments *between* values, but the demandingness and multi-faceted-ness of mutual respect means that new priority questions will arise *internal to* that value.

A discouraging upshot wouldn't make the argument unsound, of course. Mutual respect *is* distributively demanding. That *does* make it easier to entertain the possibility of lexical priority. But we still might ask: Is this welcome news? Because mutual respect is demanding and multi-faceted, the rankings of verdictive justice will depend heavily on the relative weight of distinct reasons sourced by that value. Should those of us who hope for justice to be practically useful take heart? I think so. Tradeoffs internal to mutual respect are tractable in principle. We can discern which protections and which reforms are more and less strongly favored by that value—and which injustices are more or less strongly condemned—by asking which interests of free and equal citizenship mutual respect prioritizes. Plausibly, for example, mutual respect's weightiest *distributive* concern is to secure the material preconditions for citizens *actually to relate to each other* on terms of mutual respect. That is, its weightiest distributive concern is to realize the adequacy threshold. Equalizing shares of social product above that threshold is favored by the value of mutual respect as well, but it is plausibly less

---

[41] Rawls 1999a, 37. Or compare the distinction between social justice and basic political justice in Pettit 2015. Much of my argument here parallels Pettit's in that paper, and my distinction between reasons sourced by aspirational social values and those sourced by the foundational value of mutual respect resembles his between social and basic political justice. Translated into that framework, my argument can be understood as follows: Mutual respect is a demand of basic political equality, which underpins basic political justice; and the material demands of basic political justice are still more distributively egalitarian than Pettit acknowledges. See especially Pettit 2015, 32.

92   THE ANATOMY OF JUSTICE

important than securing the preconditions for interpersonal mutual respect. In Chapter 5, I consider another weighting question internal to mutual respect, showing how we can adjudicate it by discerning the relative priority of interests of free and equal citizenship.

Applied to actual social arrangements and social reforms, judgments of mutual respect will often be messy and may depend on circumstances in complicated ways. We shouldn't hope to eliminate the role of intuition in particular cases. But weighting questions internal to the value of mutual respect admit of principled adjudication, and that accounts for part of the appeal of a value-monistic theory of justice based in mutual respect. A pluralism about justice that casts mutual respect as the lexically weightiest value realizes a great deal of that appeal, without relinquishing the conviction that other things matter in their own right: most notably, distributive equality.

Meanwhile, appreciating the demanding distributive implications of mutual respect dissolves a seeming inconsistency among some common theoretical and practical convictions: Failing to establish the institutional conditions favored by mutual respect among free and equal citizens is categorically worse than failing to realize fair shares of social product. But this doesn't entail, implausibly, that we must defer concern about distributive inequality as such until after the basic liberties are optimally institutionally protected. Nor need we stretch to make the case against inequality *on the back* of the basic liberties. Across a broad range of circumstances of injustice, aggressive efforts to mitigate inequality are called for on the basis of the fundamental democratic commitment to cooperating on terms of mutual respect despite all that divides us.

Insofar as we want our theory to provide guidance for political practice in circumstances of injustice, we should regard this chapter's conclusions as encouraging ones. Still more clearly, insofar as we want theory to guide practice, we should want to know how morally weighty the values in play actually are. Recognizing a presumption of distributive equality as a demand of mutual respect is practically important in assessing the political *dis*-value of inequality.

The Anatomy of Justice: On the Shape, Substance, and Power of Liberal Egalitarianism. Gina Schouten, Oxford University Press. © Gina Schouten 2024. DOI: 10.1093/9780191999772.003.0004

4
Relational Equality as Legitimacy

My conceptual schema of justice features both an *aspirational* and a *verdictive* concept of justice. Verdictive justice gives an ordering of social arrangements by value once all sources of political value are considered. Aspirational justice is one source of value. Substantively, on the anatomy of justice, luck egalitarian distributive equality is aspirational justice. Relational egalitarian values also feature in the substantive anatomy. But whereas some relational values, like community and solidarity, stand alongside distributive fairness as aspirational values, one relational value, mutual respect among free and equal citizens, occupies an importantly different place in the anatomy: Mutual respect comprises my account of liberal legitimacy, and as such, it's evaluatively lexically prior with respect to aspirational social values.

In Chapter 3, I argued that this priority ranking withstands some apparent objections based on extensional adequacy. It withstands those objections, I argued, because on the anatomy of justice, the priority value affirms a great deal of what aspirational social values favor. But I have not yet adequately motivated that priority ranking on principle; nor have I adequately motivated the casting of mutual respect in the role of legitimacy; nor have I responded to all worries about the anatomy from the perspective of distributive egalitarianism. This chapter undertakes these tasks by exploring the ways in which the casting of mutual respect as the ideal at the heart of legitimacy makes the anatomy a version of political liberalism. I contextualize mutual respect as politically liberal legitimacy, draw from political liberalism the grounds and context for a ranking of mutual respect as the lexically weightiest political value, and make further strides toward defending the anatomy by addressing a worry about the role of aspirational values in political liberalism.

Section 4.1 does the contextualizing. Rawls writes in *Political Liberalism* that protection for the basic liberties in their central range of application "is a condition of the adequate development and full exercise of the two moral powers of citizens as free and equal persons."[1] Because the basic liberties are a fundamental interest of citizenship, protection for those liberties has priority over other social aims. It acts as a constraint on any reasonable liberal political conception of justice: To be reasonable, a political conception of justice must specify and protect

---

[1] Rawls 1993, 297.

94 THE ANATOMY OF JUSTICE

"certain basic rights, liberties and opportunities"; assign a "special priority to those rights, liberties, and opportunities, especially with respect to claims of the general good"; and ensure for all citizens "adequate all-purpose means to make effective use of their liberties and opportunities."[2] The priority of basic liberties is not new in *Political Liberalism*; it is present already in Rawls's earlier work. But in political liberalism we can find the value of mutual respect—a respect based on our shared interests as free and equal citizens—as *the grounds for* the priority of the basic liberties; and from political liberalism we can draw a set of conceptual resources—like the idea of a reasonable conception of justice—for situating the evaluative significance of protections called for by mutual respect. In the face of inevitable reasonable disagreement over matters of political value, political liberalism hopes to maintain mutual respect among free and equal citizens by ensuring that the terms of social cooperation are *mutually justifiable* and by protecting certain key interests that we are understood to share by virtue of that very aspiration of preserving mutual respect. Mutual justifiability requires that we exercise our shared democratic power—in authorizing social arrangements and political action within those arrangements—only in ways that can be justified using values that all relevant parties can recognize as reasons-giving, whatever else sets them at odds.[3] Among the reasons that are shared in this sense are our reasons to ensure protection for basic liberties: Doing so is favored by the demand to arrange our cooperation on terms of mutual respect among equals. Because they are called for by the fundamental value motivating justificatory reciprocity in the first place, protections for basic liberties are not only permissible; they are a *condition for reasonableness*: No conception of justice can be *reasonable* if it fails to call for those protections. And, I'll add, no social arrangement can be fully *legitimate* if it fails to secure them.

To situate my argument within this framework is to argue that more things than Rawls acknowledged are constraints on reasonable conceptions of justice: Such a conception must not *only* protect basic liberties, afford them some priority, and secure all-purpose means for making use of them. To be reasonable, a conception of justice must also recognize a baseline of equal shares and deem talent unfit to justify deviations from that baseline.[4] And a society that fails to secure the distributive demands of mutual respect is to that degree not only less (verdictively) just, but less (verdictively) just *because less legitimate*. This is so, I'll argue, because the distributive demands of mutual respect are relevantly like the

---

[2] Rawls 1993, 6; see also xlvi, 137.   [3] See Rawls 1993, for example xliv.

[4] That's not to say that any citizen who fails to recognize all demands of mutual respect is an *unreasonable citizen*. Mutual respect is complex and multi-faceted, and discerning its demands is difficult. What matters for membership in the justificatory community is acceptance of the fact of reasonable pluralism and, correspondingly, *willingness to* cooperate on terms that are publicly justifiable. We can be *willing* to engage on terms of shared reasons without always getting it right about what those shared reasons are.

more widely accepted substantive constraints on a reasonable conception of justice. And, in circumstances of injustice, ameliorating problems of legitimacy always yields more value on the whole—more verdictive justice—than ameliorating shortcomings by the lights only of aspirational values.

This brings us to the final piece of unfinished work enumerated above. Chapter 2 defended a distributive egalitarian account of fair shares by emphasizing its position as a lexically subordinate value, outweighed by any concerns of the lexically prior value of mutual respect. Chapter 3 defended the lexical priority of relational egalitarian mutual respect over distributive egalitarian fair shares largely by arguing that mutual respect is *itself* substantively very distributively egalitarian. This can all make the distributive egalitarian suspect that *her* egalitarianism does no real work within the anatomy. This suspicion will only be heightened in section 4.1 of this chapter, where I cast the anatomy as a political liberalism. In light of the subordinate status of distributive equality, sections 4.2 and 4.3 take up the job of arguing to distributive egalitarians that the anatomy of justice redeems the surpassing political importance of mutual respect without unduly eclipsing the distributive egalitarian commitment to mitigating unearned disadvantage as a source of reasons of justice in its own right. I show how distributive equality can "speak up" even from within its lexically subordinated role—how the anatomy enables considerations of fairness to remain practically relevant even when legitimacy condemns acting on them. Finally, section 4.4 answers objections and (re)considers the relationship between legitimacy and authority.

4.1 Mutual Respect and Legitimacy in Political Liberalism

In a liberal society, reasonable citizens will inevitably be in deep disagreement about matters of value. In a liberal *democratic* society, this disagreement matters morally. Preserving space for citizens to make important decisions *themselves* about how to live, and *collectively* about how to live together, can make a social arrangement more valuable in ways that don't rely on the value of what they choose.

John Rawls's focus in *Political Liberalism* is on questions of liberal democratic legitimacy. He defends principles we must abide by as we seek political solutions to our shared social problems, given that we will disagree, reasonably, both about what constitutes a problem and about what costs we should be willing to incur to fix it. As I'll understand it, legitimacy encompasses two importantly different types of demands: *Procedural* demands are determined by citizens' will expressed through democratic decision-making. *Substantive* demands impose the constraints within which procedural demands actually work to confer legitimacy. The substantive demands of legitimacy delineate the space of *reasonable* political conceptions of justice compliance with which is a requirement of legitimacy. On

96 THE ANATOMY OF JUSTICE

my reading, these constraints on the reasonable comprise the relational egalitarian strand of Rawlsian political liberalism: The substantive demands of legitimacy are the institutional requirements entailed by the ideal of social cooperation on terms of mutual respect among free and equal citizens.[5] Legitimacy's substantive demands in turn constrain its procedural demands, because democratic verdicts that frustrate mutual respect frustrate the very ideal in virtue of which those processes are *presumptively* legitimacy conferring.[6]

We can get to this conclusion from another direction by considering political liberalism's motivating question: How can we achieve mutual civic respect when any social arrangement and any exercise of democratic power within it inevitably will be opposed by some citizens and inevitably will burden some citizens' reasonable values? On my reading, political liberalism's answer is that we can maintain mutual respect among free and equal citizens by ensuring that the terms of social cooperation be *mutually justifiable*: by making sure that we exercise our shared democratic power only in ways that can be justified to all parties as free and equal citizens, using reasons that all parties as free and equal citizens can recognize as such, whatever else sets them at odds.[7] Among the reasons we can all recognize as such are those we can infer from the very aspiration to arrange our social cooperation on terms of mutual respect befitting free and equal citizens.[8]

---

[5] The view I'm spelling out diverges from what Kolodny refers to as "a common view, perhaps the dominant view, in political philosophy": that "even the fact that the decision is substantively ideal is not enough to make it legitimate" (Kolodny 2014, 316). That's because on my view, one substantive ideal *does* suffice for legitimacy: namely, the ideal of mutual respect among free and equal citizens. Although on my view substantive ideality by the lights of mutual respect suffices to make a political action *legitimate*, it may nonetheless be true that that action would be better *in some other way* were it also approved by democratic processes. Conversely, when substantive constraints of legitimacy impugn the verdict of an otherwise legitimate democratic process, that process may make the verdict *authoritative*, or otherwise better, even as it remains illegitimate on grounds of substantive illegitimacy.

[6] By Rawls's lights, too, the legitimacy-conferring power of democratic procedures is subject to substantive constraints. For him, though, legitimacy is a "purely procedural" concept, and the substantive constraints on it comprise certain substantive demands of *justice*: For a procedure to confer legitimacy, "It is of great importance that the constitution specifying the procedure be sufficiently just...But it may not be just and still be legitimate, provided it is sufficiently just in view of the circumstances and social conditions" (Rawls 1993, 428). Later he clarifies: "Neither the procedures nor the laws need to be just by a strict standard of justice, even if, what is also true, they cannot be too gravely unjust. At some point, the injustice of the outcomes of a legitimate democratic procedure corrupts its legitimacy, and so will the injustice of the political constitution itself" (428). On my view, the substantive constraints on the legitimacy-conferring power of democratic procedures are themselves constraints *of legitimacy*. This section makes the case for such a two-part construal of legitimacy.

[7] In defense of a mutual-respect-based take on political liberalism, see Larmore 1999; Nussbaum 2011; Schouten 2019. Apart from realizing the value of mutual civic respect, the strictures of political liberalism are instrumental for achieving stability, and it's this achievement that is standardly taken to motivate the project and, relatedly, the case for justificatory reciprocity. In a society that abides by a principle of reciprocity—in which citizens hold themselves to burden one another only in ways that are mutually justifiable—ideologically divided citizens can reasonably assent to their political arrangement even when they are personally burdened by it. See Rawls 1993, xli–xlii. On the question of what motivates justificatory community or reciprocity, see also Leland 2019.

[8] See Rawls 1993, for example xliv.

These reasons favor shared self-governance, but *within the confines of our most foundational shared interests* as free and equal citizens. In this way, legitimacy's substantive and procedural demands are unified, both underpinned by the ideal of mutual respect.

Just as legitimacy comprises both substantive and procedural demands, an important distinction separates two types of the shared reasons that inform those demands. First, we have shared reasons drawn from the particular reasonable conception of justice that orders—or, in circumstances of injustice, that is *meant to order*—our society: This is the conception supported by an overlapping consensus of reasonable citizens, based on the shared moral and political convictions implicit in our public political culture. These reasons can legitimately be invoked to justify political action. But they are *contingent* in that they *could reasonably* have been different than they are. In justice as fairness, our shared reasons to comply with the difference principle rather than fair shares differently construed are thought to exemplify this type.[9] Similarly with other accounts of fair shares: Any such account generates shared reasons only if it enjoys an overlapping consensus. I've argued that the right account of fair shares is stringently distributively (luck) egalitarian. I now add: That account generates shared reasons only when it enjoys an overlapping consensus. As we'll see, this means we legitimately may act through political institutions to pursue luck egalitarian aspirational justice only by first bringing that account into overlapping consensus.

Second, we have shared reasons supplied directly by the bedrock value of mutual respect among free and equal citizens. That value justifies imposing the reciprocity requirement in the first place, it constrains the reasons sourced by aspirational values, and it can even rule out some conceptions of aspirational value on their face, setting them outside the family of reasonable such conceptions. Because in political liberalism mutual respect constrains the space of reasonable conceptions of justice, these substantive shared reasons flowing directly from mutual respect operate as *mandatory* shared reasons: We are compelled by reasonableness to recognize them as reasons. In this way, the value of mutual respect constrains not only political action but also political *inaction*. This it does by issuing positive *demands of legitimacy*. Because protection for the basic liberties in their central range of application "is a condition of the adequate development and full exercise of the two moral powers of citizens," and because securing conditions favorable to the development of citizenship is a reason supplied by the value of mutual respect among free and equal citizens, a social arrangement that fails to protect the basic liberties cannot be fully legitimate. More generally, when the ideal of mutual respect among free and equal citizens decisively favors some exercise of political power, we cannot legitimately *decline* to act on it. To put it

---

[9] See Estlund 1996.

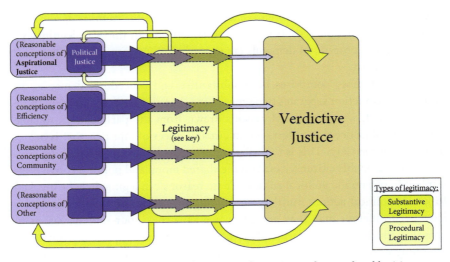

Figure 4.1 The anatomy of justice, depicting substantive and procedural legitimacy

roughly, mutual civic respect *just makes* demands: Its reasons *just are* the substantive demands of legitimacy.

These substantive demands of legitimacy have so far been depicted with yellow arrows that flow from legitimacy to verdictive justice. We can now begin to represent the complexity of legitimacy: Its *substantive* demands—informed by the weight of mandatory shared reasons—reach forward, directly influencing the rankings of verdictive justice; and they reach backward, describing the family of reasonable conceptions of aspirational justice (and, plausibly, describing the family of reasonableness for other aspirational values as well). Its *procedural* demands encompass democratic decision-making in light of a shared conception of justice, as well as the selection of a shared conception of justice from within the family of reasonable such conceptions: the process of forming an overlapping consensus. (Figure 4.1.)

Democratic enfranchisement is among the substantive demands of legitimacy, and it is for this reason that the outcomes of legitimate democratic processes become legitimate by virtue of their procedural provenance. Just as mandatory shared reasons favor protection for basic liberties which thereby becomes a requirement of substantive legitimacy, mandatory shared reasons favor the preservation of democratic decision-making processes and render their verdicts presumptively legitimate.[10] But those verdicts are *in fact* legitimate only insofar as they comply with the very value that grounds their *presumptive* legimacy: mutual

---

[10] I take this statement about the grounds of democracy's legitimacy conferral to be largely compatible with a range of accounts that base the value of democracy in the interests of free and equal citizenship. For a canonical example, see Christiano 2004. In this book, I do not weigh in on the *authority* of democracy, only its legitimacy.

respect among free and equal citizens. A democratic verdict can certainly be legitimate without being aspirationally just, and it can be legitimate without promoting aspirational value on the whole. But it cannot be legitimate if it violates substantive demands of legitimacy—that is, if it fails to respond to the mandatory shared reasons of mutual respect.[11] Thus does mutual respect both call for the preservation of some space for collective democratic ends-setting and decision-making and constrain the space within which democratic processes confer legitimacy.[12]

Because the substantive demands of legitimacy on my account are so extensive, so too are the constraints on the legitimacy-conferring capacity of democracy. We'll consider this more concretely in due course. For now, just note that, even when democratic processes do not confer legitimacy, we may have sufficient reason to defer to those processes. For example, deference might be our best hope of achieving legitimacy in the long run. Or deference might be our best hope of *accurately discerning* legitimacy's demands now. But democratic processes don't confer legitimacy on political measures that frustrate substantive demands of mutual respect. Such measures remain illegitimate, even if we sometimes ought to defer to process.[13]

In Chapter 2, I argued that distributive equality comprises *the truth* about aspirational justice. I argued, in other words, that fairness *in fact* demands equality. Now, in filling out the anatomy so as to make it a version of political liberalism, I effectively *alienate* the truth about justice from political evaluation in one important respect. To see how this is so, notice what "gets through" to verdictive justice: First are the mandatory shared reasons of mutual respect—liberal

---

[11] For Rawls, only *grave injustice* can render a democratic verdict illegitimate (Rawls 1993, 428). For me, a democratic verdict is illegitimate if it is impugned by the substantive demands of mutual respect. From that description alone, it is unclear how widely our views diverge in extension, but because I regard mutual respect as highly demanding, one might infer that the divergence is significant. It isn't clear how liberally Rawls would use the designation "gravely unjust," but he does give some clues. He identifies three "urgent matters" of injustice for the U.S. constitution: that it "woefully fails in public financing for political elections, leading to a *grave* imbalance in fair political liberties" (emphasis mine); that it "allows a widely disparate distribution of income and wealth that seriously undermines fair opportunities in education and employment, all of which undermine economic and social equality"; and that it lacks "provisions for important constitutional essentials such as health care for many who are uninsured" (Rawls 1993, 407). This passage raises some doubts that Rawls's "grave injustice" is so *very* different than the considerations of mutual civic respect that constrain democratic processes on my view, though Rawls clearly did not endorse the distributive demands of mutual respect (as such) that I argued for in the last chapter.

[12] This argument does not presume that the political liberties are less important than or "subordinate" to other liberties, like freedom of speech. (See Rawls 1999a, 202, 396.) The argument is that all the basic liberties are underpinned by the same value, and that the interactions among them should be settled in light of that value.

[13] The space within which we all things considered should defer to democratic processes may be *significantly* larger than the space within which those processes confer legitimacy. This point is crucial given that on my view the space within which democratic processes actually confer legitimacy is smaller—because the substantive demands of legitimacy are more extensive—than we may have thought. (Remember, not all substantive demands of legitimacy need be *constitutional* essentials; some will be matters of basic justice properly left to legislation.)

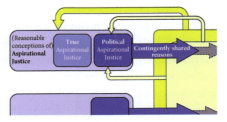

Figure 4.2 Aspirational justice, depicting reasonable, true, and political conceptions

legitimacy's substantive demands. Second are the reasons sourced by aspirational social values *when those values are supported by an overlapping consensus and when the reasons are voiced by legitimate democratic processes*—when the reasons become *procedural* demands of liberal legitimacy, by virtue for example of being enacted by citizens' duly chosen representatives or by regulatory regimes sanctioned by those representatives.

Suppose we have an overlapping consensus on an account of aspirational justice that is different from the account I have defended as the right one: Suppose I'm right that stringent distributive equality is the *true* account of aspirational justice, but some less demanding account is the one that enjoys an overlapping consensus. In that case, we might say that the less demanding account comprises *political* (aspirational) justice but not *true* (aspirational) justice. Because in this case political justice is (by supposition) distinct from true justice, we may not realize true justice by pursuing political justice. But only political justice can issue contingently shared reasons compliant with mutual respect. In Figure 4.2, we get a close-up view of aspirational justice. Substantive legitimacy describes the large purple box: the family of reasonable conceptions of aspirational justice. *Procedural* legitimacy, through overlapping consensus, describes the particular reasonable conception of aspirational justice that sources political reasons. True justice, as we can see, may not be the conception that enjoys an overlapping consensus. Even so, the conception that enjoys an overlapping consensus is the conception that issues contingently shared reasons. (Figure 4.2.)

I said the anatomy of justice alienates the truth about justice in one important respect. Let me now make that more precise: As a political liberalism, the anatomy alienates the truth about justice *with respect to the reasons bearing on how to arrange our political institutions*. But this does not entail that the truth about justice is alienated from political theorizing or political evaluation altogether.[14]

---

[14] See Rawls 1993, 94. While Rawls wrote that political liberalism "applies the principle of toleration to philosophy itself," I propose we understand it instead (as the discussion surrounding that quotation seems to do) as applying the principle of toleration to *political justification* itself. Rawls 1993, 10. This is broadly consistent with the approach taken by Cohen in J. Cohen 2009 and needn't be *in*consistent with that taken by Estlund in Estlund 1998. On the compatibility of constructivist political liberalism with rational intuitionism as a moral realism, see Rawls 1993, 95.

RELATIONAL EQUALITY AS LEGITIMACY   101

I've invoked the notion of "the truth about aspirational justice" liberally over these paragraphs, in service of the point that it is political justice and not true justice that issues (contingently) shared reasons compliant with mutual respect. This possibility, that evaluative truths matter for political evaluation and theorizing even if they play no role as such in justifying political action, bears on the plausibility of the anatomy, as we'll see.

Now, some political liberals will want to alienate the notion of truth even from political theorizing. Such political liberals will nonetheless allow that conceptions of justice can be better or worse in *some* way relevant to theorizing. They may allow, for example, that among the reasonable conceptions of justice that qualify to issue (contingently) shared reasons, some are *more* reasonable and some *less* so. This allowance is enough for my purposes: By pursuing *political* justice—or justice as understood by the overlapping consensus—we may fall short of realizing justice as construed by the most reasonable conception of justice. When this is so, it is the former that issues contingently shared reasons compliant with mutual respect. But "the most reasonable conception of justice" still refers to something, and it's a something that we can refer to in our theorizing without crossing the boundaries of political liberalism.

Later in this chapter, we'll arrive at a question that's crucial to assessing the anatomy's acceptability to distributive egalitarians: Can the *truth* about some aspirational value give us any reasons at all when the true account is not the one that enjoys an overlapping consensus? Or: Can the *most reasonable* account of justice give us reasons when *it* doesn't enjoy an overlapping consensus? For now, let's return to the distinction between contingent and mandatory reasons of mutual respect: A failure to act on the reasons supplied by the account of aspirational justice that enjoys an overlapping consensus is a failure of *political justice*. It can *become* a failure of *legitimacy*, but this occurs only when democratic processes call for some pursuit of the value in question and the measure called for is not subsequently enacted. In such a case, we have a failure of *procedural* legitimacy: a failure to enact some particular measure that's been democratically elected. Contrast such failures with failure to act on the *mandatory* shared reasons of mutual respect, including our *general* reasons to extend equal franchise in democratic processes through which we set shared ends within the substantive constraints of legitimacy: *These* failures are *always* failures of liberal legitimacy—even when they are approved by democratic processes.

Now we can better appreciate the principled case for affording mutual respect lexical priority relative to mere political justice. In Chapter 2, I began to motivate that ranking. I wrote of a principled reason to think that the value of mutual respect among free and equal citizens trumps other social aspirations that are reasonably disputed: Mutual respect is plausibly the very value that should guide us in thinking about whether and how disputed values should be pursued politically in a liberal democracy. I acknowledged that the value of mutual respect may *itself* be disputed, and it will be more contentious still if its distributive demands are as robust as I've since argued they are. But disagreement over mutual respect is different than disagreement over aspirational social values. The ideal of mutual civic respect in a liberal democracy gives reasonable disagreement over other values normative significance: It is because we want to preserve mutual respect that we must find a way to deal fairly with disagreement. Thus, if some political strategy could bring about greater compliance with fair shares but at a cost to mutual respect, it is plausible on principle that pursuing that strategy would result in a categorically distinct kind of loss. Is it also plausible that it would result in a less good social arrangement no matter the magnitudes of the gain and cost in question? I think it might be. Mutual respect among free and equal citizens is certainly not the only important value realizable by social arrangements, and different accounts of other values, and of their relative importance, account for differences among conceptions of justice. But mutual respect defines the very extension of the family of reasonable conceptions of justice. It's one thing to fail to secure for every citizen her fair share. It's another thing, arguably categorically worse, to fail to secure an institutional arrangement commensurate with her status as a free and equal citizen owed mutual respect and membership in the justificatory community.

This argument certainly will not convince every reader to be a political liberal or to embrace the lexical priority of mutual respect. That's okay. The goal of this book is to show that the schema and the anatomy of justice can benefit our thinking about justice. I can accomplish that even if I haven't gotten it just right with my substantive accounts of the values that populate the anatomy or with my substantive account of the priority relationships among those values. Where readers think I have gone *very* wrong, I invite them to consider the substantive accounts as mere illustrations of justice theorizing that aims to produce evaluative discernment rather than normative principles.

I do hope to make a strong case for the substantive accounts in question. But it's okay for a second and more important reason that the principled case for the lexical priority of mutual respect won't compel all readers: That principled case was never meant to be dispositive. I've identified the motivating question of political liberalism as: How do we establish or preserve mutual civic respect despite inevitable reasonable disagreement? My hunch is that part of the answer is simply: We afford the institutional reasons issued by mutual respect a very high degree of priority with respect to other values that set us at odds. My case offers nothing to readers who are unmoved by the question, and even a reader who finds it pressing indeed may be unmoved by the lexical version of my hunch. She might ask: Can't we establish or preserve mutual respect without *lexically* prioritizing the institutional demands of that very value? And maybe we can! But resistance to lexical priority owes less to the lack of a dispositive principled case for lexical priority and more to its predicted implications: to the extreme suppression of other values that lexical priority seems to entail. My strategy has been to consider the strongest version of my hunch—if you really want to preserve mutual respect, you need to afford that value *lexical* evaluative priority—and to argue that the priority value cares enough about the reasons sourced by the secondary values to render even lexical subordinations palatable. Mutual respect favors a great deal of what is called for by luck egalitarian fairness, and I've suggested that the same is true about the parts of efficiency and community that we'd balk at lexically subordinating. To establish a society of mutual respect, we'll have to afford the institutional reasons supplied by that value (at least) a great deal of priority in (at least) most foreseeable circumstances. If I'm right about what that value gives us reason to do, then neither distributive egalitarians nor champions of other values like community should reflexively dismiss this possibility as unacceptable.[15] Meanwhile, if principled considerations ultimately tolerate something short of lexical priority, the substantive convergence of mutual respect and aspirational values will remain relevant both to substantive political evaluation and to the question of how champions of egalitarian aspirational values should receive a strong, but not quite lexically strong, prioritization of mutual respect.

Like the case for affording mutual respect evaluatively lexical priority, the case for construing lexically prior mutual respect as an account of legitimacy falls short of dispositive. That case appeals simply to the fitness of a strongly prioritized mutual respect to play the role legitimacy sets out. Conceptually, legitimacy comprises a moral assessment of social arrangements and exercises of political power. Liberal legitimacy assesses the ends and means of such arrangements and exercises: It assess the ways in which we act politically and the various values we might pursue in so acting. I have argued that, at least for those who find political liberalism's motivating question compelling, the institutional demands of mutual respect comprise a plausible tool for moral assessment of social arrangements,

---

[15] Consider the attempt to "dethrone democratic legitimacy" in Stemplowska and Swift 2018. Stemplowska and Swift argue against the "conventional view," exemplified by Rawls, that "democratic decisions are permissibly enforceable unless they are *gravely* unjust—perhaps when they blatantly violate basic human rights" (3, italics theirs; for an original statement, see Rawls 1993, 428). Against this conventional view, Stemplowska and Swift argue that "social injustice does not need to be grave in order to render impermissible the enforcement of the decision with the democratic provenance. Rather, whether it is the democratic provenance or the just content of the decision that determines the permissibility of its enforcement depends on whether, on a case by case basis, we have a greater reason…to advance…justice or legitimacy" (Stemplowska and Swift 2018, 4). On this formulation, legitimacy *just amounts* to having democratic provenance. Because I argue that legitimacy's *substantive* demands are so robust, my position might be regarded as friendly to their project of dethroning legitimacy understood as mere democratic provenance; but in any case, I think my view can answer the concerns they raise for a view that "thrones" legitimacy. It answers those concerns precisely by subordinating legitimacy's procedural verdicts to its substantive demands. (Stemplowska and Swift do at one point grant that legitimacy may impose some substantive demands, but maintain that "the demands of social justice, fully and properly understood, may differ from, and conflict with, the demands that result even from perfectly legitimate democratic procedures" (7). I agree, of course, but think that once we locate the conflict in question, it is fully intuitive that legitimacy, embodying the institutional demands of mutual respect, should always carry the day.)

104 THE ANATOMY OF JUSTICE

social ideals, and exercises of political power. And I have argued for a quite strong if not lexical priority of mutual respect over the other values that we might hope to realize through social arrangements and exercises of political power. I've argued, that is, that the adjudicatory value has quite strong priority over the various considerations that it adjudicates. This all seems tantamount to casting mutual respect as the value at the heart of liberal legitimacy: to making liberal legitimacy a matter of respecting the institutional implications imposed by the commitment to preserving mutual respect among free and equal citizens.

The case seems stronger still when we recognize that one such implication involves the terms on which we justify and the procedures by which we authorize enactments of democratic power: A liberal legitimacy based on mutual respect is a *democratic* legitimacy. In a diverse, liberal democratic society, no social arrangement will be maximally congenial to all of us, and none will at once *optimally* realize *all* the values bearing on a social arrangement. But we can realize legitimacy in part by ensuring that our social arrangement is justifiable by a reasonable balance of values, each recognizable as such even by those who are burdened or aggrieved by some aspect of that social arrangement. Foremost among these shared values is the value of mutual respect among free and equal citizens that motivates this requirement of justificatory reciprocity to begin with. Failure to live up to the mandatory reasons that value sources is of a kind with a failure to institutionalize protections for the political liberties. It is a violation of substantive legitimacy.

Suppose a reader rejects *this* non-dispositive argument. As I noted above, the case for the usefulness of the anatomy survives the rejection of the substantive accounts of its components. But even the substantive picture I'm advancing in this chapter can get by with more minimal premises than the ones I'm trying to motivate. If you think that mutual respect plausibly enjoys *some* priority, you can come along on the substance even if you still resist *lexical* priority and even if you resist calling the institutional demands of mutual respect demands of *legitimacy*. You can regard these simply as highly stringent demands of justice—just the kind of demands that underwrite the liberal case for the equal basic liberties.

Conjoining this point with the conclusion of Chapter 3, we see that the substantive anatomy I'm forwarding is *radically* egalitarian: Distributively egalitarian aspirational justice is egalitarian, of course, and we'll turn presently to the question of what that means for verdictive justice. *Legitimacy*—or if you like, *highly stringent justice*—is *also* distributively egalitarian. It imposes the distributive demands implied by the ideal of mutual respect among free and equal citizens, and those demands include a defeasible baseline of equality and the impermissibility of talent to overturn that presumption. An inegalitarian conception of fairness thus cannot set inequality beyond verdictive justice's reproach, even if that conception enjoys an overlapping consensus and democratic support. By pursuing such a conception, we would render our social arrangement not only unjust by the lights of *true* justice; we would bring about injustice of the same category as a failure to secure the basic liberties. And the priority of mutual respect ensures that we always or nearly always generate more value by bringing our social arrangement into compliance with mutual respect—into the domain of the reasonable—than we do by making it compliant with any particular conception of value within that domain. Mutual respect does favor strong protections for basic liberties as the conventional wisdom has it, but it favors protections for other fundamental interests of free and equal citizenship, too. Those interests subsume a lot of what is normatively weightiest about distributive fairness. And once that is clear, it becomes a far easier pill to swallow that the parts of distributive fairness that are *not* seconded by mutual respect take a strong backseat to the parts that are.

Let's take stock. On the view I'll move foward with, the relational ideal of mutual respect among free and equal citizens underpins liberal legitimacy. That relational ideal acts as a trump: It is lexically morally weightier than and constrains the pursuit of aspirational political justice and all other aspirational social values. And that relational value limits the legitimate scope of—and should inform—democratic decision-making. In an ideal theory orientation, mutual respect—including its distributive demands—constrains the space of reasonable political conceptions of justice. In circumstances of injustice, further compliance with mutual respect—including with its distributive demands—always yields more political value than full compliance with reasons sourced only by one particular conception of justice, be it the true conception or the most reasonable, or the one that enjoys an overlapping consensus of support in our society. And when we lack any such consensus, we can know nonetheless that progress toward mutual respect is progress toward verdictive justice, because it is non-contingently progress toward legitimacy.

4.2 Distributive Justice Silenced?

All this can easily make the distributive egalitarian wonder what's in the anatomy *for her*. On the one hand, I've argued that verdictive justice is stringently distributively egalitarian even *without* aspirational justice, because mutual respect imposes such strong distributively egalitarian demands. On the other, I've argued that aspirational justice takes a very strong backseat to mutual respect whenever the two values diverge. Distributive egalitarians won't object to the anatomy on the grounds that it situates equality alongside other values that inform what we ought to do; unlike relational egalitarians, distributive egalitarians standardly regard their favored conception of equality as only one among the things that matter for political evaluation. What *will* strike distributive egalitarians as an objectionable demotion of distributive justice is the *way* in which distributive

106   THE ANATOMY OF JUSTICE

equality is constrained: Because mutual respect renders much of distributive equality redundant and constrains what it doesn't render redundant, the anatomy appears to afford distributive equality vanishingly little weight as an input into verdictive justice. The concern extends: If liberal legitimacy (nearly) always wins in conflict cases, then champions of all values other than mutual respect stand to worry that their favored social consideration gets short shrift.

To feel the weight of the worry, let's recall an example first introduced in Chapter 1 (1.3): There, I claimed that distributive egalitarian aspirational justice plausibly disfavors *all* inequalities among children, along whatever metric matters for fairness. Whatever role voluntary choice might play in sanctioning inequality *generally*, the choices of children simply do not have the kind of moral status to render resulting disadvantage just, whatever other deference those choices deserve. Suppose I'm right. In that case, plausibly, aspirational justice directs educational institutions and other institutions that influence children's life prospects to ensure that all children enjoy equally good life prospects as they enter the point in their lives at which their choices *do* begin to license distributive inequalities among them.

Now, other aspirational values will weigh against aspirational justice. Even as aspirational justice favors equal prospects, we may have other aspirational-value-based reasons that limit the extent to which, for example, schooling should discount the interests of relatively advantaged students. But to isolate the effects of legitimacy, let's again simplify matters and pretend that educational equality is what the balance of aspirational social values favors.

Legitimacy will impugn some of what this balance of aspirational values calls for. Recall our supposed strategy for realizing educational equality (1.3): starkly means-testing public primary education, leaving all those with private means to find their way in a private education market while concentrating public educational resources on those who lack private means. Suppose this really would promote educational equality. Even so, plausibly, means-testing primary education is inimical to the legitimacy value of mutual respect, because actually achieving the standing as equal citizens that mutual respect favors requires that prospective citizens be educated together with other students from all walks of life, not segregated by economic class as they would be if those with means were opted into a separate private system.[16] Accepting these suppositions, then, legitimacy will condemn means-testing primary education, and verdictive justice will rank as less valuable a society that means-tests relative to one that does not, other mutual-respect-related things equal. It will render this verdict even though means-testing is (we've supposed) favored by the weight of aspirational values.

---

[16] See Anderson 2007.

RELATIONAL EQUALITY AS LEGITIMACY   107

Or consider a different case, suggested to me by Tom Parr.[17] This is the case of *Fallen Utopia*, which Parr describes like this:

> We live in a utopia, in which each of us is guided exclusively by sound reasons, including those derived from sound political values. Accordingly, we have a national health service that funds a variety of life-saving medical procedures, but not all such procedures, since we correctly identify some as being too expensive to be worth state-funding. Now, let us suppose that some dissenters emerge, and eventually become dominant: their views meet the demands of mutual respect, but they insist that the national health service should be funded less generously. Their policy is enacted and, as a result, I am denied a life-saving medical procedure on the grounds that it is too expensive.

Parr's judgment, and mine, is that procedural legitimacy *rightly* outweighs aspirational justice in this case—that our foregone realization of aspirational justice and the loss of fictional Tom Parr's life in *Fallen Utopia* are a price we should be willing to pay to preserve mutual respect. Here we have mutual respect outweighing aspirational justice, and that strikes many of us as the right verdict for a theory to render. But real-life Tom Parr starts to worry when the number of deaths grows. Suppose further cuts with democratic backing result in increasing premature death. Isn't there some number of premature deaths, real-life Tom Parr asks, above which aspirational justice matters more than mutual respect?

In fact, as premature death and underfunding increase, I think *mutual respect itself* takes offense. At some point, it is no longer credible to regard our fallen utopia as a society in compliance with the substantive demands of legitimacy, within which legitimacy's procedural demands actually confer legitimacy. Collectively, we do not treat the medically vulnerable with respect as free and equal citizens, with morally equal interests in pursuing their conceptions of the good, if we fund health services so scantily that premature deaths abound. And in real-life iterations of this case, we'd arguably be failing to express mutual respect as well toward the least advantaged and toward other oppressed groups, who in unjust societies figure disproportionally among the medically vulnerable. In other words: As the number of premature deaths increases, it becomes less credible that the parameters of the case still obtain: namely, that the citizens who favor de-funding are guided by sound reasons compliant with mutual respect.

But of course, there is a point at which medically avoidable premature deaths offend against the balance of aspirational social values—namely, against aspirational justice—but are not yet plentiful enough to offend against mutual respect. In that space, on the anatomy I'm forwarding, procedural justice wins the day: The more

---

[17] I reproduce and discuss it here with his permission.

108 THE ANATOMY OF JUSTICE

meagre funding level is tolerated by substantive legitimacy and favored by procedural legitimacy, and legitimacy trumps even at a cost to aspirational justice. (Indeed, in some such cases, legitimacy plausibly comes at a cost to aspirational relational values like community and solidarity as well.) Accepting these suppositions, legitimacy condemns reversing the de-funding trend, and verdictive justice will rank as less valuable a society that reverses the trend relative to one that does not, other mutual-respect-related things equal. It will render this verdict even though restoring the higher funding levels would be favored by the weight of aspirational values.

These two cases feature mutual respect impugning as illegitimate a measure that (by supposition) aspirational social values favor. To many of us, it seems *right* that aspirational values give way in these cases. To *most* of us, it will seem right that distributive equality *sometimes* defers, even if not in these cases. But even so, I submit that it can also seem *regrettable* that it should be so. It seems like things would be better if the conflict could be avoided and both values realized at once. That conviction suggests that, even when distributive fairness gives way to mutual respect, it is not thereby *evaluatively silenced*. And it suggests that even when outweighed, fairness is not rendered practically impotent. The anatomy of justice can seem to contradict that judgment. But in the next section, I argue that distributive egalitarian aspirational justice is reasons-generating *even when* it is strongly constrained by legitimacy—indeed, even when legitimacy condemns acting on it. Legitimacy is partially fact dependent, and some of the facts that matter to the question of how tightly legitimacy constrains the pursuit of aspirational justice are subject to being changed by social processes. So, when legitimacy rules out further pursuit of some genuine social value like aspirational justice, that value can generate reasons to change the social facts that make it the case that legitimacy rules out its pursuit: These include reasons to bring true aspirational justice into overlapping consensus and reasons to push democratic decision-making toward greater support for aspirational justice.

4.3 The Substantive Role of the Aspirational: Distributive Justice Speaks Up

To generate reasons bearing on how we ought to arrange our social institutions, aspirational social values must be *political*: They must enjoy the support of an overlapping consensus. And for compliance with aspirational values to yield value on the whole—for compliance to increase *verdictive justice*—the action those values favor must be consistent with the mandatory shared reasons issued by mutual respect. But distributive egalitarians should reject an account of pluralist justice on which distributive equality can be rendered evaluatively impotent

RELATIONAL EQUALITY AS LEGITIMACY 109

whenever mutual respect impugns it or it lacks the support of an overlapping consensus. They should reject such an account even if relationally egalitarian legitimacy is demandingly distributively egalitarian on its own. Luckily, the anatomy of justice is not such an account. The right account of aspirational justice retains evaluative and practical significance, even when its demands are impugned by mutual respect and even when it doesn't enjoy an overlapping consensus.

One way in which aspirational justice may remain relevant bears mentioning, though it won't be the backbone of my argument. On the conventional view, political values issue demands of justice to individual people only indirectly, in a manner mediated by political structures and institutions. Consider Rawls's duties of justice for individuals: In circumstances of justice, individuals have a duty of justice to support just institutions; in circumstances of injustice, they have a duty of justice to work to bring just institutions into being. But for Rawls, individuals don't have a duty to promote the values of justice *directly*. Suppose I'm offered a higher wage than I'd be able to command in a justly regulated labor market. On this conventional view, I have no duty of justice to refuse the surplus. Maybe I *should* refuse it, but if so, refusing is a matter of virtue or ethics and not a duty of justice. One way to make aspirational justice speak up even when it's constrained by legitimacy, then, is to reject this institutional focus of distributive justice. Perhaps the values of justice *do* generate duties of justice that apply directly to individuals.[18] In *Fallen Utopia*, when procedural legitimacy impedes the realization of aspirational justice by favoring underfunded public health services, perhaps aspirational justice comes to command individuals to take up the slack and crowd-fund life-saving treatments. If they did, we could respect procedural legitimacy by reducing public funding of health services, but still avoid the loss to aspirational justice that de-funding threatens by increasing individual giving to take up the slack. My argument here won't rely on the view that justice applies to individual behavior in such a way, though I will explore this issue further in Chapter 6. For now, I want to argue that aspirational values remain practically relevant even when legitimacy forbids acting on them *and* even if the values of justice don't command individuals directly.

My answer to the worry depends on this simple fact: The two relevant questions—whether luck egalitarianism is a political conception of justice that enjoys an overlapping consensus and whether legitimacy approves political action to pursue it—both partially depend on social contingencies that individuals have a hand in shaping. Recall that, on the anatomy of justice, legitimacy is fact dependent in two important ways: First, some shared reasons are only *contingently* shared; second, the procedural demands of legitimacy are set by

[18] Or perhaps the scope of the Rawlsian duty of justice is more expansive than it's typically taken to be. See Cohen 1992; Shiffrin 2010.

110 THE ANATOMY OF JUSTICE

verdicts of democratic processes. When aspirational justice is obstructed by the contingent reasons of mutual respect, it can find voice by condemning the very contingencies in question and giving us reason to change them. When it's obstructed by democratic processes, it can find voice by condemning the outputs of those processes and calling on us to work toward better outputs next time. In sum: When legitimacy precludes institutions from fully realizing aspirational justice, aspirational justice can generate reasons to ease the constraints of legitimacy by changing the circumstances that generate the preclusion—by changing the voting behavior of citizens or the conception of aspirational justice that enjoys an overlapping consensus of support and that thus generates contingently shared reasons. Citizens can adjust and ease legitimacy's constraints by working through persuasion, deliberation, consciousness raising, advocacy, activism, and procedural democracy to increase the extent to which the right or most reasonable account of aspirational justice—and the right or most reasonable account of other aspirational social values—influences verdictive justice.

To make this case, let's begin a few steps back. Recall that the invariant requirements and constraints of legitimacy are set by the mandatory shared reasons issued by the ideal of mutual respect among free and equal citizens. Mutual respect invariantly demands that we intervene politically in one another's lives only in ways that can be justified on terms we can all accept; and mutual respect invariantly demands substantive protections for certain fundamental shared interests of equal citizenship. The basic liberties illustrate what it means, and what it *doesn't* mean, that these demands are invariant: *Which* interventions or institutional arrangements are necessary to protect basic liberties depends on social circumstances; but the fact that mutual respect demands the needed protections (whatever they are) is set. Similarly, *which* economic system and *which* economic policy best realize the distributive demands of mutual respect depends on circumstances, but the fact that mutual respect imposes these demands is invariant. Finally, the invariant constraints limit political deliberation about what to do with our shared democratic power to the space of reasonable conceptions of aspirational social value. *Which* institutional configurations any such reasonable conception will call for depends on the circumstances; but the fact that we are constrained to the family of conceptions that heed the mandatory shared reasons of mutual respect is invariant. Call these invariant constraints and requirements the "minimal condition" for legitimacy: A social arrangement is legitimate only if it falls within the range of arrangements that comply with all the constraints and requirements imposed by mandatory shared reasons of mutual respect. I call this the "minimal condition" because it is necessary but not sufficient for legitimacy.[19]

---

[19] We might say that a society satisfying the minimal condition is one that is legitimate in its constitution and in matters of basic justice. See Rawls 1993, 10.

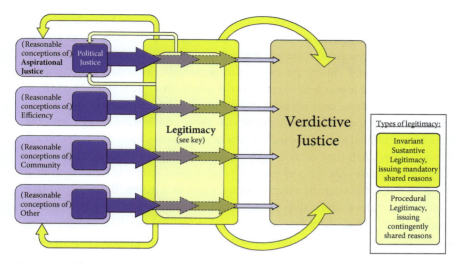

Figure 4.3 The anatomy of justice, depicting substantive and procedural legitimacy and their respective type of shared reasons

But as the distributive demands of mutual respect attest, these requirements and prohibitions are far from minimal in substance.

The minimal condition doesn't *suffice* for legitimacy because the ideal of mutual respect also imposes a procedural requirement which favors deliberative democratic ends-setting and decision-making and restricts the reasons invoked in democratic deliberation about what to do to those which flow from an overlapping consensus. A *fully* legitimate social arrangement, then, is one that falls within the range delineated by the invariant requirements and constraints implied by the ideal of mutual respect among free and equal citizens, that pursues political values as sanctioned by an overlapping consensus, and that is ordered in compliance with the verdicts rendered by legitimate democratic processes. In other words: A fully legitimate social arrangement is one that heeds both the mandatory and contingent shared reasons implied by the ideal of mutual respect, and that is sanctioned by democratic decision-making. (Figure 4.3.)

This standard of full legitimacy is striking in its demandingness. But distinguishing its layers enables us to see that, demanding as legitimacy is, we should want *still more* than full legitimacy: First, but less importantly for our purposes, we should want our social arrangement to *realize* political justice—not only for us to *be constrained* to considerations of political justice, but for us to realize political justice fully—and we should want that *whether or not* political justice is the true or most reasonable conception of justice.

Second, and distinctly, we should want our overlapping consensus to fall on the *true* or *most reasonable* conception of justice, and we should want procedural legitimacy to approve our pursuit of it. A social arrangement is truly (or most reasonably) aspirationally just, in addition to being legitimate, insofar as the contingencies of legitimacy converge with the facts about justice: insofar as the arrangement which realizes the contingently shared reasons of mutual respect and enjoys the support of democratic processes *also* complies with demands of aspirational justice to the extent that the minimal condition allows. Because those contingencies of legitimacy *are contingencies*, and because society is really more just to the extent that those contingencies align with the facts of aspirational justice, the facts of aspirational justice can remain practically relevant even when they do not enjoy an overlapping consensus or democratic support. We never win value by pursuing aspirational justice at a cost to mutual respect—this is the sense in which legitimacy acts as a trump. But trumped true aspirational values don't stop being values because circumstances make it illegitimate to pursue them politically. They don't become evaluatively impotent. Rather, their evaluative force is redirected: Trumped true aspirational values can bear on the question of *what it would be good for legitimacy to approve, to proscribe, or to demand*.[20] They give citizens reason to change the contingencies that presently bring aspirational values into conflict with mutual respect. Citizens and representatives can promote aspirational justice by working democratically for aspirationally just institutional arrangements when mutual respect permits this, and they can promote aspirational justice by working to bring the reasons it supplies more fully into the domain of fundamental political ideas we can legitimately invoke compliant with the justificatory reciprocity demands of mutual respect.[21] In short, citizens can influence the contingent facts of democratic decision-making on which depend those matters of verdictive justice that are not settled invariantly by the ideal of mutual respect.

To the degree that they comply with the invariant constraints and requirements that comprise legitimacy's minimal condition, then, the demands of true distributive egalitarian aspirational justice remain practically and evaluatively relevant. Whatever invariant requirements of legitimacy are imposed by the ideal of mutual respect among citizens construed as free and equal political persons, relational egalitarian legitimacy leaves some matters of political value—as well as some matters of what to do—to be determined by citizens. This is the space within which we might shift our overlapping consensus—and with it, our contingently shared reasons—and the space within which we may vote to authorize representatives to act on our behalf. It may include some space within which the demands of public reason simply do not apply: issues on which citizens are free to vote on the basis of *all* the reasons they find relevant, including to further the comprehensive conception of justice they believe to be true. If such space exists,[22]

---

[20] But see Cohen 2003.

[21] Rawls 2001, 5–6. Compare the discussion of the difference principle in Estlund 1996.

[22] On this question, see Quong 2011, chap. 9; Watson and Hartley 2018, chap. 3.

RELATIONAL EQUALITY AS LEGITIMACY 113

then citizens can bring legitimacy more fully into alignment with distributive egalitarian aspirational justice simply by voting to authorize equalizing measures—progressive taxation, labor market reform, socialization of services beyond those mandated by relational egalitarianism—that *become* legitimate just in virtue of their approval by citizens. Beyond this space, and even if there *are* no issues on which citizens can participate democratically on the basis of the full moral truth as they see it, aspirational justice can give citizens reason to work through democratic deliberation, activism, and consciousness raising to further the extent to which distributive equality is endorsed by an overlapping consensus of citizens, each from within her own reasonable conception of the good.

Is this cold comfort to champions of aspirational values? At the end of the day, does my pitch to distributive egalitarians amount to any more than a reminder that they are free to try to persuade others to share their convictions about justice? It's much more than that. The anatomy of justice elevates aspects of distributive equality as well as community or solidarity to the same category of evaluative significance as protections for the basic liberties. What aspects of those values it *doesn't* elevate, it also doesn't treat as a matter of taste. It doesn't say to champions of particular values: "If you care about this then you are free to try to persuade others." It says to *all* of us: "Aspirational justice (or community or solidarity) *tasks you* with trying to persuade others." If luck egalitarianism gets it right about fairness, then its champions aren't pursuing some optional social end by trying to build a consensus in its favor. They are doing as justice directs them to do. The substantive anatomy *is* politically liberal: The truth of our convictions about aspirational value doesn't suffice to justify just any political pursuit of it. In *Fallen Utopia*, even if luck egalitarianism is true, we may not circumvent the legitimate democratic process to achieve it. By the same token, even if the threat of eternal damnation were real, those who could save us from it may not circumvent the minimal condition of legitimacy to impose the needed spiritual values. But genuine values that bear on our social arrangement don't only *permit* us to act to ease legitimacy's contingent constraints *if we're so inclined*; they positively prevail on us to do so. The substantive anatomy I endorse doesn't feature spiritual aspirational values because I don't think there are genuine spiritual values that bear as such on the goodness of our social arrangement. But the anatomy does endorse demands of distributive egalitarian fairness that go beyond even the robust distributive demands of mutual respect. My appeal to distributive egalitarians is: You can be political liberals and you can accept the stringent priority of mutual respect without treating your egalitarian convictions as politically optional, as political hobbies. The anatomy doesn't regard them as such. Nor does it regard it as innocent when *opponents* of genuine aspirational values obstruct their realization. Those who vote to de-fund the public health service in *Fallen Utopia* act legitimately, but they also act in violation of aspirational justice.

114   THE ANATOMY OF JUSTICE

We can say all these things even if justice applies primarily to the institutional structure of society.[23] In each case, the reasons for citizens to act are reasons to change the facts that constrain what institutional arrangements we may pursue or what we authorize institutions to do; they are *not* reasons to pursue the values of justice directly. In *Fallen Utopia*, aspirational justice may or may not ask individuals to crowd-fund life-saving care; I've not taken a stand either way. What I've argued for is that true aspirational justice asks individuals to work politically to bring distributive equality into overlapping consensus, to oppose the political forces that favored de-funding, and to work to build democratic consensus around investing in public health services. Even if the truth about aspirational justice doesn't compel individuals to further the value of egalitarian fairness directly, it calls on them to change legitimacy's contingent reasons in order to bring our social arrangement into greater compliance with the true demands of fairness. In Figure 4.4, we see the complete anatomy of justice. In the scenario pictured, the truth about aspirational justice is not the conception of aspirational justice that enjoys an overlapping consensus. Yet even without an overlapping consensus, the truth matters: It gives reasons that target *contingent legitimacy*. Only through legitimacy do those reasons influence verdictive justice. Figure 4.5 zooms in on the evaluative significance of the truth about aspirational justice.

I've claimed that true aspirational justice tasks citizens with acting democratically to authorize equalizing measures beyond what mutual respect demands. But the priority of legitimacy means that verdictive justice favors *whatever* institutional arrangement citizens select, compliant with the minimal condition, even if that arrangement doesn't include the further equalizing measures that true aspirational justice favors. If verdictive justice orders all political values, how do we reconcile the all-things-considered nature of its judgments with the claim that aspirational values can give reason to change them?

In fact, there is no tension here to be reconciled, because the social arrangement that verdictive justice favors at one moment is not the same as the most

---

[23] Distributive egalitarians who believe that "it is bad in itself if some people are worse off than others" can go on believing that, and if they're right, the badness can go on being practically relevant (Parfit 2000, 84). I've written as if the anatomy regards distributive equality only as *conditionally* non-instrumentally bad: as non-instrumentally bad only when it *arises within an arrangement of social cooperation*. This gets us a lot if arrangements of social cooperation come in different forms with different associated egalitarian considerations (as I believe they do). This bounded non-instrumental egalitarianism charts a middle course between cosmopolitan globalism, according to which demands of equality apply everywhere with the same strength, and strong statism, according to which those demands operate only within states. On my view, like on that advanced by Martin O'Neill, "the degree of [cooperative] interaction between different individuals, peoples, or societies can determine the extent to which a distributive inequality between them is objectionable" (O'Neill 2008, 138). But it's also open to the proponent of equality to argue that it bears on the goodness of *our* social arrangement that it regard *any* inequality as bad, even among non-contemporaries and unrelated distant strangers. If such a claim is true, we may have reasons to bring still more distributive egalitarian considerations into overlapping consensus.

RELATIONAL EQUALITY AS LEGITIMACY 115

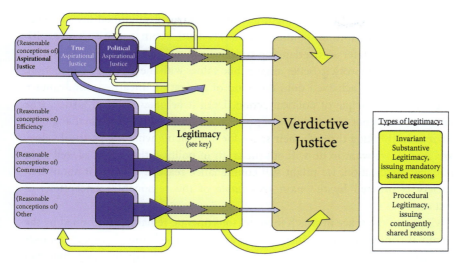

Figure 4.4 The anatomy of justice, depicting the evaluative significance of the truth about aspirational justice

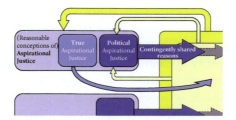

Figure 4.5 Aspirational justice, depicting the evaluative significance of the truth about aspirational justice

valuable arrangement that *we can hope to achieve*. We can have reason to make accessible more valuable ranges on the verdictive justice ranking by easing the tradeoffs among the values it orders. If we are luck egalitarians, we needn't regard a society with avoidable disadvantage as fully just, even if it is the most verdictively just arrangement we can achieve within the contingent constraints of legitimacy. That's because true aspirational justice calls on us to change the contingent constraints of legitimacy, and thereby to expand political possibility. It calls on us to make legitimacy and true aspirational justice more co-realizable: to vote or agitate for better realization of egalitarianism within the space of open democratic contestation and to deliberate to bring the badness of unearned disadvantage into the stock of shared ideas we can invoke in public reason, thereby enabling that badness to serve as political justification. Should we do this successfully, luck egalitarianism can *become* political justice, even though the citizens who helped to make it so were motivated by their convictions about *the truth* of

116   THE ANATOMY OF JUSTICE

aspirational justice.[24] On this picture, reasons of true aspirational justice never serve *illicitly* as reasons for political action. The truth about justice only gives citizens reason to prefer an overlapping consensus in support of *these* values rather than *those*, and to work to better align public values with the preferred conception. Only once this is achieved does the good of mitigating unearned disadvantage operate as a principle of political action. Until it *becomes* political justice, *true* justice operates not as a principle of political action but as a principle that guides citizens in thinking through their space for influencing what the political values *are*. And, if we want to do without the truth in political theorizing as well as in political justification, we might still countenance reasons to bring it about that society is ordered by the *most reasonable* of the reasonable conceptions of justice.[25]

Crucially, the space in which these reasons operate remains constrained by the minimal condition on legitimacy. Even as the ideal of mutual respect imposes positive requirements that bring us closer to distributive equality as a matter of legitimacy, it also imposes constraints that effectively preclude perfect alignment of verdictive justice with aspirational justice. Plausibly, for example, the minimal condition of legitimacy demands for individuals some degree of occupational discretion. Because legitimacy constrains aspirational justice, this occupational prerogative must be preserved even at a cost to aspirational justice. If we have good reason to attach different social rewards to different social contributions, then assuming our capacity to contribute is to some degree unearned, occupational discretion will preserve unearned disadvantage. Plausibly too, the minimal condition demands freedom of association, which might shield acts of partiality toward loved ones, including transfers of competitive advantage that are pure bad brute luck from the perspective of those thereby disadvantaged. Legitimacy's minimal condition thus forecloses the political machinations necessary to arrange institutions optimally to pursue luck egalitarian justice, at least when some citizens demand salary differentials for valued social contributions or favor the material interests of their loved ones over others.

Even so, there remain significant possibilities for legitimate, democratically enacted legislation to bring verdictive justice into closer alignment with luck egalitarian aspirational justice than mutual respect calls for on its own through its invariant distributive demands. Educational institutions illustrate one avenue by way of which a fully legitimate basic structure can lessen the inequality-generating behavior of its citizens: Schools could promote an egalitarian ethos of justice as a component of a politically liberal civic education—for example, by bringing students into careful and open deliberation about such values as justice, fraternity, and solidarity. Such an ethos could be sustained without restricting the

---

[24] See Rawls 1993, 12.   [25] Compare Tomlin 2012, 392–4.

occupational prerogative or compromising the protections for partiality that relational egalitarian legitimacy demands. The point is that a range of institutional arrangements will be approved by the minimal condition for legitimacy, and aspirational justice can guide us within the space between the distributive equality that mutual respect invariantly demands and the equalizing measures it invariantly rules out as illegitimate.

In this way, the anatomy can account for the clear conviction that, while certain aspects of human nature bear on the question of how we ought to arrange the terms of social cooperation, those aspects are not immune to criticism at the bar of justice. Suppose that, in *Fallen Utopia* or some other fully legitimate society, self-interestedness precludes further progress toward (re)achieving aspirational justice because the better off will not vote to authorize policy that would remove their (aspirationally) unjust surplus and because democratic processes cannot authorize such policy without their approval. In this case, we can criticize their acquisitiveness on that basis—we can regard it as "justice-tainting"[26] for example—while still maintaining that verdictive justice, within the invariant constraints of legitimacy, heeds the actual judgments of actual citizens. We can condemn behavior that frustrates the ends of aspirational justice, while still maintaining that verdictive justice should not take humans to be other than what we are.[27]

To a considerable extent, the requirements of legitimacy are set: A legitimate liberal democratic society must protect essential interests that follow from the ideal of mutual respect among free and equal citizens. The invariant demands of that ideal extend far beyond protections for the basic liberties. They include robustly distributively egalitarian demands, which, because they are called for by the same consideration that justifies protections for basic liberties, carry the same type of evaluative importance as those protections. The invariant demands of the minimal condition of legitimacy also include the demand to protect some space for actual citizens to set shared ends and make decisions together about how to pursue those ends. This space of democratic ends-setting and decision-making includes a possibility of pursuing luck egalitarian aspirational justice beyond its overlap with relational egalitarian legitimacy. Citizens not only *may* but *should* work toward equalizing measures—progressive taxation, labor market reform, socialization of services that go beyond those demanded by mutual respect, educational curricula conducive to the development among citizens of an egalitarian ethos—that *become* legitimate only in virtue of their approval by citizens. So, even if principles of aspirational justice don't directly impugn individual behavior that frustrates equality, they give citizens reasons to work democratically for a

[26] Estlund 2011, 227. See also Gilabert 2011; Gilabert and Lawford-Smith 2012; Gheaus 2013; Southwood 2016.
[27] See Cohen 2001. I'll have more to say about this possibility in Chapter 6.

118   THE ANATOMY OF JUSTICE

social arrangement that restricts their capacity to frustrate equality effectively. These are reasons to work for policies that reform institutions to realize distributive equality beyond legitimacy's minimal condition.

4.4 Justice, Legitimacy, Authority

Even as mutual respect seconds a great deal of the distributive equality that aspirational justice also favors, and even as it constrains aspirational justice where the latter is more demanding than mutual respect, aspirational justice can find its voice. Yet in circumstances of profound injustice, like ours, we fall short of achieving even the minimal condition for legitimacy. In such circumstances, the space within which aspirational justice needs to find a voice feels distant, because so much more urgent work remains undone. There's a silver lining: In such circumstances, we can *know* that bringing our social arrangement more fully into compliance with mandatory shared reasons of mutual respect constitutes a gain by the lights of verdictive justice. The how-to depends on circumstances, but the mandatory shared reasons that comprise the minimal condition are invariant: We must protect the equal basic liberties and their fair value including by preserving robust equal opportunity; we must equalize shares when no apt reason overturns that presumption; and we must treat unequal talent as inapt to constitute such a reason. Progress toward realizing these conditions is always progress toward verdictive justice, no matter our starting point, because it is non-contingently progress toward verdictive justice's overriding value, mutual respect.

Notice that we can say all these things without yet invoking any shared conception of aspirational social value. We needn't even *have* an overlapping consensus to know that we can make progress in the ways just described. Insofar as no overlapping consensus yet exists, we can work to bring one about over the truth of aspirational justice. Plausibly, we often may not vote on the basis of the whole truth, or act on that basis in our capacities as political representatives, until *after* the true account is brought into overlapping consensus. But plenty of spaces for deliberation, persuasion, and learning exist outside the official public political arena, and that's where an overlapping consensus can be built favoring the true or most reasonable conception of justice. There too, if an overlapping consensus already exists, we can work to shift it toward truth. The anatomy of justice accommodates a plausible pluralism about the value of equality. It accommodates a plausible pluralism about the concept "justice." It enables us to theorize at the level of ideals of justice while still generating action guidance that can be helpful across ideal and very non-ideal circumstances. It enables us to grasp a plausible public reasons liberalism which acknowledges that sometimes our public reasons aren't yet what they should be, and that what they should be can still make a difference. The anatomy can give theory focus without oversimplification. On my picture, many of the most important questions about justice crucially turn on matters of legitimacy, and in particular on legitimacy's invariant constraints and requirements.[28] Aspirational justice and other aspirational social values matter and can be made to matter more. But on the anatomy of justice, questions of legitimacy are of utmost importance, in theory and practice, to verdictive justice. Both our theory and practice should reflect this.

This observation might also prompt an important objection to the proposed anatomy: On my picture, legitimacy can't plausibly serve as a minimally demanding, necessary condition for a regime to have authority to govern. The ideal of mutual respect that underpins liberal legitimacy is *highly* demanding, and we cannot plausibly think that any regime that fails fully to realize its demands thereby loses authority to govern or to (presumptively) morally compel compliance. Is this a problem for the anatomy?

I don't think so. It's true that fully realizing the institutional demands of mutual respect can't plausibly be necessary for authority to govern. But authority and legitimacy can come apart. Plausibly, a political regime can be authoritative, with its citizens presumptively obligated to comply, even if that regime fails to live up to all the demands of legitimacy. It's not particularly counterintuitive to think that distinct considerations underpin citizens' presumptive obligation to comply on the one hand and the moral permissibility of particular institutional arrangements and political actions on the other. If that's right, we should not expect legitimacy and authority to converge neatly. And they might yet converge in *some* significant way, because legitimacy admits of thresholds: for example, the threshold at which we meet the institutional preconditions for interpersonal mutual respect, which we've seen are less demanding than the institutional conditions fully befitting a society of mutual respect among free and equal citizens. Maybe a regime achieves authority when it reaches some significant threshold of legitimacy.

But perhaps the most pressing objection in this vicinity is not that on the anatomy legitimacy can't plausibly co-extend with authority; perhaps the most pressing objection invokes the sheer fact of legitimacy's demandingness. Can legitimacy plausibly be so very difficult to realize? For example, can an account of legitimacy plausibly entail that no currently existing social arrangement is fully legitimate?

I think it can. Notice first that my account of legitimacy is not distinct from more orthodox conceptions in its entailment that few if any societies achieve full legitimacy. To offer up the obvious example, the Rawls of *Political Liberalism* also must conclude that few if any societies we've known have been ordered by a reasonable political conception of justice, since any reasonable such conception will,

---

[28] See Williams 2005; Miller 2016.

120 THE ANATOMY OF JUSTICE

by his lights, provide for the fair value of political liberties. Though Rawlsian political liberalism arguably doesn't wear its demandingness on its sleeve, its conditions for reasonableness turn out to be anything but minimal.[29] Yet the ideal of mutual respect on which they're based is what justifies a heightened normative status for the basic liberties. If that ideal makes still further demands, we should elevate those demands, not demote the ideal. I submit that nobody who finds my arguments otherwise compelling should reject the substantive account of legitimacy on grounds of its surprising demandingness. Legitimacy might just be surprisingly demanding, and alternative ways of theorizing it are not exactly *un*demanding. But even if we ultimately depart from my terminology and reserve "legitimacy" for a different, more substantively minimal concept, we should retain the insight that mutual respect imposes demands that have overriding normative importance in both political theory and political practice.

My conclusion so far is this: In both political theory and political practice, we have much to gain by locating our claims and our disputes within a substantive and conceptual anatomy like the one I've put forward. But even if I'm wrong about luck egalitarianism as aspirational justice or relational egalitarian mutual respect as legitimacy; even if I'm wrong about what legitimacy demands or how much priority mutual respect enjoys; even if I'm wrong about the helpfulness of employing distinct concepts of justice, still, I hope to have shown that we can make some progress in the theory and the practice of justice by working at the level of the various things that matter that a social arrangement can realize.

The Anatomy of Justice: On the Shape, Substance, and Power of Liberal Egalitarianism. Gina Schouten, Oxford University Press. © Gina Schouten 2024. DOI: 10.1093/9780191999772.003.0005

---

[29] As noted before, Samuel Freeman argues that in order for a conception of justice to satisfy the all-purpose means requirement, that conception must provide for: "(i) public financing of political campaigns and ways of assuring the availability of information on matters of public policy...(ii) fair equality of opportunity especially in education and training; (iii) a decent distribution of income and wealth; (iv) society as an employer of last resort, needed in order to provide security and meaningful work so that citizens can maintain their self-respect; and (v) basic health care assured to all citizens." See Freeman 2007, 402. In making this case, Freeman cites Rawls 1993, lviii–lix.

5

Values Tradeoffs under Injustice

The Feminist Debate over Basic Income

This chapter aims to show that the anatomy of justice can provide plausible and illuminating guidance in circumstances of injustice, including in confronting intersecting social and economic injustices. Liberal egalitarians, feminists, and liberal egalitarian feminists should all be committed to finding political solutions to the social challenges associated with justice in caregiving: the challenges of ensuring that dependents receive the care to which they are entitled while also ensuring that the care*givers* are not unfairly burdened in virtue of performing this valuable role. And they should be committed to doing this within the context of pervasive and intersecting social inequalities. To be genuinely helpful, theorizing should provide guidance in weighing the tradeoffs we face, among distinct aims of liberal egalitarian feminist justice, when it comes to devising social policy approaches for addressing injustice.

Consider a policy that illuminates these tradeoffs. Unconditional basic income would materially benefit disadvantaged citizens, including unpaid caregivers. But it is likely to have a side effect: As we'll see, it is likely to lessen women's labor market attachment more than it lessens *men's* labor market attachment, thus reinforcing the gendered division of labor. Several empirical projections are packed into this putative social policy tradeoff, and the tradeoff plausibly arises only because of a particular combination of injustices in the social arrangement. For example, only within a context of pervasive gender norms would basic income result in patterns of choice that further exacerbate gender inequality in caregiving. But suppose for now that the tradeoff is genuine: In our circumstances, basic income would benefit unfairly disadvantaged citizens but also reinforce the gendered division of labor. What should those of us committed to gender egalitarianism *and* to distributive egalitarianism make of this tradeoff?

Plausibly, decision-makers should ultimately decide which values to prioritize partly on strategic grounds—for example, on the basis of feasibility, political will, and calculations about our prospects for making meaningful progress on this front or that. Mine is a prior question that largely sets those contingencies aside. I want to ask about the relative *moral* importance of distinct policy aims, which will inform but not settle the matter of what we ought to do in any particular set of circumstances.

122   THE ANATOMY OF JUSTICE

The tradeoff between gender egalitarianism and distributive egalitarianism seems straightforward enough at the extremes. Indeed, we probably have strong enough convictions at the extremes to use as provisional fixed points for moral reflection. Here is one of mine: Poverty is a direr social injustice than the gender norms that incline women to step back at work when caregiving demands mount. But of course, we do not operate politically only at the extremes, and we should want values to guide us, with as much precision as they can supply, in navigating the difficult terrain in between. I want to show that the guidance we need can be found in the anatomy of justice, and that the guidance it provides matches the provisional fixed point just expressed, which I expect is widely shared. More importantly, I hope to show that the anatomy is more illuminating and helpful in the face of this tradeoff than an incommensurability pluralism or a theory that offers normative principles rather than evaluative discernment.

First, some preliminaries: I use "gender egalitarianism" to refer to a social ideal whereby any differences in social roles between women and men concerning work are not determined or reinforced by social norms or social institutions that promote gendered allocations of work. I use "gendered division of labor" to refer to the norms and institutional arrangements that influence individuals' labor allocations under the status quo. Full realization of gender egalitarianism—full erosion of the gendered division of labor—is consistent with unequal shares of caregiving and labor market work between women and men within particular domestic arrangements or even in aggregate. What matters is that, in a fully gender egalitarian society, choices about how to share work and caregiving won't be reinforced by social norms about gender or by institutional design that makes equal sharing difficult. Defined in this way, gender egalitarianism and, conversely, the gendered division of labor, are principally about the *norms and institutional arrangements that sustain prescriptive gender roles*, and *not* about inequality between women and men as measured by their shares of some distributable goods. The tradeoff I address arises between—on the one hand—the social aim of eroding the gendered division of labor so understood and—on the other—the social aim of lessening unjust disadvantage in holdings of social goods, including unjust disadvantage in holdings that results from women's disproportionate share of caregiving.

As we will see, liberal egalitarian feminists have particular cause *as feminists* to care about both social aims. Indeed, for precisely that reason, some may object to my defining "gender egalitarianism" to exclude concerns about the distribution of social goods. But nothing substantive hangs on this stipulated definition. Clearly, the gendered division of labor is a cause of women's subequal shares of social goods,[1] and the stipulation does not presume otherwise. It simply holds clearly

---

[1] For the canonical text on this, see Okin 1989. For a more recent picture, see Goldin 2021.

open the possibility that some policy could improve the lot of disadvantaged citizens by enhancing their shares of social goods while also exacerbating the gendered division of labor. If anyone wants to insist that "gender egalitarianism" be understood to subsume the two social aims I am keeping distinct, they can simply translate this chapter into one about the tradeoffs that arise between two distinct aims of gender egalitarianism (and, too, between one of those aims and distributive egalitarianism more broadly). Although I will explain how the tradeoff in question arises and why forms of social support like basic income plausibly require us to address it, skeptical readers are invited to take this as supposed for the sake of argument, or to consider whether my argument might fruitfully be applied to social aims that *they* regard as worthy, under circumstances that *they* take to call for tradeoffs. My aim, after all, is to show that the anatomy can provide guidance across a range of circumstances, and I can do that whether or not the circumstances I'll describe are ours precisely.

Even setting aside its effects on gender egalitarianism, basic income may not be the best way to promote liberal egalitarian justice.[2] For the most part, this chapter steers clear of that debate. I focus on basic income because it presents a vivid tradeoff for liberal egalitarian feminists. Policies can present values tradeoffs either because of structural features of the policies or of the context of implementation, or simply because resources and political will are scarce and we can't do everything we need to do to combat injustice in one fell swoop. If critical commentators are right to think that basic income will effectively subsidize women's withdrawal from paid labor and thereby set back gender equality, then it's a policy proposal that illustrates both opportunity cost tradeoffs and structural tradeoffs.

Section 5.1 explains why basic income presents a values tradeoff for liberal egalitarian feminists. Section 5.2 considers the tradeoff in the terms of distributive justice so far used in the feminist debate over basic income: Basic income can improve conditions for the very worst off in society. This is clearly an urgent demand of distributive justice. On the other hand, given existing gender norms, basic income risks subsidizing women's disproportionate withdrawal from paid work to perform unpaid caregiving—for example, to take care of their young children or aging parents. Although basic income lessens *everyone's* dependence on earnings from paid work, given existing gender norms, relatively more men will use it to *supplement* their earnings while relatively more women use it to *replace* their earnings. Because women's proportionally greater withdrawal from paid work will likely fuel discriminatory processes, it risks exacerbating unequal opportunities between women and men in competitions for scarce positions in the labor market. So, we have here a tradeoff within distributive justice: We could

---

[2] Compared, for example, with unconditional provision of basic goods (as distinct from cash) and/or means-tested (as opposed to unconditional) provision of cash or in-kind goods. See Bergmann 2004.

124   THE ANATOMY OF JUSTICE

be moved *against* universal basic income by the threat that it will exacerbate unequal opportunity between women and men in competitions for rewarding jobs, or we could be moved *in favor* of basic income by the prospect that it will benefit the disadvantaged broadly by supplementing their earnings from paid work.

Although there is a great deal about this diagnosis that I endorse, I argue in section 5.3 that it overlooks a fundamental value commitment of liberalism. In previous work, I argued that the gendered division of labor is best diagnosed as a problem of mutual respect and thus of liberal legitimacy, rather than a problem of egalitarian distributive justice.[3] If that's right, then the downside of basic income in speeding women's withdrawal from paid work is weightier than the distributive justice assessment implies. It's not only for the sake of equalizing employment opportunities between women and men that we should worry about women's withdrawal from paid work; it's because gendered trends in participation in paid labor reinforce gender *norms* that are impugned by the value at the heart of legitimacy. Thus, the aim of gender egalitarianism is weightier than it appears to be when we focus only on distributive justice.

In sections 5.4 and 5.5, I reconsider our tradeoff case in light of the argument just previewed and the anatomy of justice, and I explore the upshots of this reframing. We might expect the implication of section 5.3's argument for our tradeoff case to be that gender egalitarianism strongly constrains distributive equality, since the former is a matter of legitimacy and the latter of mere aspirational justice. But we saw in Chapters 3 and 4 that distributive equality and distributive adequacy are *also* matters of legitimacy. The argument's implications concerning the relative priority of gender egalitarianism and distributive egalitarianism are thus quite surprising: On my diagnosis, the tradeoff doesn't arise internal to distributive justice, and it is a tradeoff only in small part between aspirational justice and relational egalitarian legitimacy. Though aspirational justice *is* involved, the most important tension arises internal to legitimacy. This illustrates the point already previewed, that many of the most difficult and interesting questions of verdictive justice rely on discerning the distinct institutional demands of mutual civic respect. The anatomy can help us answer such questions. In the end, this chapter's assessment of basic income shows that if we locate them within the anatomy of justice, the tradeoffs we face when assessing policy alternatives in circumstances of injustice are not intractable. The anatomy of justice underpins a subtle and multi-layered priority ranking that is intuitively plausible and appropriately responsive to changing circumstances on the ground.

[3] Schouten 2016, 2017, 2019.

5.1 Basic Income and Values Tradeoffs

We can situate the feminist debate over basic income within the ongoing conversation among feminists about the potentially pernicious effects of certain caregiver support policies. Despite progress toward gender equality along several dimensions, household divisions of labor remain highly unequal, with women in every industrialized country continuing to do the vast majority of housework and childcare.[4] Among the most widely discussed interventions to promote a more equal sharing of paid and unpaid caregiving work are various forms of caregiver support policies. But recent evidence suggests that some forms of caregiver support will be ineffective at eroding the gendered division of labor. Indeed, given prevailing social norms and against an institutional background of structurally embedded gendered incentives, these forms of caregiving support can even be detrimental to the aim of gender egalitarianism.[5]

Consider subsidized leave that provides partial wage replacement so a parent can stay home to care for a new child. Even when such leave is offered on equal terms to women and men, women are likelier than men to take it.[6] This is true for myriad reasons: Gender role attitudes have changed greatly over recent decades, but prevailing norms continue to favor women specializing in caregiving once caregiving needs arise, even if not to the exclusion of paid work. Social surveys show that "traditional" attitudes about gender persist, with a robust and widespread conviction "that women should work full-time before having children and after the children have left home, while they should work only part-time or not at all when they have children living at home."[7] Meanwhile, gendered socialization in upbringing prepares women and men for gendered specialization, even if not for such strict specialization as it once did.[8] Finally, straightforward household economic considerations make women's leave-taking, on average, less costly than men's: In part because many women choose less-well-paid jobs that offer flexibility for caregiving and in part because of cumulative effects on earnings potential of prior choices to prioritize caregiving, men on average face higher opportunity costs of leave-taking, both in terms of career progression and (where wage replacement is only partial) of forgone income.[9] Because women are likelier to use leave and other family-friendly workplace amenities and because patterns of behavior like leave-taking reinforce norms about such behavior, such amenities

---

[4] Lachance-Grzela and Bouchard 2010; Goldin 2021.
[5] See, for example, Zippel 2009; Blau and Kahn 2013; Bertrand 2018.
[6] Kleven, Landais, and Søgaard 2019.
[7] Kleven, Landais, and Søgaard 2019, 6. See also Gerson 2010; Bertrand, Kamenica, and Pan 2015; Parker 2015.
[8] See England 2010. See also Okin 1989.
[9] See, for example, Gornick and Meyers 2003; Kleven, Landais, and Søgaard 2019.

126 THE ANATOMY OF JUSTICE

have limited capacity to erode the gendered division of labor. In some contexts, they can even risk reversing hard-won progress toward gender equality.[10]

Basic income would provide income unconditional on caregiver status, and so it is not naturally thought of as a form of caregiver support. But because basic income also does not condition the benefit on labor market participation, it does *effectively* support caregiving. It increases the material standing of unpaid caregivers, and it can act as partial earnings replacement so that working parents can reduce their labor market participation. Like the dedicated caregiver support just discussed, then, basic income will plausibly increase women's share of caregiving work and reduce their participation in paid labor by weakening their financial incentive to stay in the workplace, or return to it, after a child is born. This raises a feminist worry about basic income. The worry does not depend on the (false, in my view) notion that caregiving work lacks value or that it is less valuable than labor market participation as a contribution to the cooperative scheme. What feminists might object to—and what I will object to later in this chapter—is the role basic income would play in reinforcing gender-norm-compliant behavior and thereby reinforcing gender norms about who *should* perform caregiving. Increased withdrawal of women from the workforce also affects employer behavior: If women are perceived as temporary workers destined to reduce or to exit employment when they become mothers or when their own parents or their spouse's parents are ailing, their perceived value as workers will diminish: Consciously or not, employers may see them as less fit for positions with growth trajectories or with implications for workplace stability and viability, less worth training, and less worth promoting. Insofar as basic income has these effects, it too can exacerbate the gendered division of labor and risk reversing progress toward gender egalitarianism.[11]

On the other hand, even as these policies risk entrenching gender norms, basic income could greatly benefit many women, both materially and otherwise. In part because they do the bulk of caregiving, women figure disproportionally among the poor for whom basic income arguably would make the most significant material difference. By lessening the material precarity of poor women, basic income could loosen the circumstantial binds which lead many poor women to take work that they regard as demeaning or which dissuade them from leaving abusive relationships. As its feminist champions have argued, basic income would also provide income for caregivers outside the formal labor market, thereby plausibly elevating the status of caregiving, easing the vulnerability of caregivers and their economic reliance on breadwinner partners, and increasing their bargaining power both within domestic relationships and, where relevant, in labor markets.

---

[10] Kleven, Landais, and Søgaard 2019.

[11] On the risk of basic income further entrenching gender norms, see Robeyns 2000, 2001; Bergmann 2004; Gheaus 2008. For a review of feminist arguments for and against basic income, see Robeyns 2000.

Effectively, basic income could ease the vulnerabilities associated with caregiving, even as it leaves intact or exacerbates its gender coding. These are distinctly feminist considerations to add to the general egalitarian considerations in favor of basic income. Alongside their reasons to oppose it, then, liberal egalitarian feminists apparently have reasons to support basic income.[12]

Barbara Bergmann considers this tradeoff by comparing universal basic income with an alternative approach to supporting citizens: a suite of Swedish-style welfare goods, which Bergman terms "merit goods," combined with narrowly targeted cash payments to those in need. Merit goods are goods to which everyone should have access, either on grounds of general public benefit or on grounds of the individual interests of the merit-good-holder. According to Bergmann, goods we should socialize on these grounds include high-quality schooling, healthcare, childcare, housing, and public transportation. Bergmann argues that modern economies do not have the capacity to generate enough revenue through taxation to provide merit goods *and* a universal basic income, and that the former—along with means-tested cash payments—should take priority. Part of her case invokes the setbacks to gender equality considered above: Because of its implications for gender norms and employer expectations, "the full-blown implementation of Basic Income schemes in the near future should not appeal to those for whom gender equality is an important goal."[13] Because *targeted* cash transfers do not risk driving large-scale gendered withdrawal from paid work and because in-kind benefits can be formulated to *disrupt* gendered behavior around work and caregiving,[14] Bergmann's Swedish-style welfare state seems preferable on gender egalitarian grounds. But this is not the end of the story, and insofar as we're evaluating Bergmann's argument without wishing away the current prevailing political ethos, one reservation in particular deserves an airing: It'll likely be harder to generate and sustain popular support for a means-tested cash transfer than for universal basic income, even if the former is combined with universal in-kind benefits. Perhaps a Swedish-style welfare state is preferable to a universal basic income in some respects, then, but it may yet be true that in our circumstances of injustice the former is politically infeasible in many places—for example, where needy would-be recipients of means-tested aid are stigmatized as "takers." And it may be true more broadly that basic income is a politically stabler way to support vulnerable citizens. If so, basic income may be preferable on (feminist) distributive egalitarian grounds.[15]

---

[12] On the benefits of basic income for women, see Robeyns 2000, 2001; Pateman 2004; Baker 2008; Elgarte 2008; Zelleke 2008. For a review of feminist arguments for and against basic income, see Robeyns 2000.

[13] Bergmann 2004, 116.   [14] See Schouten 2019.

[15] I don't claim to have audited all the considerations bearing on this case. Perhaps basic income has the advantage of avoiding unemployment traps, which occur when people lose benefits as they gain employment income. Means-testing might leave people without support they still need but for which they no longer meet eligibility requirements, or it might discourage them from taking jobs for

128 THE ANATOMY OF JUSTICE

While the comparative projected effects of a universal basic income and alternative social support policies continue to be studied and debated, what seems clear is that the effects will point in different directions and will fluctuate over time and across policy context. What's wanting, in addition to contextualized empirical projections, is a framework for ordering the moral importance of the various achievements and liabilities likely to be projected. We need a framework—a theory of justice—within which to understand the moral significance of the costs and benefits of the policies under consideration.

5.2 The Values at Stake: A Distributive Justice Assessment

Unsurprisingly given the kind of policy it is, normative analysis of basic income from a feminist and egalitarian perspective has largely focused on *distributive* considerations. We just saw that basic income could significantly benefit the least advantaged members of society, who in gender unequal societies are disproportionally women. The women who stand to benefit most from basic income are women with low earning capacity or low labor market attachment including full-time housewives, many single mothers, many women with disabilities, and many refugees and non-Western immigrants.[16] Basic income promises better financial standing and personal security for these women. These are clear gains at the bar of egalitarian distributive justice. A Swedish-style welfare regime might seem to promise many of these same distributive justice gains, but if means-testing cash transfers is stigmatizing, or if it makes the transfers politically untenable or unstable, or if in-kind goods are rejected by voters who prefer universal cash benefits, then basic income may be the best policy to realize these distributive justice gains all things considered, whether or not some alternative is better on its intrinsic merits.

Yet even as it promises certain distributive justice gains, basic income risks reinforcing gender inequality, and just like its projected egalitarian gains, basic income's projected (gender) egalitarian liabilities have been construed largely in terms of distributive egalitarian principles. In line with this distributive focus, much of the feminist criticism of basic income invokes the risk that it will fuel statistical discrimination.[17] Statistical discrimination occurs when employers (consciously or unconsciously) use aggregate group characteristics to make inferences about the likely behavior of employees, or prospective employees, about whom they know relatively little else.[18] Women's larger share of caregiving is

which they qualify. Other considerations surely bear on the case for basic income, but those sketched in the main text will suffice to show how the anatomy of justice can help.

[16] Robeyns 2000, 131.   [17] See for example Gheaus 2020, 5.
[18] Poeschl 2008; Gittell 2009; Ross-Smith and Chesterman 2009.

one such characteristic. Women are (known to be) likelier than men to have commitments to caregiving reduce their time available for paid employment; thus, women, and especially mothers, come to be perceived as less committed employees. In part because of this perception and the consequent hiring and promoting decisions of employers, women are less likely to occupy the most prestigious positions and they continue to earn less than their male counterparts even if they *don't* take time out for caregiving.[19] This apparently violates a widely accepted requirement of justice: equality of opportunity.[20]

So, basic income can serve egalitarian ends by improving the lot of the least advantaged, but it risks reinforcing the gendered division of labor and thus frustrating equal opportunity between women and men in competitions for scarce positions in labor markets and in politics. This way of framing the tradeoff might incline some to look for a resolution in Rawls's theory of justice. Because Rawls's theory lexically prioritizes fair equality of opportunity over the prioritarian difference principle,[21] it might seem to issue the judgment that the distributive justice costs of basic income are lexically more important than the distributive justice gains. But in fact, if Rawls's theory gives guidance in our case, it does so less straightforwardly than this first-pass gloss suggests. Most obviously, *both* distributive requirements in play are lexically secondary to the basic liberties principle, which is surely implicated in our case. More importantly for our purposes, Rawls's principles and their ranking apply in circumstances of full compliance and in reasonably favorable circumstances—including, for example, in circumstances where a basic needs principle is already met.[22] More broadly, Rawls's theory comprises normative principles that apply only within a particular range of circumstances. To see what guidance they provide outside that range, we need to consult the values or ideals those principles are formulated to realize. If the values apply even outside the specified range—for example, if benefitting the least advantaged matters even in circumstances of injustice—then an evaluative specification can help us where corresponding normative principles don't apply. But where we try to apply the normative principles directly outside their range of application, they can give the wrong answer: Whatever priority equal opportunity may have in a fully just society, it is implausible that it automatically wins the day in the actual, unjust circumstances we inhabit. In our circumstances, intuitively, benefitting the least advantaged matters more than it does when basic needs are already met—and more than equal opportunity in competitions for positions in the labor market.

---

[19] Glass 2004; Correll, Benard, and Paik 2007; Coltrane 2009; Zippel 2009.

[20] Making this case specifically about the debate over basic income, see Robeyns 2000, 2001; Gheaus 2020.

[21] Rawls 1999a, 52–4.   [22] See Rawls 1993, 7.

Anca Gheaus argues for a particularly strong version of this claim.[23] In our unjust society, she argues, "it is mostly better off women who have an interest in equal opportunities to positions of advantage"; and inequalities of opportunity for positions of advantage between advantaged women and men matter relatively little, or not at all, from the perspective of justice.[24] We therefore have little reason to care about the putative liability of basic income at the bar of equal opportunity, or even to regard it as a liability at all. If basic income would improve conditions for the least advantaged women, Gheaus argues, its distributive justice gains clearly outweigh its distributive justice cost of driving unequal opportunity.

Gheaus advances two arguments for discounting equal opportunity in this context: First, many of the positions in competition for which women are disadvantaged are positions that confer an unjustly large share of social rewards. Nobody has a right to such positions, Gheaus argues; thus, we ought to discount the value of equal opportunity to realize such positions. Second, in societies wherein most people are excluded from the positions in question, those who are competing for them generally already have had more than their fair share of opportunities. Nobody has a claim to more than their fair share of opportunities; thus, most women applicants to such positions do not have a claim to more opportunities for such positions than they have already had.[25] In short: equal opportunity is discounted as a moral liability in the case of basic income, either because the positions in question confer unjust rewards or because the women in competition for them already enjoy richer opportunities than justice allows. Gheaus concludes that, if the case for basic income is otherwise strong, egalitarian feminists should endorse it even if it sets back women's opportunities to attain positions of advantage.

I agree with Gheaus this far: In very distributively unequal societies, a benefit to the least advantaged has more moral value than a benefit (of equal magnitude) to the relatively more advantaged; and this is true even if the latter (and not the former) is a gain at the bar of equal opportunity. The case is stronger still when the least advantaged are not only *relatively* worse off, but very badly off by absolute standards as well. Easing the hardships of the very worst off simply matters more than equalizing opportunity in competitions for highly rewarded social positions. I think this weighting of priorities holds even when the least advantaged are considerably better off than they are now, but the case is clearest in our present circumstances, where improving the lot of the least advantaged means ameliorating the absolute bad of living in poverty. Indeed, I took it to be a

---

[23] Gheaus 2020.   [24] Gheaus 2020, 2.

[25] Gheaus allows that there is expressive dis-value when men vastly outnumber women in highly rewarded positions, but she argues that that dis-value can be addressed without realizing the more demanding ideal of equal opportunity in competitions for such positions. Gheaus 2020, 5.

provisional fixed point that, in circumstances like ours, eroding gender norms matters less than improving the plight of the most badly off.

Yet while I share that particular conviction, I think the distributive justice assessment of the tradeoff is too narrow. It misses a fundamental ideal of liberal egalitarianism that is not subsumed by principles of distributive justice but that in fact constrains our legitimate pursuit of those principles. Equal opportunity for positions of advantage between women and men is not all that is at stake in eroding the gendered division of labor. The previous section foreshadowed just what a focus on discrimination leaves out: Women's withdrawal from paid work risks entrenching or exacerbating gender *norms* that impose constraints and harms extending far beyond their effects on employer behavior, and certainly beyond their effects on employer behavior at the relatively advantaged end of the labor market. Because something more is at stake, it's distorting and reductive to hold, as Gheaus does, that "the main feminist complaint against care-supporting policies is that they will increase a kind of discrimination against women."[26] And this mistaken reduction is practically significant, because research increasingly shows that the explanation for the gender gap that persists in developed countries lies elsewhere than in employer discrimination.[27]

What more is at stake, I'll argue, is our realization of mutual respect. By the lights of this fundamental constraining value of liberalism, poverty amelioration remains the prevailingly morally important social aim. But mutual respect also impugns the gendered division of labor as currently manifested in our social practices. By surfacing this ideal, we can see clearly and accurately *why* promoting distributive equality by benefiting the least advantaged is our most morally urgent political end right now. And only by understanding the *why* can we correctly discern the evaluative facts even as circumstances change—including, hopefully, as our social arrangement gains legitimacy and the tradeoffs become a closer call.

5.3 Mutual Respect and Gender Egalitarianism

This section argues that liberal values weightier than distributive justice are at stake when it comes to gender egalitarianism; it concludes that gendered labor norms are a morally weightier liability of basic income than the distributive justice assessment of the case suggests. The anatomy of justice offers a different way of looking at the tradeoffs we confront. I begin by disputing the presumption that basic income's primary liability is a threat to equal opportunity at the high end of the occupational structure.

---

[26] Gheaus 2020, 5.   [27] See, for example, Kleven, Landais, and Søgaard 2019; Goldin 2021.

132　THE ANATOMY OF JUSTICE

One way to dispute this presumption is to argue that the distributional maladies of the gendered division of labor apply broadly: that the gendered division of labor undermines the fairness of competitions in which the less advantaged take part and harms less advantaged citizens in absolute terms as well. I think that this case can easily be made. The gendered division of labor sustains gender injustices across the population, frustrating equal opportunity among privileged *and* disadvantaged women. It sustains glass ceilings that constrain women at the top of the employment structure, *and* it accounts for the de-valuation of caregiving and the (partially consequent) feminization of poverty. It is for this reason that many feminists regard the institution of the family and its gendered division of labor as the "linchpin" of gender injustice.[28] If some labor market reform can dismantle the gendered division of labor, it can benefit women across the income distribution—even those outside of the formal labor market altogether.

This means that the distributive assessment sketched in the previous section is too narrow, even within the parameters of distributive justice. Not *only* privileged women stand to gain, distributively, from the erosion of gender norms. But I want to focus on a different way to dispute the notion that basic income's main liability from the perspective of liberal egalitarianism is its threat to equal opportunity at the high end of the occupational structure: not (only) to deny that the problems of distributive justice befall only those at the high end of the occupational structure, but to deny that basic income's liability with respect to gender egalitarianism is reducible to a problem of distributive justice in the first place.

Ultimately, we want our theorizing to shed light on practical questions about what we should do—like: Should non-parents be taxed to help defray the costs to parents of raising children, for example through subsidized parental leave? And: Should parental leave be arranged to incentivize equal parenting among cooperating domestic partners? In order to settle practical political questions about what we should do, we need to consult aspirational values about what ends we should ideally seek to bring about, and we need to consult the value considerations that constrain our political pursuit of aspirational aims. The anatomy of justice systematizes this natural thought. Distributive justice is an aspirational social aim. Questions of distributive justice are questions about what would make society fair, setting aside such considerations as the worry that in our circumstances, we cannot achieve a fair arrangement short of political intrusions that constitute objectionable government overreach. By casting fairness as aspirational justice, we accommodate this point that while circumstances matter to the question of how far we may go to equalize people's material conditions, the content of fairness does not vary so easily with circumstances.

---

[28] See Okin 1989, especially 173. See also Gheaus 2012.

To figure out what course of action has most value all things considered, we have to get it right about the relevant aspirational ideals, and we have to correctly discern the ways in which our pursuit of those ideals is constrained by political legitimacy. Legitimacy, I've said, concerns the permissibility of social arrangements and political intervention to pursue social ideals given the fact of reasonable disagreement about the ideals in question and the democratic conviction that reasonable disagreement about social ideals matters. In a liberal society, reasonable disagreement is inevitable. In a liberal *democratic* society, political interventions are regarded as exercises of shared democratic power. A liberal democracy seeks to exercise the shared power of citizens only in ways that respect the authority of each to live out a life of her own choosing—on my construal, only in ways that preserve mutual respect by complying with a justificatory reciprocity requirement. Liberal democratic legitimacy assesses the degree to which social arrangements and political interventions live up to this commitment. Some interventions, like protections for basic liberties, don't rely on democratic approval for their legitimacy. Standing in contrast are interventions necessary only to pursue *aspirational* social values. To abide by the reciprocity requirement, *those* interventions must be called for by a *political* conception of aspirational justice and approved by legitimate democratic processes. Such interventions must surmount these procedural hurdles because although they can *be compliant with* mutual respect, they are not *positively called for* by mutual respect the way protections for basic liberties are.

As the basic liberties have illustrated throughout, mutual respect positively calls for the pursuit of our shared interests that follow from the very project of finding fair terms of cooperation for a society of free and equal citizens. An idealized conception of citizenship can helpfully systematize these interests we share: Because we assume that the project of seeking fair terms of cooperation is not *futile*, we idealize citizens as capable of modulating their behavior to comply with principles of justice. Because we assume that we are seeking terms of cooperation for a pluralist society wherein individuals can be held accountable for the values they live by, we idealize citizens as capable of forming and rationally revising a conception of the good. Because we aim to specify conditions under which a just society can stably persist over time, we attribute to them an interest in protecting these moral powers of idealized citizenship.

From this characterization, we can infer still further interests of idealized citizenship. Most straightforwardly, there is a citizenship interest in protecting a prerogative for each actual citizen to pursue her conception of the good, free from state intrusion. This interest might be thought to generate a sort of liberal presumption against political intervention—the general justificatory burden political liberalism imposes. But the presumption is overridden whenever intrusion can be justified as an essential positive means of protecting other shared interests of citizenship. Intrusions justified in this way include protections for the basic

134 THE ANATOMY OF JUSTICE

liberties that we have a shared idealized-citizenship interest in protecting. Whether or not actual citizens actually endorse the protections in question, the idealization of citizenship licenses us to treat those protections as *in their interest*. That idealization systematizes the interests implied by a project we are all taken to endorse: finding fair terms of cooperation for a democratic society of free and equal citizens.

Reciprocity thus constrains the political strategies available to us for pursuing distributive justice or any other aspirational social end, and, itself underpinned by the ideal of mutual respect among free and equal citizens, reciprocity also positively requires that we recognize as reasons-giving those fundamental interests we share in common as citizens. The citizenship capacity to form and revise a conception of the good generates a strong interest in protections for the freedom to, for example, espouse a religion of one's own choosing or none at all. Similarly with the other basic liberties, with the prioritization of the basic liberties, and with the provision of the material necessities for the effective exercise of those liberties: Because shared citizenship interests demand that these conditions be secured, any society that fails to secure them violates the requirement of reciprocity—it violates the *mandatory shared reasons*, and thus the *invariant demands*, of mutual respect. In this way, the requirement of reciprocity takes some social arrangements off the table from the start. It is, as Rawls puts it, the "limiting feature" of a reasonable political conception of justice.[29] In these invariant demands of mutual respect, we find resources to ground a complaint against gender norms *as well as* against a great deal of distributive inequality.

One such resource is well known: We can criticize the gendered division of labor as a violation of invariant demands of mutual respect insofar as the norms that comprise the gendered division of labor cause or constitute a basic liberties violation. Some gendered practices clearly do constitute basic liberties violations: Forced prostitution should be an uncontroversial example. More mundane cases may implicate basic liberties as well: Perhaps the association of women with caregiving generates an obstacle to their candidacy for high public office. If so, then legitimacy might demand special protections for women's political liberties. This might involve elevating the status of caregiving and educating citizens to see that traditionally feminine work and traditionally feminine skills can be sources of qualification for public service. If such a social project is essential to protecting the basic political liberties of women, then omitting to undertake it is illegitimate.[30] Broadly, if the gendered division of labor undermines protection for women's basic liberties and if basic income exacerbates the gendered division of labor, this would be a morally far weightier liability than if the gendered division of labor

---

[29] Rawls 1993, 450.
[30] Remember, an illegitimate act or omission does not entail that a regime's mandates do not generate moral duties to comply or that it lacks authority to govern. These are distinct questions.

only sustained statistical discrimination. But, plausibly, we can adequately protect the basic liberties without fully eroding the gendered division of labor.[31] If that's right, then the basic liberties case doesn't yet show that the liabilities of basic income go beyond frustrating equal opportunity in competitions for jobs.

What about equal opportunity itself, *as a prerequisite for the effective use* of the basic liberties? For Rawls, recall, one condition on a reasonable political conception of justice is that it ensure for each citizen adequate "all-purpose means" to make effective use of her basic liberties.[32] According to Samuel Freeman, in order for a liberal political conception to satisfy the all-purpose means requirement, that conception must provide for, among other things, "fair equality of opportunity especially in education and training."[33] We might think, then, that the equal opportunity that Gheaus saw gender norms infringing—the equal opportunities of privileged women in competition for jobs at the top of the occupational hierarchy—is a condition for reasonablness, and thus a requirement for legitimacy.

That is not my argument. I agree with Freeman that *some* version of equal opportunity is a requirement for a reasonable political conception of justice. But notice his qualification: *especially in education and training*. Robust, fair equality of opportunity is an invariant demand of mutual respect, on my view, when it concerns crucial *developmental* opportunities. For example, given education's important role in modern democratic societies, equal *educational* oportunity is an invariant demand of mutual respect. Perhaps mutual respect also condemns *overt discrimination* across the occupational hierarchy, including condemning overt discrimination for positions that wouldn't even exist in a just society. And of course, some *aspirational* social value may favor robust equal opportunity even in competitions for unjustly privileged positions. But whatever else may favor it, robust fair equality of opportunity for positions at the top end of the occupational hierarchy is not among the invariant demands of mutual respect. It is not a condition on a reasonable conception of justice. Gender norms *are* a problem of legitimacy, we'll see, but not by way of their deleterious effects on privileged women's promotion prosects. On my view, those deleterious effects are not problems of legitimacy, even though unequal opportunities in education and in other domains are.

So, the norms comprising the gendered division of labor are not a problem of legitimacy as such because they constitute a basic liberties violation; nor are they a problem of legitimacy because they impede the part of fair equal opportunity that's called for as an invariant demand of mutual respect. If not by fueling discrimination or by constituting a basic liberties violation, how *are* gender norms objectionable by the lights of mutual respect's mandatory shared reasons?

---

[31] See Schouten 2019, especially chap. 2.   [32] Rawls 1993, xlvi, 6; see also 137.
[33] Freeman 2007, 402. Freeman cites Rawls 1993, lviii–lix.

136   THE ANATOMY OF JUSTICE

Christie Hartley and Lori Watson argue that political liberalism's criterion of reciprocity demands political interventions necessary to eliminate "pervasive social hierarchies that thwart the give and take of public reasons among free and equal citizens" and to ensure "the social conditions necessary for recognition respect among persons viewed as free and equal citizens."[34] The criterion of reciprocity makes these demands, on my way of framing things, because mandatory shared reasons decisively favor the shared citizenship interests that these demands protect: Idealized citizens cannot accept circumstances under which others fail to recognize and respect them as citizens; thus the criterion of reciprocity demands that society establish and preserve the conditions necessary for citizens to relate to one another in this capacity.

According to Hartley and Watson, this has implications for the gendered division of labor. They argue that, because caregiving is necessary for sustaining society over time and because we all have an interest in receiving care when we're children, caregiving should be regarded as socially necessary work for which we share responsibility as a society, and those who do it should not be disadvantaged when participating in various other social spheres central to citizenship. To allow otherwise is a failure to recognize caregivers as equal citizens. Because women's greater share of caregiving disadvantages them in labor markets, and because labor market participation is a dimension of social life central to citizenship, the criterion of reciprocity licenses political interventions aimed at dismantling the gendered division of labor.[35] If this argument is successful, then the gendered division of labor does indeed frustrate essential interests of idealized citizenship; and insofar as a policy like basic income is counterproductive by this metric, that constitutes a relatively more serious evaluative liability.

In previous work, I have argued that Hartley and Watson's politically liberal complaint against the gendered division of labor is flawed.[36] Surely there is nothing *intrinsic* to caregiving that entails that full-time caregivers will be, or be regarded as, second-class citizens. If caregiving were appropriately esteemed, caregivers would not need to supplement that role with significant labor market participation in order to stand as social equals. Imagine a society in which we recognize that caregiving is inadequately rewarded in the marketplace, and so we impose mechanisms to socialize the costs of remunerating it fairly. We rightly appreciate the indispensable social contribution made by caregivers, and their social status and compensation are made commensurate with that contribution. Without the (surely false) premise that caregiving on its own is an inherently inadequate basis for equal social standing, Hartley and Watson's argument lacks

---

[34] Hartley and Watson 2010, 8. Hartley and Watson draw on the concept of recognition respect as developed by Stephen Darwall. See Darwall 2009.
[35] Hartley and Watson 2009, 533–5, 2010, 17; Watson and Hartley 2018.
[36] Schouten 2015, 2019, 2023b.

resources to find fault with this arrangement. No hierarchy of breadwinning over caregiving relegates caregivers to second-class citizenship, and so we evidently have no failure to respect caregivers as equal citizens. Hartley and Watson argue that the failure of respect persists as long as caregivers face some opportunity costs in the labor market in virtue of their investment in caregiving. But it is a fact of life that investment in one domain imposes opportunity costs in others. To say that caregiving uniquely is not permitted to come at such costs is to treat it as distinctly unfit to underwrite equal standing on its own and to place undue importance on labor market participation as a requirement for equal standing in society. In short, once we rid their argument of its false premise, Hartley and Watson can't find fault with the non-hierarchical specializing arrangement imagined above.

And yet, I've argued, the gendered division of labor and the *injustice* of the gendered division of labor can persist in that imagined arrangement. If the institutionalized presumption persists that individuals will specialize as breadwinners or caregivers—if, for example, jobs continue to be structured as if on the assumption that workers have no significant caregiving responsibilities—and if individuals continue to be systematically socialized to specialize based on sex, then injustice persists. To put it roughly, I've argued that there is injustice not only in the hierarchical gendered "stacking" of traditionally masculine over traditionally feminine work, but also in the gendered "steering" of individuals into roles based on sex. The latter might persist even if we were to genuinely esteem caregivers commensurate with the importance of the work they do. Hartley and Watson's strategy does not equip us to impugn gendered steering, because it can find fault only with the hierarchy of paid labor participation over (private) caregiving.

So, if we dispense with the (false) premise that caregiving specialization is *always* hierarchical because it competes with labor market participation, then Hartley and Watson cannot impugn mere gendered steering. Dispensing with that premise, their strategy may yet diagnose a great deal of what is wrong with the gendered division of labor: The hierarchy of breadwinning over caregiving is certainly objectionable from the perspective of mutual respect, and for reasons including those that they invoke. The problem that I worry their approach does *not* address concerns the *social mechanisms that sustain* the gendered division of labor. This problem survives the elimination of relational and material inequality between caregivers and other social contributors. And once we identify the problem that afflicts even the hypothetical, gender-esteeming, non-hierarchical *but still gender-norm-sustained* division of labor I asked us to imagine above, we will see that it is a problem by the lights of mutual respect.

The problem lies in the steering of women and men into certain roles on the basis of a socially embedded assumption that one's sex rightly dictates the kind of work one does. The *source* of this steering—the socially embedded assumption that sex rightly dictates work specialization—is objectionable from

138   THE ANATOMY OF JUSTICE

the perspective of our mandatory shared reasons based on shared interests of citizenship. Let me briefly explain how I support that claim.[37]

The socially embedded assumption that sex rightly dictates work specialization is objectionable from the perspective of free and equal citizenship because that assumption is *inimical to autonomy*. A robustly autonomous person can reflect upon, revise, and reject the social roles and affiliations that fundamentally shape her life. Her choices in domains central to her identity are not effectively determined by normalized and institutionally embedded assumptions that members of a social group to which she belongs are best suited to populating particular roles. We can be autonomous in a gendered society like ours, because social norms don't *effectively determine* our choices. And while gender norms attach contingent social costs to the options we choose among, that alone is no problem from the perspective of autonomy; our options *always* carry contingent social and material costs. What *is* objectionable is the specific configuration of costs that gendered work norms sustain. Our social arrangement is inimical to autonomy because it *presumes that citizens will behave non-autonomously* in their cooperative domestic lives: that they will specialize into caregiving and labor market roles. It does not make gender-equal caregiving impossible, and it does not make autonomous choice impossible. But a social arrangement can affront a value even without making that value impossible to realize. Most notably, a social arrangement affronts a value when the arrangement is predicated on the assumption that citizens will not realize or aspire to realize that value.

Because our social arrangement institutionalizes the assumption that one's sex will dictate the work that one does, it presumes that citizens will not autonomously choose for themselves what configurations of paid work and private caregiving to undertake. Whether or not individual decision-makers within institutions make this assumption, the institutional design takes it for granted. Decent jobs are still designed as if for workers with "someone else at home," a caregiving specialist partner to see to the caregiving and other domestic work that needs to be done so that the supposed breadwinning specialist partner can devote himself fully to wage earning.[38] Employers impose demands on workers that are incompatible with workers simultaneously having serious personal caregiving commitments, and job success often requires living up to such demands. The institutionalized assumption that sex will determine work specialization also explains the dearth of support for substitute caregiving in the U.S.: Because we have assumed parents—mothers—will internalize the costs of caring for children, we have neglected to develop social solutions for meeting the needs of dependents or for sharing the costs. And that assumption explains increasingly labor-intensive parenting norms: Because we presume that the costs of caregiving will be internalized and borne by

---

[37] The following paragraphs summarize an argument from Schouten 2019.
[38] See, for example, Williams 2000.

VALUES TRADEOFFS UNDER INJUSTICE 139

caregiving specialists, we have increasingly expected caregivers to develop the skills and commitment that typify work specialization.[39]

The entrenched presumption of work specialization is a remnant or a manifestation of the longstanding presumption of *sex-based* work specialization. And that presumption makes it socially and materially costly to *avoid* specialization.[40] A social arrangement that institutionalizes such a presumption—and that in so doing makes it costly to arrange one's domestic life in defiance of that presumption—is an affront to autonomy. Accordingly, these institutional arrangements and social norms are objectionable on grounds of autonomy even though individuals can autonomously choose whether to comply with them or to flout them.

Now, the robust, *comprehensive* kind of autonomy that this argument invokes cannot straightforwardly justify political intervention in a society that abides by the criterion of reciprocity.[41] But there *is* a reciprocity-abiding case to make based on the *instrumental* value of comprehensive autonomy: It is instrumentally valuable for all of us when some citizens manifest behavior that is or that seems to be comprehensively autonomous. That's because in manifesting such behavior, they perform a kind of public service: They provide assurance to all of us that each of us *could* acquire the capacities involved in using our moral power to revise our conception of the good. Because some threshold of behavior manifesting comprehensive autonomy is a necessary condition for reasonable assurance that every citizen's capacity for a conception of the good is protected, comprehensive autonomy is instrumentally politically valuable by the lights of political liberalism. So, when our social arrangement burdens enactments of comprehensive autonomy or presumes that individuals will behave comprehensively non-autonomously, it burdens or impugns a way of life whose manifestation is politically valuable by the lights of political liberalism. That's a big problem: For our social arrangement to impugn a way of life whose exercise is instrumentally politically valuable is for it to jeopardize a kind of stability that we have a shared citizenship interest in preserving.

Insofar as citizenship interests favor stability, and insofar as stability is jeopardized when our social arrangement is predicated on an institutionalized assumption that affronts comprehensive autonomy, we have a mutual-respect-based grounding for gender egalitarian reservations about basic income: The gendered labor norms that basic income risks exacerbating run afoul of the requirement of reciprocity, which regulates society's pursuit of aspirational social values. Those norms are thus a direr political problem—and the liabilities of basic income correspondingly morally weightier—than if they merely disrupted equal opportunity in competitions for positions at the high end of the occupational structure.

---

[39] See, for example, Gerson 2010; Ramey and Ramey 2010. [40] See Goldin 2021.
[41] See Rawls 1993, xlii–xliii, for further discussion of the difference between political and comprehensive autonomy.

5.4 The Values Tradeoff and the Anatomy of Justice

Because considerations of liberal legitimacy take priority over concerns of aspirational justice, we have a weightier reason to erode the gendered division of labor than we would appear to have were we to look only at the demands of distributive justice. At a first glance, we might think this means that we should opt against basic income even at a high cost to distributive equality, because our reasons of legitimacy to erode the gendered division of labor trump our reasons of aspirational distributive justice to benefit the least advantaged by implementing some social support intervention like basic income. Consulting my provisional fixed points, I think that if the anatomy of justice did issue that ordering of priorities, we would have very good reason to reject the anatomy. But of course, it *doesn't* issue that ordering, because our reasons to benefit the least advantaged are themselves not *only* reasons of aspirational justice. The distributive reasons crucially at stake in the feminist debate over basic income figure among the invariant demands of mutual respect. To see this, we needn't even consult the ambitious argument from Chapter 3 to the conclusion that mutual respect imposes a baseline of distributive equality from which deviations require a permissible justification. We need only recall the conventional wisdom about the distributive demands of mutual respect: Each person is entitled to meet a robust threshold of distributive adequacy. Indeed, one way to understand the aspiration of universal basic income is precisely in terms of this distributive requirement for us to relate as equals: A generous basic income may act as a guarantor of material status adequate for equal standing. And equal standing is demanded, rather than being merely countenanced, by the ideal of mutual respect among free and equal citizens.

Under some circumstances, including ours, gendered labor norms are a problem of legitimacy. Under some circumstances, including ours, distributive inadequacy is also a problem of legitimacy. This means that considering the tradeoffs of basic income in terms of distributive justice is unhelpful insofar as we want our theorizing to provide guidance for the normative and evaluative questions we actually face. Though they don't use the terms of the anatomy, parties to the feminist debate over basic income do treat the considerations in play as aspirational in my sense of the term: They invoke values whose realization makes our social arrangement more just, not the regulative value that *adjudicates* other values and our political pursuit of them. Someday, when we have reformed or remade our social arrangement to comply as much as we can with the institutional demands of mutual respect, we *will* need to consider social policy like basic income in terms of aspirational values. Even now, doing so is not without practical significance. But theorizing about justice can *best* contribute to our thinking about the policy tradeoff that basic income presents by helping us to distinguish reasons supplied by aspirational ideals from reasons supplied by regulative ideals, and by helping us to discern the relative priority of different demands of mutual respect. That is just what the anatomy of justice aims to do.

Distinguishing the aspirational from the regulative and noticing all that the latter encompasses raises the stakes of the basic income tradeoff. If the sole or main evaluative liability of basic income were that it fueled stereotype threat and thus eroded equal opportunity in competitions for very advantageous social positions, our policy tradeoff question would be easy. However we locate the bad of the unequal opportunities that Gheaus described and rightly demoted, they are not problems of legitimacy, and so the importance of mitigating poverty clearly trumps. But what we have instead are projected gains *and* losses in terms of legitimacy. Basic income could help solve distributive legitimacy problems, but at the cost of exacerbating illegitimate gender norms. Even if the evaluatively favored course of action were clear, getting it right about the terms of evaluation is crucial to appreciating the gravity of the tradeoff.

So, the anatomy of justice correctly locates the principal tradeoff in the basic income case internal to legitimacy; it thereby raises the stakes. Does it also help us to *navigate* that tradeoff? Can it render principled verdicts on the relative moral importance of divergent citizenship interests? For example, can it render a principled judgment to match our considered conviction that poverty is the direr problem of legitimacy? I think it can.

To begin to see how, recall that in Chapter 3, I paused to address a point in my argument that might confuse: My argument presumes that the ideal of mutual respect supplies institutional reasons that go beyond reasons to secure the institutional prerequisites for interpersonal mutual respect to obtain. I illustrated with solidarity: We might say that solidarity favors condition X because, even though X is not *necessary* for securing solidarity, a society with condition X is in some other way more befitting a society that rightly esteems solidarity. So too with the surprising demands of mutual respect. Perhaps all that is necessary distributively to preserve interpersonal relations of mutual respect is robust distributive adequacy. But mutual respect gives us reason to do still more, distributively, than to secure the preconditions for its interpersonal instantiation. Perhaps all that is strictly necessary to preserve relations of mutual respect *vis-à-vis* gender is to erode gender hierarchies. But mutual respect gives us reason to do more to counteract gender norms than to render them non-hierarchical. We have reason to bring about the institutional conditions that a commitment to mutual respect calls for, where those might include conditions befitting a society that rightly esteems mutual respect, even if those conditions are not necessary to enable interpersonal mutual respect to prevail. A society without gender stacking *and* without gender steering is more befitting a society of mutual respect, as is one that respects a presumption of distributive equality in addition to an adequacy threshold. These are thus institutional conditions called for by a commitment to that value.

142   THE ANATOMY OF JUSTICE

One dimension of priority setting internal to mutual respect tracks this distinction between the institutional necessities for interpersonal mutual respect and the institutional conditions that mutual respect calls for though they aren't necessary to securing its interpersonal realization. Plausibly, the morally weightiest work of mutual respect is to secure the institutional preconditions for interpersonal mutual respect to obtain. Beyond that, securing institutional conditions befitting a society of mutual respect is a mandate of legitimacy, but a less urgent one than actually enabling a society of equals. This means that when we face policy tradeoffs that implicate mutual respect, we have more to gain—at least other things being equal—by securing the institutional preconditions for mutual respect than by pursuing compliance with mutual respect beyond that. Among the distributive demands of mutual respect, we get more value by ensuring that everyone has enough to stand as an equal than we do by equalizing above that threshold. That, intuitively, is just as it should be. On the other front, where gender norms truly prevent women from standing as social equals, rectifying this brings more value, by the lights of mutual respect and thus verdictive justice, than does eroding norms that do not inhibit interpersonal mutual respect but that are impugned by mutual respect on other grounds. So, while the stability problem I identified in my earlier work is a problem of legitimacy, it is a less urgent problem of legitimacy than, say, the feminization of poverty. A society without gender norms is one that better realizes mutual respect, but the full erosion of gender norms is not a precondition for citizens to actually stand as equals. Rectifying gendered material deprivation and vulnerability is.

If all that's right, then mutual respect's first orders of business are to realize an effective adequacy threshold and to correct for the subordination of women along dimensions crucial to citizenship—for example, by ensuring that women and girls enjoy equal developmental opportunities including job re-entry opportunities after time out of the workforce. Mutual respect's *second* orders of business are to correct for distributive equality condemned by its more robust distributive demands and to erode gender norms that are impugned by mutual respect but that do not prevent women from standing as equals along dimensions crucial to citizenship. The anatomy of justice can thus issue the verdict that our considered convictions call for: If basic income is the most effective way to generate gains by the lights of the actual preconditions for all to stand as equals, then it promises to yield a more valuable arrangement on the whole, and this is true despite the projected short-term losses with respect to the erosion of gender norms.

An incommensurability pluralism might also render this verdict, but it offers no principled explanation that we can invoke in public deliberation to justify particular policy upshots. And in foregoing principle, it offers no corresponding insights in other tradeoff cases. In contrast, the principled resolution offered by the anatomy of justice extends, as my earlier discussion of caregiver support policy foreshadows: If unconditional support for caregivers can effectively mitigate poverty and enable disadvantaged women to stand as equals, then that yields a gain on the whole, even if it further entrenches gender norms in the short run, and even if we could avoid that cost by opting for alternative forms of support.

Finally, by offering this principled systematicity and, relatedly, by clarifying the stakes of the tradeoff, the anatomy of justice helps us to identify further empirical questions we should ask. Bergmann offered a principled case for prioritizing a Swedish-style welfare state over basic income: Basic income will not ensure provision of crucial merit goods to all citizens, and it faces other morally important drawbacks like exacerbating gender inequality. At the same time, she acknowledged some extrinsic considerations that point the other way: Welfare states are subject to problems and abuses like inefficient provision or deteriorating funding over time. And means-tested social support can be a harder sell to parts of the electorate that wield the most power; they can thus be politically infeasible or unsustainable. On these grounds, we might reasonably favor basic income even acknowledging the merits of Bergmann's case. But understanding the stakes of the tradeoff should prompt us to scrutinize these extrinsic considerations. Gheaus wrote that her argument in defense of basic income "echoes the current popular debates between a feminism interested in the fate of poor and marginalised women and so-called 'boardroom feminism'."[42] Her argument, she says, comes down in support of the former. But the feminist liabilities of basic income aren't liabilities only of "boardroom" feminism. Gender norms are a legitimacy problem. Universal merit good provision plus means-tested cash transfers *could* realize legitimacy's adequacy threshold without exacerbating gender norms. In contrast, basic income is likely to help with one of these legitimacy problems at the cost of exacerbating the other. If these empirical projections are right, then before we accept an inferior policy solution on grounds of political feasibility or expediency, we should also inquire about the prospects for expanding the space of the politically feasible. What hangs in the balance is not a frivolous concern of "boardroom feminism," because gender norms concerning work and caregiving affect us all and bear on the legitimacy of our social arrangement.

When circumstances force tradeoffs, we have reason to prioritize the social policies we judge most effective at ameliorating the most egregious problems of legitimacy: in our case, poverty and gendered vulnerabilities that prevent disadvantaged women from standing as equals. But we should not lose sight of what is at stake in this tradeoff. Insofar as the gendered division of labor also constitutes a problem of legitimacy, social policy to erode it should be weighted considerably more heavily than if it generated only a problem of unequal opportunity among the most advantaged citizens. The gendered division of labor frustrates the fundamental liberal values that regulate our use of political power in pursuit of

---

[42] Gheaus 2020, 3.

144 THE ANATOMY OF JUSTICE

distributive justice. It is a less urgent problem of legitimacy than distributive inequality so long as those on the losing end of inequality fall below the threshold for standing as equals. But it comes to weigh equitably with distributive equality once the least advantaged are materially well enough off to stand in relations of social equality and effectively to exercise their basic liberties. I think that this is a quite high threshold of distributive equality, and, even above it, distributive inequality doesn't cease to be unjust. It doesn't cease, even, to be a problem of legitimacy, so long as the inequality is impugned by mutual respect's less recognized distributive demands. At that point, we have a tradeoff between two institutional demands of mutual respect neither of which is a prerequisite for actual interpersonal equal standing. Even here, we do not have incomparability. We can ask which is more strongly condemned by mutual respect: an obstacle to stability for the right reasons, or a failure (for example) to treat talent as morally irrelevant.

5.5 Reframing Gender Egalitarianism, Reframing Justice Theorizing

This reframing of the feminist debate over basic income has important upshots extending beyond basic income. The first concerns the framing of gender egalitarianism. Although gender equality is naturally thought of in terms of distributive justice, the gendered division of labor and gender norms broadly are not injustices that we should ameliorate only for the sake of equal opportunity among relatively privileged women and men at the high end of the occupational hierarchy. This is true first because gender norms sustain injustice that harms the least advantaged women as well as the most advantaged, because they sustain the very social attitudes that account for the de-valuation of caregiving work and the feminization of poverty. But gendered labor norms matter even apart from their frustrating equal opportunity at the high end of the social hierarchy *and* sustaining feminized disadvantage at the bottom: They matter because they frustrate essential interests of citizenship that liberals must regard as morally very important indeed. If some caregiver support policy threatens to exacerbate the frustration of those interests, we have a strong reason to prefer other forms of caregiver support that avoid the tradeoff in question.

A second upshot concerns priority questions broadly: Circumstances matter for the weighting of social aims. Using the language of the anatomy of justice, we might say that, in the abstract, problems of legitimacy are weightier than problems of distributive justice. But some distributive injustices *are* problems of legitimacy. And among those, some are worse problems of legitimacy than others. Similarly, whether a gender-correlated distribution of caregiving is a problem of legitimacy depends on whether it maintains social hierarchies and whether it is sustained by institutionalized social assumptions that are inimical to autonomy.

The values in the anatomy are invariant, but the reasons they supply and the political responses they call for depend crucially on circumstances. As we've seen, circumstances also make a difference to which tradeoffs we face in the first place. For instance, basic income risks setting back gender equality only because social norms influence the relative likelihood of women and men opting out of paid work in favor of caregiving if their financial circumstances allow it. Circumstances matter to the tradeoffs we face for a simpler reason, too: Social resources and political will are scarce, and this means we will always face opportunity costs. But all these circumstances are politically malleable, and one worthy target of political energy might be to ease the tradeoffs themselves. We should want to get it right about how dire the tradeoffs are, because the constraints we face and the tradeoffs they force are themselves a product of political decisions. Those decisions can be influenced by efforts to change the contingently shared reasons of legitimacy, for example by resisting the tendency to regard recipients of means-tested transfers as "takers." These points will matter greatly in the coming chapters.

Most importantly for now, I hope this discussion shows that the anatomy of justice has ample resources for rendering plausible and nuanced verdicts concerning the evaluative merits and demerits of social policy. Basic income is only one example. That caregivers are vulnerable and that caregiving is gendered constitute social problems that we can recognize as such by invoking the anatomy of justice, and the anatomy of justice does not reduce these to problems of distributive justice. Unlike on a pluralist intuitionism, principled evaluative discernment informs the tradeoffs and is available for public deliberation and extension across cases. Unlike on an approach that spotlights normative principles, the evaluative discernment the anatomy provides can guide us robustly across a range of circumstances, including when an invariant evaluative ranking gives rise to shifting priorities among normative mandates as circumstances improve. That discernment can underpin critical and normative arguments that we can invoke robustly across circumstances, in political deliberation, in movement building, and in democratic practice generally. Even concerning nuanced questions of priority setting, democratic practice needn't reduce to competing self-interest or competing moral intuition. The anatomy of justice shows that liberal egalitarian theory can find fault with the social norms comprising the gendered division of labor and with a great deal of distributive inequality, and that it can order faults so as to provide helpful, principled, and plausible guidance for political action in circumstances of injustice. This too will matter as we move into the final two chapters.

The Anatomy of Justice: On the Shape, Substance, and Power of Liberal Egalitarianism. Gina Schouten, Oxford University Press. © Gina Schouten 2024. DOI: 10.1093/9780191999772.003.0006

6
Liberalism, Culture, and the Subject Matter of Justice

"Liberal feminism" has at times been treated as something of an oxymoron. Here's Anne Phillips describing a particular stage in the development of feminist thought:

> Feminism re-emerged in the 1960s and 70s in a period when liberalism was shorthand for everything stodgy, unambitious, and dishonest: a glorification of rights and freedoms that paid scant attention to the inequalities of income and power; a discourse of complacency designed to keep things as they are. In that moment in history, to be radical was almost by definition not to be liberal: witness the familiar taxonomy from the 1970s that divided feminisms into their liberal, socialist, and radical varieties, and rather patronized the liberal sort.[1]

More recently, the most influential variants of liberalism have been *non*-complacent, at least insofar as they have been *principally* concerned with inequalities of income and power. Feminist and egalitarian liberals argue that, properly understood, liberal values underpin a deep critique not only of sexism but of racism and economic inequality as well. Beyond critique, these liberals draw from liberalism an egalitarian vision for a more just social arrangement and normative insights about how to get there from here. To take one prominent example, Martha Nussbaum emphasizes the critical and normative potency of liberalism: "In a world governed by hierarchies of power and fashion, this is still, as it was from the first, a radical vision, a vision that can and should lead to social revolution."[2] I agree with Nussbaum that properly understood, liberalism's vision is radical. And I find feminist, left-liberal defenses of liberalism to be largely satisfying. But to my mind, some feminist concerns about liberalism have not yet fully been answered. This chapter takes up one such concern: that liberalism is inadequate insofar as it focuses on the state and political institutions as the primary subject of justice theorizing.

---

[1] Phillips 2001.
[2] Nussbaum 1999, 79–80. See also Laden 2001 for a different approach, maybe better than that pursued here.

The concern is difficult to adjudicate for several reasons. For one thing, feminist critics of liberalism are not always clear about what kinds of entities they think normative political theory needs to judge, and on what terms, in order for that theory to be adequate. Nor are they always clear about what commitments of liberalism they think exclude the judgments in question. Meanwhile, liberals disagree among themselves about the so-called "primary subject of justice,"[3] and even with a specified subject matter, questions remain about the practical significance of any particular inclusion or exclusion. If liberal justice cares about the shape and behavior of political institutions, for example, then liberal theorists seemingly *must* care about social norms, because norms influence political participation and—in a liberal democracy—political participation influences the shape and behavior of political institutions. Conversely, political institutions affect social norms, patterns of individual behavior, and even the preferences we come to develop. In what sense, then, would it even be *possible* to restrict the subject matter of justice to political institutions? And what can a theorist who *does* impose that restriction say about culture?

This chapter aims to provide some clarity. The clarity gained shows state-oriented liberalism to be more plausible than critics take it to be, because it shows that a state-oriented liberalism can be a demandingly feminist and demandingly egalitarian liberalism. I draw on the anatomy of justice to make my case. To foreshadow: A state-oriented liberalism can do more critical and normative work than its critics give it credit for, because it must care about a wide range of social entities even if it conceptualizes justice so that, strictly speaking, only arrangements of political institutions can be unjust. I don't argue that we should all be state-oriented liberals. I only defend state-oriented liberalism against the criticisms on offer, clarifying the dispute in a way that serves largely to deflate it. I believe the criticisms should be taken seriously, and so I think the capacity of the anatomy of justice to address them not only deflates the dispute; it reflects favorably on the anatomy of justice.

Section 6.1 elaborates the complaint against state-oriented theorizing that I'll subsequently use the anatomy of justice to answer. Section 6.2 locates the variants of liberalism that must answer that complaint, and it previews the contribution of the anatomy of justice to my defense against it. Sections 6.3 and 6.4 comprise the substance of my defense, with section 6.3 assessing state-oriented liberalism's capacity to underpin radical feminist and egalitarian critique and section 6.4 assessing state-oriented liberalism's capacity to underpin radical normative guidance for reform. I conclude that the practical and theoretical limitations of state-oriented theorizing about justice have been overstated by critics. Section 6.5 briefly considers upshots for liberal feminism and for the anatomy of justice.

---

[3] Rawls 1999a, 6.

6.1 Culture and Ideology Critique

A common thread runs through much feminist opposition to liberalism: the conviction that liberalism's fundamental commitments render it overly status quo deferent. Reflecting on liberalism's commitment to preserving individuals' freedom to live their lives according to their own values, for example, Alison Jaggar writes that the "inevitable result" is "the tacit acceptance of conventional or dominant values."[4] Catharine MacKinnon describes "the strategy" of liberalism like this: "first to constitute society unequally prior to law; then to design the constitution ... so that all its guarantees apply only to those values that are taken away by the state; then to construct legitimating norms so that the state legitimates itself through noninterference with the status quo." On this strategy, "so long as male dominance is so effective in society that it is unnecessary to impose sex inequality through law ..., not even a legal guarantee of sex equality will produce social equality."[5] And bell hooks argues that feminisms underpinned by the liberal values of autonomy and social equality fail to appreciate that race and class oppression are "feminist issues with as much relevance as sexism."[6] These theorists' arguments are distinct, but they're united in the claim that liberalism's signature commitments render it overly deferent to the status quo—even when the status quo is patriarchal, sexist, racist, or economically unjust.

The most powerful feminist defenses of liberalism coopt these challenges for *internal* critique. Martha Nussbaum argues, against Jaggar, that liberalism *rightly* values agency, and that while some strands of liberalism have deferred overly to convention, they have done so *to the detriment of* agency and thus actually "did not follow the vision of liberalism far enough."[7] Addressing MacKinnon's charges, Nussbaum argues that liberalism can and should include a commitment to substantive equality. MacKinnon's criticism of certain legal decisions is apt, then, but not an apt criticism *of liberalism*.[8] In response to charges of neglect for race and social class, Nussbaum again spotlights the egalitarian and anti-racist credentials of liberalism's foundational normative commitments, which plenty of liberals historically have wrongly theorized in complacent, inegalitarian ways. She says:

> As a liberal feminist, one is also, by the entailment of one's very feminist position, also an antiracist ... and a supporter of fair equality of opportunity across classes. One's feminism is not mere identity politics, putting the interests of women as such above the interests of other marginalized groups. It is part of a systematic and justifiable program that addresses hierarchy across the board ...[9]

---

[4] Jaggar 1983, 189.   [5] MacKinnon 1989, 163–4.   [6] hooks 2014, 27.
[7] Nussbaum 1999; but see Phillips 2001.   [8] Nussbaum 1999, 68–9.
[9] Nussbaum 1999, 71.

LIBERALISM, CULTURE, AND THE SUBJECT MATTER OF JUSTICE   149

I think this aspiration to address hierarchy across the board is manifest in recent liberal feminist scholarship, including in the liberal feminist arguments reviewed in the previous chapter. That is not to say the aspiration is *realized*. But if the arguments are sound, this scholarship stands as a possibility proof: It demonstrates liberalism's radical potential to challenge the status quo. Yet doubts about the possibility of a truly feminist liberalism persist. Liberalism's feminist critics by and large don't press their criticisms of liberalism by engaging with liberal feminist scholarship that advances substantive normative and critical arguments. For instance, they do not proceed by showing that arguments like mine or Hartley and Watson's are unsound and thus cannot serve as arguments by demonstration for the radical potential of liberalism. Instead, they continue to invoke headline features of liberalism that *seem* as though they would limit its critical and normative resources. One concern in that mold centers the role of culture and ideology in sustaining injustice. Though she addresses her criticism not to liberalism *per se* but to "mainstream" normative political theorizing broadly,[10] Sally Haslanger's work on methods of social critique lends force to this concern. For her, we'll see, "ideology" refers to informal social practices, or parts of culture, that sustain injustice. In her critical case, Haslanger addresses structural commitments she attributes to "mainstream" normative political theory that she thinks render it inadequate for ideology critique. Those commitments include a focus on the state as the primary subject of justice. Since a restricted subject matter of justice is famously characteristic of liberalism and since sexist culture and ideology are primary culprits in the maintenance of gender inequality, liberal egalitarian feminists will need to answer this challenge.

While criticizing the "mainstream," Haslanger forwards her own favored method of social critique.[11] I don't want to disparage that method or Haslanger's many contributions to our thinking about justice. Liberalism needs ideology critique and social theory. But on my view, both our thinking about justice and our efforts to ameliorate *in*justice should be guided, too, by liberal normative theory. I'll argue that liberal theorizing has radical critical and normative potential in part *because* it spotlights the role of political institutions as tools for remediating injustice. I think Haslanger underappreciates that potential. But her criticism of state-oriented political theory yields insights that can help move us beyond the longstanding impasse between liberal feminists and liberalism's feminist critics: Because of Haslanger's vigilance about the role of culture in sustaining injustice, the challenge for state-oriented liberalism that I find in her work can help us to think well about what a framework for theorizing justice needs to equip us to say about culture, and what it needs to direct us to do, in order to be adequate.

---

[10] Haslanger 2017, 153.   [11] Haslanger 2021b, 2017, 2020.

150 THE ANATOMY OF JUSTICE

Haslanger is hardly alone in finding state-oriented justice theorizing to be inadequate.[12] At times, I will sharpen her complaints by allying her critical arguments with those of G. A. Cohen. In whole, the critical arguments I consider appear to surface two important shortfalls. First is a *diagnostic* shortfall: a divergence between the critical work that state-oriented liberal principles of justice can do and the critical work we should want our justice theorizing to do. Second is *normative* shortfall: a divergence between the political remedies for injustice that state-oriented liberal principles of justice can approve and the remedies we should want justice theorizing to approve. I argue that the diagnostic and normative limits of state-oriented theory are not as Haslanger and Cohen describe them. Perhaps there is yet some diagnostic or normative shortfall that we should deem an inadequacy of state-oriented theorizing. But I think that, once we see how robust a state-oriented theory's diagnostic and normative resources can be, critics will be hard-pressed to sustain a categorical rejection of all state-oriented theory as inadequate.

To appreciate the critical case that needs answering, begin with this simple and undeniably true observation: Justice can be undermined by sexist culture, where that sexist culture operates within the informal practices of a society and isn't sustained by overtly sexist law. The problem, says Haslanger, is that "within mainstream moral philosophy, normative analysis seems to focus on either individuals or the state. Culture is almost entirely left out of the picture."[13] Mainstream *political* philosophy evidently takes the latter focus: Following John Rawls, many theorists take the primary subject of a theory of justice to be the "basic structure" of society, or the structure by way of which "the major social institutions distribute fundamental rights and duties and determine the division of advantages from social cooperation."[14] Since Rawls is the primary target of Haslanger's general criticism of the mainstream, and since her criticism assails the restriction of normative appraisal to "the state," some defenders might want to correct the record: The Rawlsian basic structure is not limited to the state; it includes other major social institutions like the family. But in this chapter, for the sake of argument, I'll strategically elide any differences between "the state," "(social and) political institutions," and "the basic structure." I want to argue that the critical and normative shortfalls of basic structural liberalism are vastly smaller than Haslanger sizes them up to be, even on a *quite* stingy construal of the basic structure. Moreover, the crucial feature of the state *or* the basic structure for purposes of Haslanger's criticism is that it excludes culture. Even understanding the basic structure on Rawls's own, relatively capacious terms, then, culture-based challenges would still

---

[12] Feminists have long charged liberalism with an undue or exclusionary emphasis on the state or on formal social and political institutions as a means of promoting justice. See Jaggar 1983, 199–203; MacKinnon 1989. On the restrictiveness of the Rawlsian basic structure in particular, see also Mills 2007, 2018; Young 2011; Nuti 2022; Richardson 2023.

[13] Haslanger 2017, 153.   [14] Rawls 1999a, 6.

need to be addressed. Focusing only on the *state's* capacities makes my case harder, so it's not unfair to critics of—and may be more interesting to defenders of—basic structuralism.

Because culture is left out, mainstream political philosophy seems impotent for the purposes of *culture critique*—for criticizing social injustices like those sustained or constituted by gender norms concerning work and caregiving. In that case, "the question is not how a particular family should divide labor. Rather, it is a question about social norms, the formation of gender identity, and the socialization of individuals through particular practices of intimacy, sexuality, parenting, and economic cooperation."[15] These practices evidently are not sustained by an unjust basic structure (nor by individual moral failing), so we evidently need theory that equips us to critique social machinery beyond (individual fault or) institutional failing. State-oriented political theory thus seems inadequate, because to adequately address injustice, theory must assess culture and not only formal institutions (or individual behavior).[16]

So, Haslanger is principally concerned with methodology for critique of culture, and she finds mainstream theorizing inadequate in part due to its focus on the state.[17] Or, to use the term she favors for unjust culture, she argues that a focus on the state as the primary subject of justice renders mainstream political theorizing inadequate for critiquing and addressing *ideology*. For Haslanger, "ideology" is pejorative by definition; and its primary unit of analysis is "culture" or "cultural technē," which is a "network of social meanings, tools, scripts, schemas, heuristics, principles, and the like, which we draw on in action, and which gives shape to our practices."[18] Social critique is the work of criticizing collections of social meanings as ideological: as cultural technē gone wrong. Culture can go wrong—it can create or sustain injustice—either by organizing us in unjust ways or by preventing us from seeing well what is really of value.[19] That some piece of culture is ideological, for Haslanger, means that it functions, in its operative context, to create and sustain injustice and oppression.[20] Haslanger's conception of ideology is distinctive, both in terms of the social entities that can rightly bear the designation and in terms of the negative evaluation that it denotes: On her view, not only beliefs or forms of social consciousness but *aspects of culture broadly* can be ideological, and they can be ideological in virtue not only of their

---

[15] Haslanger 2020, 8.   [16] Haslanger 2020, 1; see also 2017.
[17] E.g. at Haslanger 2017, 168, 153, 2020, 1.   [18] Haslanger 2017, 155–6, 2021b, 26–7.
[19] Haslanger writes: "An ideology is a cultural technē 'gone wrong.' It prevents us from recognizing or creating forms of value, and/or, organizes us in unjust ways. This account of ideology is functionalist, pejorative, but not doxastic. It is functionalist because the evaluation of a technē as ideological depends on how it functions in a context; it is pejorative because, in being ideological, it functions to create or sustain injustice; and it is not doxastic because a cultural technē is not a set of beliefs, but is, rather, a set of public meanings (though some parts of it may be internalized as beliefs and other attitudes). The cultural technē both provides resources to interpret and also shapes the material world." Haslanger 2021b, 2.
[20] Haslanger 2017, 2021b.

152   THE ANATOMY OF JUSTICE

epistemic consequences but also by sustaining unjust arrangements more directly.[21] Haslanger's implied criticism of state-oriented normative theory is correspondingly broad. She claims that because ideological culture contributes to injustice, state action is insufficient to secure justice and "our political efforts (and the normative inquiry that guides them) should not be focused entirely on the possibilities of state action and other policy changes."[22]

Beyond gender norms, Haslanger's argument draws on the U.S. Supreme Court case *Brown v. Board of Education* and subsequent legislative and judicial attempts to de-segregate racially segregated schools. She observes that racial achievement gaps and racial educational segregation persist now despite the court's de-segregation orders in the wake of the 1954 *Brown* decision. These racial achievement gaps are sustained, among other things, by patterns of residential segregation, which persist even in the face of court-mandated de-segregation of schools. After *Brown*, Haslanger argues, the state intervened "in an attempt to improve the economic and political position of the subordinated"; but collections of social meanings—ideological culture—mediated the space in between social policy and individuals' response to that policy in such a way as to make the policy fail: Injustice persists because of oppressive culture even when that injustice isn't sustained by state action.[23] Indeed, injustice persists even when the state acts in ways that attempt to correct for the injustice: "At the heart of these patterns of racial injustice is a structure of social relations that is ideologically sustained in spite of legislative, judicial and individual efforts to change it."[24]

We might wonder what these particular legislative and judicial efforts can prove about the prospects for reform through state effort generally. The failure of any isolated attempt to mitigate injustice doesn't show that state action as such is impotent, particularly when that attempt is flawed or undermined by state action at another level. We'll return to this. For now, we can get Haslanger's point off the ground with a fairly mundane observation: Ideological culture clearly contributes to (sustaining) injustice. But following Rawls, liberal justice theorizing tends to treat arrangements of social and political institutions as the primary subject of justice. Haslanger's point that ideological culture lies at the heart of injustice seems to challenge such theorizing: If in focusing on institutions, liberalism neglects culture, and if culture lies at the heart of injustice, then liberalism is an inadequate framework for theorizing injustice.

---

[21] See, for example, Haslanger 2012, 18, 413, 2017, 159–60, 2021b, 23. For a construal of ideology on which "ideological" is primarily predicated of beliefs or forms of social consciousness, see Shelby 2003, 157–60. For a construal which is (I think) distinct from both Haslanger's and Shelby's, see Mills 2017, 79.

[22] Haslanger 2017, 150; see also 2012, 16.   [23] Haslanger 2017, 155.

[24] Haslanger 2017, 152.

6.2 Varieties of Liberalism and the Basic Structural Focus

State-oriented theorists of justice are perfectly well positioned to countenance a wide array of normative claims and a wide array of value-laden descriptive claims about a wide array of social entities. Some piece of culture or a social practice may be *racist* or *sexist* or *patriarchal*, and those designations themselves carry condemnation. Similarly, individual behavior can be racist or sexist. State-oriented liberals needn't and shouldn't think that state-oriented principles of justice capture all social normativity. For this reason, *some* of what Haslanger says simply misfires, even when applied to the most abstemious of liberalisms. For example, state-oriented liberals can agree with Haslanger that "political efforts (and the normative inquiry that guides them) should not be focused entirely on the possibilities of state action and other policy changes."[25] Many liberals focus on the state; Haslanger focuses on culture; both could think the other contributes something important to social and political normativity.

The wrinkle for liberals comes when we ask about the terms of evaluation: about what things certain liberals regard as directly compelled by principles of justice. As we've seen, Rawls applied his principles of justice primarily to the basic structure of society. Principles of justice do also judge individual behavior, but only derivatively: We are each required by justice only to do our part in supporting or bringing about a just basic structure. To illustrate, consider Rawls's difference principle, which favors the arrangement of social institutions within which the worst off are better off than under any other arrangement. The difference principle clearly encodes special concern for the least advantaged, but it doesn't ask *individuals* to act to benefit the least advantaged *directly*. On the contrary, the difference principle asks individuals only to support and comply with (or to support the formation of) the arrangement of political institutions that's favored by the difference principle.[26]

Haslanger's challenge clearly needs response from liberal theorists who follow Rawls in regarding the arrangement of social and political institutions as the primary subject of justice. But disputes about the restriction of justice to institutions arise among liberal theorists just as they arise between liberals and their critics. Beyond arguing that *culture* should be susceptible to condemnation at the bar of justice, some liberal critics of the Rawlsian basic structure restriction argue that a theory of justice should judge individuals' behavior, not only derivatively but even when that behavior has no bearing on whether political institutions are just. Following G. A. Cohen, these critics tend to focus on two kinds of behavior: "market maximizing," the behavior of economic agents who demand incentives

---

[25] Haslanger 2017, 150.   [26] Rawls 1999a, 293–9; see also 99, 154, and 415.

154   THE ANATOMY OF JUSTICE

to exercise talents in socially valuable ways,[27] and "housework shirking," a too-narrow label for gender-norm-sustaining choices domestic partners make about how to share out the work of income generating and caring for dependents.[28]

The primary argument for including such behavior in the direct subject matter of justice draws on an observation about how behavior relates to culture and what it functions to do: Market maximizing and housework shirking comprise patterns of behavior that sustain *social norms* that profoundly impact the lives of both those who participate in them and those who want to defect. Referring to a culture or "ethos" of justice, Cohen argues as follows: "To the extent that we care about coercive structure because it is fateful with regard to benefits and burdens [of social cooperation], we must care equally about the ethos that sustains gender inequality and inegalitarian incentives."[29] And because individuals can directly help or hinder the goals of justice through their behavior—for example, by contributing to a culture of material acquisitiveness that makes things worse for the least advantaged—individual behaviors should not be beyond the direct reach of principles of justice.

So, important strands of liberalism are animated, just as Haslanger is, by the conviction that culture matters deeply to the justice of a society;[30] and some infer from this that culture and individual behavior can be unjust. This means that only *some* liberals need answer Haslanger's inadequacy charge against state-oriented theorizing. Let's distinguish three pieces of social machinery to which we might apply critiques and demands of justice: institutional arrangements, norms or culture, and individual behavior. Call theorists "conceptually permissive" who are happy to subject all three things—individual behavior, culture, and institutions—to demands of justice. Cohen is conceptually permissive. Now notice that while Cohen moves from arguing that culture impacts the goals of justice to inferring that *individual behavior* can be (non-derivatively) unjust, we *could* stop at culture.[31] Call theorists "conceptually moderate" who would subject institutional arrangements and norms or culture, but *not* individual behaviors, to demands of justice.[32] Haslanger often seems motivated by the view that culture can be unjust and that culture is not reducible to individual behavior.[33] Conceptually moderate liberalism seems well positioned to accommodate that view. Finally, still other theorists, like Rawls, are what I'll call "conceptually

[27] Cohen 1992, 1995, 2000; Murphy 1998.
[28] Okin 1989, 1994, 2005; Lloyd 1994; Nussbaum 1999; Neufeld 2009.   [29] Cohen 2008, 138.
[30] Cohen himself is only *arguably* a liberal (see, for example, Cohen 2008, 10, 12). But see, in addition to others cited in the paragraph above, Allen 2004, 138; Chambers 2008, 2017, 190; Schemmel 2021.
[31] But see Cohen 2008, 145–6.
[32] I read Christian Schemmel as developing a culturally moderate liberal relational egalitarianism in Schemmel 2021, for example at 116, 165, and 195. See also Young 2011.
[33] See, for example, Haslanger 2012, 20, chap. 11. But also see Haslanger 2020, 1, where she clarifies that the "site" of social critique includes individuals and the state.

stingy": They subject only institutional arrangements to direct demands of justice. *Individuals* act unjustly—and *culture* is unjust—only derivatively: when that behavior or that piece of culture undermines (the formation of) just institutions.

So, conceptually permissive liberals, conceptually moderate liberals, and conceptually stingy liberals take opposing positions on the question of how far the demands issued by principles of justice extend: Do principles of justice regulate and condemn only institutional arrangements, or also culture and individual behavior?[34]

The anatomy of justice sheds light on this disagreement. The first step toward illumination is to notice that the disagreement arises *downstream of* the anatomy. Recall that verdictive justice ranks social arrangements according to their realization of political value—of the things that matter from the perspective of justice. Recall too that the amount of political value realized by a social arrangement is indexed to the circumstances of the society so arranged, including to facts about patterns of individual behavior, culture, and history. For example, in a society without a racist history, a political regime that prohibits racial preferences in hiring might realize more political value than a regime that permits such preferences. But in a society *with* a racist history, the reverse might be true, even holding fixed all other institutional features. We might better realize the values of mutual respect, distributive fairness, and/or community if we act to address ongoing and structural effects of racism, for example by implementing some degree of affirmative consideration for members of targeted social groups in hiring and admissions. As I've emphasized throughout, different circumstances call for different institutional configurations and political practices to realize a constant set of values of justice.

Now suppose a conceptually permissive liberal, a conceptually moderate liberal, and a conceptually stingy liberal walk into a bar. Sitting down to talk about justice, they agree on all the values of justice and all the facts about the relative importance of those values. They agree, say, that the anatomy of justice captures the truth about aspirational political values and political legitimacy, and they agree fully on the ranking of social arrangements that verdictive justice gives. Since our three liberals in the bar all agree on the anatomy of justice, they agree for example that distributive inadequacy is a problem of legitimacy and that distributive inequality is always a problem of fairness. They agree with both Haslanger and me that the gendered division of labor makes our current social arrangement worse with respect to (verdictive) justice: that our social arrangement realizes less (verdictive) justice than it could because of "the social norms, the formation of gender identity, and the socialization of individuals

---

[34] Do the parties accuse each other of making a *conceptual* mistake? Only sort of: Here unlike in earlier chapters, the disagreement under consideration is not about the concept "justice." I think we *can* understand the disputants as disagreeing about the concept "principle of justice," but I wouldn't fight for that characterization. I use the modifier "conceptual" mainly to set up the point that stingies, moderates, and permissives can agree on much *of substance*.

156 THE ANATOMY OF JUSTICE

through particular practices of intimacy, sexuality, parenting, and economic cooperation."[35] Our three liberals in the bar can therefore agree on quite a lot about justice, despite being starkly at odds on the question of what social entities normative principles of justice judge.

Their *disagreement* arises only when we ask about apt terms of condemnation and prescription. Our conceptually permissive liberal in the bar may think that individuals behave unjustly insofar as they comply with the practices and norms that comprise the gendered division of labor; that those norms and practices are unjust; and that the state acts unjustly insofar as it omits to disrupt them. Our conceptually moderate liberal might say that gender norms and gendered institutional arrangements are unjust, but that individual behavior that (directly) sustains those norms cannot be so impugned. She agrees with her more permissive companion that individual behavior makes a social arrangement *less valuable by the lights of what matters for justice*, because that behavior makes realizable only a lower range on the ranking of verdictive justice. But she thinks such behavior is ineligible to be impugned as unjust. Finally, our stingy liberal might think that political institutions act (omit) unjustly when they fail to interrupt the norms comprising the gendered division of labor, but that the norms themselves and the behaviors that sustain them cannot be so regarded. *She* agrees with *her* more permissive companions that norms and individual behavior influence the range of verdictive justice we can access, and so can make a social arrangement less valuable by the lights of justice. But she thinks *both* individual behavior and cultural practices are inapt for being impugned as unjust.

The anatomy of justice's key contribution to this debate is to illuminate this possibility that liberals across conceptual camps can agree on so much of substance. It excavates the conceptual space within the evaluative underpinnings of normative principles to make the possibility vivid, and it provides theoretical resources to talk about the places of agreement. But the possibility of extensive substantive agreement across these three camps is not an exotic point: After all, Cohen and Rawls—conceptually permissive and conceptually stingy respectively—agree in large part about *what things matter* from the perspective of justice. Their *disagreement* concerns the particular *form* of social critique and normative recommendation that's derivable from those things that matter: It concerns which entities are judged directly by principles of justice. Similarly, our three liberals in the bar agree, we've supposed, about *what matters* for justice. And they agree about how much each thing matters relative to other things that matter. Their disagreement arises only when we ask about apt terms of condemnation and recommendation: about which social entities are required directly to promote the things that matter for justice, and which are *unjust per se* for failing on that count.

---

[35] Haslanger 2020, 8.

Just as those within different conceptual camps can agree on quite a lot about justice, those within the *same* camp can *disagree* about a lot. Both a liberal and a staunch critic of liberalism can be conceptually permissive about justice. Within liberalism, too, permissives can disagree with permissives, moderates with moderates, and stingies with stingies about *which* behaviors, norms, or basic structures really are unjust. Haslanger's charge of structural inadequacy against state-oriented theory threatens to undermine all and only conceptually stingy theorizing. The crucial question for our purposes in this chapter, then, concerns the substantive costs of conceptual stinginess: What critical and normative work is stingy liberalism left unequipped to do by virtue of restricting the subject matter of justice to political institutions and institutional arrangements? What data points about justice and injustice is it structurally ill-fit to accommodate? I consider this question on behalf of the liberal egalitarianism that the anatomy of justice aims to develop. To what extent can a conceptually stingy advocate of the anatomy accommodate the extensional data points that egalitarian and feminist critics of the political institutional focus think stinginess sets beyond reach?

6.3 What Can Stingy Liberal Justice Impugn?

Let's first consider stingy liberalism's *diagnostic* adequacy: Does stingy liberalism's focus on the state as a subject of (in)justice prevent it from doing crucial diagnostic or critical work in identifying injustice? The feminist or egalitarian case against stingy liberalism invokes data points that critics like Haslanger and Cohen think stingy theorists can't accommodate. To start, recall the mundane observation that culture contributes to sustaining injustice. This observation is enough to raise questions about stingy liberalism's adequacy: If culture can sustain injustice but stingy liberals can't deem culture unjust, how can their theories be adequate? For example, if the basic structure restriction renders Rawls's theory unable to deem culture unjust, how can that theory guide us when culture functions to sustain injustice?

The observation is enough to *raise* the questions, but it's not enough to answer them. While stingy liberals will deny that culture can be unjust, they easily can allow that culture *creates and sustains* injustice. To assess its diagnostic adequacy, then, let's examine the terms on which stingy liberals *can* find culture and individual behavior at fault.

First, as already noted, stingy liberals can accommodate social theoretic claims that a social practice or piece of culture is *racist* or *sexist*, or that (some of) those who participate in racist or sexist practices are racists or sexists. Justice doesn't encompass all normativity or even all *political* normativity, and injustices are not the only wrongs. These terms and others can carry clear moral condemnation and a clear call for reform. Of course, when it comes to wrongs and bads like

158   THE ANATOMY OF JUSTICE

racism and sexism, we often do think in terms of justice. Stingy liberalism can accommodate this, too. A stingy liberal operating with the anatomy of justice can appreciate the myriad ways in which cultural practices and individual behavior lead to less valuable social arrangements by the lights of verdictive justice. A culture of materialist consumerism can make the least well off worse off than they'd be if a different ethos prevailed. A racist or sexist culture can undermine the equal standing of women or people of color and is plausibly corrosive to verdictive justice in other ways as well. However we analyze designations like "racist" or "sexist," stingy liberals can use the values comprising verdictive justice to substantiate these condemnations of culture or individual behavior without calling culture or individual behavior *unjust per se*. A stingy liberal feminist can regard her uncle as a sexist or a racist when he makes a deplorable remark at Thanksgiving, and she can regard the culture that emboldens him as sexist or racist as well. She can defend these claims by showing how patterns of such behavior impede our realization of a more valuable span of verdictive justice. Stingy liberals only deny that these charges translate automatically to charges of being *unjust per se*.

Second, conceptually stingy liberals can and should attend to the ways in which culture and individual behavior affect political institutions. For Rawls, while justice doesn't ask individuals to work to further the values of justice directly, it does require individuals to support and comply with a just basic structure, or to work to bring it into being. So, while any moral mandate to benefit the worst off *directly* isn't a demand of justice, justice does condemn individuals who omit to act to contribute to building and supporting *institutions* that optimize the position of the least well off. And, when a racist uncle's deplorable remarks contribute to social practices that prevent adequate institutional protection for the equal political enfranchisement of people of color, that uncle acts unjustly by failing to support just institutions. In short, when individual behavior affects institutions, that behavior can be condemned as *unjust per se*. And even when individual behavior *doesn't* affect institutions, it can be condemned as showing a deficient sense of justice, if an effective sense of justice requires embracing the institutional principles of justice *and their major justifications*.[36] Since any plausible principles of justice will owe their justification in part to the moral or political equality of all citizens regardless of race, racist attitudes and behaviors will generally manifest a deficient sense of justice in this way.

Third, stingy liberals can and should attend to the other direction in the interaction: to the ways in which political institutions influence and *can* influence culture or behavior. While stingy liberals cannot call racist or sexist or materialist culture "unjust," they can say that *institutions* are unjust when those institutions fail to do their part to reform racist or sexist or materialist culture.

---

[36] See Shiffrin 2010.

LIBERALISM, CULTURE, AND THE SUBJECT MATTER OF JUSTICE   159

So, a conceptually stingy liberal feminist might say that while gender norms are not themselves unjust, institutions are unjust insofar as they fail to erode those norms—for example, by incentivizing norm-transgressive behavior to reform norms over time. She can issue this judgment on the grounds that the norms in question impede our realization of a more valuable span of verdictive justice. We'll see that this potential of political institutions to target norms is a powerful source of diagnostic capability for the stingy liberal.

Finally, just as stingy liberals can issue the critical claim that *institutions* are unjust insofar as they omit to reform social norms that impede our realization of more value by the lights of verdictive justice, so too can they issue corresponding critical diagnoses of the *norms themselves*: They can critique some norm or social practice, or its constituting behaviors, as *justice-impeding*. Here again, stingy liberals can issue such charges on grounds that norms, social practices, and individual behaviors influence the span of verdictive justice that a society is able to realize. When they do so by obstructing a more valuable range, stingy liberals can diagnose those norms and practices, not as *unjust*, but as justice-impeding or as calling for rectification as a matter of justice. A racist or sexist culture that emboldens the despicable uncle is justice-impeding and calls for rectification as a matter of justice. The devaluation of caregiving and the association of women with devalued work are justice-impeding and call for rectification as a matter of justice. And, more broadly, the myriad social practices that allocate power unequally along lines of class, race, and gender are practices that call for rectification as a matter of justice.

The key to understanding these diagnostic capacities of stingy liberalism is to notice a possibility that the anatomy of justice elucidates: A piece of social machinery like a cultural practice might lessen the degree to which our social arrangement realizes justice without being *itself unjust*. When stated plainly, this possibility can seem bizarre or even incoherent. It is neither. The need to put food on the table may lessen the extent to which there is beauty in the world, because the need to put food on the table limits the time which those of us who aren't professional artists can devote to art-making. The need to put food on the table might be regrettable or condemnable on that basis. But the need to put food on the table is not *ugly* by virtue of lessening our realization of *beauty*. The imperative to protect the vulnerable may limit the extent to which there is mercy in the world, because some protective practices might be ineliminably punitive. But the imperative to protect the vulnerable is not *vicious* by virtue of lessening our realization of *mercy*. Whether it is regrettable or condemnable is a substantive question. Similarly, some social practice can lessen the extent to which we realize verdictive justice without thereby being *unjust* by the lights of a set of normative principles of justice inferred from the anatomy of justice. Whether that practice is condemnable on other terms and how we should act on it are distinct substantive questions.

160 THE ANATOMY OF JUSTICE

The anatomy *illuminates* this possibility, but it's not uncharted territory. A great bulk of left-liberal feminist scholarship, including the contributions reviewed throughout this book, could leave entirely open the question of which pieces of social machinery can be *unjust per se*. This scholarship examines the ways in which and the grounds on which certain social practices call for rectification as a matter of justice. These practices include gendered caregiving and labor market participation, pornography, prostitution, marriage, and religious exemptions from equal protection statutes.[37] The scholarship considers promising levers of rectification and asks of these levers which constitute permissible exercises of political power. If we read these contributions through a conceptually permissive lens, we might read them as concluding that the practices in question are *unjust*. If we read them through a stingy lens, we'll read their conclusion differently: The practices call for rectification as a matter of justice because they prevent us from realizing some of what matters from the perspective of justice; and *institutions* are unjust insofar as they fail to do what they can to provide or induce or incentivize the rectification in question. Because the critical upshots diverge so subtly, a reader need never know whether the author would limit the purview of justice's direct condemnations beyond the limits imposed by the substance of what matters itself—that is, by constraints of legitimacy. For example, stingy or not, the substance of legitimacy tells us that we mustn't criminalize housework shirking. How we might act politically on housework shirking short of criminalizing it and when individual shirkers act wrongly or are to blame are matters of substantive disagreement among liberal feminists. The terms on which we condemn that behavior or the culture it sustains take a back seat, in these discussions, to questions of when and how individuals should act otherwise and whether and how institutions can induce them to do so.

In large part, then, contemporary liberal feminist arguments proceed without any clearly discernible commitment to or against stinginess. This fact gives some reason to doubt that stinginess comes at any great substantive cost. But the force of this point will seem to some readers to cut *against* stinginess. I've been suggesting that the critical divergence between stinginess and permissiveness, with respect to culture, comes down to a difference between impugning culture as *unjust* and impugning it as *calling for rectification on grounds of justice*. But if the substantive implications of stinginess are so minimal, why not just abandon the commitment that forces all those extra words?

So far, we've focused on the set of data points that critics of stinginess emphasize in their criticisms: data points that stinginess (merely) appears not to accommodate. But stingy liberals reserve "unjust" for institutional (in)action in order to

---

[37] Beyond the standing examples of Nussbaum (1999), Watson and Hartley (2018), and Schouten (2019), see also Brake 2012; Watson 2015; and several of the feminists writing on basic income discussed in the previous chapter, just for a sampling.

LIBERALISM, CULTURE, AND THE SUBJECT MATTER OF JUSTICE 161

accommodate a different set of data points, which some critics of stinginess ignore: We should be able to have a demandingly feminist, demandingly egalitarian theory of justice without condemning as unjust every behavior or bit of culture that disrupts equality. In our circumstances, inequality is ubiquitous, and because of that, some patterns of perfectly mundane behaviors obstruct the path toward rectification. A lot of that behavior is rightly subject to moral condemnation. But nobody should adopt the view that any norm of behavior is *unjust* if that norm or behavior *fails to optimize with respect to justice*. Yet that's just what normative principles of justice direct institutions to do.

To illustrate, recall the Rawlsian difference principle: For Rawls, justice favors the institutional arrangement within which the cumulative effect of individuals' production and consumption choices is to promote the good of the least advantaged. That means institutions should elicit certain kinds of behaviors. For example, the difference principle might favor an arrangement of labor markets that incentivizes pediatricians working in rural areas, but that calibrates wage differentials carefully: We should pay rural pediatricians more if and only if paying them more is necessary to bring them where they're needed; and we should pay them *only as much* more as is necessary to achieve that end.

Now, if I'm a pediatrician, the least advantaged are *best* served by my working in a rural area *but foregoing the additional salary* meant to draw me there. Nonetheless, for conceptually stingy Rawls, justice permits me to accept the higher salary, even if the least advantaged would be better off if I took the same job at lower pay. In no sense is the difference principle violated by my choice to take the offered pay differential for working in the underserved area, even though the values that just institutions are arranged to realize would be better realized if I chose differently. This is true, too, of *patterns* of such behavior, even when they come to exert pressure as acquisitive social norms or a market-maximizing culture. A stingy liberal like Rawls needn't police other theorists' terminology, but he can defend his proposed principles of justice as an answer only to the basic structural question of justice: His principles of justice are meant to impugn neither individual behaviors that neglect to promote the ideals those principles embody nor the informal culture those behaviors contribute to. Perhaps such behavior and norms should be impugned—that's a distinct, substantive question. But they are not unjust by the lights of his principles.

One appeal of stinginess, then, is that stingy principles of justice can be highly demandingly egalitarian while protecting some space for individuals to pursue their own private projects. Stinginess enables the offloading of some kinds of impartial moral concern to institutional configurations.[38] How much concern gets offloaded and how demanding justice is notwithstanding that offload are

---

[38] But by no means *all* impartial moral concern. For discussion, see Cohen 2008, 8–11.

162   THE ANATOMY OF JUSTICE

determined by the substance: by the content of what matters and especially by the constraints and demands of legitimacy.[39] But *some* cases of offload comprise data points that *all* parties will be concerned to account for: Even critics of stingy liberalism, even if they think justice issues very stringent demands, probably don't think our rural pediatrician must decline the salary offered to her in favor of a lower one *anytime* doing so would further the realization of the egalitarian principles of distributive justice they favor. If her brother lives in the city, and she likes seeing him regularly, but she likes it marginally less than she would like the additional income she could get with the salary incentive for moving to the country, surely justice doesn't ask that she move to the country *and* forego the salary incentive, even if that's the choice that would maximize the good of the least well off. Cohen agrees with this verdict, saying that justice must permit us all to be more than only "slaves to social justice."[40] Cohen accommodates the data point not by being conceptually stingy but by appending a personal prerogative that sometimes permits us not to optimize with respect to the values of justice. But he never specifies just what this prerogative allows or how permissive it is. The stingy liberal approach to accommodating the data point that we are more than slaves to social justice is principled: The pediatrician does not behave unjustly for the simple reason that justice is principally about institutions. We will still need to ask when some individual or cultural failure to optimize is morally condemnable, and on what terms. But because it is an individual or cultural failure, though it may be condemnable as justice impeding, we know it is not condemnable *as unjust.*

Notice that, on this way of motivating stinginess, we needn't *start out* with any deep commitment to restricting the subject of justice to institutions. We start out only with a well specified subject for a moral question. *Whatever* justice ultimately judges, the stingy liberal *begins* her thinking about justice with the question of institutions. Because she's doing moral theorizing, she knows she'll be guided in some way by considered convictions about actual cases of injustice. She doesn't *know* how far institutional principles extend, but in case the best principles for institutions *don't* apply to individuals, she doesn't want to mistake noise for signal when she *tests* theory: She doesn't want to reject a good principle for institutions on grounds that it tells us something implausible if we apply it directly to individuals or culture. So, she asks the narrow question: What principles for basic structure? Then, once she has an answer to that question that provides guidance we can accept on reflection, the stingy liberal sees that some of the demands justice makes of institutions would be implausible, or misfire, if applied to individuals or

---

[39] For stingy liberals, the restricted application of justice may not be a foundation-level commitment but rather a pattern that emerges from the judgments issued by the things that matter, especially legitimacy. See Schouten 2013.
[40] Cohen 2008, 10.

culture. So she concludes: Those institutional principles don't *directly* compel individuals, because (verdictive) justice does not ask us to try, with every decision we make, to predict the long chain of consequences including implications of our behavior for culture, and to act only in ways that optimally realize the values that just institutions promote.[41] Perhaps *aspirational* justice asks us to do just that. But verdictive justice, with its mutual-respect-based constraints on our pursuit of the aspirational, does not. We should want our terms of social cooperation to be just, but individual conscientiousness is not only *insufficient* to secure justice (on which, more later); that degree of conscientiousness is too much for justice to ask, because justice is demanding and because we each are more than just slaves to promoting it.

As Cohen's personal prerogative attests, restricting the reach of justice is not the only way to respect this datum that justice is demanding but that we are sometimes innocent for not optimizing with respect to it. But it is one principled way. It explains why our rural pediatrician may sometimes be innocent of injustice, even if by acting differently she would enable our social arrangement to realize more verdictive justice. In the next section, when we examine the *normative* adequacy of stingy liberalism, we will see another part of the case for stinginess. Our primary question for now is what important diagnostic data points we give up by being stingy. So far, we might seem to have given up some elegance: In some cases of culture or behavior that seems to call for censure, we cannot say straightforwardly that that behavior or culture is unjust.

But this inelegance seems not to undermine the capacity of liberal egalitarian feminists to derive demanding content from liberal commitments. Above, I canvassed some diagnostic resources of stingy liberalism with respect to culture and individual behavior: First, stingy liberalism allows for political condemnations other than being unjust, so we can say that our deplorable uncle acts *immorally* or *as a racist or sexist* in some circumstances where he obstructs realization of verdictive justice. Second, stingy liberal justice does require individuals to contribute to building and securing *just institutions*. In some circumstances, then, even our innocent-seeming rural pediatrician might behave unjustly for taking the better paid job, because by acting differently she could have helped to bring about institutional change to better realize justice. (Suppose she is a social media influencer during a cultural tipping point with respect to material acquisitiveness, such that by publicly opting for a below-market salary she could build a constituency in favor of egalitarian labor market reform.) Meanwhile, stingy liberal justice requires *institutions* to intervene on culture or on individual behavior when doing so furthers verdictive justice, and it condemns institutions as unjust when they

---

[41] See the discussion of pure procedural justice in Rawls 1999a, 73–8. These considerations may be underwritten by still deeper reasons in favor of stinginess. See, for example, the considerations of publicity harnessed in Williams 1998. For Cohen's response, see Cohen 2008, 344–71.

164 THE ANATOMY OF JUSTICE

fail to so intervene. So, for example, we might say that educational institutions are unjust insofar as they omit to inculcate gender-egalitarian social norms or anti-racist attitudes, or to draw students into discussion of material acquisitiveness so those students come to see that their behavior as producers and consumers is subject to moral appraisal. Finally, when some bit of culture obstructs realization of verdictive justice, we can condemn that culture as calling for rectification on grounds of justice.

Stingy liberalism can therefore be highly demandingly egalitarian. For one thing, securing egalitarian justice requires an institutional arrangement very different from the one we've got. It's easy to forget, for example, that Rawls impugned welfare-state capitalism as unjust by the lights of his two principles of justice.[42] Instead, he argued, justice requires market socialism or a democratic economic system built to ensure and sustain broad dispersal of ownership of productive resources, including to the least advantaged. So, lest our rural pediatrician prime us to think about doctors demanding massively high salaries to work where they're needed or choosing obscenely lucrative specializations that serve a small market of customers with vast disposable income, we should remember that stingy liberalism is perfectly well equipped to diagnose institutions as unjust when those institutions allow medical care to work this way. It is perfectly well equipped to diagnose the corresponding culture as calling for rectification on grounds of justice. It is perfectly well equipped to diagnose individual behavior as stingy or meanly acquisitive, or showing a deficient sense of justice, and it is perfectly well equipped to diagnose individual behavior as unjust when individuals fail to do their part—perhaps quite a lot—to work for institutional reform. Some stingy liberals will not want to endorse these diagnoses, just as some conceptually permissive or moderate liberals may not want to endorse them. But stinginess does not preclude a theory of justice from issuing them.

Stingy liberalism's diagnostic capacities with respect to gender norms and gendered behavior parallel its capacities with respect to market maximizing. Liberal feminist arguments impugn gender norms and gendered social practices on grounds of liberal values like mutual respect and social equality. If those arguments are sound, we can conclude from them that gender norms and gendered social practices cause our social arrangement to rank lower by the lights of verdictive justice. Stingy liberals can argue on this basis that justice favors political interventions to act on culture and influence individual behaviors. They can argue, as I have, that justice requires structuring paid leave to incentivize gender transgressive leave-taking. This might involve making leave non-transferrable or penalizing workplaces when male leave-taking falls below some set threshold.

---

[42] See Rawls 1999a, xiv–xv. Against this reading, some canonical criticisms of liberal feminism claim, wrongly, that liberalism is unable to level "any direct challenge to the capitalist system" Jaggar 1983, 199.

Stingy liberals can diagnose institutions as unjust insofar as those institutions fail to act on culture in the relevant ways, and they can support *that* diagnosis using a diagnosis about culture: that the norms and social practices that comprise the gendered division of labor are justice-impeding and call for rectification on grounds of justice. They can diagnose individual behavior as sexist or patriarchal and manifesting deficient sense of justice, and they can diagnose individual behavior *as unjust* when by behaving differently individuals could have effected institutional change for the better. Again, stingy liberals aren't committed by stinginess to any of these substantive claims. But stinginess doesn't preclude them, either.

Stingy liberals and their critics both need to walk a line. On one side, we want to avoid *too much* condemnation. The thing about culture, after all, is that it can often go wrong even when it's sustained by individual behavior that, taken in isolation, seems wholly unobjectionable. Intuitively, a (non-influencer) pediatrician who takes the salary she's offered because it enables her to work where she's needed but also visit her brother in the city does nothing even defeasibly unjust. A woman who foregoes a promotion because it would require her to spend a lot of time away from her children does nothing even defeasibly unjust. These are data points we all should want to account for. On the other side, though, we risk *too little* condemnation. Justice is demanding, and we fall far short of realizing it. Many social norms and practices call for condemnation in justice-rich terms. Often, so do the individual behaviors that comprise or sustain those norms. Critics of stingy liberalism walk this line either by invoking a personal prerogative the content of which is left unspecified, or by ignoring it, invoking data points on only one side of it and charging stingy theorists of justice with neglecting them. In contrast, the anatomy of justice illuminates a principled stingy liberal pathway for walking the line: The rural pediatrician does not behave unjustly, but her behavior may nonetheless contribute to a culture that calls for rectification on grounds of justice, because a more solidaristic culture would better serve the interests of the worst off among us. The woman who foregoes the promotion does not behave unjustly, but her behavior might contribute to a culture that calls for rectification on grounds of justice, because a more gender-egalitarian culture would be one in which jobs at all levels impose fewer tradeoffs in terms of parents' time with their children. These critical claims can be substantiated by showing that the behavior and the culture to which that behavior contributes impede our realization of verdictive justice. And, we'll see, the rectification called for might include political measures to change the incentive structure against which individuals make such choices, to render verdictive-justice-furthering behavior relatively more attractive and verdictive-justice-obstructive behavior relatively less so.

My burden has been to show that stinginess is not bought at the price of diagnostic inadequacy. The anatomy of justice enables me to make this case because it

166 THE ANATOMY OF JUSTICE

equips us to make sense of the crucial kind of condemnation: Even if culture cannot be unjust, it can nonetheless call for rectification on grounds of justice. Even if individual behavior is not unjust, it may be legitimately susceptible to political pressure on grounds of justice. These diagnoses enable liberals to talk in plausible and justice-rich terms about culture and individual behavior without relinquishing conceptual stinginess, and without relinquishing their capacity to accommodate data points on the other side of the line in a principled way. Culture can change over time, and institutions can exert pressure on it.[43] Institutional arrangements can reform culture by shifting attitudes directly (through education or political rhetoric, for example) and indirectly (by incentivizing certain behaviors and burdening others, thus shaping norms and culture over time). I'll discuss these normative possibilities next. But already we see that the approach I'm forwarding addresses culture, individual behavior, and their role in sustaining injustice by making the diagnostic ride on the normative: For a stingy liberal feminist to say that gender norms call for rectification on grounds of justice is for her to say that justice favors social institutions that work to dislodge them. For a stingy liberal feminist *egalitarian* to say that norms of acquisitiveness call for rectification on grounds of justice is for her to say that justice favors institutions that work to inculcate norms of economic solidarity. It is to say that we can unlock a more verdictively just span of social arrangements by acting now, through institutions, to reform culture, in part by influencing individual behaviors. Stingy liberal feminist egalitarians can say these things on grounds of the plain truth that norms and patterns of behavior can frustrate the values that just institutions would be arranged to realize. When norms frustrate the things that matter for justice, those norms call for rectification on grounds of justice, and institutions are unjust insofar as they aren't arranged to provide rectification. And, when institutions are unjust, *individuals* can behave unjustly by omitting to act in ways that prompt institutional reform.

One last thing: Suppose the normative runs out before we've diagnosed all that warrants criticism. Suppose we've exhausted all legitimate institutional means of behavior nudges and culture reform: Institutions are doing all they legitimately may do—which liberals like me think is quite a lot—to shape culture and behavior in justice-conducive ways. And yet, suppose, market-maximizing culture persists. Here again, liberals will disagree on the substance: about whether anything in this case is actually worth impugning. But suppose a culture of market maximizing in our imagined scenario continues to impede realization of verdictive justice. If we're stingy, then that culture is not assessable *as unjust*. Nor can

---

[43] Danielle Allen writes that institutions "inevitably extend the reach and force of the cultural norms around which they are shaped. A shift in how people interact will inevitably also transform their institutions, just as when the snail changes direction, its shell turns too. But the cultivation of new cultural habits is not the only way to reorient institutions. They can also be reconfigured by intentional policy; a body constituted to amplify the effect of one set of norms in the world may reconstitute itself so as to amplify another set of norms." Allen 2004, 172; see also Haslanger 2021a.

institutions be diagnosed as unjust in our scenario, for by assumption institutions are doing all they legitimately may do to influence the culture in justice-furthering ways. What diagnostic resources remain for the stingy liberal when no normative resources remain upon which a diagnostic critique might ride?

The stingy liberal can continue to impugn behavior and culture that impedes the realization of liberal values as justice-impeding even when political institutions cannot legitimately act to nudge that behavior or reform that culture. The anatomy of justice can substantiate this designation. Suppose market-maximizing culture lessens our realization of aspirational justice, but we've already acted to rectify that culture in all the ways that legitimate democratic processes will approve. In this case, market-maximizing culture offends against the aspirational values that just institutions would be arranged to realize, but legitimacy condemns further action to rectify the situation.[44] Stingy liberals can impugn market-maximizing culture for undermining aspirational value even when institutions have done all they legitimately may do to intervene. The culture remains justice-impeding simply because it relegates us to a less valuable span on verdictive justice's ranking than would otherwise be within reach. This diagnosis is normatively significant, though it doesn't respond to anything we ought to do right now: It tells us that, should the constraints of legitimacy ever shift, justice would reissue its demand that institutions act on the culture. And this can give individuals some kinds of reasons to act now, to shift institutional capacity and the constraints of legitimacy over time.[45]

Haslanger insists that *culture* gone wrong, and not objectionable state action or inaction, at least sometimes lies "at the heart" of injustice.[46] Stingy liberals needn't disagree. They can recognize that culture can cause and sustain injustice. They can recognize that culture can call for reform on grounds of justice. They can diagnose culture as justice-impeding, and they can maintain that diagnosis even when legitimate institutional reforms are exhausted. These diagnostic distinctions track meaningful differences that liberals and critics alike have reason to observe. A critic might yet insist that justice theorizing is inadequate unless it can designate ideological culture as *unjust per se*. But given all that stingy liberalism can say on the diagnostic front—and depending still on what it can permit and prescribe us to *do* about injustice—a rejection of conceptual stinginess on grounds of its diagnostic incapacity begins to look like a question-begging rejection on a technicality: an insistence that a theory of justice must be able to condemn culture as unjust, using just those words. Given that the critics never meant to be fighting over the use of a word,[47] it begins to look like their objection loses its bite.

---

[44] For a more richly described case that meets these specs, we can think of *Fallen Utopia* from Chapter 4.

[45] See Chapter 4 for further discussion of these reasons.   [46] Haslanger 2017, 152.

[47] For her part, Haslanger confirms and indeed emphasizes this in personal conversation.

168   THE ANATOMY OF JUSTICE

6.4   What Can Stingy Liberal Justice Prescribe?

Turn now to critics' doubts about stingy liberalism's *normative* adequacy: Does stingy liberalism's focus on the state *as a means of remedying injustice* render it impotent to prescribe redress for ideological culture? Haslanger regards state-oriented theorizing as normatively inadequate with respect to ideology, and she supports her view by invoking the failure of state-mandated school integration to realize educational justice. In school integration, through courts, the state intervened "in an attempt to improve the economic and political position of the subordinated," yet their economic and political position remains dire. Thus, oppressive culture can persist, and can sustain injustice, even when institutions try to set things right.[48] Beyond a charge of *diagnostic* inadequacy, Haslanger finds here a shortfall in the *normative* resources of state-oriented theory: in what theory tells us to do about injustice.

Haslanger offers no explicit standard of normative adequacy. Because her own theorizing focuses on critiquing injustice but not on thinking through what we ought to do about it, we have few clues as to what she thinks normative political theory should tell us to do.[49] I propose to examine stingy liberalism's structural normative *limitations* and ask whether a critic might plausibly regard them as *inadequacies*. First, we'll look closer at the limitation Haslanger focuses on. I'll argue that the failure of Supreme-Court-mandated school integration to secure educational justice does not establish the normative inadequacy of stingy theorizing. We'll also consider a limitation that Cohen finds, as well as one more candidate case for surfacing stingy liberalism's normative inadequacy. I'll argue that the normative limitations of stingy liberalism are less significant than either Haslanger or Cohen takes them to be, and not plausibly regarded as normative inadequacies of stingy liberalism.

To my mind, court-mandated school integration in the U.S. is a surprising choice for Haslanger's purposes. For one thing, once actually implemented, court-mandated integration *was working* to improve education for Black children, but affirmative measures to promote school integration were too quickly abandoned. And integration was working *despite* having to work against explicitly racist policy at other levels of government and racial inequality solidified by decades of racist government at all levels.[50] We shouldn't saddle Haslanger with an implausibly strong inference from the case. But the argument clearly relies on *some* premise about the potential of governmental action to confront injustice, and it bases that premise on the failure of an isolated and half-hearted attempt to

---

[48]   Haslanger 2017, 155.

[49]   As she puts it, "the social critic's role is primarily negative." Haslanger 2021b. She does, however, articulate social aspirations in various places, for example in Haslanger 2012, chap. 8.

[50]   See, for example, Rothstein 2017; Darby and Rury 2018; Hannah-Jones 2019. This is a point that Haslanger clearly agrees with. See, for example, Haslanger 2017, 152.

undo a wrong that government itself spent lifetimes helping to create. The case offers little insight into what government policy *can* accomplish.

It's surely true that school integration wouldn't *suffice* to secure educational justice, even if affirmative steps toward integration had persisted and even if state and local governments had supported them. Fully racially integrated schools won't produce equal educational outcomes so long as patterns of residential segregation and racial wealth gaps persist outside of school. Suppose we read Haslanger's argument this way: Even if aggressive state action to secure school integration had persisted, residential segregation, wealth gaps, and other racial injustices outside of schools would have undermined the pursuit of educational equality. Does this true counterfactual support any inferences about what governmental action can accomplish?

No, because *schooling* policy is not the only way that state policy affects *education*. Haslanger insists that the source of persisting educational injustice is racist culture. I think that lets racist policy off the hook too easily. Surely the source is a complicated cocktail including culture and the state. Whatever the proportions, individual behaviors sustain and partly comprise racist culture, and material conditions mediate the effects of racist culture on education.[51] This matters to an assessment of stingy liberalism's normative adequacy, because the state can act to disrupt material inequalities and patterns of behavior. Zoning ordinances requiring that new housing be economically heterogenous, public investment in underserved communities, cash transfers, steep taxes on inheritance, and labor reform are just a few examples of institutional action or institutional reconfiguration that would promote educational justice in part by disrupting racializing patterns of behavior.[52] Stingy liberalism can also call for rectification of racial educational injustice by calling for institutions to target racist culture directly: for example, through anti-racist curricula in racially integrated schools. Just as liberalism can diagnose cultural practices as calling for rectification on grounds of justice, it can normatively call for that rectification. Because racial injustice within and outside of schools sustains educational injustice, and because the state clearly has underutilized means of eroding racial injustice within and outside of schools, even perfectly implemented school integration wouldn't support a pessimistic conclusion about what governmental policy and institutional reconfiguration *can* accomplish. Here again, stingy liberals will disagree among themselves about what rectification is called for. But stinginess doesn't preclude calling for institutional reform to promote the values of justice, whether what impedes those values is unjust institutions or justice-impeding culture. The timeline for rectification will be different—culture takes time to change—but this presents no problem for the normative adequacy of stingy liberalism. By acting now to reform culture, we can access a more valuable span of verdictive justice in the future.

---

[51] See for example Posey-Maddox 2014.   [52] See Kelly 2017.

170   THE ANATOMY OF JUSTICE

Finally, we can't forget that stingy liberals do countenance derivative individual obligations of justice: Individuals are obligated to comply with or work toward realizing just institutions. In circumstances of profound injustice, the duty to work toward realizing just institutions may directly condemn as unjust a great deal of behavior that sustains housing segregation and educational disadvantage. After all, that behavior undeniably delays the realization of just institutions. When the behavior is motivated by racist beliefs, it reveals a deficient sense of justice. What behavior *does* the duty of justice call for in circumstances of injustice when, among other things, just institutions are needed to usher in *culture* reform? Must we act *now* as a reformed culture would prescribe? That these are substantive open questions for stingy liberals shows how little normative work stinginess itself precludes.

Now consider a case Cohen uses to challenge the Rawlsian restriction of justice to the basic structure: In 1988, the ratio of top executive salaries to production worker wages was 6.5 to 1 in West Germany and 17.5 to 1 in the U.S.[53] Cohen thinks the German distribution was clearly more just. Alas, he argues, Rawlsian stingy liberalism cannot render that verdict, "since the smaller inequality that benefited the less well off in Germany was not a matter of law but of ethos."[54] But Cohen's case misfires in the same way that school integration misfires as an attempt to surface the inadequacies of stingy liberalism: It is simply not credible that *no legal or policy changes* could have been enacted in the U.S. to change the ratio of executive salaries to worker wages. If justice favors benefitting the least well off, as both Rawls and Cohen think it does, then it favors the institutional arrangement that benefits the least well off *in our circumstances*. Just institutions for a society of market-maximizers might feature not only tighter regulation of markets for goods and labor or more restricted use of such markets, but also interventions for *norm reform*, such as wealth taxes or civic education, to build a culture of economic solidarity. If distributive equality or prioritizing the least well off matters for justice, then institutional reform is called for by a needlessly high ratio of executive salary to worker wage. And, in circumstances of injustice, the individual duty of justice to work toward just institutions may call on (some of) us to stop market maximizing now, even in advance of the egalitarian social norms that more just institutions would foster.

Finally, consider stingy liberalism's normative capability with respect to gender. The liberal feminist arguments sketched in the previous chapter surface problems of justice with gender norms and cultural practices, showing that stingy liberalism can impugn those norms and practices: Gender norms undermine

---

[53] Unsurprisingly, the earnings disparity in the U.S. between workers and executives has only grown worse. To consider a different measure than Cohen's: In 2020, chief executives of big companies made, on average, 320 times as much as their typical worker. In 1989, that ratio was 61 to 1. See Mishel and Kandra 2020.

[54] Cohen 2008, 143.

social equality among citizens; they give rise to distributive inequalities that liberalism clearly condemns; and gendered patterns of behavior constrain choice in ways that frustrate interests we share as equal citizens. On these grounds, liberal feminists argue that liberalism impugns the cultural practices in question and favors policy and institutional reconfiguration to interrupt them: for example, caregiver support which incentivizes paternal caregiving and maternal labor market attachment, reform to labor markets to make jobs more flexible and to revalue female-coded work, and support for and regulation of paid caregiving. Here too, liberalism licenses state action to promote the values of justice, whether by reforming culture or more directly. And here too, the stingy liberal duty of justice may compel individuals to pre-enact the reformed culture to help realize just institutions.[55]

These three cases show that stingy liberals can address culture by licensing political action targeting the patterns of behavior that sustain it: for example, by making market maximizing less lucrative, or encouraging gender-norm transgression, or discouraging the "white flight" that sustains racial educational injustice. Stingy liberals can also call for institutions to act on ideology directly, for example by mandating a civic education to encourage anti-racism and by preserving democratic culture. And they can invoke the duty of justice: that individuals do their share to bring about just institutions. Neither gender norms, nor *Brown*, nor salary ratios can establish that institutional reform is inadequate for securing justice, because none of these are cases in which institutional capacity has been exhausted.

Critics of stingy liberalism might insist that *non*-institutional action is a quicker or more effective path to realizing the values of justice. Stingy liberals needn't deny this. Indeed, because they are committed to some degree of procedural democratic decision-making, they should agree that, other things equal, justice reform will come faster insofar as individuals are motivated to vote and agitate for it.[56] Similarly, critics might argue that just institutions rely upon culture reform because without culture reform, we simply cannot see certain injustices as injustices. For example, state action to address sexual harassment first required the cultural achievement of *naming* sexual harassment.[57] Stingy liberals needn't deny this either: It's no surprise that fully just institutions would be unrealizable in a democracy absent certain cultural preconditions. We might add that such cultural achievements and developments in social ontology can equip us to perceive parts of the verdictive justice ranking that were previously opaque. Stingy liberals should welcome ideology critique because (institutional) justice will be sooner and better realized—and better theorized—with a justice-conducive culture than without it.

---

[55] Schouten 2019, 138.   [56] Chambers 2017, 191.
[57] Thanks to Ding for raising this question and surfacing the example.

172 THE ANATOMY OF JUSTICE

Critics of stingy liberalism might insist that institutional action is inadequate for realizing justice *even though* the cases on offer don't demonstrate that inadequacy. Haslanger punctuates her discussion of *Brown* by noting that, "at this point in time, the idea that racism is going to be dismantled by state action is no longer credible."[58] I'm not sure it ever *was* credible. But for Haslanger to have an opponent in stingy liberalism, our incredulity must target a more specific claim: Is it incredible that *justice's demands with respect to racism* flow primarily through institutional structure? With stingy liberalism as its target, Haslanger's claim might be read like this: Even if we (somehow) achieved a fully just institutional arrangement despite persisting racist culture, *that racist culture* should be deemed unjust, and justice should prescribe (non-institutional) rectification. The charge of normative or diagnostic inadequacy rests ultimately on an appeal to the intuition that theory *should enable us to do more than this*: that it should enable us to criticize more, or to prescribe more or different remediation. For stingy liberalism to be structurally inadequate is for it to be possible that we fully realize its prescriptions and exhaust its condemnations *and yet* something persists that we ought to regard and respond to as (not only immoral or condemnable but) *distinctly unjust.*

Let's imagine that political institutions are arranged to maximally promote the values of justice in the circumstances at hand, including legitimate political means to foster justice-promoting culture. Suppose we nonetheless fall short of optimally realizing the values of justice because, though individuals *do* discharge their duty of justice to support just institutions, they don't pursue the values of justice within their space of discretion. Perhaps they choose where to live without treating the racial and economic justice implications as overridingly important factors. Does adequacy require that we diagnose this behavior or culture as *unjust*? Or is it enough to register them as *justice-impeding*? Does adequacy require that justice always defeasibly ask individuals to act in less justice-impeding ways or work to disrupt justice-impeding culture? Or is the mere diagnosis of the culture and behavior as justice-impeding enough?

I find the questions difficult to take in. Insofar as I have any intuition at all, I wouldn't use it to underpin a standard of theoretical adequacy. The suppositions take us too far from where we are, and my uncertainty about the perfectly just institutional arrangement for our circumstances leaves me ill-equipped to imaginatively make the journey. We could dispense with the stipulation, in the framing of the question, that institutions are doing all they can to promote justice. If we do, we need a different way to control for the intervening variable that undermines Haslanger's inference from school integration and Cohen's inference from earnings ratios: In those cases, the true intuition—*this remains unjust*—arguably

---

[58] Haslanger 2017, 152.

LIBERALISM, CULTURE, AND THE SUBJECT MATTER OF JUSTICE   173

is due to the fact that *institutions remain (very) unjust* and not to the verdict that *something other than institutions must be unjust here.* Instead of stipulating that institutions are in some sense perfectly just, then, we might try to discern the *nature* of remediation called for in circumstances of institutional *in*justice: Are individuals obligated by justice to promote the values of justice directly? Or are they obligated by justice only to work (maybe quite hard) for institutional reform? We have an intuition that challenges conceptual stinginess only if we perceive individual obligations to work *directly* to promote the values of justice, only if we perceive that these are obligations *of justice*, and only if our intuition is clear enough to be treated as an *adequacy test.*

Remember, too, that *something* normative arguably follows simply from the stingy liberal diagnosis of behavior as "justice-impeding." When a behavior or pattern of behavior is justice-impeding, when it obstructs a more valuable range of verdictive justice, *that very fact* may give us reason to desist, whether or not the behavior is, on its own, morally objectionable. The fact that gender norms, market maximizing, and patterns of residential segregation are justice-impeding may give me a reason to defect from those patterns of behavior, even if my own continued participation would be morally innocent and certainly not unjust.[59] This is a justice-relevant reason, even if a failure to heed it isn't unjust. And my reason to abstain from morally permissible behavior that erodes some value of justice plausibly is stronger when that value is badly realized or when I'm so situated that my individual behavior can make a significant difference.[60] Beyond my *duty of justice* to work for fairer social institutions, then, I may have *justice-relevant reasons* to act directly to further the values a just society would realize: for example, to self-tax and give to the least advantaged or to transgress gender norms even when I prefer not to. These might include reasons to cultivate a *sense* of justice, including motivations that cohere with institutional principles and don't oppose the values those principles realize.

Critics may again wonder why anyone would be caught talking this way. I use these distinctions defensively: The distinctions enable liberals to be conceptually stingy while still doing the work that Haslanger and Cohen think state-oriented theory leaves undone. Of course, that's a *virtue* only if this is work that theory should do and only if stinginess is worth rescuing. Within this dialectic, I needn't motivate either condition. I embrace the critics' demanding standard of substantive adequacy and argue that justice theorizing can clear that standard even when the theory retains the feature alleged to be adequacy-undermining. Still, this is a chapter addressed to critics of stingy liberalism, and it defends stinginess by introducing distinctions that some critics might regard as fussy philosophers' distinctions. So, it's fair to ask why stinginess is worth preserving. Above we saw

---

[59] On reasons to resist residential segregation, though, see Anderson 2010a; Shelby 2014.
[60] See Murphy 1998.

174 THE ANATOMY OF JUSTICE

some of the case for stinginess: In setting out to think about *institutional* justice, we don't want to assume that the same principles will directly compel individuals. And once we have on hand demandingly egalitarian principles for institutions, we see that *those* principles plausibly *don't* compel individuals directly, at least if we want to maintain space for individuals to pursue projects other than promoting justice. If this left justice without teeth, we'd need to reconsider the approach; but stingy liberalism isn't toothless.

Still, in the face of racial and economic and gender injustice, and allowing that culture can affect our lives as profoundly as laws or social policies, why *begin* normative political theorizing with the question of institutions?

Crucially, *critics* don't have to. To defend stingy liberalism against these criticisms isn't to say that everyone should be a stingy liberal! It's only to deny that stingy liberalism is inadequate in the way it's often claimed to be. It's to insist that *someone* might forward principles specifically for the basic structure of society, and that those principles might be worth having even if they'd be implausible were we to apply them directly to individual behavior. And it's to show that even if we *don't* apply those principles directly to individual behavior, we can still have a theory that gives plausible and sometimes radical guidance in response to injustice. One can think all these things and still want to let other flowers bloom. We need lots of people asking different kinds of justice-relevant questions about different bits of social machinery.

But here's why *I* start with political institutions: Justice concerns our interests and entitlements as free and equal political persons, and when it comes to the most fundamental of those interests, we're entitled not only to have the interests protected or weighed fairly in deliberations. We're entitled to *assurance* that our interests will be fairly considered. And the justificatory burden faced by political institutions in a liberal democracy gives them an important role in providing assurance. I needn't think political institutions are more important or more impactful than culture. On the contrary: Because the effects of culture are so profound *vis-à-vis* our entitlements of justice, I think culture should lie within the reach of political institutions. We should act politically on culture in ways we can justify to each other as equals. We should ask how we may and how we *must* act on culture, through institutions, to preserve mutual respect among citizens construed as free and equal. Maybe we can serve the values of justice more efficiently by giving money to the least advantaged, taking a below-market salary, or openly transgressing gender norms. Stingy liberals can explain our reasons to do these things: They'll increase the extent to which the values of justice are realized. Stingy liberals can even say we sometimes should do these things when it imposes opportunity costs with respect to institutional reform: With our limited time and energy, we might have stronger reason to promote the values of justice directly than to discharge our duty of justice to promote institutional reform. But when direct action doesn't contribute to institutional change, they'll say, it doesn't discharge our duty of justice. However much it benefits the unjustly badly off, it doesn't provide assurance that their basic entitlements of justice are robustly protected against the same informal structures and bits of culture that so provoke the critics of stinginess I'm responding to. To approach culture from the direction of the state is to give culture its due as something with effects so profound that it's an apt subject of democratic deliberation and political action. It's to appreciate a kind of assurance that only the democratic state can legitimately provide. In part *because* of the influence of ideology and culture, certain fundamental interests warrant protection backed by the state. They shouldn't depend on the informal voluntary and coordinated recognition of others.

Restricting judgments of justice to political institutions makes sense for another reason, too. The behavior of political institutions can be directed by individual agents responding to the demands of justice, and those institutions can act on culture by influencing the behavior of individual agents in turn. This puts rectification front and center by connecting our critique with the acts of agency that can put things right. This seemingly should be a virtue in Haslanger's eyes, for her work powerfully underlines the importance of correcting injustice: "The project [of social critique] is anti-utopian"; it acknowledges that "injustice is rampant" and that "rectification is a priority."[61] Yet, according to Haslanger:

> Culture is a proper target of critique, for culture is a crucial component of social structures; state actions alone are not sufficient to bring about social change for the better. Social critique is also not, or not obviously, situated within ethics, narrowly construed. The question is not simply what should I do, as an individual, given my concerns with the actions of others in their personal consumption of pornography, or with actions that marginalize certain children or families. The questions are about what social norms should govern us as a community, what values we uphold, how we should live together.[62]

Stingy liberals can easily ask these questions. (I think the social norms that should govern us are those conducive to our realizing verdictive justice.) But because liberal egalitarian feminists are also concerned with rectification, they are asking questions not only about what social norms should govern us but also about *what individual agents or political institutions under the influence of individual agents ought to do to right the ship*. This includes asking what individual agents and political institutions ought to do to bring into effect the social norms that should govern us. In asking this question, liberal feminists may be cast as technocrats or aspiring philosopher queens. But even as we ask what we should do to bring about culture reform, we can affirm that such matters should be

---

[61] Haslanger 2020, 1.   [62] Haslanger 2020, 1. In this passage, Haslanger cites Haslanger 2017.

settled collectively; we can explain why that is so; and we can identify the sorts of exigent circumstances in which the value of collective self-governance gives way to other values. In contrast, it is decidedly *not* anti-utopian to ask what norms should guide us if we are not also to ask what anyone should or may do to bring those norms into being. Culture is not a normative agent the way people are. We get rectification—which, I agree, *is* the priority—not only by asking what should be the case but by asking what we should do to make it so. In asking both questions, stingy liberalism is a powerful tool for justice theory and practice.

Liberalism needs ideology critique. Culture as well as individual behavior matter to the question of how well realized are the values of justice. And stingy liberals should not police the terms on which other theorists refer to ideology and behavior. But stingy liberals have reasons for taking care with these designations. To say that I am obligated *by justice* to defy gender norms in my intimate partnerships, or to send my child to the neighborhood public school, or to choose a job based on its social value rather than only on its personal value, is to say that others are entitled *by justice* to my doing those things. Some liberals think individuals should be compelled to send their children to neighborhood schools precisely on the grounds that others are entitled as a matter of justice to the social goods achieved when everyone sends their children to common schools. This is a substantive commitment of justice that brings school-shopping behavior into the purview of justice by approving institutional arrangements to restrict that behavior. And we've seen that some liberal feminists think that gender-norm-transgressive behavior should be institutionally encouraged, even if not legally compelled. Again we see that conceptually stingy liberals may be substantively progressive. They may fully agree with critics of liberalism about which individual behaviors should be regulated by political institutions and which of the behaviors that *aren't* so regulated are nonetheless apt for criticism in justice-rich terms. These arguments have relied on fine distinctions among justice-rich designations. But whether we carve the conceptual space as I have or in some other fashion, all of us who want to think carefully about political normativity need to track the differences these distinctions mark.

Critics of stingy liberalism assume that conceptual stinginess entails a substantive incapacity that renders stingy liberalism inadequate. But we haven't found that incapacity where those critics thought we would. Using the anatomy of justice, stingy liberals can impugn culture and individual behavior in justice-rich terms, even as they abstain from assessing (some) such behavior as *unjust* or designating (some) such behavior as *demanded by justice*. Are these abstentions nonetheless inadequacies? Maybe. Maybe at the end of the day we should abandon stinginess. But we shouldn't do it under the misguided notion that stinginess leaves us with too impoverished a set of diagnostic and normative resources to condemn or to correct for ideological culture or norm-compliant behavior. In the previous work referenced earlier, I argued that the state may legitimately act to reform gendered cultural practices over time by incentivizing norm-transgressive behavior in the here and now. That is a claim about how the state ought to act to promote verdictive justice: Justice requires the intervention; the state is unjust insofar as it omits to so intervene. But I supported these claims precisely by arguing that cultural practices comprising the gendered division of labor *call for rectification as a matter of justice*, because they obstruct our realization of the things that matter from the perspective of justice. Am I a stingy liberal? I haven't decided yet.

A stingy liberal, a moderate liberal, and a permissive liberal walk into a bar. They have a lively discussion about justice. They talk about what matters and about how we can better realize more of what matters without sacrificing some of what matters more. They talk about what is wrong and what we should do about it. They talk *to* each other rather than *past* each other. Maybe we should abandon stinginess. But insofar as what we care about is thinking well and carefully about what's wrong and what we should do to make things better, I can't see that it matters all that much. Armed with an anatomy of justice that helps us to focus on the things that matter from the perspective of justice, we see that the theoretical cost of some liberals' focus on political institutions has been overstated. The real contested space between stingy theorists and critics of stinginess is smaller than the critics seem to think.

6.5 Liberal Feminism and the Anatomy of Justice

This book has argued that liberals should orient their theorizing and their pursuit of justice around the realization of certain values. That's what matters: that the values be realized. Political institutions affect how much those values get realized, but so do various other pieces of social machinery, including individual behavior, patterns of behavior, social norms, and cultural practices. All these things are relevant to the question of how institutions ought to be arranged, because the basic institutional structure of society is less just to the extent that it's not best arranged to realize the things that matter *given the patterns of choice, norms, and cultural practices that characterize our society.* Insofar as patterns of choice, norms, and cultural practices obstruct realization of the things that matter, the basic structure may be less just by virtue of omitting to disrupt those patterns to realize more verdictive justice.[63]

This way of seeing things reveals that Haslanger's criticism of state-oriented normative political theory fails on its own terms. For all she says, liberal

---

[63] I often have David O'Brien to thank for explaining my arguments to me more clearly than I myself can manage. This paragraph owes a great deal to a conversation with David in which he summarized my view to me.

egalitarian feminism can be conceptually stingy and still provide a theoretical underpinning for the critical claims she wants to issue and the normative claims to which she seems committed. Haslanger is right that theorists should ask about the norms that should govern us. But we can't stop there. Insofar as we are concerned with making things better, we should care about what steps moral and political agents should take to bring about greater realization of justice both directly and by changing institutions, norms, and practices. Stingy liberalism spotlights just those questions, even as it can answer the charge that conceptual stinginess entails substantive incapacity.

If stingy liberalism has all the diagnostic and normative capability I have claimed for it, then feminist opponents of liberalism should abandon non-specific complaints to the effect that liberalism or mainstream normative political theorizing is too state oriented or too institution oriented, and instead examine the particular substantive verdicts issued by its various contemporary liberal feminist formulations. Liberal feminists' arguments can still stand as a possibility proof that liberalism's feminist potential is not undermined by that theory's most conspicuous and most widely derided commitments. Meanwhile, Haslanger's work on ideology can fuel productive internal critique for liberal feminism. That critique supports theorizing justice within a framework like the anatomy of justice.

The Anatomy of Justice: On the Shape, Substance, and Power of Liberal Egalitarianism. Gina Schouten,
Oxford University Press. © Gina Schouten 2024. DOI: 10.1093/9780191999772.003.0007

7
Reflective Equilibrium and Social Critique

We saw in Chapter 6 that liberalism has long been regarded by its critics as "a glorification of rights and freedoms that [pays] scant attention to...inequalities of income and power; a discourse of complacency designed to keep things as they are."[1] And we saw that in response, left-liberal feminists argue that, properly understood, liberal values entail a deep critique of sexism, racism, and economic inequality, and furnish an emancipatory, democratic vision for progress toward a more just society.

Alongside this substantive debate about liberalism's feminist, anti-racist, and egalitarian credentials, a distinct and seemingly deeper set of challenges targets liberalism's method of moral justification. This chapter asks whether liberal feminist attempts to redeem the radical potential of liberalism, including this book's attempt to fill in the theoretical underpinnings for a feminist left liberalism, are undermined by their use of *reflective equilibrium*. I argue that they are not. I make my case, again, by engaging with work from Sally Haslanger—this time with her arguments to the conclusion that reflective equilibrium cannot generate adequate social critique. Her criticism of reflective equilibrium is broad, as is my defense against it: As we'll see, this book, and liberal egalitarian feminism broadly, are far from unique in employing reflective equilibrium! But her criticism and its shortcomings are especially illuminating when it comes to assessing the adequacy of liberal egalitarian feminists' use of reflective equilibrium, because her criticism focuses on reflective equilibrium's perceived non-responsiveness to a kind of data about injustice that egalitarians and feminists should be especially concerned to incorporate.

Haslanger's charge against the epistemology of "mainstream" normative theory resonates with a still deeper criticism directed at liberalism in particular: Not only is liberalism inadequate for social and ideology critique; in its defense of ideals or principles that transcend circumstances, liberalism positively *acts as an ideology*.[2] That might be because its principles are flawed or because *any* principle on behalf of which we claim such transcendence will come to function ideologically—for example, by sidelining the wisdom to be learned from social

---

[1] Phillips 2001.
[2] An importantly different criticism charges that *ideal theory* is ideology. See Mills 2017, chap. 5.

180   THE ANATOMY OF JUSTICE

movements. On this charge, liberalism is *worse* than inadequate. This chapter focuses on Haslanger's criticism of reflective equilibrium and argues that normative political theory employing reflective equilibrium *can* issue the critique that Haslanger's argument denies it can issue. But in concluding, I briefly consider the stronger allegation, that such theorizing is *ideological*, bringing to bear my response to Haslanger's argument for the inadequacy of reflective equilibrium.

Section 7.1 reviews work in liberal feminism that apparently accomplishes what Haslanger denies can be done: It apparently uses principles discerned and justified using reflective equilibrium to criticize sexist ideology and to issue prescriptions for correction. Section 7.2 emphasizes the breadth of Haslanger's critical argument by briefly sketching the alternative moral epistemology she favors. Sections 7.3 through 7.5 comprise the bulk of my defense. Section 7.3 refutes Haslanger's claim that reflective equilibrium excludes so-called "outlier judgments," like those advanced by social movements. Section 7.4 defends against the argument that normative theory produced by reflective equilibrium is *unnecessary* for social critique, and section 7.5 defends against the argument that such theory is *inadequate* to underpin critique and guidance for correction because it cannot respond to the ways in which (dis-)value is created *in medias res*, through our social practices. I conclude that the defects in reflective equilibrium that Haslanger claims to have unearthed are merely apparent. The candidate possibility proofs of liberalism's radical feminist potential withstand her methodological criticism, just as they withstood her institutionalist criticism. Throughout the chapter, I draw on the anatomy of justice to develop my defense and to illustrate the kind of theorizing that Haslanger's critical argument claims to undermine. This chapter thus constitutes a defense of the anatomy against criticism targeting its methodology and further illustration of what it can do for left-liberal theorizing.

7.1 "Applied Ideal Theory"

Beyond its focus on institutions, Haslanger argues that much of "mainstream" justice theorizing is unfit for ideology critique due to its common "moral epistemology," which she terms *"applied ideal theory."*[3] Applied ideal theory aims to identify injustice and guide corrective political action by reference to some *theory of justice*. Such a theory may feature principles, ideals, or values of justice. The applied ideal theorist *applies* those principles, ideals, or values to identify *injustice*s, or failures to live up to the principles, ideals, or values in question.

---

[3] Haslanger 2020, 5. On related challenges to "mainstream" methodology in political philosophy on grounds of inadequate action guidance, see also Sangiovanni 2008, 2016; Valentini 2009, 2011; Estlund 2011, 2020; Erman and Möller 2015; Enoch 2018.

I'll adopt Haslanger's own terminology for purposes of engaging with her arguments, but I'll also claim presently that Haslanger's so-called "applied ideal theory" includes much of what more commonly goes under the name "non-ideal theory." It includes principles of reform and revolution, principles of rectification, and principles to guide individuals' responses to injustice, where those principles refer to some ideals or ideal-theory principles of justice.[4]

Haslanger describes applied ideal theory as comprising a certain kind of process: First, the theorist formulates and justifies a theory of justice. Second, she draws on social science and policymaking expertise to *apply* that theory to two ends: She conjoins theory with empirical social science to discern and critique injustice, and she uses that critique in harness with input from policymakers to propose responses to the injustice so discerned. Haslanger's criticism targets the first step of applied ideal theory, wherein we formulate and justify the fundamental theory by reference to which we subsequently critique injustice and prescribe reform. She describes the standard methodology for theorizing as a "relatively *a priori*" process that aims to bring considered convictions about normative matters into broad coherence.[5] Rawlsian reflective equilibrium is the primary target of Haslanger's criticism, and indeed Rawls named the method "reflective equilibrium" and used it to formulate and justify his principles of justice.

Now, the two-step process Haslanger calls "applied ideal theory" is clearly *not* an "*a priori*" exercise. Conjoining theory *with empirics* in order to *diagnose injustice* and *prescribe reform*, this process is known outside of Haslanger's critique as "non-ideal theory." So, no applied ideal theorist need disagree with Haslanger when she writes that, "in undertaking social critique, we need to understand the complexity of the actual situation to diagnose the problem."[6] This is why so-called applied ideal theory draws on the empirical social sciences. Haslanger's objection to applied ideal theory targets its eschewal of the empirical in reflective equilibrium, at the point of *formulating theory*: Though our *use* of theory to critique and prescribe surely invokes empirical complexity, the fundamental theory by reference to which we level critique *itself* makes no reference to the empirical particulars of our situation. Indeed, it is precisely by abstracting away from empirical particulars that such theory can hope to apply broadly across circumstances. But for Haslanger, no normative theory can achieve broad relevance *and* provide an adequate standard for critiquing injustice. The applied ideal theorist's ambition is hopeless. Invoking familiar liberal egalitarian ideals to make her case, she writes that "uncontroversial but vague notions such as *reciprocity* and *equal respect* do not give the social critic adequate normative resources to challenge the status quo."[7] To support her charge, she describes informal practices and gender norms about work and caregiving, such as the

---

[4] See Shelby 2013, 154.   [5] Haslanger 2020, 5.
[6] Haslanger 2020, 3; see also 2012, 16–17.   [7] Haslanger 2020, 8–9; italics mine.

182 THE ANATOMY OF JUSTICE

"social norms, the formation of gender identity, and the socialization of individuals through particular practices of intimacy, sexuality, parenting, and economic cooperation."[8] Liberal ideals like reciprocity and equal respect come up short, on Haslanger's telling, not only because mainstream theorists apply these ideals to assess institutions, but also because the ideals are theorized using the methodology of reflective equilibrium: Reciprocity and mutual respect are held out as broadly appealing, "relatively *a priori*" ideals that furnish normative guidance across circumstances;[9] but according to Haslanger, their versatility and *a priority* are purchased at too high a cost to their critical power.

A vast body of work from liberal feminists and other non-ideal theorists employs the method of reflective equilibrium, and several of the arguments comprising this body of work purport to generate just the kind of critique of injustice that Haslanger describes in the quotation above: that is, critique of the "social norms, the formation of gender identity, and the socialization of individuals through particular practices of intimacy, sexuality, parenting, and economic cooperation." Such arguments would appear antecedently to refute Haslanger's impossibility claim, that the methodology of reflective equilibrium cannot produce such critique. Moreover, some of these apparent possibility proofs deploy the very ideals Haslanger invokes to illustrate reflective equilibrium's alleged impotence: Using reflective equilibrium, this work draws on ideals like reciprocity and equal respect to do the kind of critical work that Haslanger finds those ideals and that methodology unfit to do. The arguments in question thus stand as *apparent* possibility proofs twice over: They use the methodology Haslanger criticizes, and they invoke the values she uses to illustrate the feebleness of that methodology. Yet they purport to reach the very conclusions that she deems that methodology unfit to generate and those values unfit to support. Haslanger's impossibility argument does not engage with these putative possibility proofs, so her criticism needs to be addressed on its own terms. But it's worth briefly recalling some of the putative possibility proofs to have on hand.

First recall the politically liberal argument from Lori Watson and Christie Hartley.[10] Watson and Hartley argue that social practices like pornography, prostitution, and the gendered division of labor are unjust and politically actionable because they undermine women's social and civic equality. Equal respect requires the elimination of social conditions that enable domination and subordination in the space of democratic deliberation, and it demands of us that we secure social conditions conducive to preserving civic respect among equal citizens.[11] Because prevailing gender norms and gendered social practices are not consistent with the treatment of women on terms of social equality and mutual civic respect— because they undermine women's equal social and civic standing—Watson and

---

[8] Haslanger 2020, 8.   [9] Haslanger 2020, 5.   [10] Watson and Hartley 2018.
[11] Watson and Hartley 2018, 160.

Hartley offer a deep critique of such norms and practices on precisely the grounds of reciprocity and equal respect.

My own work on liberalism and gender also spotlights the values of reciprocity and equal respect.[12] I agree with Watson and Hartley that the liberal ideal of mutual respect gives reason to eliminate social hierarchies, like the hierarchy of male-coded over female-coded work. But I argue that there's something objectionable too in the gender coding *itself*: in steering people into work specialization based on sex. So, we have reason to elevate the status of caregiving—Hartley and Watson's argument secures this conclusion—and we have *independent* reason to draw more men into caregiving, to erode the gender coding. Liberalism has the resources to issue these reasons: Beyond its condemnation of hierarchal stacking, a commitment to preserving mutual respect among free and equal citizens also impugns the steering of individuals into normatively prescribed gender roles. That's because the source of the steering is the institutionalized assumption that sex dictates work specialization, an assumption that is objectionable at the bar of mutual respect because it is inimical to autonomy. The assumption is inimical to autonomy, I argue, because it presumes that citizens will behave non-autonomously: that they will specialize by sex into caregiving and labor market roles.

These arguments explicitly purport to ground a critique of the gendered status quo atop the liberal ideals of reciprocity and equal respect. Those ideals are theorized using reflective equilibrium, and subsequently conjoined with empirical social science to critique unjust gendered social practices and to prescribe correction. These are paradigmatic cases of so-called applied ideal theory. They are sketched more expansively in Chapter 5 for those who want a fuller picture. I re-present them here only in barest outline because my case does not depend on establishing that they are sound. I need show only that their *methodology* does not render their conclusions *unachievable*. If Haslanger's criticism succeeds, then such arguments can't help but fail in what they purport to do. This chapter shows that the example arguments' status as putative possibility proofs is not undermined by Haslanger's criticisms of reflective equilibrium.

7.2 The Epistemic Problem of Ideology

To understand the breadth and significance of Haslanger's criticism, it helps to glimpse her own preferred approach to social critique. For Haslanger, the task of social critique is "to reveal the systematic and harmful forms of social coordination as they unfold in a particular historical context and to promote change."[13] Because informal social practices play the pivotal role in sustaining injustice,

---

[12] Schouten 2019.   [13] Haslanger 2020, 1.

184 THE ANATOMY OF JUSTICE

such practices are social critique's most important target; but *ideology* presents an epistemic problem for the practice of social critique. For Haslanger, recall, ideology is any set of social meanings, or "cultural technē," that functions, in its operative context, to create and sustain injustice and oppression.[14] Social meanings can be ideological by deceiving us about injustice or simply by organizing us in unjust ways.[15] But precisely because ideology can work to "mask or occlude what's valuable,"[16] it can resist detection: Both oppressors and the oppressed may misperceive ideology as benign culture. Conversely, many may misperceive benign culture as ideology. How are we to avoid these errors?[17] As theorists, as citizens, or as participants in social movements, how can we recognize ideology for what it is so that we can resist it?

We just saw that Haslanger rejects "the standard methods of political episte-mology."[18] But Haslanger does not resort to relativism. Like me, she believes "there is a fact of the matter about what is just and unjust, good, and valuable."[19] So, how can we distinguish ideology from benign culture without normative the-ory of the sort produced by reflective equilibrium? Her preferred approach to discerning these evaluative facts relies on consciousness raising, a collective activity that "prompts a paradigm shift in one's orientation to the world."[20] On its own, consciousness raising only relocates the epistemic problem posed by ideology: Some attempts at consciousness raising—by anti-vaxxers and Neo-Nazis, for example—rest on *false* claims of injustice.[21] How do we know which claims of injustice are true? How do we distinguish a worthy paradigm shift from one that abandons truth for ideology or trades one ideology for another? Haslanger's solu-tion is to draw on "critical social theory" as a "value-laden empirical inquiry."[22] For this, we rely on discernment acquired through first-personal knowledge that "a moral wrong or injustice is being done to me or to us,"[23] and on a form of "tested" consciousness raising.[24]

---

[14] Haslanger 2017, 2021b. Haslanger writes: "An ideology is a cultural technē 'gone wrong.' It pre-vents us from recognizing or creating forms of value, and/or, organizes us in unjust ways. This account of ideology is functionalist, pejorative, but not doxastic. It is functionalist because the evalu-ation of a technē as ideological depends on how it functions in a context; it is pejorative because, in being ideological, it functions to create or sustain injustice; and it is not doxastic because a cultural technē is not a set of beliefs, but is, rather, a set of public meanings (though some parts of it may be internalized as beliefs and other attitudes). The cultural technē both provides resources to interpret and also shapes the material world." Haslanger 2021b, 2.

[15] It is a distinct feature of Haslanger's view that a set of social meanings can be ideological simply in virtue of organizing us in unjust ways, where this injustice is not mediated by any kind of problem-atic belief. See, for example, Haslanger 2012, 18, 413, 2017, 159–60, 2021b, 23. For a construal on which "ideological" is primarily predicated of beliefs or forms of social consciousness, see Shelby 2003, 157–60.

[16] Haslanger 2017, 160.

[17] A distinct question concerns standing to proclaim on these matters. See Chambers 2017, 177.

[18] Haslanger 2021b, 2.   [19] Haslanger 2017, 165.   [20] Haslanger 2021b, 14.

[21] Haslanger 2021b, 20.   [22] Haslanger 2020, 11.   [23] Haslanger 2017, 166.

[24] Haslanger 2021b, 17–21. This is a process previewed in Haslanger 2012, 423–6, 472–5, and more fully developed in Haslanger 2021b.

REFLECTIVE EQUILIBRIUM AND SOCIAL CRITIQUE   185

In her own engagement with Haslanger's work, Clare Chambers rejects this approach, arguing that ideology and benign culture are distinguishable only by invoking normative theory:

> We cannot critique ideology by saying that it shapes the thoughts, concepts and practices of its members, because [benign] culture does the exact same thing, and because we are necessarily speaking from within a culture ourselves. Instead, the critique has to be that ideology shapes knowledge badly, where this is a normative and not an epistemological bad.[25]

Like Chambers, I find Haslanger's moral epistemology unpromising. It may well capture genuine ideals for how social movements should respond to consciousness raising attempts. But I doubt that readers who are antecedently inclined to deny that we can derive an "ought" from an "is" will find it to be a satisfying account of what to believe about (in)justice. Consciousness raising can inform normative theorizing by publicizing neglected dimensions of injustice, but on its own, it offers at best partial discernment of facts about the injustice of our social practices and about how to make them better. For instance, it apparently offers no adequate basis for adjudicating among divergent claims of injustice or moral salience in difficult cases.[26] Even if Haslanger can respond to these challenges, reflective equilibrium still seems to its defenders to be "the best way of making up one's mind about moral matters."[27] Some think it's the *only* viable way: that "apparent alternatives to it are illusory."[28] But can it answer Haslanger's objections?

7.3 Reflective Equilibrium's Abstemiousness and Outlier Judgments

Reflective equilibrium aims for justification by way of coherence. It involves

> working back and forth among our considered moral judgments about particular instances or cases, the principles or rules that we believe govern them, and the theoretical considerations that we believe bear on accepting these considered judgments, principles, or rules, revising any of these elements wherever necessary in order to achieve an acceptable coherence among them."[29]

---

[25] Chambers 2017, 182.

[26] Whether I'm right about this depends on the success of semantic externalism and ameliorative epistemology, which Haslanger pursues elsewhere in her work. See Haslanger 2012, chap. 16. See also Srinivasan 2020.

[27] Scanlon 2003a, 149.   [28] Scanlon 2003a, 149.

[29] Daniels 2015, 711. The literature on reflective equilibrium is vast. For especially relevant seminal contributions, see Hare 1973; Daniels 1979; Rawls 1999a, 1999b, chap. 1; Scanlon 2003a; Freeman 2007, 29–42.

186 THE ANATOMY OF JUSTICE

The kind of coherence we aim for is one that defers to convictions in proportion to their likelihood of being true, or—on another formulation—in proportion to their having been "made under conditions conducive to avoiding errors of judgment."[30] We might have extra confidence in judgments formed under certain kinds of circumstances, for example, or in judgments that happen not to serve our interests and so are less likely to be products of motivated reasoning.[31] Then, treating the most reliable considered convictions as provisional fixed points, we work to bring our moral convictions at all levels of generality into coherence; and it's (in part) by featuring in the system that offers the best "fit" of our provisional fixed points—or that guides revision of those convictions in plausible ways—that some (set of) principle(s) is justified. Crucially, to do reflective equilibrium *well* is to do it in broad conversation with others. People from different backgrounds and with different life experiences have different insights and liabilities when it comes to moral discernment. Through deliberation across difference, we can develop new convictions, uncover contradictions, and gain greater clarity about which of our own judgments deserve to be treated as provisional fixed points.[32]

Reflective equilibrium understandably prompts worries of status quo bias because its initial raw materials are the judgments that inquirers already endorse at the time of inquiry. Defenders have tried to assuage those worries elsewhere,[33] but Haslanger's objection is a new and specific version. She attaches a modifier—*"domain specific"* reflective equilibrium—to clarify that hers is not an objection to all coherentist justification, but only to reflective equilibrium that aims specifically to illuminate the *normative* domain.[34] This is the standard use, described by Daniels above, of the process that Rawls named "reflective equilibrium." That process undertakes to justify normative principles by reference to broad coherence among considered normative judgments in particular cases, the normative principles we believe govern them, and the theoretical normative considerations we believe bear upon those judgments and principles. It's because the coherence we seek is among specifically normative provisional fixed points that Haslanger describes reflective equilibrium as "relatively *a priori.*" But we need greater clarity about what this means. After all, one type of provisional fixed point comprises normative judgments *about particular cases.* This is the sort of judgment we make when we think, "that is clearly unjust" upon learning that job seekers with

---

[30] Daniels 1979, 258. Throughout this chapter, I help myself to the idea of moral truth that Rawls and Scanlon do without. For them, our provisional fixed points for reflective equilibrium include convictions especially likely to be *justified* or to be "supported by good and sufficient reasons" Scanlon 2003a, 140.

[31] But see Kelly and McGrath 2010.

[32] For Rawls, the ideal is wide (not narrow) and general (not individual) reflective equilibrium. See Rawls 2001, 31.

[33] See, for example, Rawls 1999a, 230–1, 508; Scanlon 2003a.

[34] Haslanger 2020, 5; see also 2012, 349–51.

REFLECTIVE EQUILIBRIUM AND SOCIAL CRITIQUE 187

"African-American-sounding" names are significantly less likely to get callbacks from prospective employers than job seekers with "White-sounding" names.[35] This judgment is hardly *a priori*—its content includes an empirical fact—yet it figures in our reflective equilibrium on equal footing with considered convictions about theory. Because normative judgments about injustice in particular cases are empirically laden, terms like "domain specific" and "relatively *a priori*" can mislead.

It's tempting to accept without scrutiny a description of Rawlsian reflective equilibrium as relatively *a priori*. That's because we associate Rawls's theory with ideal theory, and because Haslanger's coined term "domain specific" to describe her target methodology invites us to imagine some peculiarly Rawlsian subspecies of the methodology. But Rawls's reflective equilibrium is no methodological subspecies. Rawls named the methodology, but he neither discovered nor invented it, and he shares it with his most trenchant substantive critics. Indeed, the methodology of reflective equilibrium described above characterizes nearly all moral theorizing. This chapter defends "Rawlsian" reflective equilibrium not to defend Rawls's substantive principles of justice but because "Rawlsian" reflective equilibrium has subsequently been employed in the arguments of this book as well as in our candidate liberal feminist possibility proofs. The methodology of reflective equilibrium is ubiquitous. Haslanger herself sometimes employs the very methodology she criticizes, for example, when she rejects theory as inadequate because of its (perceived) inability to condemn racist cultural practices that survived state-mandated school integration. In that argument, discussed in Chapter 6, a normative judgment about a particular case serves to overturn a normative judgment about theory. And, like all judgments about particular cases, Haslanger's is empirically laden.

Because Rawlsian reflective equilibrium clearly makes use of empirically laden normative judgments, we need to precisify the descriptor "relatively *a priori*" by distinguishing among the various justificatory abstentions we might practice in reflective equilibrium. By "justificatory abstentions," I mean the systematic setting aside or discounting of certain kinds of premises at certain stages of reflective equilibrium, depending on the question we are using that methodology to answer. For example, in his original position argument, Rawls undertakes to justify his principles without invoking *particular contingent facts* about the circumstances of any particular society those principles are proposed to regulate.[36] Haslanger characterizes Rawls's use of reflective equilibrium at that stage as employing yet another distinct kind of abstention: the setting aside of *controversial* descriptive facts for purposes of justifying theory.[37] Her allegations as to the inadequacy of reflective equilibrium begin with that characterization: "Outlier judgments are

---

[35] Bertrand and Mullainathan 2004.
[36] Rawls 1999a, 118–19.   [37] Haslanger 2020, 5–6, 2021b, 9.

188 THE ANATOMY OF JUSTICE

set aside. However,...redescriptions of the social domain and resulting outlier judgments are typically the source of social critique."[38] If we need outlier judgments for social critique, and if reflective equilibrium sets such judgments aside, then reflective equilibrium is evidently an inadequate methodology for social critique.

To assess this criticism, let's begin by asking: Why be empirically abstemious at all? Answering this question will help us to see how best to clarify the justificatory abstentions of reflective equilibrium. My answer, and the answer I read Rawls as giving, invokes the very point of having a theory to begin with: We want *theory*, rather than simply a collection of distinct judgments, because we want guidance across cases and even when we confront new cases. This motivates the Rawlsian abstention from the particular: We eschew particular contingent facts in theorizing in order to make theory more robust across changing circumstances. If we want foundational principles to provide systematic guidance and to be justified across circumstances, then we should avoid invoking particular, contingent empirical facts—facts about *our circumstances*—for the purposes of formulating or justifying those principles.

Haslanger focuses on what kinds of premises abstention (apparently) rules *out*, but with this case for abstention on the table, we can also discern the myriad kinds of premises our principled abstention *allows in*. First, we can achieve robust guidance across circumstances without eschewing *conditional projections* about what some normative commitment *would* tell us to do in some specified set of circumstances. Second, we can achieve robustness without eschewing *general* descriptive facts about human societies—for example, basic laws of economics. Since Rawls's use of reflective equilibrium is Haslanger's primary target, let's illustrate using his fair equality of opportunity principle: Using reflective equilibrium, Rawls argues that our prospects for attaining social positions to which income and wealth accrue should not be influenced by social-class origins.[39] The argument is complex, but in basic outline, he derives his equal opportunity principle from the conviction that our social-class origins are morally arbitrary with respect to our share of income and wealth, and then he *confirms* the principle by testing it against our considered convictions about particular cases across a range of circumstances. So, from a premise about the moral arbitrariness of our contingent social circumstances and a set of considered convictions about cases, Rawls defends a robustly egalitarian principle to the effect that prospects for attaining advantageous social positions should not be influenced by our social-class origins. Crucially, he derives that principle without invoking any particular facts about, for instance, racialized social closure *in our circumstances*. But he *tests* the

---

[38] Haslanger 2020, 6.   [39] Rawls 1999a, 16–17, 118, 122.

principle by asking what it *would* impugn and prescribe across a range of social circumstances.[40]

Now, famously, the range of circumstances across which Rawls tests his theory is limited to circumstances of full compliance: roughly, circumstances in which people are doing their best to realize and comply with a just institutional structure. But *ours* is a question about the adequacy of Rawlsian reflective equilibrium for the purposes of *applied* ideal (that is: non-ideal) theory. To *that* end, reflective equilibrium might have us testing the Rawlsian principle—or, on the anatomy of justice, the ideal that principle encodes—by asking if and on what grounds that ideal impugns racialized social closure across a range of *un*just circumstances. We may ask: What would the ideal behind fair equal opportunity condemn, and what would it prescribe, in circumstance wherein white wealth or employment or college-going far outpaces Black wealth or employment or college-going, and wherein this is due to a long history of severe racial injustice and oppression? We may reject a candidate ideal of equal opportunity as inadequate if, for example, it entailed that affirmative hiring would be unjustified in such circumstances whether or not affirmative hiring would achieve its desired effects. To do this, we needn't invoke the premise, "these are *our* circumstances." And a principle or ideal that stands the tests can remain operant and applicable within some range of *changing* circumstances.

This case illustrates that empirical abstemiousness may be motivated simply by the hope that foundational normative theory could provide unified but responsive guidance across variation in the circumstances, culture, and history of the societies to which it's applied. Rawls is explicit in acknowledging that we might have to ease our abstention—to go back and incorporate more empirical particulars into our initial justification for the principles.[41] If so, the resulting principles will have a correspondingly narrower range of justification. But we start with the hope that we can formulate theory to be informative and to give guidance about what we should do across a wide range of liberal democratic societies. Insofar as theory is supported by premises about what judgments that theory *would* render in thus-and-such circumstances, rather than by premises about thus-and-such being *our* circumstances, its applicability can range more broadly.

This case makes vivid a second point, crucial to addressing Haslanger's criticism: In reflective equilibrium, no one *type* of considered conviction is

---

[40] Rawls 2001, 136. Rawls assesses conditionalized judgments of the difference principle at Rawls 2001, 66–72. Like Haslanger, I characterize the *deliberative* model of reflective equilibrium, which aims to determine what to believe about justice. This is in contrast with the *descriptive* model that Rawls sometimes seems to have in mind, on which we aim only to describe our own particular conception of justice. See Scanlon 2003a.

[41] Rawls 1999a, 18.

190   THE ANATOMY OF JUSTICE

privileged.[42] Neither our convictions about particular cases of (in)justice nor our convictions about the principles or rules or ideals that we believe govern those cases are treated as categorically likelier to be reliable. This means that even when we're *formulating and justifying theory*, we're invoking our considered convictions about *actual instances of injustice*, like, "it would be unjust if white wealth or college-going outpaced Black wealth or college-going due to a history of racial injustice." Haslanger describes applied ideal theory as cleanly separating theory from application: Step one, we *theorize*. We develop a normative theory "that does justice to our considered moral judgments and intuitions concerning normative matters."[43] Step two, we *apply*. We conjoin the normative theory just developed with social science and policymaking expertise *to critique injustice* and *prescribe correction*.[44] This characterization isn't inaccurate, but it's liable to mislead. In reflective equilibrium, when we're *developing theory*, we're already asking what applied judgments a theory under consideration (conditionally) would render. We're testing theory against our considered convictions about supposed cases of injustice: Suppose things were like this. Would our candidate theory guide us implausibly or generate implausible critique? If so, then so much the worse for that theory. All this occurs at step one, in formulating theory using reflective equilibrium.

Notice what this means for outlier judgments. If we commit to eschewing particular facts about our social circumstances in formulating and justifying principles of justice, then we can't invoke outlier judgments *as judgments predicated of our particular circumstances*. But this doesn't single out outlier judgments; we also can't invoke facts from the *conventional wisdom* in judgments predicated of our circumstances. On the other hand, *non-indexical* outlier judgments, like the judgment that certain racialized inequalities are unjust, *can* figure among the judgments that inform our reflective equilibrium. If a theory well accommodates conditionalized versions of the outlier judgments that operate as provisional fixed points, that tells favorably of the theory. And testing theory against such judgments in no way restricts the applicability of the theory to circumstances in which the conditions obtain. If an outlier moral judgment is held with the conviction that makes it fit to fuel a social movement, nothing about reflective equilibrium precludes a conditionalized formulation of that judgment figuring in moral deliberation. Indeed, such outlier judgments are as apt to challenge theory as theory is to challenge them.

So far, we have a case for abstention from *particular* facts in formulating and justifying theory. That abstention doesn't exclude outlier judgments. What about abstention from *controversial* facts? Though Haslanger claims to be "following Scanlon's interpretation of Rawls" in characterizing reflective equilibrium's

---

[42] Daniels 1979, 265.   [43] Haslanger 2020, 5.   [44] Haslanger 2020, 5.

abstemiousness,[45] neither Rawls nor Scanlon actually requires that judgments used in reflective equilibrium be empirically uncontroversial. On the contrary, for Rawls and Scanlon, the considered judgments we invoke to justify principles of justice must be empirically *informed*: Scanlon writes that to be fully probative, a considered judgment must be formed with awareness "of relevant facts about the issue in question."[46] To illustrate, consider Rawls's argumentative device employing reflective equilibrium: Though ignorant of *particular* features of their society, the contractors in the original position know "whatever *general* facts affect the choice of the principles of justice," notably including principles of economic theory and laws of human psychology.[47] Rawls continues: "There are no limitations on general information, that is, on general laws and theories, since conceptions of justice must be adjusted to the characteristics of the system of social cooperation which they are to regulate, and there is no reason to rule out these facts."[48] Whether some *general* fact is also *uncontroversial* is an open question—even premises that *should* be broadly shared can turn out to be objects of intense controversy. So, although Haslanger describes Rawlsian reflective equilibrium as eschewing controversial descriptive facts as such, neither Rawls nor Scanlon takes controversy as such to constitute principled grounds for abstention.[49]

Now, some liberals—*political* liberals—do effectively eschew many controversial premises for purposes of political justification. Although the constraint is standardly taken to apply to the moral or religious convictions that make up a person's value system or conception of the good, some of the controversial metaphysical and empirical premises that Haslanger thinks reflective equilibrium excludes are arguably components of conceptions of the good.[50] Nonetheless, on my view, the politically liberal eschewal of controversial premises isn't best construed as a requirement *of reflective equilibrium*. It is not a constraint on a methodology for determining what to believe about justice. Rather, it flows from a view about what constraints we ought to impose *on public political deliberation about what to do* in a liberal democracy. For political liberals, eschewing certain kinds of divisive premises in political justification is a downstream substantive demand of normative commitments that themselves may be justified using

---

[45] Haslanger 2020, 5. [46] Scanlon 2003a, 143. [47] Rawls 1999a, 119; italics added.
[48] Rawls 1999a, 119; see also 137–8, 384. On *complex* empirical facts, see 122–3.
[49] Haslanger 2020, 5–6, 2021b, 9. Haslanger quotes Scanlon writing that for Rawls, justice "has no controversial empirical or metaphysical presuppositions" (Scanlon 2003a, 146). But in this brief remark, Scanlon is pointing out that our reasons for taking morality seriously don't derive from claims outside of morality—from physics or psychology, for example. That our reasons for caring about morality don't depend on controversial non-normative claims doesn't entail that moral principles must be justified without invoking controversial non-normative claims.
[50] On empirics in conceptions of the good, see Rawls 1993, 55–8; Kelly and McPherson 2001; Fowler 2019.

192   THE ANATOMY OF JUSTICE

reflective equilibrium.[51] For example, political liberals might use reflective equilibrium, as I have in this book, to describe mutual respect as a foundational liberal value. They might use it to discern that mutual respect favors abstemiousness in justifying social policy so as to preserve justificatory community within a liberal democracy—that is, to discern that mutual respect permits only broadly sharable premises for political justification. In short, even for liberals whose applied theorizing *does* favor non-controversial premises in some sense, the signature preference for broadly sharable premises is not a methodological commitment *of reflective equilibrium*.

Here, some readers might suspect that Haslanger is simply *conflating* reflective equilibrium and political liberalism, the former being a methodology that characterizes nearly all moral theorizing and the latter being a substantive view imposing constraints on normative deliberation when that deliberation is an instance of public political justification. Although this would be surprising in light of her emphasis not on moral or religious disagreement but on empirical disagreement, it does sometimes seem that Haslanger's targets include both reflective equilibrium *and* political liberalism. This possibility is no problem for my defense. If political liberalism is among Haslanger's targets, then our possibility proofs would be possibility proofs not twice but *thrice* over. That's because both the liberal feminist arguments sketched above and the anatomy of justice forwarded in this book take on board the justificatory constraints of political liberalism, yet the theorizing in question purports to issue just the kind of social critique that Haslanger claims reflective equilibrium (and political liberalism?) cannot furnish.

I've argued that Rawlsian reflective equilibrium and politically liberal reflective equilibrium are not aptly characterized as imposing a methodological abstention from controversial premises. But reflective equilibrium is the methodology of nearly all moral theory, and moral theorists using reflective equilibrium can disagree about which judgments are most probative and by what margin. Some may favor discounting judgments that sustain the status quo; others may favor discounting controversial judgments, just as Haslanger characterizes Rawls as doing, on grounds that controversial judgments are more susceptible to error. Some favor *total* eschewal of the empirical—controversial or particular or not—in justifying foundational principles: While Rawls thinks that "both general facts as well as moral conditions are needed even in the argument for first principles of justice," this claim is famously disputed.[52] And, of course, there's always a mundane reason for moral deliberators to discount the controversial: Any argument is in one way better insofar as it relies on fewer controversial premises, since

---

[51]   I don't say Rawls agrees. On reflective equilibrium in political liberalism, see Rawls 2001, 29–32; Daniels 2020.

[52]   Rawls 1999a, 138. For a case against, see Cohen 2008, chap. 6.

interpersonal justification must proceed from some consensus.[53] So, it's worth seeing what reflective equilibrium can do if we characterize it as eschewing both the particular *and* the controversial.

My defense so far extends straightforwardly to cover reflective equilibrium that eschews both the particular and the controversial. That's because, just as we can invoke suitably conditionalized *particular* judgments without invoking the particular in any problematic way, so too can we invoke suitably conditionalized *controversial* judgments. As we've seen, we can test a theory by asking if it can accommodate a considered conviction that "it's unjust for racial wealth disparities to persist due to a history of racial injustice," even if that descriptor happens to match our actual circumstances. Because we can use the test case without using an *indexical* version of the test case, we can also use the test case even if the causal claim, that the disparities persist *due to racial injustice*, would be *controversial* if predicated of our circumstances. This is true for a simple reason: The non-indexical version *doesn't* predicate it of our circumstances.

The upshot is that "outlier judgments" and "redescriptions of the social domain" needn't be excluded from reflective equilibrium. And it bears emphasizing that all this care with conditionalizing the premises need only be taken in theory *building*, because we want theory to apply broadly. In theory *application*, reflective equilibrium clearly permits invoking particular and controversial facts about what our society is like.[54]

This refutes Haslanger's initial case for thinking that "applied ideal theory is not the best strategy for social critique,"[55] because it shows that, even at the stage of theory formulation, applied ideal theory can admit the very outlier judgments that, by Haslanger's lights, hold our best hope of escaping ideology. But Haslanger's complaint about the exclusion of outlier judgments from reflective equilibrium doesn't exhaust her case against that methodology. Let's recall her description of applied ideal theory's approach to social critique: In step one, we develop a coherent normative theory "that does justice to our considered moral judgments and intuitions concerning normative matters, specifically, judgments and intuitions that are empirically and metaphysically uncontroversial."[56] In step two, we *apply* that theory: We use the normative theory in harness with social science and policymaking expertise to critique injustice and make suggestions about how to bring about change to better realize justice as specified by our theory.[57] I read Haslanger as leveling two further charges against applied ideal theory, concerning the *necessity* and the *internal adequacy* of the kind of theory step one uses reflective equilibrium to build: First, that kind of theory is

---

[53] See Rawls 1999a, 512–13.

[54] Political liberalism does impose its justificatory constraints at the stage of theory application. But as we'll see, those constraints do not rule out the critique Haslanger deems reflective equilibrium incapable of generating.

[55] Haslanger 2020, 6.   [56] Haslanger 2020, 5.   [57] Haslanger 2020, 5.

194   THE ANATOMY OF JUSTICE

unnecessary for critiquing injustice and guiding correction. Second, that kind of theory is *inadequate* to underpin critique and guidance for correction, because (even if it admits outlier judgments as I've so far argued) reflective equilibrium cannot respond to the ways in which social practices create (dis-)value.

These two charges, I think, comprise the strongest reconstruction of Haslanger's remaining criticisms. These are criticisms I will need to answer, because this book uses reflective equilibrium to forward an evaluative theory by reference to which I claim feminist and egalitarian social critique and guidance for reform can be derived. This book as well as the liberal feminist arguments reviewed above are clear cases of "applied ideal theory" and of theorizing that uses reflective equilibrium.

7.4 Is Normative Theory Necessary?

Let's use "normative theory" to refer to normative theory developed by reflective equilibrium that sidelines or discounts controversial facts and particular facts about our social circumstances. A major thread of Haslanger's case against applied ideal theory consists in arguing that normative theory is *unnecessary* for critique or correction. But several of the necessity claims Haslanger argues against are claims that nobody need affirm. For example, Haslanger claims that applied ideal theory "presupposes" a "priority thesis": that "to make a (warranted) judgment of injustice, one must apply a (warranted) principle of justice."[58] This is a thesis that "the social critic should reject," she argues; thus, the applied ideal theory that relies on that thesis is not a good methodology for social critique.[59] It would indeed be a problem for applied ideal theory to presuppose the priority thesis. That thesis is manifestly false. Suppose I wade into a cold lake to save a drowning child, motivated simply by the reflexive judgment that I should do so. That judgment might be warranted even if I don't stop to apply a principle. Indeed, I might intentionally cultivate virtuous habits to minimize my need to apply principles. But this is no problem for applied ideal theory, because rather than presupposing the priority thesis, applied ideal theory actually presupposes the very possibility that thesis denies.[60]

Reflective equilibrium proceeds by refining and testing principles in light of what *seem pre-theoretically* to be clear moral judgments at different levels of generality. If theories give the wrong answers by the lights of our considered pre-theoretical judgments about what theory should tell us to do, that gives us reason to reject or revise the theories. We might ultimately overturn our considered judgments in light of what the best theory tells us—reflective equilibrium doesn't

---

[58] Haslanger 2020, 5.   [59] Haslanger 2020, 7.
[60] Haslanger acknowledges this herself; see Haslanger 2021b, 6–7.

assume that our considered pre-theoretical judgments are *true*—but the methodology does rest on the conviction that some pre-theoretical judgments can have warrant. Such judgments are among the provisional fixed points by which we can test theory for adequacy. They're among the provisional fixed points to which I've subjected the anatomy of justice over the course of this book. So, no defender of applied ideal theory should defend the "priority thesis" that one must apply a warranted principle of justice in order to make any warranted judgment of injustice.

It follows from not needing to apply a principle that we needn't have a *complete moral theory* to make a warranted judgment of injustice, either. Yet Haslanger goes to the trouble of arguing against that claim, too: "We do not need to *know what justice is* or have a complete moral theory to engage in social critique. We can know, in some cases, when a practice is unjust, without knowing why it is."[61] I agree that we can.

Elsewhere, Haslanger argues against a necessity claim not about critique but about remediation: She denies that "we need to know what justice is in order to remedy current injustice."[62] I think that correction is more theory reliant than critique. For example: I don't need theory to tell me that poverty-in-the-midst-of-plenty is a problem of justice; I regard that as a provisional fixed point. Yet the question of what we should do about the problem does seem to me to call for theory. We might want theory, for example, to help adjudicate the tradeoffs we face on the road to correction. In Chapter 5, we explored a case in which the anatomy of justice provides guidance for managing evaluative tradeoffs that we can't get without theory. Yet this hardly commits me to thinking that we need to know what justice is in order to remedy *any* current injustice. In fact, I should deny that claim for the same reason I denied the noted necessity claims about critique: Reflective equilibrium *takes for granted* that normative theory is unnecessary for successfully recognizing some injustices as such. In reflective equilibrium, we scrutinize principles of justice by asking how well they match and how well they explain our pre-theoretical considered convictions about (in) justice. Because reflective equilibrium assumes we can have warranted pre-theoretical judgments that a practice is unjust, it also allows that we can do some corrective work without theory.

Haslanger contradicts yet another claim about the necessity of theory for corrective work: She insists that we can work to make things better without knowing what's best; indeed, she argues, we needn't even assume there *is* a best.[63] Here she denies a necessity claim that shows up in the literature on ideal and non-ideal

---

[61] Haslanger 2021b, 6; italics hers. See also 2020, 7, 2012, 23.

[62] Haslanger 2020, 2. Haslanger writes that Tommie Shelby "explicitly embraces" this thesis at Shelby 2018, 11, 13. See Haslanger 2020, 2. I don't find Shelby endorsing that thesis on those pages, explicitly or otherwise.

[63] Haslanger 2021b, 7–8.

196 THE ANATOMY OF JUSTICE

theory: In Amartya Sen's discussion of comparative judgments of justice, he points out that we can compare the heights of Kanchenjuga and Mont Blanc without knowing that Everest is the tallest mountain in the world.[64] Haslanger and Sen are surely right this far: We can make comparisons without knowing what's best. But this possibility seems beside Haslanger's point, since, once again, normative theorists needn't and shouldn't deny it. Reflective equilibrium assumes we can recognize some injustice pre-theoretically; it follows that we can make some other-things-equal comparisons, too.

Haslanger wants to reject normative theory on the grounds that we don't need it, but to do so, she saddles it with necessity claims that are false by the lights of the very theory she wants to reject. Normative theorists shouldn't deny that we can get *any* critique or *any* correction without theory; their very methodology assumes we can. What theory can give us is *more* critique and *better* critique, and through it better and more principled guidance for correction. Is there an argument here against *that*?

It might seem that the mountains' heights help make the case, since the point surely applies beyond Kanchenjuga and Mont Blanc: We can rank *lots* of mountains without knowing which is the tallest in the world. But the mountain analogy is inapt for Haslanger's purposes, because applied ideal theorists needn't infer comparative from transcendental judgments at all. Theorizing with the anatomy of justice, we make no attempt to discern the tallest mountain. Instead, we undertake to discern and precisify the notion of *height*. Or, to dispense with metaphor, the anatomy systematizes our considered moral judgments in reflective equilibrium to discern the *things that matter* that our social arrangement may (fail to) realize. The things that matter include the very ideals of reciprocity and equal respect that Haslanger regards as vague and uncontroversial. The theorist's hope of robustness is the hope that some set of things that matter will matter across circumstances, including in various circumstances of injustice. Though their guidance will vary with the circumstances, it will be unified and principled: Justice favors whatever social arrangement we need in these circumstances to realize the things that matter.[65]

Return to our example of Rawlsian fair equal opportunity, now understood as a thing that matters and not as a narrow prohibition against awarding positions based on considerations of race. In a just society, fair equal opportunity as a thing that matters probably does prohibit awarding positions based on considerations

---

[64] Sen 2006, 222.

[65] Remember: To construe a theory of justice as a weighted, worked out scheme of the things that matter is not to make justice consequentialist. Rawlsian justice—famously deontological—is itself underpinned by things that matter, like the ideal of citizenship that underwrites the moral importance of the basic liberties. These things that matter justify the features of the original position and veil of ignorance; and the principles of justice are those that would be chosen in the original position—the principles that realize the things that matter in a well-ordered society.

of race; it probably calls for straightforward anti-discrimination protections. But, under deep racial injustice, I've suggested, equal opportunity as a thing that matters plausibly calls for radical economic reform, progressive educational practices, strict regulation of inheritance, and affirmative hiring and selection practices.[66] After all, we won't reach a point at which our prospects for attaining desirable positions are unaffected by our race or social class—which is the thing that matters—if we don't reverse the mechanisms by way of which race and class do presently influence our prospects. If we value robustly equal opportunity as a thing that matters, we should always deem a social arrangement less just insofar as that arrangement tolerates barriers to robust equal opportunity. But what equal opportunity so understood tells us to do will depend, as it should, on the nature of the barriers in question.

If we think of normative theory as I have proposed we do, as a project of discerning, precisifying, and weighting the things that matter so that those things supply guidance across circumstances, then the non-necessity of normative theory doesn't follow from the non-necessity of knowing the tallest mountain. We can make progress toward justice without knowing much about the *most* just society, and certainly without being able to describe its institutional structures. Still, for many comparative judgments of justice and certainly for many prescriptive judgments about how to make an unjust society better, we plausibly do need to know what things matter for justice, and how much they matter relative to other things that matter. In short, we need to know in virtue of what a society may be more or less just.

Though not the ones Haslanger attacks, then, I think normative theorists could defend some necessity claims: Without normative theory, we could not render *all* the warranted complaints of injustice that normative theory can underpin, and we would certainly lack its guidance for correction, including its guidance for managing values tradeoffs. Haslanger seems to agree when she writes that "we may need something like a moral theory—or modal knowledge of what sorts of things make something an injustice—to solve *all* of our problems."[67] If we need it to solve all our problems, presumably we need it, too, to know when a solution to one problem comes at the cost of exacerbating another.

Still, I'm not sure normative theorists should bother much trying to prove normative theory's necessity. Instead, I propose that they carry on working to *demonstrate its usefulness*. Using reflective equilibrium, this book undertakes to set forth an anatomy of justice comprising a weighted set of things that matter, which can guide corrective action across circumstances of injustice. The anatomy can also serve as a framework of shared commitments to draw upon in public

---

[66] On corrective justice and fair equality of opportunity, see, Shelby 2004, 2013; Shiffrin 2004; Mills 2013. Or, in a different vein, see Fishkin 2014.

[67] Haslanger 2020, 7; italics hers.

198   THE ANATOMY OF JUSTICE

political deliberation. The liberal feminist work sketched at the outset of the chapter uses reflective equilibrium to theorize mutual respect as a thing that matters. Subsequently drawing on social science, that work claims to furnish an illuminating critique of our gendered practices and better guidance for correction. In Chapter 5, I used reflective equilibrium to explore the urgency of correcting the injustices so critiqued so that we can make better normative judgments when correction comes at a cost in terms of other things that matter. Even if all these arguments are unsound, plenty of others can serve to make the same point: Evidently, by using reflective equilibrium to inform critique and correction, we can make nuanced judgments about where injustice lies in our circumstances, what we should do about it, and at what cost we should do it. We can make our inferences to such judgments legible to those who disagree with us about them.

However normative theorists should assert the value of their contributions, Haslanger's non-necessity case against normative theory fails, because those who employ applied ideal theory need make no categorical claims as to the necessity of normative theory for making any warranted critiques of injustice or for guiding correction. Indeed, their very methodology presumes such claims are false. Some social movements or consciousness raising groups presumably are advancing a lot of true and warranted claims about injustice. Defenders of normative theorizing shouldn't deny this. Those of us who think that theory is worth having don't presume that no justified true moral belief can be had without it.

7.5 Is Normative Theory Adequate?

In applied ideal theory, critique occurs in step two, when principles developed through reflective equilibrium are conjoined with facts about the circumstances we inhabit. Normative theory does not generate critique on its own for the simple reason that we need to know descriptive facts about our society in order to know what normative theory has to say about it. The charge of inadequacy, then, is not the charge that theory needs empirics for critique, which nobody denies, but rather the charge that normative theory generated by domain-specific reflective equilibrium cannot furnish adequate critique even when it is conjoined with empirical facts. It's the charge that step one cannot accomplish even what it claims to accomplish—that reflective equilibrium cannot yield normative theory that's *fit for* critique.

Just as the adequacy of normative theory isn't challenged by the need for empirics in theory application, it also isn't challenged by observations about what kind of awareness *theorists* should cultivate. Plausibly, normative theorists should be responsive to a broad range of salient descriptive facts about their circumstances. Among the empirical facts that reflective equilibrium sidelines as indexical facts about our circumstances, some are products of the social sciences; others are products of consciousness raising and of claims advanced by social movements. Plausibly, theory will be better insofar as theorists cultivate awareness on both fronts. For example, theorists who know Raj Chetty's "mobility report card" research might refine theory to be more responsive to the realities of social closure in the U.S.[68] Those familiar with the Movement for Black Lives may be more alert to the role of social movements in a democracy;[69] that awareness should surely inform theory's priorities. And normative theorists owe feminist consciousness raising for putting certain injustices on our radar. Theorists who are aware of justice-salient social science and social movements, or who are in conversation with those who are aware, can treat these as especially salient conditional test cases for reflective equilibrium. But none of this means that theory must reference particular facts or movements as indexical facts about our circumstances, or that it must rely on those facts for justification.

Haslanger's inadequacy charge withstands these clarifications. She argues that social practices cannot be judged by reference to freestanding theoretical normative standards of the sort developed through reflective equilibrium because (dis-)value *is created by* social practices. Normative theory can't comprise freestanding standards by which to judge existing practices, then, because what critique is warranted *depends upon* the practices.[70] Haslanger invokes the unavoidability of social loss to illustrate:

> Practices are valuable and produce goods that are internal to the practice. For example, in a division of labor, there will be a division of expertise. Even if the division of labor is unjust, individuals marked for a particular set of tasks may develop a set of skills, a sensibility, solidarity with each other, by virtue of participation in a particular position in the structured set of practices. Goods may accrue to the participants, even if overall the structure is problematic and should be changed. In such cases, sacrifice is inevitable.[71]

Haslanger seems to argue here that there's value in the practices and meanings we've created together, even if they're unjust, because changing existing practices and meanings invariably involves sacrifice. Her argument resonates strikingly with a liberal case for status quo deference: People form their life plans against a set of social meanings and practices, and respect for their life plans gives us *some* reason to carry on as we've been doing. Liberalism treats these reasons as very defeasible: Our example liberal feminist arguments conclude that the reasons give way in the face of gender injustice, for example. The question at hand is whether (liberal) normative theory can recognize these *as* reasons—whether it

---

[68] Chetty et al. 2017.   [69] Woodly 2018.   [70] Haslanger 2021b.
[71] Haslanger 2021b, 8. On the inevitability of loss and sacrifice in democracy, see Allen 2004, especially chap. 4.

200 THE ANATOMY OF JUSTICE

can recognize some value in the status quo as such. Clearly it can. We all have interests in avoiding frustrated expectations, and social change frustrates expectations. Both facts are general and non-controversial. Theory should tell us both when an interest frustration is morally relevant and when, though morally relevant, it gives way to weightier concerns. The anatomy proceeds by refining the ideals by reference to which expectations matter and the ideals that may call for disruptive social change even at the cost of frustration.

A second way in which value is created by social practices goes beyond a standing defeasible status quo deference and raises deeper concerns. Haslanger quotes J. M. Balkin to help make her case:

> Before culture there are no electric guitars, violins, or orchestras...no idea of jazz or the blues...Throughout human history people develop different ways of making and organizing sounds, which they test against their developing sense of beauty and interest. Their sense of the beautiful and the interesting in turn is developed through exposure to and use of the cultural tools available to them within their culture.[72]

Similarly, with ethical value:

> We concretize our indeterminate value of justice by creating human institutions and practices that attempt to enforce it and exemplify it...Of course, because justice is an indeterminate standard, there is no necessary way to exemplify it. The value of justice does not tell us, for example, whether a democratic legislature should have one, two, or three houses. Hence the institutions that people construct to exemplify justice may be different in different eras and different lands.[73]

It's surely true that different circumstances call for different institutions to realize justice. But this is no challenge to the adequacy of normative theory. Even on Haslanger's characterization of reflective equilibrium, we first discern principles and then figure out what institutional configuration those principles favor *in our circumstances*. This does not render justice "an indeterminate standard"; it just means that theory offers higher level guidance—and guidance more robust across circumstantial change—compared with prescriptions about legislative design: A theory of justice offers standards by way of which we might assess or justify such prescriptions in light of circumstantial facts. Just as we might draw on the anatomy of justice and facts about our society's racist history to argue that realizing equal opportunity requires affirmative hiring practices, so too might we draw

---

[72] Balkin 1998, 28; quoted at Haslanger 2020, 7.
[73] Balkin 1998, 30–31; quoted at Haslanger 2020, 7–8, 2021b, 8.

on the anatomy and on our history and the sociology of representation to argue for expanding the U.S. House of Representatives.[74]

Haslanger insists that "there is an important difference between 'applying a principle' and, as Balkin puts it, 'concretizing our indeterminate sense of justice'."[75] Reflective equilibrium renders principles we can *apply*, she thinks, but the work that needs doing is more complex than application: We need to *concretize* something *indeterminant*. But as her prime example concerns the number of legislative houses, the distinction seems not to do the work she asks of it. With Haslanger, normative theorists will deny that theory developed using reflective equilibrium normatively *determines* legislative design; they nonetheless think that such theory can supply illuminating normative guidance about legislative design when conjoined with information about our culture, history, and circumstances. The guidance isn't easily derived. It requires significant further argumentation about which there will be both moral and empirical disagreement. Remember, it was Haslanger who coined "applied ideal theory" to refer to the practice of using reflective equilibrium and normative theory to critique injustice and prescribe correction. Pressed with her distinction between "applying" and "concretizing," defenders of that practice might point out that theory application is hard work; this is evidenced by the many rich literatures in which writers who agree broadly on some theoretical convictions *dis*agree about how those convictions bear on an issue of social importance. Alternatively, defenders of the practice might deny that the term fairly characterizes their approach to thinking about injustice. Either way, the sense of shallowness that the term "application" sometimes carries doesn't show the methodology of reflective equilibrium to be inadequate. A critic can't ground her rejection of a method of inquiry on a shallow-sounding term that she herself has coined.

To see what "application" or "concretization" looks like in practice for those who use reflective equilibrium to consider legislative design, we can invoke Haslanger's most explicit target. Rawls's principles of justice make no mention of how many houses the legislature should have or what form the economy should take. Still, they provide guidance on such matters once we apply them to our particular circumstances. Rawls's process for deriving institutional guidance from the principles of justice is called the "four-stage sequence,"[76] and by the time we ask about the shape of the legislature, we are permitted a great deal of information about our society. First, we derive principles of justice. Second, we consider constitutional design. For this, we invoke the general facts we drew on to derive the principles and also all relevant particular facts about our society, including facts about its natural circumstances and resources, economic circumstances, political culture, and history.[77] We ask what constitutional design best protects

---

[74] See Drutman et al. 2021. [75] Haslanger 2020, 9.
[76] See Rawls 1999a, 171–6. [77] Rawls 1999a, 172–4.

202 THE ANATOMY OF JUSTICE

our entitlements of justice and supports legislation that realizes the principles of justice given those facts.[78] For the Rawlsian non-ideal theorist, these facts might include facts about the society's *racist* history. To return to our running example, we may ask at the constitutional stage whether equal opportunity in our circumstances favors affirmative practices or only prohibitions against discrimination.

At the third stage of Rawls's process for applying/concretizing principles of justice, we ask about the justice of particular laws and policies. Here we know the full range of facts about our society; we abstain only from invoking facts about the circumstances of particular people.[79] With full knowledge of our society, we ask which laws will best realize justice. At this stage, for example, Rawls asks which *economic* system is just. Depending on the history and circumstances of the society, he argues, it will be either market socialism or property-owning democracy. His remarks on this choice are illuminating:

> Which of these systems and the many intermediate forms most fully answers to the requirements of justice cannot, I think, be determined in advance. There is presumably no general answer to this question, since it depends in large part upon the traditions, institutions, and social forces of each country, and its particular historical circumstances…A conception of justice is a necessary part of any such political assessment, but it is not sufficient.[80]

For Rawls, then, the principles of justice, all on their own, limit the range of economic institutions that *can* be just. Welfare state capitalism, for example, is ruled out as unjust, even before we know the particulars of the society in question. But within that range of *possibly* just economic arrangements, the *most* just arrangement will depend on circumstantial facts of just the sort that Haslanger rightly insists we cannot be without when we turn to matters of institutional design. And, within the range of the possibly just, an argument for a particular economic system—like an argument for the number of houses in a legislature—should proceed from principles of justice in harness with those circumstantial facts. Though they don't *settle* answers to these institutional questions, then, Rawls's principles give guidance by narrowing the range of possible answers and by specifying the considerations that adjudicate among them.[81]

Recall, too, that the guidance we get as we concretize a theory of justice can also serve to confirm or disconfirm that theory. If we're egalitarians, we might find Rawls's theory more plausible when we see that it rules out welfare state capitalism as unjustly inegalitarian. If we're anti-racist, we might find an approach to theorizing less plausible when we believe it ignores the injustice that would

---

[78] Rawls 1999a, 194.   [79] Rawls 1999a, 175.   [80] Rawls 1999a, 242.

[81] I omit discussion of the fourth and final stage, "that of the application of rules to particular cases by judges and administrators, and the following of rules by citizens generally." See Rawls 1999a, 175.

survive state-mandated school integration. (If we later see that it actually *attends to* that injustice, we will need to revise our earlier judgment.) If we are feminists, we might find a proposed anatomy of justice more plausible when we see that it would license and in fact positively call for social policy to erode pernicious gender norms, or that it can provide plausible guidance in cases of values tradeoffs. All these are ways in which the judgments rendered as we "concretize" theory reflect back, via reflective equilibrium, on the theory itself.

Haslanger is surely right that social practices can create (dis-)value. In reflective equilibrium, a theory gains justification by virtue of providing plausible guidance across a range of circumstances. Guidance is plausible insofar as it accommodates or credibly revises our considered convictions about what guidance justice *should* provide, and insofar as it responds in plausible ways to historical, sociological, and material circumstances, including to the ways in which those circumstances affect how value gets created. Using reflective equilibrium, I've argued that the anatomy of justice provides guidance across a broad range of circumstances, including circumstances of justice and of profound injustice. I've argued that the anatomy responds to the (dis-)value created by social practices, and that it can prescribe circumstance-responsive reform including in the form of *new* value-creating practices. I have used conditionalized premises about our circumstances to assess the anatomy's plausibility while still preserving its broad applicability. If we learn later that our actual circumstances fall elsewhere within our tested range than I thought, the anatomy needn't be any less justified, because justification relies on its giving good guidance *in thus-and-such circumstances*, not on thus-and-such being *our* circumstances. This is how we get theory that is robust across circumstances *and* that has bite: theory that responds to the ways in which social practices can create (dis-)value.

Recall the kinds of social awareness I said theorists might rightly cultivate for the sake of theorizing better. With those kinds of awareness, applied ideal theorists might ask questions of a theory of justice like these: Does this theory give plausible guidance for a society in which children from the top 1 percent of the income distribution are seventy-seven times likelier to attend an Ivy League college than children from the bottom quintile?[82] Or in which a massive, socially transformative movement is saying "this hurts us" about racist policing and doing real, tangible, self-protective work?[83] We can ask: Could our theory, in response to the Combahee River Collective Statement of 1977, have impugned the distinct tradeoffs that Black women face between intellectual and social pursuits?[84] There are countless moral judgments of injustice against which we *could* test theory. Our provisional fixed points can certainly come from social movements, and we can certainly rely on consciousness raising to determine which fixed points are

---

[82] Chetty et al. 2017, 1.   [83] Campbell 2021.   [84] Taylor 2017; Haslanger 2021b, 15.

204   THE ANATOMY OF JUSTICE

the most salient test cases for us, now. That a theory of justice gives plausible critique and plausible guidance across a range of circumstances is a mark in its favor—and theorists get to choose what circumstances to consider. That a theory's guidance changes in plausible ways as circumstances change is yet another win. We needn't compromise a theory's breadth of application by asking these questions when we assess it.

Haslanger invokes still other cases meant to show that social practices create (dis-)value in ways that normative theory cannot appreciate: Diachronically, "normative questions arise about parenthood, surrogacy, parental responsibility, human enhancement, eugenics, all with an overlay of concerns about gender, race, class, sexuality, and disability... [T]he biotechnology revolution has disrupted, contested, and changed 'family values' as well as what counts as a family and even what counts as human."[85] Synchronically,

> any 'sense of justice' or appreciation of the 'value of reciprocity' (etc.) that might provide a basis for moral theorizing across social and cultural differences is indeterminate...and our efforts to articulate it in a way that renders it determinate will inevitably incorporate particular socio-historical elements that make it apt for some contexts, or some communities, but not others.[86]

Haslanger is right that foundational normative theory will make no reference to surrogacy or eugenics, just as it makes no reference to the number of legislative houses. But theory making no mention of such practices can still provide guidance that's responsive to the value or dis-value they create in different circumstances and that attends to the "overlay of concerns about gender, race, class, sexuality, and disability." If techniques for human enhancement exacerbate class injustice or stigmatize people with disabilities, adequate normative theory will regard those as bad-making features. On the anatomy of justice, for example, mutual respect clearly condemns social stigma and subordination based on disability. Whether some technology has these bad-making features can depend on the context. Similarly, mutual respect may impugn some practice in one cultural context but approve it in another. We need to theorize mutual respect to discern its judgments, and when we "concretize" that single determinate ideal, its guidance will surely vary from context to context.

Haslanger's purported problem cases for applied ideal theory are anything but. Those cases illustrate that social practices can change how existing values get instantiated and even create new bearers of value or dis-value. But they don't challenge the thought that one robust set of ideals explains *what it is in virtue of which* these bearers are (dis-)valuable. Indeed, her cases all seem well

---

[85] Haslanger 2020, 8.   [86] Haslanger 2021b, 9.

REFLECTIVE EQUILIBRIUM AND SOCIAL CRITIQUE 205

accommodated by reference to the very ideals that liberal egalitarian applied ideal theorists commonly invoke: mutual respect, equal consideration, reciprocity, and distributive fairness. Haslanger's cases may illuminate something important about value, but all this can remain true: Ideals like mutual respect matter robustly; we realize those ideals in different ways in different contexts; and we should theorize the ideals precisely by asking whether the guidance they provide across a range of salient cases matches our provisional considered convictions about those cases or prompts revision in ways we can accept upon reflection.

Let's bring the discussion full circle. The liberal feminist arguments we sketched at the outset work to refine and "concretize" the ideals of social equality and mutual respect in part by considering the guidance those ideals supply within a particular empirical context.[87] The arguments also invoke social equality and mutual respect to surface injustice in practices like sex work or the gendered division of labor, where that injustice is commonly thought to lie beyond (political) liberalism's diagnostic resources, thus revealing those ideals' underappreciated critical power. For all I establish in this chapter, these liberal feminist arguments may be unsound. My burden is only to show that their methodology does not render their conclusions inaccessible. Haslanger's case against reflective equilibrium implies that the claimed accomplishments of these liberal feminist arguments are *impossible*: "Either we establish principles that are precise enough to guide action, and they will be continually overthrown; or we make do with vague articulations of our sense of justice and we reformulate them in response to our confrontation with social reality."[88] The liberal feminist arguments claim to have refined theory by confronting it with social reality. But the theorists' aim is to contribute to the work of building theory that is both robust and precise enough to be helpful. Haslanger's argument that such theory cannot be had returns us to our gender case:

> Suppose we are considering the division of labor in the family. The question is not how a particular family should divide labor. Rather, it is a question about social norms, the formation of gender identity, and the socialization of individuals through particular practices of intimacy, sexuality, parenting, and economic cooperation...[F]eminist critics reject the existing gendered division of labor and the processes by which individuals are shaped to fit its requirements. But what are the uncontroversial empirical and metaphysical claims the feminist is entitled to rely on in developing the critique? For example, can we assume that men and women have the same capacities for nurturing young children? This is not only a radical claim in the context of the history of the family, but it remains controversial in many contemporary contexts. Insofar as it is a controversial

[87] See also Nussbaum 1999, 2000.   [88] Haslanger 2020, 10.

206   THE ANATOMY OF JUSTICE

> empirical claim, it cannot play a role in the normative reflective equilibrium that yields our [applied] ideal theory...Uncontroversial but vague notions such as reciprocity and equal respect do not give the social critic adequate normative resources to challenge the status quo. But such challenges are the task of social critique.[89]

By now we can recognize three problems for Haslanger's attempted case in point. First, reflective equilibrium *needn't* exclude controversial empirical and metaphysical claims. Rawls, Haslanger's primary target, insisted that theorizing could not proceed without facts. If it is true that men and women have the same natural capacities for nurturance, then that *general* fact is akin to the general laws of psychology or economics that Rawls liberally and explicitly invokes in his original position argument.

But suppose we do want to eschew the controversial empirical. Haslanger's case fails for a second reason: She misdescribes the methodology when she describes it as eschewing any empirical claims at all when it comes to *critiquing gendered social practices*. Nothing in applied ideal theory precludes invoking true empirical facts at the point of applying theory to critique and rectify injustice. Plenty of applied ideal theorists regard empirical facts about gender socialization as highly relevant to the question of what principles of justice have to say about gendered behavior.[90] Liberal feminists don't invoke the social construction of gender to explain *why mutual respect or reciprocity matter*. But they can and do invoke true empirical premises—controversial or not—to explain what normative theory directs us to do in our circumstances. The entire point of applied ideal theory, recall, was to apply theory in harness with empirical data and policy-making expertise. So (liberal) applied ideal theorists *can* criticize the "norms, formation of gender identity, and the socialization of individuals through particular practices of intimacy, sexuality, parenting, and economic cooperation" by refining theory through reflective equilibrium and subsequently concretizing it in light of the facts about gender's operation in our society. That includes facts about the social causes of observed gender differences. And, crucially, the verdicts that theory renders can reflect well or badly on the theory itself. This means we are invoking our (conditionalized) convictions about instances of injustice even at the point of formulating, revising, and refining theory.

Haslanger's case in point fails for yet a third reason: Applied ideal theory can criticize the norms and social arrangements that sustain gendered relations in the family even without invoking the claim that men and women have equal (natural) capacities for nurturing children. As discussed in Chapter 4, the anatomy of justice is a version of political liberalism. As such, it does impose a kind of

---

[89] Haslanger 2020, 8–9.   [90] See, for example, Okin 1989; Chambers 2008.

non-controversiality constraint on the moral convictions we can invoke to justify political action.[91] To comply with this constraint and still answer Haslanger's charge, the anatomy must support critique of the gendered division of labor that eschews premises which we can accept only if we embrace certain controversial conceptions of the good.[92] It must eschew such premises *especially* at step two. The arguments I've invoked throughout this and the previous two chapters claim to do just that: By the lights of these arguments, if the gendered division of labor undermines mutual respect by sustaining social hierarchies or by offending against foundational interests entailed by our social equality, then it is unjust and calls for rectification *whether or not* women and men have equal natural capacities for nurturance. Thus, while it might seem that Haslanger's strongest case isn't against the methodology of reflective equilibrium but rather against the substantive commitments of political liberalism, her criticism fails even there. Arguments from politically liberal feminists explicitly claim to use reciprocity and equal respect for critique without invoking any forbidden premises at either stage of applied ideal theory. Haslanger may want to show that those arguments are unsound, but she hasn't successfully shown that what they claim to do cannot be done using reflective equilibrium.

Haslanger's criticisms of reflective equilibrium are unsuccessful. They mischaracterize reflective equilibrium's empirical abstention, attribute necessity theses that its defenders needn't and sometimes shouldn't endorse, underappreciate its responsiveness to the ways value is created through social practices, and wrongly declare ideals like equal respect unfit to challenge the status quo.

7.6 Is Liberalism Ideology?

Haslanger makes another point meant to challenge applied ideal theory: "We are situated inquirers, and the question is how we should go on from here...There may be some practices...in which we can rely mainly on experts to decide the best way to go on. But in the social domain, we should figure this out collectively."[93] Liberalism—using applied ideal theory—can fully appreciate this insight. Liberal democratic theory tells us that we should often defer politically to the verdicts of

---

[91] See, most notably for our purposes, Rawls 1997, 786. For other substantive commitments that impose something like a non-controversiality constraint in certain circumstances, see Rawls 1999a, 187–9.

[92] I count claims about women's and men's natural capacities for caregiving as depending on disputed conceptions of the good. Compare Fowler 2019. If I'm wrong about that—if such claims reflect *mere* empirical disagreement—and if political liberals needn't take the same care with empirical disagreement as with normative or evaluative disagreement, then my defense against Haslanger's criticisms is, if anything, on firmer ground.

[93] Haslanger 2021b, 7. On democracy in justice as fairness (both political and comprehensive), see Cohen 2003.

inclusive, deliberative democratic procedures, even when those verdicts don't align with what our normative theory tells us is most just. Liberalism as I have understood it in this book *does* attempt to discern and systematize normative facts that can be true independent of anything that we situated inquirers would say on the matter. But it also tells us that some of what matters is realizable only through the process of deciding together. And it tells us that some normative facts—perhaps a great many—*simply don't exist* until we set our shared ends together. The importance of broad, democratic deliberation in social reform is no challenge to reflective equilibrium; it is among the considered convictions that should fuel it. And insofar as democratic deliberation is an *instance of* reflective equilibrium, it must be broad and inclusive in order to be reliable. We should empower everyone to take part, and we should listen keenly to the oppressed, whether or not they have privileged knowledge,[94] simply because everyone should be empowered to speak, and voices that have long been ignored may need amplification now in order to be heard equitably.

These remarks presuppose a distinction between what to *believe* about injustice in our society and what to *do* about it. I have argued that reflective equilibrium is more promising than Haslanger takes it to be as a means of uncovering what we should believe about injustice. Even if I'm right, her own methodology of consciousness raising and deference to social movements may be a good account of how social-justice-minded citizens ought generally to proceed with their activism once they've chosen a good movement to align with. Haslanger may deny that what we should believe about injustice is distinct from how we should proceed as social-justice-minded citizens. I think that denial would come at a high cost. We should be able to endorse the view that critique is best leveled in democratic practice through consciousness raising and movement building, without thereby being analytically committed to the view that those practices also determine what we should believe about injustice. We might also like to have moral guidance on what movements to align with. We might like to have moral arguments to offer our political opponents, and hope that by treating (some) opponents as reasonable we can come to fruitfully exchange reasons. But asserting my conviction on these matters clearly doesn't settle them. What I've *argued* for is this: Haslanger's criticism notwithstanding, reflective equilibrium *can* accomplish what the anatomy of justice and what liberal egalitarian feminists take it to accomplish. Haslanger may argue that we shouldn't bother trying to accomplish that. But that's a different argument than the one she's so far given, and the importance of figuring out collectively where to go from here doesn't cut against the value of reflective equilibrium's work.

---

[94] See Dror 2022.

What about collective, deliberative ideals in *theory building*? Remember the old joke about the police officer who sees a drunk man searching for his house keys under a streetlight. The officer helps look for a while before asking the man, "are you sure you lost the keys here, in this spot?" The man says, "no, I lost them in that park across the street." "Then why search *here*?" the officer asks. The man responds, "because this is where the light is."[95] In political philosophy, liberal theory has long been where the light is. It commands massive theoretical attention. We should ask: Are we like the drunk man, looking here only because this is where the light is, and looking here despite a good reason to look across the street? But our suspicion shouldn't be insurmountable. I *don't* think we're like the drunk man. I think we have good reason to think the keys are here, and I think the proffered reasons to think they *aren't* here come up short. And, while the light itself isn't a reason to look here, on its own it's not a reason not to, either. A theory that commands massive theoretical attention might command it for good reason.

What if, in addition to being bathed in light, liberal theorizing is *ideological*? Recall that, on Haslanger's definition, a set of social meanings functions ideologically whenever it functions to sustain injustice. A lot then hangs on what it means to say that some normative framework "functions in a context...to create or sustain injustice."[96] Haslanger seems to think that justice is demanding and that our current arrangement falls very far short. I think she's right on both counts. If she is, then on her definition, *lots* of sets of social meanings arguably will function ideologically in lots of unjust circumstances. Just how many yet depends on precisely what is meant by "functions in a context." To establish that liberalism *operates to* sustain *some* injustice in our circumstances, we need only observe that many still associate it with minimally restrained capitalism and a minimal welfare state. But if that suffices to make it ideology, then *any* normative and any *critical* theory can come to function ideologically if it affects the world at all: Influential ideas can always be distorted or misunderstood in ways that sustain injustice. And notice that, on this construal of ideology, liberal theory may function ideologically and nonetheless comprise a true, deep, illuminating, and potentially emancipatory set of ideals.

Whether we find in this observation grounds to resist this construal of ideology, we should at least find in it a reason to believe this: While ideology on this construal might still be pejorative by definition, it cannot plausibly be *dispositively* pejorative by definition. Whether a normative theory functions ideologically depends, on this construal, on contingencies of our social environment, like on whether the powerful are able to use or distort a theory to further justice-obstructing ends. But features of theories like their truth, depth, insight, and explanatory or critical power surely (also) matter to whether or not we should

---

[95] I was reminded of this parable reading Guerrero 2018.   [96] Haslanger 2021b, 2.

espouse them. Even if unfavorable social contingencies bear on theory selection, too, they can't plausibly on their own justify discarding a theory that accurately discerns and deeply illuminates political values; that diagnoses injustice and critiques the status quo in coherence with our most secure and reflective pretheoretical judgments; that prescribes deep structural reforms to redress injustice so critiqued; and that prioritizes reforms in coherence with provisional fixed points.

Some social and normative theories will be such that, even properly understood, they intrinsically *lend themselves* to sustaining injustice, or *tend to* mislead, or otherwise function to sustain injustice in some more exacting sense of "function."[97] If this book's arguments about the anatomy of justice are sound, liberalism isn't like that. Rightly understood, liberalism has radical critical and normative power. And if a normative theory functions ideologically only for reasons of contingent social circumstance, we face a choice: Either we abandon the theory, or we fight for the theory against the social contingencies that make it function to sustain injustice in our circumstances. Surely, the right course of action should depend at least in part on whether there is truth or depth or insight or critical power in the theory worth fighting for.

Whether there *is* truth or depth or insight is a question best answered by looking in the light and beyond it, and by talking to those who find insight in different places. That is just what reflective equilibrium advises. I hope that, through broad reflective equilibrium, we'll find that there is truth in the anatomy of justice, and that the evaluative discernment it offers can helpfully guide corrective action, including to correct social circumstances that enable liberal theorizing to be misused, or misunderstood, to the detriment of justice. Rather than abandoning good theory to the social contingencies that obstruct reform, we should make the case, from fundamental shared values, for what liberal theory gets right about injustice.

The Anatomy of Justice: On the Shape, Substance, and Power of Liberal Egalitarianism. Gina Schouten, Oxford University Press. © Gina Schouten 2024. DOI: 10.1093/9780191999772.003.0008

---

[97] For helpful discussion of the meaning of function in functional critique, see Shelby 2022, 87–119.

Bibliography

Allen, Danielle S. 2004. *Talking to Strangers: Anxieties of Citizenship since Brown v. Board of Education.* Chicago, Ill.: University of Chicago Press.

Anderson, Elizabeth. 1993. *Value in Ethics and Economics.* Cambridge, Mass.: Harvard University Press.

Anderson, Elizabeth. 1999. "What Is the Point of Equality?" *Ethics* 109 (2):287–337. https://doi.org/10.1086/233897.

Anderson, Elizabeth. 2007. "Fair Opportunity in Education: A Democratic Equality Perspective." *Ethics* 117 (4):595–622. https://doi.org/10.1086/518806.

Anderson, Elizabeth. 2010a. *The Imperative of Integration.* Princeton, N.J.: Princeton University Press.

Anderson, Elizabeth. 2010b. "The Fundamental Disagreement between Luck Egalitarians and Relational Egalitarians." *Canadian Journal of Philosophy* 40 (sup1):1–23. https://doi.org/10.1080/00455091.2010.10717652.

Arneson, Richard J. 1989. "Equality and Equal Opportunity for Welfare." *Philosophical Studies* 56 (1):77–93. https://doi.org/10.1007/BF00646210.

Arneson, Richard J. 2000. "Luck Egalitarianism and Prioritarianism." *Ethics* 110 (2):339–49. https://doi.org/10.1086/233272.

Arneson, Richard J. 2008. "Justice Is Not Equality." *Ratio* 21 (4):371–91. https://doi.org/10.1111/j.1467-9329.2008.00409.x.

Arneson, Richard J. 2010. "Democratic Equality and Relating as Equals." *Canadian Journal of Philosophy* 40 (sup1):25–52. https://doi.org/10.1080/00455091.2010.10717653.

Baker, John. 2008. "All Things Considered, Should Feminists Embrace Basic Income?" *Basic Income Studies* 3 (3). https://doi.org/10.2202/1932-0183.1129.

Balkin, J. M. 1998. *Cultural Software: A Theory off Ideology.* New Haven, Conn.: Yale University Press.

Bergmann, Barbara. 2004. "A Swedish-Style Welfare State or Basic Income: Which Should Have Priority?" *Politics & Society* 32 (1):107–18. https://doi.org/10.1177/0032329203261101.

Berlin, Isaiah. 2002. *Liberty: Incorporating Four Essays on Liberty.* Edited by Henry Hardy. 2nd edition. Oxford: Oxford University Press.

Berlin, Isaiah. 2013. *The Crooked Timber of Humanity: Chapters in the History of Ideas—Second Edition.* Edited by Henry Hardy. 2nd edition. Princeton, N.J.: Princeton University Press.

Bertrand, Marianne. 2018. "Coase Lecture—the Glass Ceiling." SSRN Scholarly Paper ID 3133423. Rochester, N.Y.: Social Science Research Network. https://papers.ssrn.com/abstract=3133423.

Bertrand, Marianne, Emir Kamenica, and Jessica Pan. 2015. "Gender Identity and Relative Income within Households." *The Quarterly Journal of Economics* 130 (2):571–614. https://doi.org/10.1093/qje/qjv001.

Bertrand, Marianne, and Sendhil Mullainathan. 2004. "Are Emily and Greg More Employable Than Lakisha and Jamal? A Field Experiment on Labor Market Discrimination." *The American Economic Review* 94 (4):991–1013.

Blau, Francine D., and Lawrence M. Kahn. 2013. "Female Labor Supply: Why Is the US Falling Behind?" Working Paper 18702. National Bureau of Economic Research. https://doi.org/10.3386/w18702.

Brake, Elizabeth. 2012. *Minimizing Marriage: Marriage, Morality, and the Law.* Oxford: Oxford University Press.

212 BIBLIOGRAPHY

Brighouse, Harry. 1994. "Is There Any Such Thing as Political Liberalism?" *Pacific Philosophical Quarterly* 75 (3–4):318–32. https://doi.org/10.1111/j.1468-0114.1994.tb00133.x.

Brighouse, Harry. 1996. "Is There a Neutral Justification for Liberalism?" *Pacific Philosophical Quarterly* 77 (3):193–215. https://doi.org/10.1111/j.1468-0114.1996.tb00166.x.

Brighouse, Harry, and Adam Swift. 2008. "Putting Educational Equality in Its Place." *Education Finance and Policy* 3 (4):444–66. https://doi.org/10.1162/edfp.2008.3.4.444.

Brighouse, Harry, and Adam Swift. 2009a. "Legitimate Parental Partiality." *Philosophy & Public Affairs* 37 (1):43–80. https://doi.org/10.1111/j.1088-4963.2008.01145.x.

Brighouse, Harry, and Adam Swift. 2009b. "Educational Equality versus Educational Adequacy: A Critique of Anderson and Satz." *Journal of Applied Philosophy* 26 (2):117–28. https://doi.org/10.1111/j.1468-5930.2009.00438.x.

Campbell, Travis. 2021. "Black Lives Matter's Effect on Police Lethal Use-of-Force." SSRN Scholarly Paper ID 3767097. Rochester, N.Y.: Social Science Research Network. https://doi.org/10.2139/ssrn.3767097.

Chambers, Clare. 2008. *Sex, Culture, and Justice: The Limits of Choice.* University Park, Penn.: Pennsylvania State University Press. http://www.jstor.org/stable/10.5325/j.ctt7v2d1.

Chambers, Clare. 2017. "Ideology and Normativity." *Aristotelian Society Supplementary Volume* 91 (1):175–95. https://doi.org/10.1093/arisup/akx008.

Chang, Ruth. 1997. "Introduction." In *Incommensurability, Incomparability and Practical Reason*, edited by Ruth Chang, 1–34. Cambridge, Mass.: Harvard University Press.

Chetty, Raj, John N. Friedman, Emmanuel Saez, Nicholas Turner, and Danny Yagan. 2017. "Mobility Report Cards: The Role of Colleges in Intergenerational Mobility." Working Paper 23618. National Bureau of Economic Research. https://doi.org/10.3386/w23618.

Christiano, Thomas. 2004. "The Authority of Democracy." *Journal of Political Philosophy* 12 (3):266–90. https://doi.org/10.1111/j.1467-9760.2004.00200.x.

Cohen, G. A. 1989. "On the Currency of Egalitarian Justice." *Ethics* 99 (4):906–44.

Cohen, G. A. 1992. "Incentives, Inequality, and Community." *The Tanner Lectures on Human Values* 13:263–329.

Cohen, G. A. 1995. "The Pareto Argument for Inequality." *Social Philosophy and Policy* 12 (1):160–85. https://doi.org/10.1017/S026505250000460X.

Cohen, G. A. 1997. "Where the Action Is: On the Site of Distributive Justice." *Philosophy & Public Affairs* 26 (1):3–30.

Cohen, G. A. 2000. "If You're an Egalitarian, How Come You're so Rich?" *The Journal of Ethics* 4 (1/2):1–26.

Cohen, G. A. 2008. *Rescuing Justice and Equality.* Cambridge, Mass.: Harvard University Press.

Cohen, G. A. 2009. *Why Not Socialism?* Princeton, N.J.: Princeton University Press.

Cohen, Joshua. 1989. "Democratic Equality." *Ethics* 99 (4):727–51.

Cohen, Joshua. 2001. "Taking People as They Are?" *Philosophy & Public Affairs* 30 (4):363–86.

Cohen, Joshua. 2003. "For a Democratic Society." In *The Cambridge Companion to Rawls*, edited by Samuel Freeman, 86–138. Cambridge: Cambridge University Press.

Cohen, Joshua. 2009. "Truth and Public Reason." *Philosophy & Public Affairs* 37 (1):2–42. https://doi.org/10.1111/j.1088-4963.2008.01144.x.

Coltrane, Scott. 2009. "Fatherhood, Gender and Work-Family Policies." In *Gender Equality: Transforming Family Divisions of Labor*, edited by Erik Olin Wright, 385–410. Real Utopias Project. London: Verso.

Correll, Shelley J., Stephen Benard, and In Paik. 2007. "Getting a Job: Is There a Motherhood Penalty?" *American Journal of Sociology* 112 (5):1297–338. https://doi.org/10.1086/511799.

Crowder, George. 2001. *Liberalism and Value Pluralism.* London: Continuum.

Daniels, Norman. 1979. "Wide Reflective Equilibrium and Theory Acceptance in Ethics." *The Journal of Philosophy* 76 (5):256–82. https://doi.org/10.2307/2025881.

Daniels, Norman. 2003. "Democratic Equality: Rawls's Complex Egalitarianism." In *The Cambridge Companion to Rawls*, edited by Samuel Freeman, 241–76. Cambridge: Cambridge University Press.

Daniels, Norman. 2015. "Reflective Equilibrium." In *The Cambridge Rawls Lexicon*, edited by Jon Mandle and David A. Reidy, 711–716. Cambridge: Cambridge University Press.

Daniels, Norman. 2020. "Reflective Equilibrium." Edited by Edward N Zalta. *The Stanford Encyclopedia of Philosophy*. https://plato.stanford.edu/archives/sum2020/entries/reflective-equilibrium/.

Darby, Derrick, and John L. Rury. 2018. *The Color of Mind: Why the Origins of the Achievement Gap Matter for Justice*. Chicago, Ill.: University of Chicago Press.

Darwall, Stephen. 2009. *The Second-Person Standpoint: Morality, Respect, and Accountability*. Cambridge, Mass.: Harvard University Press.

Dror, Lidal. 2022. "Is There an Epistemic Advantage to Being Oppressed?" *Noûs* n/a (n/a):1–23. https://doi.org/10.1111/nous.12424.

Drutman, Lee, Jonathan D. Cohen, Yuval Levin, and Norman J. Ornstein. 2021. "The Case for Enlarging the House of Representatives." Our Common Purpose Report. American Academy of Arts and Sciences.

Dworkin, Ronald. 1981. "What Is Equality? Part 2: Equality of Resources." *Philosophy & Public Affairs* 10 (4):283–345.

Dworkin, Ronald. 2000. *Sovereign Virtue: The Theory and Practice of Equality*. Cambridge, Mass.: Harvard University Press.

Dworkin, Ronald. 2003. "Equality, Luck and Hierarchy." *Philosophy & Public Affairs* 31 (2):190–98.

Dworkin, Ronald. 2011. *Justice for Hedgehogs*. Reprint edition. Cambridge, Mass.: Belknap Press, an imprint of Harvard University Press.

Elgarte, Julieta M. 2008. "Basic Income and the Gendered Division of Labour." *Basic Income Studies* 3 (3). https://doi.org/10.2202/1932-0183.1136.

England, Paula. 2010. "The Gender Revolution: Uneven and Stalled." *Gender and Society* 24 (2):149–66.

Enoch, David. 2018. "Against Utopianism: Noncompliance and Multiple Agents." *Philosophers' Imprint* 18 (16):1–20. http://hdl.handle.net/2027/spo.3521354.0018.016.

Erman, Eva, and Niklas Möller. 2015. "Practices and Principles: On the Methodological Turn in Political Theory." *Philosophy Compass* 10 (August):533–46. https://doi.org/10.1111/phc3.12245.

Estlund, David. 1996. "The Survival of Egalitarian Justice in John Rawls's Political Liberalism." *Journal of Political Philosophy* 4 (1):68–78. https://doi.org/10.1111/j.1467-9760.1996.tb00042.x.

Estlund, David. 1998. "The Insularity of the Reasonable: Why Political Liberalism Must Admit the Truth." *Ethics* 108 (2):252–75. https://doi.org/10.1086/233804.

Estlund, David. 2011. "Human Nature and the Limits (If Any) of Political Philosophy." *Philosophy & Public Affairs* 39 (3):207–37. https://doi.org/10.1111/j.1088-4963.2011.01207.x.

Estlund, David. 2020. *Utopophobia: On the Limits (If Any) of Political Philosophy*. Princeton, N.J.: Princeton University Press.

Eyal, Nir. 2006. "Egalitarian Justice and Innocent Choice." *Journal of Ethics and Social Philosophy* 2 (1):1–19. https://doi.org/10.26556/jesp.v2i1.19.

Fishkin, Joseph. 2014. *Bottlenecks: A New Theory of Equal Opportunity*. Oxford: Oxford University Press.

Fowler, Tim. 2019. "Public Reason, Science and Faith: The Case of Intelligent Design." *Law and Philosophy* 38 (1):29–52.

Fraser, Nancy. 1997. *Justice Interruptus: Critical Reflections on the "Postsocialist" Condition Routledge*. New York: Routledge.

Fraser, Nancy. 2001. "Recognition without Ethics?" *Theory, Culture & Society* 18 (2–3):21–42. https://doi.org/10.1177/02632760122051760.

Freeman, Samuel. 2007. *Rawls*. London: Routledge.

Galston, William A. 1995. "Two Concepts of Liberalism." *Ethics* 105 (3):516–34.

Galston, William A. 2002. *Liberal Pluralism: The Implications of Value Pluralism for Political Theory and Practice*. Cambridge: Cambridge University Press.

Galston, William A. 2005. *The Practice of Liberal Pluralism*. New York: Cambridge University Press.

Gerson, Kathleen. 2010. *The Unfinished Revolution: Coming of Age in a New Era of Gender, Work, and Family*. Oxford: Oxford University Press.

214 BIBLIOGRAPHY

Gheaus, Anca. 2008. "Basic Income, Gender Justice and the Costs of Gender-Symmetrical Lifestyles." *Basic Income Studies* 3 (3). https://doi.org/10.2202/1932-0183.1134.

Gheaus, Anca. 2012. "Gender Justice." *Journal of Ethics and Social Philosophy* 6 (1):445–64.

Gheaus, Anca. 2013. "The Feasibility Constraint on the Concept of Justice." *The Philosophical Quarterly (1950–)* 63 (252):445–64.

Gheaus, Anca. 2018. "Hikers in Flip-Flops: Luck Egalitarianism, Democratic Equality and the Distribuenda of Justice." *Journal of Applied Philosophy* 35 (1):54–69. https://doi.org/10.1111/japp.12198.

Gheaus, Anca. 2020. "The Feminist Argument against Supporting Care." *Journal of Practical Ethics* 8 (1):87–113.

Gilabert, Pablo. 2011. "Feasibility and Socialism." *Journal of Political Philosophy* 19 (1):52–63. https://doi.org/10.1111/j.1467-9760.2010.00383.x.

Gilabert, Pablo, and Holly Lawford-Smith. 2012. "Political Feasibility: A Conceptual Exploration." *Political Studies* 60 (4):809–25. https://doi.org/10.1111/j.1467-9248.2011.00936.x.

Gittell, Ross. 2009. "Constrained Choices and Persistent Gender Inequity: The Economic Status of Working Women in a High-Income, Low-Poverty State with Lessons for Others." *American Behavioral Scientist* 53 (2):170–92.

Glass, Jennifer. 2004. "Blessing or Curse? Work-Family Policies and Mother's Wage Growth over Time." *Work and Occupations* 31 (3):367–94.

Goldin, Claudia. 2021. *Career and Family: Women's Century-Long Journey toward Equity.* Princeton, N.J.: Princeton University Press.

Goodin, Robert E. 1995. "Political Ideals and Political Practice." *British Journal of Political Science* 25 (1):37–56.

Gornick, Janet, and Marcia Meyers. 2003. *Families That Work: Policies for Reconciling Parenthood and Employment.* London: Russell Sage Foundation.

Guerrero, Alexander. 2018. "A Brief History of a New Course at Rutgers University: Philosophy 366—African, Latin American, and Native American Philosophy." *American Philosophical Association Newsletter on Native American and Indigenous Philosophy* 17 (2):4–9.

Hannah-Jones, Nikole. 2019. "It Was Never about Busing." *The New York Times,* July 12 (Sunday Review). https://www.nytimes.com/2019/07/12/opinion/sunday/it-was-never-about-busing.html.

Hare, R. M. 1973. "Rawls' Theory of Justice." *Philosophical Quarterly* 23 (91):144–55.

Hartley, Christie, and Lori Watson. 2009. "Feminism, Religion, and Shared Reasons: A Defense of Exclusive Public Reason." *Law and Philosophy* 28 (5):493–536.

Hartley, Christie, and Lori Watson. 2010. "Is a Feminist Political Liberalism Possible?" *Journal of Ethics and Social Philosophy* 5 (1):1–21.

Haslanger, Sally. 2012. *Resisting Reality: Social Construction and Social Critique.* New York: Oxford University Press.

Haslanger, Sally. 2017. "Culture and Critique." *Aristotelian Society Supplementary Volume* 91 (1):149–73.

Haslanger, Sally. 2020. "Methods of Social Critique." *Publications of the Austrian Ludwig Wittgenstein Society* 28:139–56.

Haslanger, Sally. 2021a. "Feminism and the Question of Theory." *The Raven: A Magazine of Philosophy.* https://ravenmagazine.org/magazine/feminist-critical-consciousness-and-the-question-of-theory/.

Haslanger, Sally. 2021b. "Political Epistemology and Social Critique." In *Oxford Studies in Political Philosophy,* Vol. 7, edited by David Sobel, Peter Vallentyne, and Steven Wall, 23–65. Oxford: Oxford University Press.

Hirsch, Fred. 1978. *Social Limits to Growth.* 2nd edition. London: Routledge.

hooks, bell. 2014. *Feminist Theory: From Margin to Center.* 3rd edition. New York: Routledge.

Hurka, Thomas. 1996. "Monism, Pluralism, and Rational Regret." *Ethics* 106 (3):555–75. https://doi.org/10.1086/233647.

Huzum, Eugen. 2011. "Can Luck Egalitarianism Be Really Saved by Value Pluralism?" *Studia Philosophia* 56 (January):41–51.

Jaggar, Alison M. 1983. *Feminist Politics and Human Nature.* Rowman & Littlefield.

BIBLIOGRAPHY

James, Aaron. 2018. "Constructivism, Intuitionism, and Ecumenism." In *The Oxford Handbook of Distributive Justice*, edited by Serena Olsaretti, 346–66. Oxford: Oxford University Press.

Kekes, John. 1993. *The Morality of Pluralism*. Princeton, N.J.: Princeton University Press.

Kelly, Erin I. 2017. "The Historical Injustice Problem for Political Liberalism." *Ethics* 128 (1):75–94.

Kelly, Erin, and Lionel McPherson. 2001. "On Tolerating the Unreasonable." *Journal of Political Philosophy* 9 (1):38–55.

Kelly, Thomas, and Sarah McGrath. 2010. "Is Reflective Equilibrium Enough?" *Philosophical Perspectives* 24 (1):325–59. https://doi.org/10.1111/j.1520-8583.2010.00195.x.

Kleven, Henrik, Camille Landais, and Jakob Egholt Søgaard. 2019. "Children and Gender Inequality: Evidence from Denmark." *American Economic Journal: Applied Economics* 11 (4):181–209. https://doi.org/10.3386/w24219.

Kolodny, Niko. 2014. "Rule over None II: Social Equality and the Justification of Democracy." *Philosophy & Public Affairs* 42 (4):287–336. https://doi.org/10.1111/papa.12037.

Kymlicka, Will. 1988. "Rawls on Teleology and Deontology." *Philosophy & Public Affairs* 17 (3):173–90.

Lachance-Grzela, Mylène, and Geneviève Bouchard. 2010. "Why Do Women Do the Lion's Share of Housework? A Decade of Research." *Sex Roles* 63 (11):767–80. https://doi.org/10.1007/s11199-010-9797-z.

Laden, Anthony Simon. 2001. *Reasonably Radical: Deliberative Liberalism and the Politics of Identity*. Ithaca, N.Y.: Cornell University Press.

Larmore, Charles. 1987. *Patterns of Moral Complexity*. Cambridge: Cambridge University Press.

Larmore, Charles. 1999. "The Moral Basis of Political Liberalism." *The Journal of Philosophy* 96 (12):599–625. https://doi.org/10.2307/2564695.

Leland, R. J. 2019. "Civic Friendship, Public Reason." *Philosophy & Public Affairs* 47 (1):72–103. https://doi.org/10.1111/papa.12141.

Lippert-Rasmussen, Kasper. 2015. "Luck Egalitarians versus Relational Egalitarians: On the Prospects of a Pluralist Account of Egalitarian Justice." *Canadian Journal of Philosophy* 45 (2):220–41. https://doi.org/10.1080/00455091.2015.1061369.

Lippert-Rasmussen, Kasper. 2016. *Luck Egalitarianism*. Bloomsbury Ethics Series. London: Bloomsbury.

Lloyd, S. A. 1994. "Family Justice and Social Justice." *Pacific Philosophical Quarterly* 75 (3–4):353–71. https://doi.org/10.1111/j.1468-0114.1994.tb00135.x.

MacKinnon, Catharine A. 1989. *Toward a Feminist Theory of the State*. Cambridge, Mass.: Harvard University Press.

Markovits, Daniel. 2008. "Luck Egalitarianism and Political Solidarity." *Theoretical Inquiries in Law* 9 (1):271–309.

Mason, Andrew. 2012. *Living Together as Equals: The Demands of Citizenship*. Oxford: Oxford University Press.

Mason, Andrew. 2015. "Justice, Respect, and Treating People as Equals." In *Social Equality: On What It Means to Be Equals*, edited by Carina Fourie, Fabian Schuppert, and Wallimann-Helmer, 129–45. New York: Oxford University Press. https://doi.org/10.1093/acprof:oso/9780199331109.003.0007.

Mason, Andrew. 2021. "What's Wrong with Everyday Lookism?" *Politics, Philosophy & Economics* 20 (3):315–35. https://doi.org/10.1177/1470594X20982051.

Miller, David. 1997. "Equality and Justice." *Ratio* 10 (3):222–37. https://doi.org/10.1111/1467-9329.00042.

Mason, Andrew. 2016. "In What Sense Must Political Philosophy Be Political?" *Social Philosophy and Policy* 33 (1–2):155–74. https://doi.org/10.1017/S0265052516000339.

Mills, Charles. 2007. "Contract of Breach: Repairing the Racial Contract." In *Contract and Domination*, edited by Charles Mills and Carole Pateman, 106–133. Malden, MA: Polity.

Mills, Charles. 2013. "Retrieving Rawls for Racial Justice? A Critique of Tommie Shelby." *Critical Philosophy of Race* 1 (1):1–27. https://doi.org/10.5325/critphilrace.1.1.0001.

Mills, Charles. 2015. "Racial Equality." In *The Equal Society: Essays on Equality in Theory and Practice*, edited by George Hull, 43–71. Lanham, Md.: Lexington Books.

216 BIBLIOGRAPHY

Mills, Charles. 2017. *Black Rights/White Wrongs: The Critique of Racial Liberalism*. New York: Oxford University Press.

Mills, Charles. 2018. "Racial Justice." *Aristotelian Society Supplementary Volume* 92 (1):69–89. https://doi.org/10.1093/arisup/aky002.

Mishel, Lawrence, and Jori Kandra. 2020. "CEO Compensation Surged 14% in 2019 to $21.3 Million." https://www.epi.org/publication/ceo-compensation-surged-14-in-2019-to-21-3-million-ceos-now-earn-320-times-as-much-as-a-typical-worker/.

Moles, Andres, and Tom Parr. 2019. "Distributions and Relations: A Hybrid Account." *Political Studies* 67 (1):132–48. https://doi.org/10.1177/0032321718755589.

Murphy, Liam B. 1998. "Institutions and the Demands of Justice." *Philosophy & Public Affairs* 27 (4):251–91.

Nagel, Thomas. 1979. "The Fragmentation of Value." In *Mortal Questions by Thomas Nagel*, 128–41. New York: Cambridge University Press.

Neufeld, Blain. 2009. "Coercion, the Basic Structure, and the Family." *Journal of Social Philosophy* 40 (1):37–54.

Neufeld, Blain. 2015. Review of *Review of Equality and Opportunity*, by Shlomi Segall. *Notre Dame Philosophical Reviews*, March. https://ndpr.nd.edu/news/equality-and-opportunity/.

Nussbaum, Martha. 1999. *Sex and Social Justice*. New York: Oxford University Press.

Nussbaum, Martha. 2000. *Women and Human Development: The Capabilities Approach*. Cambridge: Cambridge University Press.

Nussbaum, Martha. 2011. "Perfectionist Liberalism and Political Liberalism." *Philosophy & Public Affairs* 39 (1):3–45.

Nussbaum, Martha C. 1986. *The Fragility of Goodness: Luck and Ethics in Greek Tragedy and Philosophy*. 2nd edition. Cambridge: Cambridge University Press.

Nuti, Alasia. 2022. *Injustice and the Reproduction of History*. New edition. Cambridge: Cambridge University Press.

O'Neill, Martin. 2008. "What Should Egalitarians Believe?" *Philosophy & Public Affairs* 36 (2):119–56.

Okin, Susan Moller. 1989. *Justice, Gender, and the Family*. New York: Basic Books.

Okin, Susan Moller. 1994. "Political Liberalism, Justice, and Gender." *Ethics* 105 (1):23–43.

Okin, Susan Moller. 2005. "'Forty Acres and a Mule' for Women: Rawls and Feminism." *Politics, Philosophy & Economics* 4 (2):233–48.

Orloff, Ann S. 2013. "Why Basic Income Does Not Promote Gender Equality." In *Basic Income: An Anthology of Contemporary Research*, edited by Karl Widerquist, 149–52. Chichester: John Wiley & Sons Inc.

Parfit, Derek. 2000. "Equality and Priority." In *The Ideal of Equality*, Vol. 10, edited by Matthew Clayton and Andrew Williams, 81–125. Basingstoke: Palgrave Macmillan.

Parker, Kim. 2015. "Women More than Men Adjust Their Careers for Family Life." Pew Research Center (blog). October 1. http://www.pewresearch.org/fact-tank/2015/10/01/women-more-than-men-adjust-their-careers-for-family-life/.

Pateman, Carole. 2004. "Democratizing Citizenship: Some Advantages of a Basic Income." *Politics & Society* 32 (1):89–105. https://doi.org/10.1177/0032329203261100.

Pettit, Philip. 2015. "Justice: Social and Political." In *Oxford Studies in Political Philosophy*, Vol. 1, edited by David Sobel, Peter Vallentyne, and Steven Wall, 9–35. Oxford: Oxford University Press.

Phillips, Anne. 2001. "Feminism and Liberalism Revisited: Has Martha Nussbaum Got It Right?" *Constellations* 8 (2):249–66. https://doi.org/10.1111/1467-8675.00229.

Poeschl, Gabrielle. 2008. "Social Norms and the Feeling of Justice about Unequal Family Practices." *Social Justice Research* 21 (1):69–85.

Posey-Maddox, Linn. 2014. *When Middle-Class Parents Choose Urban Schools: Class, Race, and the Challenge of Equity in Public Education*. Chicago, Ill.: University of Chicago Press.

Quong, Jonathan. 2010. "Justice Beyond Equality." *Social Theory and Practice* 36 (2):315–40.

Quong, Jonathan. 2011. *Liberalism without Perfection*. Oxford: Oxford University Press.

BIBLIOGRAPHY 217

Ramey, Garey, and Valerie A. Ramey. 2010. "The Rug Rat Race." *Brookings Papers on Economic Activity* 1:129–76. https://doi.org/10.1353/eca.2010.0003.

Rawls, John. 1993. *Political Liberalism*. New York: Columbia University Press.

Rawls, John. 1997. "The Idea of Public Reason Revisited." *The University of Chicago Law Review* 64 (3):765. https://doi.org/10.2307/1600311.

Rawls, John. 1999a. *A Theory of Justice, Revised Edition*. Cambridge, Mass.: Harvard University Press.

Rawls, John. 1999b. *Collected Papers*. Edited by Samuel Freeman. Cambridge, Mass.: Harvard University Press.

Rawls, John. 2001. *Justice as Fairness: A Restatement*. Cambridge, Mass.: Harvard University Press.

Raz, Joseph. 1986. *The Morality of Freedom*. Oxford University Press.

Raz, Joseph. 1999. *Engaging Reason: On the Theory of Value and Action*. Oxford: Oxford University Press.

Rhode, Deborah L. 2011. *The Beauty Bias: The Injustice of Appearance in Life and Law*. Oxford: Oxford University Press.

Richardson, Henry. 2023. "Why Rawls's Ideal Theory Leaves the Well-Ordered Society Vulnerable to Structural Oppression." In *Rawls's A Theory of Justice at 50*, edited by Paul Weithman, 181–98. Cambridge: Cambridge University Press.

Robeyns, Ingrid. 2000. "Hush Money or Emancipation Fee? A Gender Analysis of Basic Income." *Basic Income on the Agenda : Policy Objectives and Political Chances; Seventh International Congress of the Basis Income European Network*, 121–36. Amsterdam: Amsterdam University Press.

Robeyns, Ingrid. 2001. "Will a Basic Income Do Justice to Women?" *Analyse Und Kritik* 23 (January):88–105. https://doi.org/10.1515/auk-2001-0108.

Robeyns, Ingrid. 2003. "Is Nancy Fraser's Critique of Theories of Distributive Justice Justified?" *Constellations* 10 (4):538–54.

Roemer, John E. 1993. "A Pragmatic Theory of Responsibility for the Egalitarian Planner." *Philosophy & Public Affairs* 22 (2):146–66.

Roemer, John E. 1994. *Egalitarian Perspectives: Essays in Philosophical Economics*. Cambridge: Cambridge University Press. https://doi.org/10.1017/CBO9780511528293.

Ronzoni, Miriam. 2008. "What Makes a Basic Structure Just?" *Res Publica* 14:203–18. https://doi.org/10.1007/s11158-008-9056-0.

Ross-Smith, Anne, and Colleen Chesterman. 2009. "'Girl Disease': Women Managers' Reticence and Ambivalence towards Organizational Advancement." *Journal of Management & Organization* 15 (5):582–95.

Rothstein, Richard. 2017. *The Color of Law: A Forgotten History of How Our Government Segregated America*. Illustrated edition. New York: Liveright.

Sangiovanni, Andrea. 2008. "Justice and the Priority of Politics to Morality." *Journal of Political Philosophy* 16 (2):137–64. https://doi.org/10.1111/j.1467-9760.2007.00291.x.

Sangiovanni, Andrea. 2016. "How Practices Matter." *Journal of Political Philosophy* 24 (1):3–23. https://doi.org/10.1111/jopp.12056.

Scanlon, T. M. 2003a. "Rawls on Justification." In *The Cambridge Companion to Rawls*, edited by Samuel Freeman, 139–67. Cambridge: Cambridge University Press.

Scanlon, T. M. 2003b. "The Diversity of Objections to Inequality." In *The Difficulty of Tolerance: Essays in Political Philosophy*, 202–18. Cambridge: Cambridge University Press.

Scheffler, Samuel. 2003. "What Is Egalitarianism?" *Philosophy & Public Affairs* 31 (1):5–39.

Schemmel, Christian. 2011. "Why Relational Egalitarians Should Care about Distributions." *Social Theory and Practice* 37 (3):365–90.

Schemmel, Christian. 2021. *Justice and Egalitarian Relations*. Oxford Political Philosophy. Oxford: Oxford University Press.

Schouten, Gina. 2012a. "Educational Justice: Closing Gaps or Paying Debts?" *Journal of Applied Philosophy* 29 (3):231–42. https://doi.org/10.1111/j.1468-5930.2012.00563.x.

218 BIBLIOGRAPHY

Schouten, Gina. 2012b. "Fair Educational Opportunity and the Distribution of Natural Ability: Toward a Prioritarian Principle of Educational Justice." *Journal of Philosophy of Education* 46 (3):472–91. https://doi.org/10.1111/j.1467-9752.2012.00863.x.

Schouten, Gina. 2013. "Restricting Justice: Political Interventions in the Home and in the Market." *Philosophy & Public Affairs* 41 (4):357–88. https://doi.org/10.1111/papa.12022.

Schouten, Gina. 2015. "Does the Gendered Division of Labor Undermine Citizenship?" In *The Equal Society: Essays on Equality in Theory and Practice*, edited by George Hull, 273–91. Lanham, Md.: Lexington Books.

Schouten, Gina. 2016. "Is the Gendered Division of Labor a Problem of Distribution?" In *Oxford Studies in Political Philosophy*, Vol. 2, edited by David Sobel, Peter Vallentyne, and Steven Wall, 185–206. Oxford: Oxford University Press. https://doi.org/10.1093/acprof:oso/9780198759621.003.0008.

Schouten, Gina. 2017. "Citizenship, Reciprocity, and the Gendered Division of Labor: A Stability Argument for Gender Egalitarian Political Interventions." *Politics, Philosophy & Economics* 16 (2):174–209. https://doi.org/10.1177/1470594X15600830.

Schouten, Gina. 2019. *Liberalism, Neutrality, and the Gendered Division of Labor*. New York: Oxford University Press.

Schouten, Gina. 2023a. "Equal Educational Opportunity: What Should It Mean?" In *Routledge Handbook of Philosophy of Education*, edited by Randall Curren, 187–98. London: Routledge.

Schouten, Gina. 2023b. "Review of Equal Citizenship and Public Reason: A Feminist Political Liberalism by Lori Watson and Christie Hartley." *Hypatia* 38 (4):1–5. Cambridge: Cambridge University Press. https://doi.org/10.1017/hyp.2023.30.

Segall, Shlomi. 2007. "In Solidarity with the Imprudent: A Defense of Luck Egalitarianism." *Social Theory and Practice* 33 (2):177–98.

Segall, Shlomi. 2014. *Equality and Opportunity*. Oxford: Oxford University Press.

Sen, Amartya. 1995. *Inequality Reexamined*. Cambridge, Mass.: Harvard University Press.

Sen, Amartya. 2006. "What Do We Want from a Theory of Justice?" *The Journal of Philosophy* 103 (5):215–38. https://doi.org/10.5840/jphil2006103517.

Shelby, Tommie. 2003. "Ideology, Racism, and Critical Social Theory." *Philosophical Forum* 34:153–88.

Shelby, Tommie. 2004. "Race and Ethnicity, Race and Social Justice: Rawlsian Considerations." *Fordham Law Review* 72 (5):1697.

Shelby, Tommie. 2013. "Racial Realities and Corrective Justice: A Reply to Charles Mills." *Critical Philosophy of Race* 1 (2):145–62. https://doi.org/10.5325/critphilrace.1.2.0145.

Shelby, Tommie. 2014. "Integration, Inequality, and Imperatives of Justice: A Review Essay." *Philosophy & Public Affairs* 42 (3):253–85. https://doi.org/10.1111/papa.12034.

Shelby, Tommie. 2018. *Dark Ghettos: Injustice, Dissent, and Reform*. Cambridge, Mass.: Harvard University Press.

Shelby, Tommie. 2022. *The Idea of Prison Abolition*. Princeton, N.J.: Princeton University Press.

Shiffrin, Seana. 2004. "Race and Ethnicity, Race, Labor, and the Fair Equality of Opportunity Principle." *Fordham Law Review* 72 (5):1643.

Shiffrin, Seana Valentine. 2010. "Incentives, Motives, and Talents." *Philosophy & Public Affairs* 38 (2):111–42.

Simmons, A. John. 2010. "Ideal and Nonideal Theory." *Philosophy & Public Affairs* 38 (1):5–36.

Skorupski, John. 1996. "Value-Pluralism." *Royal Institute of Philosophy Supplements* 40 (March):101–15. https://doi.org/10.1017/S1358246100005890.

Sleat, Matt. 2015. "Justice and Legitimacy in Contemporary Liberal Thought: A Critique." *Social Theory and Practice* 41 (2):230–52.

Southwood, Nicholas. 2016. "Does 'Ought' Imply 'Feasible'?" *Philosophy & Public Affairs* 44 (1):7–45.

Srinivasan, Amia. 2020. "Radical Externalism." *The Philosophical Review* 129 (3):395–431. https://doi.org/10.1215/00318108-8311261.

Stark, Cynthia A. 2018. "The Presumption of Equality." *Law, Ethics and Philosophy* 6 (0):7–27.

BIBLIOGRAPHY 219

Stemplowska, Zofia. 2008. "Holding People Responsible for What They Do Not Control." *Politics, Philosophy & Economics* 7 (4):355–77. https://doi.org/10.1177/1470594X08095749.

Stemplowska, Zofia. 2009. "Making Justice Sensitive to Responsibility:" *Political Studies* 57 (2):237–59.

Stemplowska, Zofia. 2011. "Responsibility and Respect: Reconciling Two Egalitarian Visions." In *Responsibility and Distributive Justice*, edited by Carl Knight and Zofia Stemplowska, 115–35. Oxford: Oxford University Press. https://doi.org/10.1093/acprof:oso/9780199565801.003.0006.

Stemplowska, Zofia, and Adam Swift. 2018. "Dethroning Democratic Legitimacy." In *Oxford Studies in Political Philosophy*, Vol. 4. Edited by David Sobel, Peter Vallentyne, and Steven Wall, 1–26. Oxford: Oxford University Press.

Stocker, Michael. 1990. *Plural and Conflicting Values*. Oxford: Oxford: Oxford University Press.

Swift, Adam. 2008. "The Value of Philosophy in Nonideal Circumstances." *Social Theory and Practice* 34 (3):363–87.

Tan, Kok-Chor. 2012. *Justice, Institutions, and Luck: The Site, Ground, and Scope of Equality*. Oxford: Oxford University Press.

Taylor, Keeanga-Yamahtta, ed. 2017. *How We Get Free: Black Feminism and the Combahee River Collective*. Chicago, Ill.: Haymarket Books.

Temkin, Larry S. 1993. *Inequality*. Oxford Ethics Series. New York: Oxford University Press.

Temkin, Larry S. 2003. "Equality, Priority, or What?" *Economics & Philosophy* 19 (1):61–87. https://doi.org/10.1017/S0266267103001020.

Tomlin, Patrick. 2010. "Survey Article: Internal Doubts about Cohen's Rescue of Justice." *Journal of Political Philosophy* 18 (2):228–47. https://doi.org/10.1111/j.1467-9760.2010.00359.x.

Tomlin, Patrick. 2012. "Can I Be a Luck Egalitarian and a Rawlsian?" *Ethical Perspectives* 19 (September):371–97. https://doi.org/10.2143/EP.19.3.2172296.

Valentini, Laura. 2009. "On the Apparent Paradox of Ideal Theory*." *Journal of Political Philosophy* 17 (3):332–55. https://doi.org/10.1111/j.1467-9760.2008.00317.x.

Valentini, Laura. 2011. "Global Justice and Practice-Dependence: Conventionalism, Institutionalism, Functionalism." *Journal of Political Philosophy* 19 (4):399–418. https://doi.org/10.1111/j.1467-9760.2010.00373.x.

Vallentyne, Peter. 2015. "Justice, Interpersonal Morality, and Luck Egalitarianism." In *Distributive Justice and Access to Advantage: G.A. Cohen's Egalitarianism*, 40–9. Cambridge: Cambridge University Press.

Voigt, Kristin. 2007. "The Harshness Objection: Is Luck Egalitarianism Too Harsh on the Victims of Option Luck?" *Ethical Theory and Moral Practice* 10 (4):389–407.

Watson, Lori. 2015. "Why Sex Work Isn't Work." *Logos* 14 (1). https://logosjournal.com/article/why-sex-work-isnt-work/.

Watson, Lori, and Christie Hartley. 2018. *Equal Citizenship and Public Reason: A Feminist Political Liberalism*. Studies in Feminist Philosophy. Oxford: Oxford University Press.

Widdows, Heather. 2018. *Perfect Me: Beauty as an Ethical Ideal*. Princeton, N.J.: Princeton University Press.

Wiggins, David. 1980. "Weakness of Will, Commensurability, and the Objects of Deliberation and Desire." In *Essays on Aristotle's Ethics*, edited by A. O. Rorty, 241–66. Berkeley, Calif.: University of California Press.

Williams, A. 2008. "Liberty, Equality, and Property." In *The Oxford Handbook of Political Theory*, edited by John Dryzek, Bonnie Honig, and Anne Phillips, 488–506. Oxford: Oxford University Press. https://doi.org/10.1093/oxfordhb/9780199548439.003.0027.

Williams, Andrew. 1998. "Incentives, Inequality, and Publicity." *Philosophy & Public Affairs* 27 (3):225–47.

Williams, Andrew. 2008. "Justice, Incentives and Constructivism." *Ratio* 21 (4):476–93. https://doi.org/10.1111/j.1467-9329.2008.00414.x.

Williams, Bernard, ed. 1973. "The Idea of Equality." In *Problems of the Self: Philosophical Papers 1956–1972*, 230–49. Cambridge: Cambridge University Press. https://doi.org/10.1017/CBO9780511621253.016.

220 BIBLIOGRAPHY

Williams, Bernard. 1981. "Conflicts of Values." In *Moral Luck*, 71–82. Cambridge: Cambridge University Press.

Williams, Bernard. 1985. *Ethics and the Limits of Philosophy*. Cambridge, Mass.: Harvard University Press.

Williams, Bernard. 2005. "Realism and Moralism in Political Theory." In *In the Beginning Was the Deed: Realism and Moralism in Political Argument*, 1–17. Princeton, N.J.: Princeton University Press.

Williams, Joan. 2000. *Unbending Gender: Why Family and Work Conflict and What to Do about It*. Oxford: Oxford University Press.

Winter, Jack. 2016. "Justice for Hedgehogs, Conceptual Authenticity for Foxes: Ronald Dworkin on Value Conflicts." *Res Publica* 22 (4):463–79. https://doi.org/10.1007/s11158-015-9285-y.

Wolff, Jonathan. 1998. "Fairness, Respect, and the Egalitarian Ethos." *Philosophy & Public Affairs* 27 (2):97–122.

Woodly, Deva. 2018. "#BlackLivesMatter and the Democratic Necessity of Social Movements: What Active Citizenship Can Look Like and What It Can Accomplish." In *#Charlottesville: Before and Beyond*, edited by Christoper Howard-Woods, Colin Laidley, and Maryam Omidi, 181–91. New York: Public Seminar Books.

Young, Iris Marion. 2011. *Responsibility for Justice*. Oxford: Oxford University Press.

Zelleke, Almaz. 2008. "Institutionalizing the Universal Caretaker through a Basic Income?" *Basic Income Studies* 3 (3). https://doi.org/10.2202/1932-0183.1133.

Zippel, Kathrin. 2009. "The Missing Link for Promoting Gender Equality: Work-Family and Anti-Discrimination Policies." In *Gender Equality: Transforming Family Divisions of Labor*, edited by Erik Olin Wright, 209–229. Real Utopias Project. London: Verso.

Index

Since the index has been created to work across multiple formats, indexed terms for which a page range is given (e.g., 52–53, 66–70, etc.) may occasionally appear only on some, but not all of the pages within the range.

adequacy threshold 72–4, 80, 83–90, 141–3.
   See also basic income
affirmative action
   and education 29–30, 135, 168–9, 189
   and hiring practices 11–12, 29–30, 189, 201–2
   and race 11–12, 155, 168–9, 189, 196–7
   vs. anti-discrimination 11–12, 29–30,
      196–7, 201–2
anatomy of justice
   action-guidingness of 2–4, 28–30, 37–42,
      44–5, 90–2, 121–3
   and circumstances of injustice 8, 28–31, 40–1,
      68, 90–2, 97, 121, 167, 197–8
   and two pluralisms about justice 4–6, 18–21
   conceptual 21–31
   introduced 2, 17–18, 22–6
   practical value of 9–10
   relation to legitimacy 22–6 (*see also* legitimacy)
   relation to Rawls 10–14, 17–18, 21, 40–1, 47–8,
      65–6, 90, 95–6
   theoretical value of 9–10, 18–21, 44–5, 156
Anderson, Elizabeth 4–5, 19–21, 34, 45 n.4,
      50–60, 72. *See also* relational equality
anti-racism 56–7, 148, 163–4, 169–71, 202–3.
   See also racism
aspirational justice
   as distinct from verdictive justice 18–31
   as fairness 17–18, 20–2
   as one value among many 18–22, 31–7
   as principles of distributive justice 22, 31–7
   its relation to legitimacy 22–5, 27–8, 31–7
   political vs. true 99–101, 104–5, 114–16
aspirational values. *See* values
authority to govern 66, 98 n.10, 119–20, 134 n.30.
   See also legitimacy
autonomy
   and the gendered division of labor 138–9, 183
   and reciprocity 139
   as a public service 139
   conditions for required by mutual
      respect 49–50, 72

basic income
   and distributive justice 122–4, 128–33,
      140–1, 144–5
   and equality of opportunity 129–32, 135, 141

   and mutual respect 131–42
   and the gendered division of labor 122–9,
      131–2, 134–8, 140–1, 143–4
   as caregiver support 125–7, 142, 144
   its tension with gender egalitarianism 121–3,
      125–30
   vs. merit good approach 127, 143
basic liberties. *See also* political liberties
   priority of 11–12, 86–7, 90–5, 129
   protection for as a standard of
      legitimacy 74, 97–9
   protection for as a standard of
      reasonableness 93–5, 134
basic needs principle 69 n.4, 129.
   See also basic income
basic structure
   and its exclusion of informal culture 150–5,
      160–3
   and legitimacy 160–2, 167 (*see also* legitimacy)
   and social change 163–6, 175–6
   and the gendered division of labor 150–1,
      153–6, 158–9, 163–6
   as non-exhaustive of normative
      theorizing 166–7, 172
   as primary subject of justice 76–7, 146–7, 149–54
   its justice as conditioned by historical
      facts 26, 155, 202
basic structure debate 73–4, 150–1, 153–7
basic structure restriction. *See also* stingy liberalism
   and feminism 146–7, 157–67
   and informal culture 150–2, 163–7
   and market-maximizing behavior
      (*see* market-maximizing behavior)
   evaluative adequacy of 150, 157–67
   in Rawls 150–1, 153–4, 158, 161
   motivation for 154, 161–3
   normative adequacy of 150, 168–77
Bergmann, Barbara 127, 143
boardroom feminism 143
Brown v. Board of Education 152, 171–2

capabilities. *See also* Anderson, Elizabeth
   and developmental opportunity 63–4, 86–7
      (*see also* fair equality of opportunity)
   and mutual respect 55–8, 72–3, 83, 87–9
   similarity to primary goods 72–3

222 INDEX

capitalism 164, 202–3, 209
caregiving
　and the gendered division of labor 34–5,
　　121–3, 125–9, 132, 134–8
　burdens of 34–5, 122, 126–9, 136–7
Chambers, Clare 185
childcare. *See* caregiving
citizenship, idealizing assumptions of 133–4, 136
civic equality. *See* relational equality
civic respect. *See* mutual respect
civil disobedience 13. *See also* duty of justice
class 11–12, 28–30, 36–7, 148, 159, 188–9,
　　196–7, 204
Cohen, G. A.
　and aspirational justice (*see* aspirational
　　justice)
　and pluralism 12 n.20, 24 n.18
　and rules of regulation 20–1
　and the basic structure debate 150, 153–5, 170
　　(*see also* basic structure debate)
　and the concept of justice 4–6, 18–31, 46–7
　and the personal prerogative 161–3
Combahee River Collective 203–4
community
　and historical facts 26, 155
　and mutual justification 33–4, 76–7, 102–3,
　　113, 191–2 (*see also* political liberalism)
　as an aspirational, relational value 19, 22,
　　24–5, 36–7, 45–6, 48
　as impugned by mutual respect 25, 36–7, 43,
　　59, 89–90
competition 60–2, 130, 135. *See also* fair equality
　of opportunity
conception of the good. *See also* autonomy;
　　two moral powers
　and political liberalism 69, 75–6, 112–13,
　　133–4, 139, 191–2
　capacity for 69, 139
　fundamental interest in pursuit
　　of 75–80, 90, 139
conceptual pluralism 21–31, 37–42, 51–2. *See also*
　　aspirational justice; verdictive justice
consciousness raising 109–10, 112–13, 184–5,
　　198–9, 203–4, 208. *See also* feminism
consumerism 157–8
corrective justice. *See* affirmative action
critical social theory 3 n.1, 149, 184.
　　See also Haslanger, Sally
culture
　and injustice 148–52, 154–5, 157–68
　and sexism 150–6, 158–9, 164–5
　　(*see also* gender norms)
　and the basic structure (*see* basic structure;
　　basic structure debate)
　as ideology 148–52
　as justice-impeding 157–67, 169, 172–3
　capacity of institutions to shape
　　158–9, 170–3

ideological critique of (*see* ideology critique)
limits of legitimate institutional interference
　　in 71–2, 161–5

democracy (*see also* political liberalism)
　and equality 19, 34, 57, 72, 84, 171, 182–3
　and legitimacy 20–5, 31–4, 47–9, 66,
　　95–105, 108–18
　and the priority of values 37, 41, 78
　and verdictive justice 26–7, 171, 174–5
democratic franchise 98–9, 101, 158
desert. *See* luck egalitarianism
developmental opportunity. *See* fair equality of
　　opportunity
difference principle
　and wage differentials 161
　as a principle of distributive justice 65–6
　as governing the basic structure 153, 161
　　(*see also* basic structure debate)
　justification for 76–8, 90–1
　lexical posteriority of 68–9, 129
disability
　and basic income 128 (*see also* basic income)
　and capabilities 57–9, 83, 87
　　(*see also* capabilities)
discrimination
　and basic income 128–31 (*see also*
　　basic income)
　and equality of opportunity 135, 196–7
　　(*see also* fair equality of opportunity)
　in hiring 11–12, 29–30, 128–9, 131, 135
　statistical 128–9, 134–5
distributive equality
　and fairness 17–18 (*see also* fairness)
　and overlapping consensus 105–18
　and talent (*see* talent)
　as aspirational justice 18–28, 31–2
　as baseline 74–80
　as ceteris paribus desirable 27, 53–60
　as distinct from relational equality 17, 31–7,
　　50–60, 95–105
　as irreducible to relational equality 17, 37–42
　　(*see also* values pluralism)
　as lexically posterior to mutual respect 53–60,
　　74–80, 95–105
　as required by relational equality 43–5,
　　71–80, 108–18 (*see also* mutual respect)
　as responsibility sensitive (*see* luck
　　egalitarianism)
　demands of 43–50, 113, 140
　deviations from 31–7, 99–102, 105–18, 161–2
　optional pursuit of 113, 161–2
distributive justice. *See* distributive equality
duty of justice 13, 109, 170–5

economic inequality
　as deviation from a baseline requiring
　　justification 74–80

INDEX 223

as impugned by fairness 46–50, 63–4, 80, 82–3
as impugned by mutual respect 71–80
education
  admissions for 11–12, 29–30, 155
  and fair equality of opportunity 11–12, 36–7,
    53, 106, 135, 152, 168–9
  as a merit good (*see* merit goods)
  as a method to shape culture, 73–4, 135,
    163–4, 168–77
  means-testing for public forms of 36–7, 106
  private forms of 36–7, 106
efficiency 4, 19–20, 22, 36–7, 51–2, 58, 65–6,
    82–4. *See also* values
egalitarianism
  distributive (*see* distributive equality)
  gender (*see* gender egalitarianism)
  liberal (*see* liberal egalitarianism)
  relational (*see* relational equality)
equality
  distributive (*see* distributive equality)
  relational (*see* relational equality)
evaluative assessment
  and democratic processes 37, 41, 84–90,
    99–102, 108–18
  vs. normative principles 1, 11–12, 14, 20–1,
    25–30

fair equality of opportunity
  and gender 128–9, 135, 148
  and social class 11–12, 148, 188–9
  and race 11–12, 148, 155, 168–9, 189, 196–7
  as a value 11–12
  under conditions of injustice 11–12
    (*see also* affirmative action)
  for unjustifiable social positions 130–1
  and education 11–12, 36–7, 53, 106, 135,
    152, 168–9
  and luck egalitarianism 50–1, 100–1
  and public insurance 53–4, 73 n.10
  and risk 53–5
  and opportunity pluralism 60–5
  in reflective equilibrium 188–9
  lexical priority of (*see* difference principle)
fairness
  as lexically posterior to mutual respect 71,
    84–90, 95–105
  and distributive equality 17–21
  and aspirational justice 17–31
  and legitimacy 31–7, 71, 84–90, 95–105
family. *See also* caregiving; feminism; gendered
    division of labor
  abolition of 51–3
  and parental partiality 82–3
feasibility 18–20, 28, 57–8, 85, 88–9, 111–14, 127, 143
feminism
  and Sally Haslanger (*see* Haslanger, Sally)
  and the critique of liberalism 146, 177–83,
    199–200, 204–7

and the gendered division of labor
  (*see* gendered division of labor)
relation to liberal egalitarianism 14–16, 121–3,
  131–9, 144–5
Fishkin, Joseph 44–5, 60–5
four-stage sequence 201–2
freedom of association 52–3, 82–4, 86, 116
freedom of religion 134
Freeman, Samuel 73 n.10, 120 n.29, 135
full compliance. *See also* ideal theory;
    non-ideal theory
  and normative principles 11, 28, 40–1, 65–6,
    129, 189
  and verdictive justice 28, 65–6

gender egalitarianism
  and basic income 121–8 (*see also* basic income)
  and gender roles 34–5, 121–2, 125–6, 183
    (*see also* gender norms)
  and the gendered division of labor
    (*see* gendered division of labor)
  tradeoff between distributive and gender
    equality 121–8, 131–9
  tradeoffs internal to legitimacy 141–5
gender norms
  as injustice-sustaining 132, 137–8, 144–5, 159,
    164–5, 167, 173
  costs to individuals of resisting 138–9
  hierarchical privileging of masculine over
    feminine 134–5, 137
  "stacking" vs. "steering" 137
  "steering" of individuals into 137–8, 141, 183
gender pay gap
  and caregiving 125–9, 131–2, 134–9, 144–5, 159
  and choice 14 n.24, 34–6, 121–2, 125–6, 138,
    165, 170–1
  and equality of opportunity 128–32
  and gender norms 8, 34–5, 121–8, 130–9, 170–1
gendered division of labor
  and autonomy 138–9, 144–5, 183
  and caregiving 34–5, 121–3, 125–9, 132,
    134–8
  and gender egalitarianism 121–3, 131–9, 144–5
  and legitimacy 35, 134–5, 140–4
  and the fair value of political
    liberties 134–5, 144
  as a problem of mutual respect 124, 131–9,
    141–2, 164–5, 174–5, 183
  as linchpin of gender injustice 132
  social mechanisms for sustaining 148–9
gendered socialization 125–6, 137, 150–1, 155–6,
    181–2, 205–6. *See also* gender norms
Gheaus, Anca 130–1, 135, 141, 143

Hartley, Christie 136–7, 149, 182–3
Haslanger, Sally
  and critical social theory 148–52, 184
  and culture 149–55, 167–9, 171, 183–5

224 INDEX

Haslanger, Sally (*cont.*)
    and ideology 149, 151–2, 168, 171, 174–6,
        179–80, 183–5, 207–10
    criticism of applied ideal theory 180–3,
        189–90, 193–6, 201, 204–7
    criticism of basic structure restriction 149–52
    criticism of liberalism 14–16, 146, 177–83,
        199–200, 204–7
    criticism of reflective equilibrium 179–83,
        185–96, 198–201, 205–6
healthcare 49–50, 72–3, 107, 127, 164
history
    its relevance for aspirational justice 202
        (*see also* luck egalitarianism)
    its relevance for verdictive justice 26, 155
hooks, bell 148
housework. *See* caregiving; gendered division
    of labor
housing 53, 127, 169–70. *See also* adequacy
    threshold
humanity (as a value) 22. *See also* values

ideal theory 10–11, 28, 40–1, 65–6, 105, 129, 179 n.2,
    180–3, 187. *See also* non-ideal theory
ideals. *See* values
ideology
    and culture 149, 151–2, 168, 171, 183–5
    and institutions 171, 174–6 (*see also* basic
        structure)
    liberalism as 179–80, 207–10
ideology critique 148–52, 171, 176, 179–83, 193–4
immigrants 128
incommensurability 37–42
in-kind provision 82 n.30, 123 n.2, 127–8.
    See also basic income; merit goods
inheritance tax 11–12, 29–30, 144, 196–7
injustice
    and culture 148–52, 154–5, 157–68
    and fair equality of opportunity 11–12, 130–1, 135
    and moral epistemology 180–90, 193–5, 197–8
    and the anatomy of justice 21–37
    failure to optimize with respect to justice as
        insufficient for 160–1
    of economic inequality 18–21, 46–50,
        74–80, 108–18
    of sexism 131–9, 149–53, 157–67
    of the gendered division of labor 8, 122–3,
        128–9, 131–2, 137–9
    vs. justice-impeding 159
integrity 77–8. *See also* values
intuitionism 5–6, 12–13, 27–8, 44–5, 50, 100 n.14,
    145. *See also* values pluralism

Jaggar, Alison 148, 164 n.42
justice
    and culture 148–52, 154–5, 157–68
    and equality (*see* distributive equality;
        relational equality)

    and fairness (*see* fairness)
    and individual behavior 27–8, 150–1, 153–9,
        161–6, 173–4, 176–7 (*see also* basic
        structure debate; Cohen, G.A.)
    and legitimacy (*see* legitimacy)
    and other forms of social
        normativity 20–1, 153
    and the basic structure (*see* basic structure)
    as a single value vs. as an encompassing
        judgment 18–21 (*see also* conceptual
        pluralism)
    as more than normative principles 1, 28–31,
        65–6, 102, 129, 145, 157–67
    aspirational vs. verdictive 20–31 (*see also*
        aspirational justice; verdictive justice)
    between generations 89
    concept vs. substance 18–21
    concepts of 21–31
    currency of 31–2, 37–42, 51 n.18, 56–7, 77 n.21,
        83, 86–7 (*see also* lexical priority)
    duty of (*see* duty of justice)
    excessive demandingness of 7, 100, 119–20,
        161–3, 165
    in political deliberation 70–1, 89–90, 99–101,
        104–5, 116
    limits to the demands of 24–5, 99–101, 145, 161–5
    pluralism about 2, 21–37
    primary subject matter of 8–9, 146–52, 157,
        168, 174–5, 191–2 (*see also* basic
        structure)
    pure (*see* aspirational justice)
    sense of (*see* sense of justice)
    substance of 19–20, 31–7, 46–50, 155–7
    true vs. political 99–101, 104–5, 111–12, 116
        (*see also* political liberalism)
justice as fairness 11, 13–14, 28, 40–1, 97. *See also*
    Rawls, John
justificatory abstentions 187–93. *See also*
    reflective equilibrium
justificatory community 32–3, 76–7, 94 n.4,
    96 n.7, 101–2, 191–2. *See also* political
    liberalism

labor market 35, 73–4, 109, 112–13, 121–2, 126–7,
    132, 136–8
legitimacy
    and democracy 20–5, 31–4, 47–9, 66,
        95–105, 108–18
    and education 36–7, 106, (*see also* education;
        fair equality of opportunity)
    and individual responsibility 59, 63–4
    and the basic liberties 74, 97–9
    and the gendered division of labor 35, 134–5,
        140–4
    as adjudicating values 5, 22–5, 27–8, 33–4
    as institutional 25, 48–9, 62–3, 66, 71–80,
        101–4, 114, 141–2 (*see also* basic structure
        restriction; stingy liberalism)

as permissibility of policies 4–5, 22–3, 93–4
as scalar 23–4, 66
contingent 31, 84–5, 97–101, 109–16
contrasted with fairness 31–7, 71,
    84–90, 95–105
demandingness of 66, 79 n.23, 91–2,
    111, 119–20
fact-dependency of 108–11
full 66, 111, 119–20
its place in the anatomy of justice 71,
    84–90, 95–105
liberal principle of 32–5
minimal condition of 93–4, 110–18
mutual respect as central value for 4–7,
    14 n.24, 23–6, 32–6, 48
non-exhaustive of mutual respect 48
positive vs. negative demands of 32–5
procedural vs. substantive demands of 95–105
vs. authority 66, 118–20
lexical priority
defended 84–90, 93–105
evaluative vs. policy-prescriptive 84–5,
    88–92
in values pluralism 31–7
its implausibility in justice as
    fairness 68–70, 84–5
of equal opportunity over distributive equality
    (see difference principle)
of mutual respect 71, 84–90, 95–105
of relational equality over distributive
    equality 71, 84–90, 95–105
of the right to the good 18 n.1
of values 84–5
opposition to 68–70, 84–5
liberal egalitarianism. See also political liberalism
alleged shortfalls of
    diagnostic 150, 157–67
    normative 150, 168–77
and ideal theory 10–11, 180–1, 187, 194–6
and non-ideal theory 180–3, 189, 194–6, 206–8
and radical social critique 9–10, 149, 156,
    175–6, 179, 194–207
and reflective equilibrium 179–82, 185–99,
    201–3, 205–8
and social movements 3, 9, 14–16, 179–80,
    198–9, 203–4
and status quo bias 9, 148–9, 181–3,
    186–7, 199–201
as non-consequentialist 1, 3 n.1, 17–18, 24,
    196 n.65
criticism from the left 3, 8–10, 148–52, 180–3,
    207–10 (see also Haslanger, Sally)
diagnostic adequacy of 157–67
feminism 121–4, 163–4, 175–6 (see also
    feminism; gender egalitarianism)
ideals as values 1–2, 17–18
ideals vs. principles 1, 12, 17–18, 28–31,
    40–1, 76–8

moral epistemology of 180–90, 193–5, 197–8
    (see also reflective equilibrium; social
    critique)
rectificatory adequacy of 168–77
liberalism
as ideology 179–80, 207–10
criticism of 3–4, 146–7, 179–83, 187–8,
    194–201
moderate 154–67, 169, 177 (see also culture;
    basic structure debate; Haslanger, Sally)
permissive 154–7, 159, 161–3, 177 (see also
    basic structure debate; Cohen, G.A.)
political (see political liberalism)
stingy 154–77 (see also basic structure
    restriction; Rawls, John)
luck egalitarianism
and bad brute luck 55–60, 63–4, 116
and bad option luck 53–5
and equality of opportunity 44–5, 51–4, 60–5
    (see also fair equality of opportunity)
and legitimacy 43–50, 71, 84–90, 95–105
and respect 43–4, 47–60, 62–6
and values pluralism 19–21, 46, 51–2, 80–4
as aspirational justice 19–21, 43–6
criticism of 50–1, 53, 55, 58–9, 61 (see also
    Anderson, Elizabeth; Fishkin, Joseph)
harshness objection to 53–5
intrusiveness objection to 58–60
mere choice as insufficient for fairness
    under 53

MacKinnon, Catherine 148
market-maximizing behavior 73–4, 76–8, 82–3,
    88, 153–4, 161–2, 166–7, 170–1.
    See also basic structure debate
markets 34–5, 56–7, 73, 170. See also labor
    market
maternity leave. See subsidized parental leave
means-testing
as politically unstable 127–8, 143
as stigmatizing 127–8, 144–5
public education 36–7, 106
medical care 49–50, 72–3, 107, 164
merit. See fair equality of opportunity;
    luck egalitarianism
merit goods
as alternative to basic income 127, 143
education (see education)
healthcare (see healthcare)
housing (see housing)
public transportation (see public
    transportation)
minimal justice 49–50, 68, 110–11, 114–19.
    See also adequacy threshold; authority
    to govern; legitimacy
moderate liberalism 154–67, 169, 177
    (see also culture; basic structure
    debate; Haslanger, Sally)

226 INDEX

moral epistemology 180–90, 193–5, 197–8 (*see also* reflective equilibrium; social critique)
moral regret 41, 108
moral remainder. *See* moral regret
mutual respect
  and a democratic constitution 32–3, 96 n.6, 110 n.19
  and an adequacy threshold 71–80 (*see also* basic income)
  and capabilities 57–8, 72–3, 83, 87–9 (*see also* capabilities)
  and equal moral importance of citizens' conceptions of the good 75–80, 90, 139 (*see also* political liberalism)
  and gender egalitarianism 35, 134–5, 140–4
  and institutions 79–80, 96–7, 141–2
  and luck egalitarianism 43–4, 47–50, 52–60, 62–3, 65–6, 109–10 (*see also* Anderson, Elizabeth)
  as deontic/mandatory 97–9, 101–4, 108–18
  as determining legitimacy 4–7, 14 n.24, 23–6, 32–6
  as especially weighty 49, 58, 90–1
  as grounds for the priority of the basic liberties 11–12, 49–50, 74, 86–7, 90–1, 95–105
  as lexically prior to other aspirational values 71, 84–90, 95–105
  as mutual justifiability 93–105 (*see also* political liberalism)
  as requiring (substantial) distributive equality 67, 72–80
  as the precondition for public political dispute over values 23–6, 49, 97–9, 101–4, 108–18
  institutional vs. interpersonal 48, 141–2
  not exhausted by legitimacy 48

non-ideal theory
  "applied ideal theory" as 180–2
  in Rawls 10–11, 13, 189 (*see also* duty of justice)
  its relationship to ideal theory 180–2, 189–90
  comparative vs. optimizing 195–6
  "priority thesis" of 194–5
normative guidance
  as settled by democratic processes 32–3, 37, 41, 98–100
  in the anatomy of justice 1–2, 5–6, 9, 11–12, 17–18
  under differing circumstances 26, 97–9, 108–18, 155
normative principles
  as merely one part of justice 1, 11, 20–1
  for institutions vs. individuals 13, 17–18, 162–3 (*see also* basic structure debate)
  vs. evaluative assessment 1, 11–12, 14, 20–1, 25–30
normative theory
  as fit for social critique 179, 194–207

  as necessary for exhaustive judgments of injustice 197–8
  as not exhausted by principles of justice 153, 157–8
  as unnecessary for judgments of injustice 194–6
  as useful 197–210
normativity
  narrow vs. broad interpretations of 3 n.1
  of shared reasons 32–3, 97–9
Nussbaum, Martha 146, 148

occupational discretion 116, 161–5. *See also* gendered division of labor
opportunity pluralism 60–5
oppression 19, 26, 29–30, 72, 107, 148, 151–2, 183–4, 207–8. *See also* injustice

Pareto efficiency. *See* efficiency
Parr, Tom 107
paternity leave. *See* subsidized parental leave
patriarchy 148, 153, 164–5. *See also* gendered division of labor; sexism
permissive liberalism 154–7, 159, 161–3, 177. *See also* basic structure debate; Cohen, G.A.
personal prerogative 161–3. *See also* basic structure debate
pluralism
  conceptual (*see* conceptual pluralism)
  opportunity (*see* opportunity pluralism)
  values (*see* values pluralism)
political institutions 1, 4–5, 66, 100–1, 146–7, 149–51, 153–4, 156. *See also* basic structure; state
political liberalism
  and legitimacy 32–4, 47–8, 95–105
  and mutual justification 32–4, 47–8, 93–7
  and non-controversiality 191–3
  and overlapping consensus 97–101, 104–5, 108–19
  and reasonableness 93–105, 109–13, 119–20, 133, 141
  and reciprocity 32–4, 93–4, 96 n.7, 97–8, 104, 111–12, 133–4
  and true vs. political justice 99–101, 104–5, 111–12, 116
  and values pluralism 31–4
  as public reasons liberalism 13
  contingent vs. mandatory reasons of 97–9, 101–4, 108–18
  motivating question for 102–4
political liberties. *See also* basic liberties; democratic franchise
  as positionally valuable 74, 83
  fair value of 72, 74, 83, 119–20, 134–5
political philosophy
  action-guidingness of 1–4, 28–30, 37–42, 44–5, 90–2, 121–3

and abstraction 15, 180–5
criticism of 8–10, 14–16, 150–1, 180–5, 207–10
  (*see also* Haslanger, Sally)
two debates within 18–21
prioritarianism 22, 51 n.20, 68–9, 129.
  See also difference principle
prostitution 134–5, 160, 182–3. *See also* sex work
public reason 112–16, 118–19, 136
public reasons liberalism. *See* political liberalism
public transportation 57–8, 87, 127
publicity
  and aspirational justice 19–20, 25–6
  and justification 32–4, 97, 111–13, 118–19,
    163 n.41, 191–2, 197–8 (*see also* political
    liberalism)
  and lexical ordering of values 114–16
  and reflective equilibrium 191–2
  and the anatomy of justice 38–40, 142, 145
  requirement 77 n.19, 111–13, 163 n.41

racial segregation
  in education 152, 168–9, 171–2, 187
  residential 169–71, 173
racism
  and community 32–3, 155 (*see also* community)
  and fair equality of opportunity 11–12, 148,
    155, 168–9, 189, 196–7
  and history 26, 155, 200–2
  and inequality 155, 168–9
  and injustice 157–9
  and policing 198–9, 203–4
  institutional vs. interpersonal 157–9, 163–4,
    168–70, 172 (*see also* basic
    structure debate)
Rawls, John
  action-guidingness of his theory 10–11
  and individual duties 13 (*see also* duty of
    justice)
  and lexical priority 5–7, 68–70, 84–5
  and liberal ideals 1, 5–6, 11
  and public reason 10–11, 13, 21, 47–8, 93–6,
    119–20 (*see also* political liberalism)
  and reflective equilibrium 181, 186–93
  and the basic structure restriction 150–1, 153–4
    (*see also* basic structure restriction)
  and values pluralism 5–6, 12–13, 27–8, 40–1
  and verdictive justice 4, 18–21
  contrast with the anatomy of
    justice 10–14, 40–1
  defense of 14
  hegemony of 15–16
  two principles of justice 10–11, 164–5
    (*see also* basic liberties; difference
    principle; fair equality of opportunity)
  usefulness of his theory 10–11
reasonably just society
  and legitimacy 93–105, 110–11, 134–5
  in Rawls 119–20, 134–5

reasons
  contingent 97–9, 108–18
  generation of 31, 93–4, 108, 134
  mandatory 97–9, 101–4, 108–18
  public (*see* political liberalism)
  shared 32–3, 94 n.4, 97–101
reciprocity. *See also* values
  and autonomy 139
  and mutual justification 32–4, 93–4, 96 n.7,
    97–8, 104, 111–12, 133–4
  and mutual respect 14, 24–5, 32–4, 43–4,
    47–8, 97–8, 111–12, 133–4
  and the gendered division of labor 136
  critique of the vagueness of 181–3, 196, 205–7
recognition 14, 34, 47–8, 136, 174–5. *See also*
    mutual respect; relational equality
redress, principle of 65–6. *See also* luck
    egalitarianism
reflective equilibrium
  as *a priori* 181–2, 186–8
  and controversial judgments 187–8,
    190–4, 205–7
  and empirical facts 186–93, 198, 205–7
  and outlier judgments 185–94
  and public reasons 191–3
  critical potential of 182–3, 205–7, 210
  criticism of 180–5, 194–6, 198–201, 204, 207–9
  done in conversation with other people 186
relational equality
  and legitimacy 4–5, 17, 31–7, 48, 112–13
  as distinct from distributive equality 19, 31–7
    (*see also* aspirational justice; verdictive
    justice)
  as irreducible to distributive equality 5–6, 21
    (*see also* values pluralism)
  as lexically prior to distributive equality 71,
    84–90, 95–105
  and mutual respect 47–8, 67–71 (*see also*
    legitimacy; mutual respect)
  as non-exhaustive of justice 48, 80–90
  as requiring robust distributive equality 71–80
  not exhausted by legitimacy or mutual
    respect 48
responsibility
  for caregiving labor 136, 204 (*see also*
    gendered division of labor)
  for justice 59, 109 (*see also* basic structure
    restriction; duty of justice; political
    institutions)
  and distributive justice 19, 45–6, 53–5, 59,
    63–4 (*see also* luck egalitarianism)
right, priority of to the good 18 n.1

Scheffler, Samuel 43–4
segregation
  class 36–7, 106
  mobility 57–8
  racial (*see* racial segregation)

228   INDEX

sense of justice 158, 164–5, 170, 173
sex work 205. *See also* prostitution
sexism 9, 146, 148–51, 153, 157–9, 163–4, 180–3.
    See also culture; feminism; gender roles
sexual harassment 171
Shiffrin, Seana Valentine 76–80, 81 n.28, 90–1
social contribution 56, 116, 136–7
social critique 9–10, 149, 151–2, 154 n.33, 156, 175,
    183–5, 205–6. *See also* basic structure
    debate; Haslanger, Sally
social ethos 20 n.12, 73–4, 116–18, 127, 154–5,
    157–8, 170. *See also* basic structure
    debate; culture
social minimum 68. *See also* adequacy
    threshold; basic income
social movements
    and feminism 9, 14–15
    and reflective equilibrium 183–5, 198–9,
        203–4
    as source of political knowledge 3, 9, 190,
        198–9, 203–4, 208 (*see also* moral
        epistemology)
    relation to liberal egalitarianism 3, 9, 14–16,
        179–80, 198–9, 203–4
socialism 164, 202
solidarity 22, 48, 54, 75, 93, 107–8, 113, 141.
    See also social ethos; values
stability 4, 18–20, 33 n.30, 139, 142–4.
    See also values
state
    as primary subject of justice 8–9, 146–52, 157,
        168, 174–5 (*see also* basic structure)
    and racist policing 198–9, 203–4
    legitimate interventions of 22–3, 58–60, 71–2,
        161–5, 176–7
    required interventions of 156, 168–9, 174–7
status quo deference 148, 181–2, 186–7, 199–201
stereotype threat 141
stingy liberalism 154–77. *See also* basic structure
    restriction; Rawls, John
subsidized parental leave 125–7, 132, 170–1.
    See also basic income

talent 76–8. *See also* difference principle; luck
    egalitarianism
two moral powers 90, 93–4, 97–8. *See also*
    conception of the good; sense of justice

universal basic income. *See* basic income

values pluralism
    and intuitionism 5–6, 12–13, 37–42, 44–5
        (*see also* lexical priority)
    and luck egalitarianism 21–37, 80–4, 105–18
    and opportunity pluralism 60–5
    and two pluralisms about justice 18–21
    as a justification for liberalism 41–2

as compatible with lexical priority /
    weighting 12–13, 37–42
conceptual vs. substantive 18–21
    (*see also* conceptual pluralism)
foundational vs. reducible 39–40
incommensurability vs. incomparability
    within 39
tension with action-guidance 37–42, 90–2
the anatomy of justice as a non-intuitionist
    form of 12–13
values. *see also* intuitionism; values pluralism
    as grounds for evaluative
        judgments 68–9, 84–5
    as liberal egalitarian ideals 1, 17–18
    as mutually irreducible 21, 37–42
    as ordered by democratic processes
        37, 41, 108–18
    as ordered in verdictive justice
        30, 114–16
    as reason-giving even when
        overridden 31, 108–18
    in justice as fairness 10–11, 13–14
    in the anatomy of justice 1–2, 11–13, 17–19,
        22–5 (*see also* anatomy of justice)
    incommensurability vs. incomparability of 39
    opportunity cost tradeoffs between 85, 123–4,
        144–5, 174–5
    political recognition of 24–5, 108–18
    realism about 25, 99–101 (*see also* political
        liberalism)
    structural tradeoffs between 123, 125–8
    "transcendence" of 179–80
    see also community; efficiency; fairness;
        feasibility; humanity; integrity; mutual
        respect; reciprocity; solidarity; stability
verdictive justice
    and opportunity pluralism 60–5
    as action-guiding 28–30, 44–5, 90–2, 108–18
    as all-things-considered ranking of social
        arrangements 20–1, 25–7, 30, 43
    as distinct from aspirational justice 21–31
    as evaluative assessment 11–12, 18–21, 25–6
    as the output of weighted values (*see* values
        pluralism)
    its relation to history and culture
        26, 109–12, 155
    its relation to legitimacy 31–7, 108–18
    maximizing with respect to 85, 111–12, 160–2

Watson, Lori 136–7, 149, 182–3
women
    and gender norms (*see* gender norms)
    disproportionate caregiving by (*see* gendered
        division of labor)
    disproportionate poverty of 130, 132, 142–4

zoning ordinances 169